ARRANGING BARBERSHOP
Volume 2: The Arranging Journey

Barbershop Harmony Society

To access recordings and hyperlinks that accompany this book, go to
www.halleonard.com/mylibrary/ and enter this code where indicated:

Enter Code
1541-0358-7245-4321

Hal Leonard Books

An Imprint of Hal Leonard LLC

T0413944

Arranging Barbershop

Volume 2: The Arranging Journey

Published in 2023 by Hal Leonard Books
An Imprint of Hal Leonard LLC
7777 West Bluemound Road
Milwaukee, WI 53213

Trade Book Division Editorial Offices
33 Plymouth St., Montclair, NJ 07042

Music permissions can be found on pages 672–699, which constitute an extension of this copyright page.

Printed in the United States

Book design by the Barbershop Harmony Society

Library of Congress Cataloging-in-Publication number 2023920560

ISBN-10: 1705191797

ISBN-13/EAN: 9781705191798

www.halleonardbooks.com

www.barbershop.org

Table of Contents

Foreword

By Joe Liles

"Let's sing a song, let's ring a song, let harmony be true. Come join the crowd, sing long and loud like good chord busters do."

From "The Chord-buster March" by W.A. Wyatt (1962)

The glorious, ringing sound of barbershop harmony has blessed our hearts, minds, and ears for a long, long time. It was the joy of singing this harmony that brought each one of us to the feast. We quickly discovered the added benefits of creating lifelong friendships and performing for cheering audiences. Rehearsing in a chorus or quartet or woodshedding with a pickup foursome can bring thrills of delight. We are held together by the magical elixir of consonant chords voiced and sung in ways to maximize the reinforcement of overtones. I am sure each of you can give testimony as to how life-enhancing, even life-changing, your own experience has been.

I was involved in church music in my early years. I wrote my first little gospel song at age six and it was published in my teens. My first immersion into four-part barbershop harmony style happened in January of 1967. It was yet another divine experience. I was astounded by the joyful sound and the dedication of the men of the San Antonio Chordsmen Chorus. I joined them and was soon invited to be their chorus director and in-house arranger. For well over 50 years, I've enjoyed harmonizing and working with barbershop singers from all over the world. I've directed choruses, sung in quartets, taught numerous courses on barbershop craft, coached, judged contests, written and arranged music, and woodshedded with many pickup foursomes.

During this journey, the primary nourishment for our singers has become obvious to me: it's the music and how it is arranged. We all thrive on songs and tags voiced in the style of music we love, that of barbershop harmony!

This new series of books, with its associated programs and activities, is for every level of arranging interests from beginner to pro. It is dedicated to the creation and preservation processes that will continue to spread the joy of singing and bind us all together in harmony forever.

Dedication

By Steve Tramack

Figure X.1

"Shine," original verse composed and arrangement by David Wright. The verse of this arrangement, written for the 1993 International Quartet Champions of the Barbershop Harmony Society (BHS), Gas House Gang, honors championship quartets that paved the way for future generations by inspiring them with their craft, musicianship, style, and excellence.

Note: "Shine," arr. David Wright, catalog no. 212661.

Dedication

We, the team of contributors to the *Arranging Barbershop* project, would like to honor those who inspired, thrilled, educated, and challenged us to become arrangers and hone our craft. Many of these giants have their work featured in this project, and thanks to the online, multimedia nature of this book, you'll be able to hear their inspirations brought to life once more. Their work—still alive in iconic performances from the past, present and, quite certainly, future—serve as a perpetual power source in keeping this artform alive and thriving. This list includes, but is not limited to:

Sylvia Alsbury	Earl Moon
Joni Bescos	Roger Payne
Dave Briner	Lou Perry
Floyd Connett	Molly Reagan
Renee Craig	Ruby Rhea
Phil Embury	Bev Sellers
S K Grundy	Lloyd Steinkamp
Warren "Buzz" Haeger	Dave Stevens
Freddie King	Burt Szabo
Walter Latzko	Ed Waesche
Joe Liles	

So many others have also continued to keep the whole world of barbershoppers singing, ringing, and believing that, through music, barriers are broken down and that anything is possible.

Editor's Note

By Steve Tramack, Lead Editor

I walked into my first rehearsal in 1982, about the time the previous Barbershop Arrangers Manual had just been published. I was a high school sophomore who had just attended the annual show held by my dad's chorus, the Nashua NH Granite Statesmen. The show featured the quartet The Harrington Brothers,[1] who were roughly my age. I also was surprised to learn that several of my high school classmates were also in the chorus. I was, in short, hooked. It could have been the harmony, which was still ringing in my ears. It could have been the songs, which told stories still rattling around in my head. It could have been the fact that singers of all ages, backgrounds, races, and creeds were equals on the risers and seemed genuinely to be having a great time. It was probably all the above; regardless, I was hooked.

During that rehearsal, I had a chance to talk with the director, Joe Kopka, not yet knowing that he would become a lifelong friend and mentor. I said, "Mr. Kopka? Um, Joe? I think I really love this barbershop thing!" After he congratulated me, I felt emboldened to ask, "Can you tell me more about what kinds of songs you sing? I happen to really love Frank Sinatra and the Rat Pack; do you sing any of those songs?"

Joe said, "Oh, no. We don't sing Rat Pack songs in barbershop."

Only slightly rebuffed, I asked, "Okay. Well, what about other Big Band songs?"

Joe said, "We only sing songs written between 1890 and 1930—and no swing songs. Only downbeat-driven songs. We only just started to hear marches." Thank you, Louisville Thoroughbreds and Ed Waesche, for opening that door with the "Mardi Gras March" at the 1981 Barbershop Harmony Society (BHS) International Convention.[2]

That seemed specific. And arbitrary. But who was I to question? I was just a high school sophomore and Joe was a past Top 20 quartet singer and longtime barbershopper. There clearly must have been a good reason. Already knowing the answer, I asked, "So, no Broadway songs? No Elvis? No Beatles?"

Joe said, "You know what? Let's sing a tag."

"A tag? What's that?" Thirty seconds later, with the overtones still buzzing around my head, I was hooked again, now for life. I figured we could talk about Sinatra and "Fly Me to the Moon" later.

Since that time, barbershop evolved. Michigan Jake, the BHS 2001 International Quartet Champion, singing songs such as "Louise,"[3] showed the barbershop world that swing can be 'shopped exceedingly well. OC Times, the 2008 Quartet Champs, sang "Love Me"[4] with harmonies and background vocals right from the King of Rock and Roll's recording and all of a sudden Elvis sure sounds like barbershop. I guess that's not too surprising, considering "Love Me Tender" features new lyrics to a song written—you guessed it—between 1890 and 1930: "Aura Lee." Like in every style of music and performance, performers have led the way, nourished by arrangements that and arrangers who ardently seek to find creative ways to honor both the song and the barbershop style.

Barbershop is not a genre of music. It is a style of arranging music that can be applied to songs of many different genres. The barbershop style features examples from the Tin Pan Alley era (1890–1930), Big Band era (1930s and 40s), Rat Pack era (1950s and early 60s), Motown era (1960s and 70s), selected artists from the Rock and Roll era (1950–1990), and the Broadway Musical stage (1930–present day). Country music, jazz standards, singer/songwriters, popular music and easy listening artists, disco, R&B… the list goes on. Barbershop harmony thrives across the world, enjoying unlimited influence on the style. As links between barbershop and the expansive a cappella and choral universe continue to strengthen, new arrangers are drawn to the style, intrigued by the power and range of development options available with just four voices.

---

1   Barbershop Harmony Society. (2020, August 22). *The Harrington Brothers: If You Were the Only Girl in the World* [Video]. YouTube. https://youtu.be/kUU0n2umN00

2   Barbershop Harmony Society. (2016, October 14). *Louisville Thoroughbreds: Mardi Gras March* [Video]. YouTube. https://youtu.be/6T-CfkF0CyA

3   Barbershop Harmony Society. (2017, June 22). *Michigan Jake: Louise* [Video]. YouTube. https://youtu.be/GdnIIPzyK2M

4   OCTenor2. (2008, August 24). *OC Times: Love Me* [Video]. YouTube. https://youtu.be/qrvai9qHvEA

Arranging Barbershop Series Overview

The reader is about to embark on a journey: arranging music in the barbershop style. The elements of this journey are not unlike an outdoor adventure, such as hiking, mountain climbing, or skiing. For some travelers, this may be their first time venturing into this wilderness; for more experienced explorers, perhaps they're looking to build the skills to tackle new challenges or seek inspiration from expert navigators and explorers. The *Arranging Barbershop* series will serve as a guide and companion along the way, and this trail map provides an overview of the experience.

Figure X.2

Overview trail map for the Arranging Barbershop series.

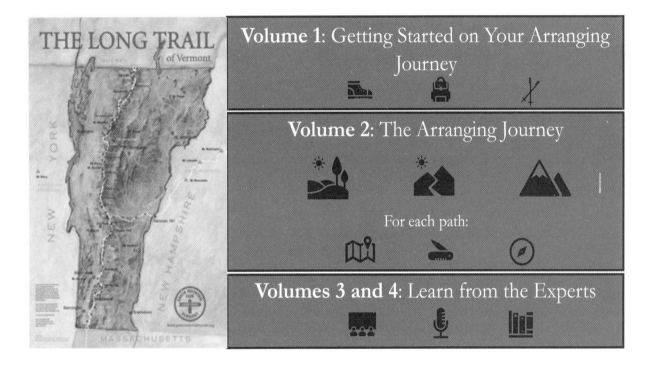

The *Arranging Barbershop* experience is broken up into four volumes: 1) *Getting Started*, 2) *The Arranging Adventure*, 3) *Visions of Excellence*, and 4) *Learn from the Experts*. Figure X.3 gives a trail-map-like visual representation of the complete series. The boxes in the left column denote the various books and the boxes in the right column describe the subdivisions of the book.

Figure X.3

Arranging Barbershop trail map.

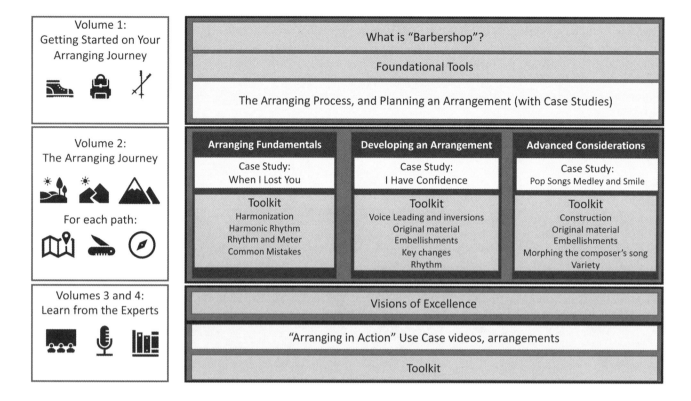

Overview of each volume

Volume 1: Before You Start Your Arranging Journey

Planning to go on a hiking adventure? Before departing, you'll need a few things to ensure your success: equipment (boots, backpack, supplies, climbing poles, etc.), a map of the area, lodging plans, and transportation to and from the hike, just to name a few. Successful planning and expertise in prerequisite skills are as important as the hike itself.

What skills and knowledge will you need along your arranging journey? This section provides a set of foundational tools and approaches that every arranging explorer will need before venturing out into the wild. This includes a glimpse into the past, a detailed overview of the style and the arranging process, a planning process roadmap, and a review of fundamental theory and musical literacy concepts that serve as a foundation for any adventure you choose. Vol. 1 includes case studies of a complete step-by-step arranging process and an example arrangement, following one arranger's process from concept to completion.

Figure X.4

Volume 1 visual description.

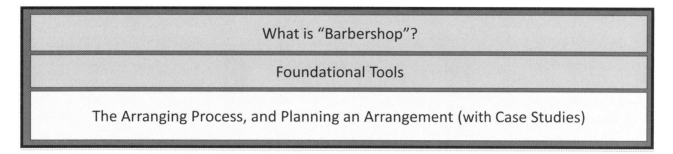

Volume 2: Choose Your Adventure

The Shenandoah National Park uses a numerical rating system to determine the difficulty of a given hiking trail. Factoring elevation and distance, the hike's rating is tied to one of five descriptors: easiest, moderate, moderately strenuous, strenuous, very strenuous. There are, of course, other factors to consider, such as the steepness of a trail over a short distance, which require more expert knowledge of the trail. Note that the ratings are tied to the terrain, not the ability of the hiker. It is up to the individual to choose their own path.

Volume 2 (this volume) takes a similar approach to arranging concepts. Rather than designate sections by skill level or experience of the arranger, this volume of *Arranging Barbershop* covers different terrains of arranging concepts:

Arranging Fundamentals focuses on the core set of skills required to harmonize a melody, leveraging the natural harmonic rhythms and implied chord progressions coupled with foundational arranging and theory-based skills to create a solid barbershop arrangement.

Developing an Arrangement focuses on the skills and approaches to bring interest and contrast into an arrangement. Starting from a foundation of core harmonization, this volume explores the use of various embellishments, the development of themes (rhythm, melody, lyrics, harmony), and creating original material such as intros and tags.

Advanced Considerations expands on these concepts, delving into a variety of challenges and choices that experienced arrangers use to create exciting musical journeys for talented performers. The case study looks at arranging for an international champion, and how this experience follows a different trajectory than the fundamental approach.

Arrangers of all levels should find value in the case studies and toolkit associated with each stage of the arranging adventure covered in Volume 2.

Figure X.5

Volume 2 visual description.

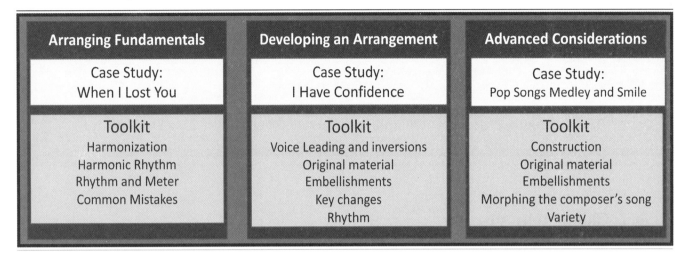

Volume 3: Visions of Excellence

Visions of Excellence is a virtual round table session of 38 arrangers who each answered the same 20 questions. You'll learn areas where there is broad agreement and where some might take a different approach. Example questions include:

- What methods do you consider when developing similar parts of an arrangement?
- Where do you draw inspiration when starting a new arrangement?
- What's the one thing you wish you'd learned sooner as an arranger?
- What trends might you predict happening to the barbershop art form in the future?

This is a most useful book that will be a constant source of inspiration.

Volume 4: Learn from the Experts

After a long day of skiing, tackling various trails of different levels of difficulty on a given mountain, skiers gather in the lodge to break bread and share the experiences from the day. It's in these gatherings where lessons learned, best practices, and things to avoid help to expand the knowledge of the community. Volumes 3 and 4 of *Arranging Barbershop* are designed to do exactly that. Volume 4 is divided into two parts: Arranging in Action and Arrangers' Toolbox.

> In the Arranging in Action section, you'll find video and audio examples of how different arrangers approached the same problems and opportunities. Learn from iconic arrangers about iconic arrangements of memorable performances from the style. You'll see how different arrangers tackle the challenges of arranging the same song with different approaches and goals. You'll see how the same arranger developed the same song differently, once as a ballad and once as an up-tempo.

> In the Arrangers' Toolbox section, you'll be able to explore individual topics such as *Arranging with Performance Staging in Mind* or *Arranging for Mixed Voices*, among others. Build your skills by learning from others, especially when it comes to these specialized topics.

Figure X.6

Volume 3 and 4 visual descriptions.

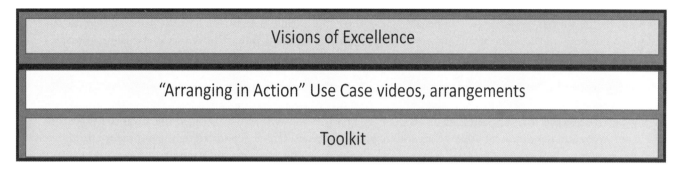

Back Matter

This guide will also contain a Back Matter section that includes the conclusion, appendix, bibliography including a detailed song list, glossary, contributor lists, sources, suggested reading, and an afterwards.

Compilation Approach

The end-to-end journey through the Arranging Barbershop adventure features contributions of note from more than 50 arrangers, over 1,000 pages of content, more than 400 arrangements featured, and roughly 50 hours of video. Each volume is presented in both a printed and online (Kindle) version.

This book is a *compilation* of topics, with lead contributors for different chapters providing relevant content and expertise in their own voice. The common threads, allowing for both individual voices and styles of communicating, while still feeling cohesive, will happen largely through formatting and structure of chapters:

- *Formatting* (use of bullets, paragraphs, etc.)
- *Style of sharing content* (verbiage, interspersed with examples from arrangements)
- *Chapter overall design and flow*: 1) Overview framing Chapter, 2) Case study, 3) Deep dives on relevant topics

Note that this leads to several examples of the same arrangement—and often the same passages—being used multiple times throughout the book to make similar points, This is due to the multiplicity of authors, the applicability of key concepts at different levels of the arranging experiences, and the fact that certain iconic arrangements are textbook examples of the barbershop style, circa 2023.

Enjoy the journey!

Who This Book is For

Arranging music is a complex, layered, rewarding musical endeavor. The arranger sits at the intersection of the creators—composer and lyricist—and performers of the music. With forethought, purpose, and sensitivity to both the original content and the performer, the arranger can help the performer successfully breathe life into the notes and words, creating a satisfying emotional journey. The arranging process includes considerations unique to the style, requiring knowledge, practice, and training to build expertise.

The *Arranging Barbershop* series is designed for anyone interested in arranging music in the barbershop style. No previous experience in the barbershop style is required; arrangers from other genres will find value in applying their theory and arranging expertise to the style. Experienced arrangers in the barbershop style will learn from the advanced problem-solving techniques and development approaches and may fill in gaps in knowledge in arranging and theory fundamentals that aid their journey. Novice arrangers will benefit from the journey, starting with the arranging process and definition of the style, advancing to the arranging fundamentals, and growing from there as their skills increase.

What You Need to Know Before You Start

Everything you need to know to leverage the full experience is found within the series itself. Specifically, if you are not an active arranger, and do not understand the difference between a major ninth and a dominant seventh chord, you'll find what you need in Vol. 1. Enough theory knowledge to understand triads and four-part chords, chord progressions, and melodic form are essential to taking advantage of Vol. 2 and beyond. Even if you are an experienced arranger, you'll likely find value in Vol. 1 with the arranging process and definition of the style aspects to warrant a review before jumping into Vol. 2 and beyond.

If you're new to barbershop, it is important to understand the barbershop voice parts and functions. The following is taken from the Barbershop Harmony Society's (BHS) website:[5]

Tenor is the highest part, harmonizing above the Lead. Notated in the top stave, tenor stems always point up. Tenor singers should have a light, lyric vocal quality. Male tenors usually sing this part in falsetto and should be approximately 10% of the sound. *This is radically different than most musical performance styles because the melody is NOT in the top voice.*

Lead is the second-highest part, singing the melody. Notated in the top stave, lead stems always point down. Lead singers should be prominent and have a dramatic and compelling vocal quality and should be approximately 30% of the sound. *This is different than most musical performance styles because the melody is in the second voice down. This "melody from inside" gives us the characteristic barbershop sound.*

Baritone sings above and below the Lead. Notated in the bottom stave, baritone stems always point up. Baritone singers should have a lyric vocal quality and should be approximately 20% of the sound. The baritone should sing louder when below the lead, and softer when above the lead. *The unusual voice leading can be very challenging, especially to the novice barbershop Baritone.*

Bass is the lowest part, singing foundational notes. Notated in the bottom stave, bass stems always point down. The Bass part should be as prominent as the Lead, with a big, robust vocal quality, and should be approximately 40% of the sound.

Throughout these volumes, you'll find examples written for high voices (e.g., SSAA), low voices (e.g., TTBB), and both (e.g., SATB or AATB). Regardless of individual voice ranges, voice parts are referred to as tenor, lead, bari, and bass.

---

5   https://www.barbershop.org/music/about-our-music

Trail Markers

Along the way, you'll see these icons to delineate sidebars that will help your learning journey.

Figure X.7

Definitions sidebars will highlight new vocabulary and their definitions. Example provided.

 A commonly used term in barbershop is *barbershop seventh*. This is a major triad with an additional minor seventh interval. Barbershop singers love the energetic nature of this chord so much that we named it after ourselves!

Figure X.8

Notes sidebars will illuminate interesting facts about the topic being discussed.

 Public domain laws vary from territory to territory. In the case of the US, songs released 96 years or more prior to the January 1st date each year are considered in the public domain.[6] In other territories, the general rule of thumb for international public domain titles is the date of the death of the last living contributor—composer or lyricist—plus 70 years.

Figure X.9

Warnings sidebars seek to share wisdom from arrangers who identify a topic as a potential trap in the arranging process. Warnings are especially helpful for new arrangers to avoid frustration. Example provided.

 Songs that feature secondary dominants that progress around the circle of fifths are well-suited to the barbershop style. Circle of fifths progressions with tritone movement in parallel half steps inherently imply dominant seventh chords, which are core to the style. Many songs, particularly those from the country, blues, and early rock genres, feature three chords: the tonic (I), the subdominant (IV) and the dominant (V). These songs move frequently from V–IV or IV–V, which lack the tension of the circle of fifths progressions. Three-chord songs featuring only V–IV or IV–V movement may not be best suited to the barbershop style. This Ritchie Valens song "Donna" provides an example of repeated I–IV–V7 movement.

---

6   For more information on public domain laws, please visit here.

Figure X.10

The barber pole sidebar indicates how the given topic is an excellent example of good barbershop and good barbershop arranging techniques. Example provided.

 The chord progression in Figure 2.10 is considered an excellent example of good barbershop arranging, as it uses eight barbershop seventh chords in a row. Note, however, that the quality of a barbershop arrangement is not determined by the sheer number of seventh chords included therein; not all melodies are well suited to this kind of harmonization.

Online Content

Barbershop is an aural art form. While looking at the examples will prove helpful for those arrangers who can hear the arrangement in their head, the art form really comes to life when you can hear and see the topic being discussed. Thus, every example in *Arranging Barbershop Vol 2* features a corresponding audio clip. Audio clips include tone-generated examples, as well as recordings from learning track makers, and, whenever possible, recordings by the original ensemble. The audio can be accessed at www.halleonard.com/mylibrary by entering the code found on the inside cover page of this book.

The audio examples correspond with the figure names.

Figure X.11

Hal Leonard MyLibrary with audio and video examples

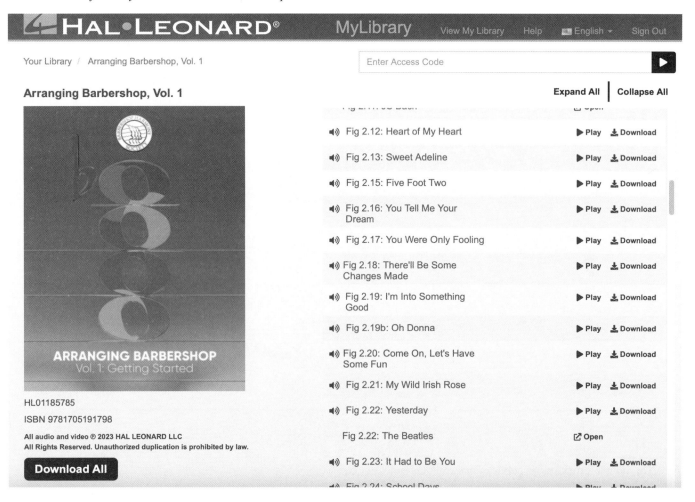

There are also examples of content from the internet throughout the books, including publicly available content from YouTube, and content specific to the *Arranging Barbershop* series, such as video interviews of arrangers discussing their process in developing referenced arrangements. The YouTube URLs are found in the footnotes, and direct links are included in the MyLibrary application.

Special Acknowledgments

The main content in *Arranging Barbershop Vol. 2*, as you're about to learn, was developed by ten individuals who selflessly donated their time, talents, expertise and experience to help capture the journey from basic harmonization of a melody through advanced arranging concepts. However, the work contained herein represents the creative efforts of hundreds of people. This book features the work of over 50 individuals arrangers, with audio and video clips featuring more than 100 ensembles. Once the material was compiled, a team of editors reviewed content, created audio files, and ensured that all of the arrangement examples followed the same look and feel. With over 700 examples, creating audio links and arrangements following a common house style was a tremendous undertaking.

We (Steve Tramack and Steve Scott) would like to acknowledge the following volunteers for their outstanding contributions:

Brian Ayers

Tona Dove

Grant Goulding

Rafi Hasib

Kohl Kitzmiller

Mendy Mendelsohn

Mike Rosen

Adam Scott

Brent Suver

Samantha Tramack

Larry Triplett

Tyler Wigginton

Arranging Barbershop: Volume II

The Arranging Journey

Contributors:

Steve Armstrong

Aaron Dale

Tom Gentry

Rafi Hasib

Clay Hine

Kevin Keller

Adam Scott

Steve Scott

Steve Tramack

David Wright

Part A.
Arranging Fundamentals

The real fun begins here: embarking on your arranging adventure. Much like hiking or skiing trails on a mountain are rated based on difficulty and experience level, this part of the book is divided into three parts: *Arranging Fundamentals*, *Developing an Arrangement*, and *Advanced Considerations*.

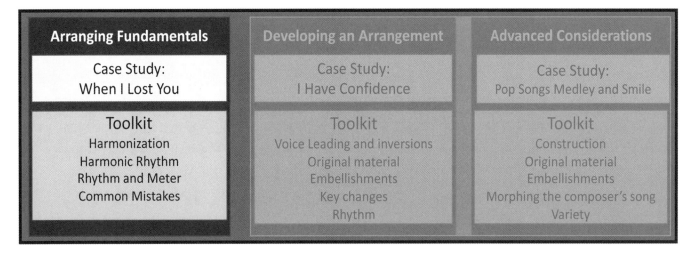

Part A

Arranging Fundamentals focuses on the core set of skills required to harmonize a melody: leveraging the natural harmonic rhythms and implied chord progressions, coupled with foundational arranging and theory-based skills, to create a solid barbershop arrangement. While this is targeted at arrangers who are new to the barbershop style, more experienced arrangers may benefit from the approaches and considerations outlined in Part A.

Chapter 13: Arranging Fundamentals Overview

Steve Tramack provides an executive summary of some of the core considerations in developing a basic barbershop arrangement.

Chapter 14: "When I Lost You" Case Study

Harmonizing a Melody Step-by-Step Case Study: Steve Armstrong walks through the process of harmonizing a melody in the barbershop style, overcoming common challenges with non-chord tones.

Chapter 15: Additional Arranging Fundamentals Considerations

Kevin Keller and Steve Tramack provide some context and content related to creating a basic arrangement in the barbershop style.

Chapter 16: Harmonic Rhythm Deep Dive

One of the most important concepts for beginning arrangers to recognize and understand is the concept of harmonic rhythm, and the associated concept of harmonic pillars. Tom Gentry, with assistance from Adam Scott and Steve Tramack, delves more deeply into these concepts, reviewing key concepts associated with harmonic rhythm.

Chapter 17: Common Mistakes

Clay Hine looks at mistakes beginning arrangers make related to harmonization and harmonic rhythm, providing before-and-after examples.

Chapter 18: Rhythm and Meter considerations

Rhythm is defined as the placement of sounds in time. In its most general sense, rhythm (derived from *rhein*, "to flow") is an ordered alternation of contrasting elements. Tom Gentry delves more deeply into fundamental considerations related to rhythm and meter as a foundation for further development in subsequent chapters of *Arranging Barbershop*, Vol. 2.

Chapter 13.
Arranging Fundamentals Overview

By Steve Tramack

Part A of this volume focuses on arranging fundamentals. These are the core set of skills required to harmonize a melody in the barbershop style. While this is targeted at arrangers who are new to the barbershop style, more experienced arrangers may benefit from the approaches and considerations outlined in this section.

What are the prerequisites required to be successful in this first stage of your arranging journey?

- Strong working knowledge of the theory of barbershop harmony, as covered in Chapter 5 of *Arranging Barbershop Vol. 1*. Of particular interest, in addition to fundamental theory skills such as keys, scale degrees and intervals, are a thorough understanding of chords and chord progressions. Understanding chord qualities, inversions and how to complete triads and seventh chords in four-part voicings are essential skills.

- An understanding of the definition of the barbershop style, as covered in Chapter 2 of *Arranging Barbershop Vol. 1*. When starting any journey, it's important to understand where one is headed and what kind of landscape one will need to traverse to be successful. Understanding how the style works and what makes for solid barbershop, will help the new arranger find success more quickly.

- A song that lends itself to being harmonized in the barbershop style. This is covered in more depth in Chapters 10 and 12 of *Arranging Barbershop Vol. 1*. Songs that feature naturally-occurring instances of secondary dominants lend themselves well to the barbershop style.

Some of the key areas covered in "Part A: Arranging Fundamentals" include:

- Approaches to harmonizing a melody, including handling of non-chord tones
- Harmonic rhythm and harmonic pillars—an important concept in making the arrangement feel organized and cohesive
- Chord vocabulary and inversions that work best in the barbershop style
- Rhythm and meter considerations
- Basic use of embellishments, e.g., echoes, swipes
- Basic approach to creating original material, e.g., tags
- Common mistakes made by fledgling arrangers

Enjoy the journey!

Chapter 14.
"When I Lost You" Case Study

By Steve Armstrong

> **Note**: This chapter was featured in *Arranging Barbershop Vol. 1* as a case study for harmonizing a melody. Because this concept is foundational for the remaining content in *Vol. 2*, we've repeated it for the sake of completeness.

Introduction

Just as it is necessary to have a solid grasp on music theory when one wishes to become an arranger, another fundamental skill is to be able to write a simple harmonization that is singable and sounds pleasing to the ear. This is really the first step. Once this skill has been sufficiently developed, it is possible to explore all the wonderful and creative ways to embellish that harmonization into a true arrangement. This chapter will outline a systematic approach to writing a harmonization that can provide that foundation and be utilized even when an arranger has become quite skilled. This chapter will also walk you through various harmonization scenarios, and end with a case study to help you understand how the process works.

Harmonic Pillars and Harmonic Rhythm

The first step is to identify the *harmonic pillars*. These are the chords that are the main harmony or harmonies for the measure, and if you were to sing the song while accompanying yourself on the guitar, these would be the chords you would play. Note that you are not going to play a different chord on each melody note. In fact, most of the time it feels right to change the chord each time you start a new measure. This is partly because rhythmically the first beat of the measure has strength, and you add strength by choosing that moment to also change the chord. This allows the listener to feel a satisfying symmetry as the chords change at consistent intervals of time. This is what we mean by harmonic rhythm: the frequency by which the main harmony, or harmonic pillars, change. In a fast song the harmonic pillars may last for two full measures. Conversely, with a slower song the pillars may change midway through the measure, e.g., in 4/4 time they might change every 2 beats, meaning they are still changing on strong beats.

 Be aware when considering appropriate harmonic rhythm and the intended delivery of the song and arrangement. It is common for up-tempo songs to have a slow harmonic rhythm (fewer chord changes) and ballads to have a fast harmonic rhythm (more chord changes).

The following are examples of inherent harmonic rhythms, moving at different paces:

Figure 14.1

"When I Lost You," words and music by Irving Berlin. Note the pillar chords change every two measures.

Figure 14.2

"Five Foot Two," words and music by Ray Henderson, Sam M. Lewis, and Joseph Widow Young. Arranged by Joe Liles. Note the pillar chords change nearly every measure.

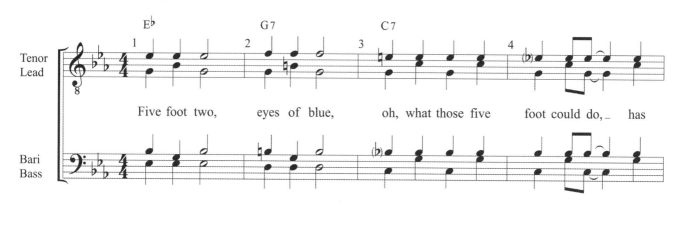

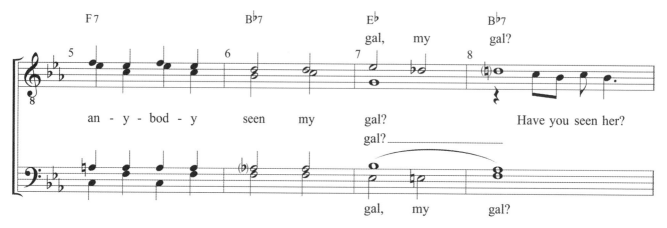

 "Five Foot Two" is a classic example of circle of fifths movement and smooth voice leading. Notice how it seamlessly moves around the circle with seventh chords back to I. The pillar progression is I–III7–VI7–II7–V7–I. Although it is not required to have so many consecutive barbershop sevenths in an arrangement, the melody naturally lends itself to these chords.

Figure 14.3

"A Nightingale Sang in Berkeley Square," words and music by Manning Sherwin. Note the pillar chords change every two beats.

For the rest of this case study, we'll use "When I Lost You."

Figure 14.4

"When I Lost You," words and music by Irving Berlin.

System Outline

While different arrangers may follow a slightly different order of steps, here are the seven steps for writing a harmonization: 1) write melody and lyrics, 2) identify harmonic pillars, 3) identify non-pillar melody notes, 4) write bass harmony, 5) write tenor harmony, 6) write baritone harmony, and 7) identify potential harmonies for non-pillar notes.

Melody and Lyricsg

Enter the melody and lyrics into your notational software. It can be helpful to print this page out for the next steps.

Figure 14.5

Example of the melody and lyrics of the song section.

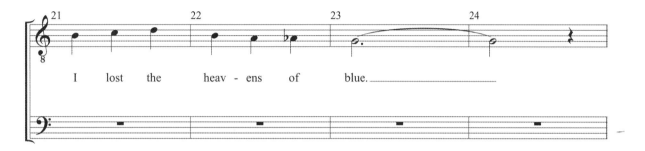

Identify Harmonic Pillars

Write or notate the harmonic pillars above the staff. Sometimes the score you are working from provides this information.

Figure 14.6

Example of harmonic pillar identification.

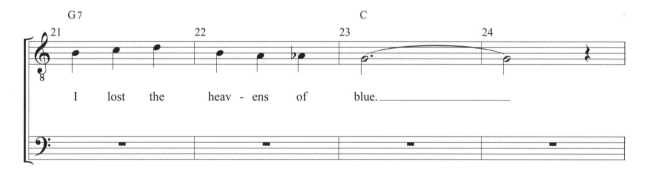

Identify Non-pillar Melody Notes

Go through the melody and circle every note that isn't readily a part of the pillar chord. These will be harmonized later.

Figure 14.7

Example of identifying notes outside the harmonic pillar chord.

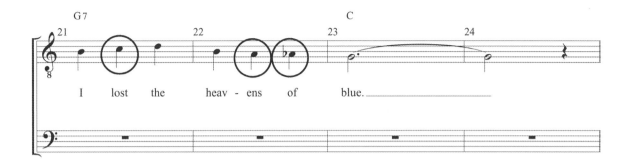

Bass Harmony

Write in the bass note for every melody note inside the pillar chord. Start the bass on the root or fifth for seventh chords and the root for triads. Try to follow the general shape of the melody so that bass notes are higher when the melody is higher and lower when the melody is lower. This will help the voicings to not become too spread. Consider bass voice leading when the harmony implies a seventh chord and the melody is not on the root or fifth.

Figure 14.8

Example of bass part harmonization of the notes within the pillar chord.

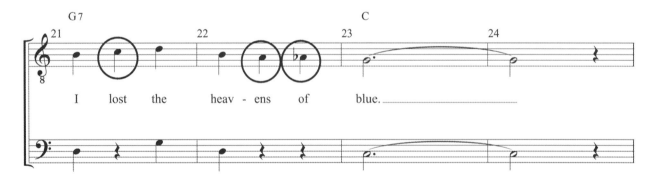

Tenor Harmony

Write in the tenor note for every melody note inside the pillar chord. Use one of the unused notes in the chord or double the root if it is a triad. Consider voice leading and seek for fewer awkward leaps. There may be times when choosing a different bass note would allow a smoother tenor part.

Figure 14.9

Example of tenor and bass part harmonization of the notes within the pillar chord.

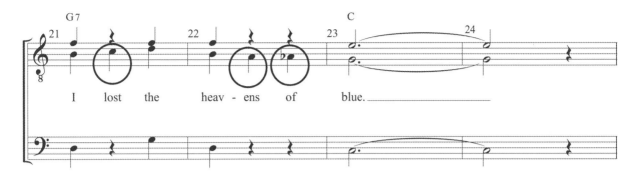

Baritone Harmony

Write in the baritone note for every melody note inside the pillar chord. Complete each chord or double the root if it is a triad. As with the tenor, try to not have the part jump around unnecessarily and consider changing the bass or tenor note if it leads to a smoother baritone part.

Figure 14.10

Example of baritone, tenor, and bass part harmonization of the notes within the pillar chord.

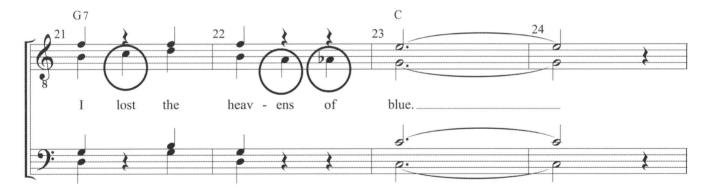

Identify Potential Harmonies For Non-pillar Notes

Now that all of the pillar harmonizations are complete, it's time to deal with the non-pillar melody notes. Examine each circled melody note and determine which of the following options from Table 14.1 could be used to harmonize it:

Table 14.1

Chord choices for non-pillar chord notes.

Option Number	Chord Type	Distance of Root From Harmonic Pillar
1	Extended chord (add 6th, 7th, or 9th)	On
2	Barbershop 7th	5th above
3	Barbershop 7th	5th below
4	Barbershop 7th	Semitone below
5	Barbershop 7th	Semitone above
6	Barbershop 7th	tritone
7	Diminished 7th	On

These options include every possible pitch. Determine which options include the melody note and try these out. Playing them on a keyboard or using notational software playback are helpful ways to hear the options that sound natural. Choose the one you like the best and write in the bass, tenor and baritone, in that order, following the same guidelines as above.

Figure 14.11

Example of non-pillar chord harmonization options.

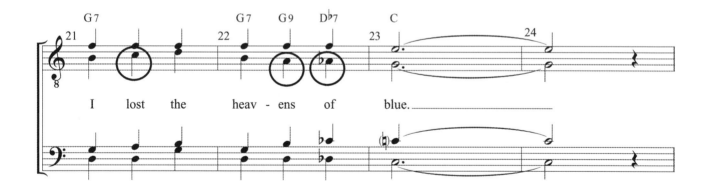

In Figure 14.11, we used a Dmin7 for the first circled note, a G9 without the root for the second one, and a Db7 for the third one.[7] Let's examine the options a little further and talk about how we arrived at these, starting in measure 22. The primary harmony is G7 and the first circled melody note is an A.

---

7   Note in the Db7, the baritone note is the properly-spelled Cb. For the sake of singability and voice leading purposes, and to avoid a non-diatonic scale tone, some arrangers may knowingly write this as a B♮.

Table 14.2

Harmonization options for the first non-pillar chord in measure 22. Prevailing harmony: G7. Melody note: A

Option Number	Chord Type	Distance of Root From Harmonic Pillar	Is this an option?
1	Extended chord (add 6th, 7th, or 9th)	On	*Yes*, the A is in G9 chord (missing the root)
2	Barbershop 7th	5th above	*Yes*, the A is the fifth of a D7 chord
3	Barbershop 7th	5th below	*No*, the A is not part of a C7 chord
4	Barbershop 7th	Semitone below	*No*, the A is not part of a F#7 chord
5	Barbershop 7th	Semitone above	*No*, the A is not part of a G#7 chord
6	Barbershop 7th	Tritone	*No*, the A is not part of C#7 chord
7	Diminished 7th	On	*No*, the A is not part of a Gdim7 chord.

From the seven options listed in Table 14.2, we see that we could harmonize this with a G9 chord (option 1), as shown in Figure 14.11. We could also harmonize the second beat of measure 22 as a D7 (option 2), as shown in Figure 14.12.

Figure 14.12

Example of non-pillar chord harmonization options.

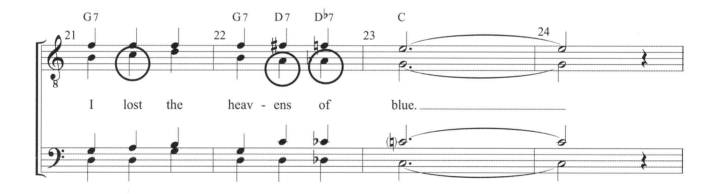

Either one seems like a viable option, but the D7 chord is more strikingly different from the first chord of the measure than the G9 is. There are times when we might prefer that, and it often comes down to personal preference, but in this case the stability of maintaining the G7 feel will be our choice and will choose option 1 (G9 chord).

For the second chord in the second measure of Figure 14.12, the choices from Table 14.3 are A♭7, Option 5, or D♭7, Option 6. The A♭7 seems a little jarring, particularly because it is the last chord in the measure, and in the next measure the primary harmony changes to C.

Table 14.3

Harmonization options for the non-pillar chord, beat 3 in measure 22. Prevailing harmony: G7. Melody note: A♭

Option Number	Chord Type	Distance of Root From Harmonic Pillar	Is this an option?
1	Extended chord (add 6th, 7th, or 9th)	On	*No*, the A♭ cannot be used to extend the G7 chord
2	Barbershop 7th	5th above	*No*, the A♭ is not part of a D7 chord
3	Barbershop 7th	5th below	*No*, the A♭ is not part of a C7 chord
4	Barbershop 7th	Semitone below	*No*, the A♭ is not part of a F#7 chord
5	Barbershop 7th	Semitone above	*Yes*, the A♭ is the root of an A♭7 (G#7) chord
6	Barbershop 7th	Tritone	*Yes*, the A♭ is the fifth of the D♭7 chord
7	Diminished 7th	On	*No*, the A♭ is not part of a Gdim7 chord.

Figure 14.13

Example of non-pillar chord harmonization option.

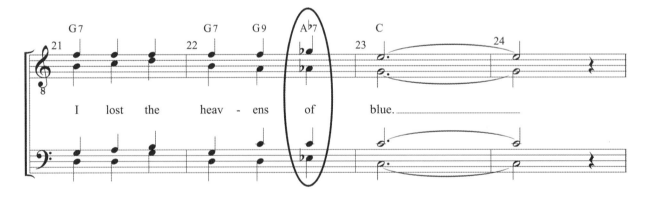

Figure 14.14

Example of non-pillar chord harmonization option.

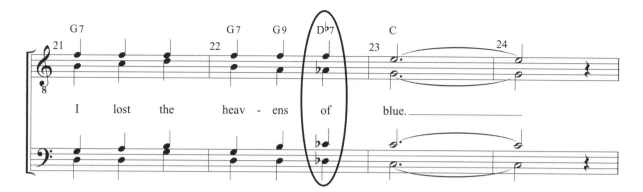

Db7, as shown in Figure 14.14, works better because it has two notes in common with the G7 chord (the tritone of F and B, or Cb)—so it is closely related to the G7. As a barbershop 7th whose root is a semitone above the harmonic pillar of the next measure, it feels like it fits in measure 22 and it moves smoothly into measure 23.

Returning to the first circled note in measure 21, the C on beat 2, the choices appear to be D7, Option 2 from Table 14.4, C7, Option 3, or Ab7, Option 5. Of all these choices, the Ab7 and especially the C7 sound jarring.

Table 14.4

Harmonization options for the non-pillar chord, beat 2 in measure 21. Prevailing harmony: G7. Melody note: C

Option Number	Chord Type	Distance of Root From Harmonic Pillar	Is this an option?
1	Extended chord (add 6th, 7th, or 9th)	On	*No*, the C cannot be used to extend the G7 chord
2	Barbershop 7th	5th above	*Yes*, the C is the seventh of a D7 chord
3	Barbershop 7th	5th below	*Yes*, the C is the root of a C7 chord
4	Barbershop 7th	Semitone below	*No*, the C is not part of an F#7 chord
5	Barbershop 7th	Semitone above	*Yes*, the C is the third of an Ab7 (G#7) chord
6	Barbershop 7th	Tritone	*No*, the C is not part of Db7 chord
7	Diminished 7th	On	*No*, the C is not part of a Gdim7 chord.

Figure 14.15

Example of non-pillar chord harmonization, option 3.

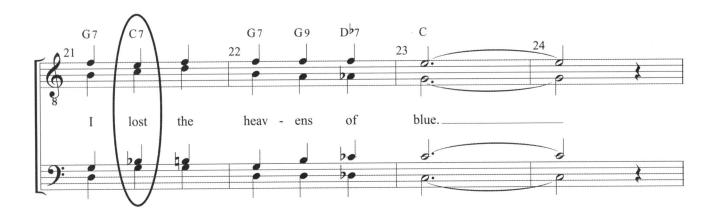

Figure 14.16

Example of non-pillar chord harmonization, option 5.

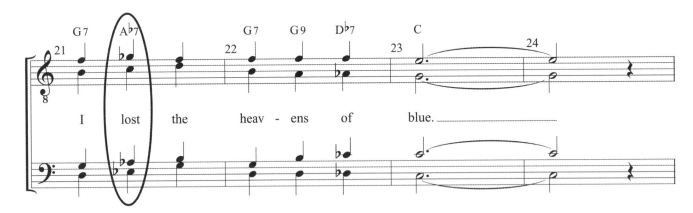

The D7 in the second beat of the first measure in Figure 14.17 sounds okay, but the same problem occurs when considering a D7 for the first circled note in the next measure, as shown in Figure 14.12; this chord is strikingly different from the first and last chords of the measure.

Figure 14.17

Example of non-pillar chord harmonization, option 2.

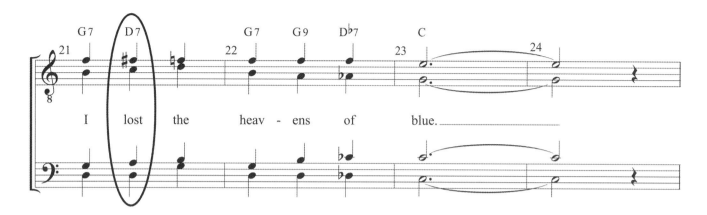

These choices might sound good, but there is another option: extending the harmonic pillar by adding the 11th. This wasn't listed as a choice in Table 14.4 because 11th chords aren't part of the barbershop chord vocabulary. 11th chords also generally consist of five chord tones: root, 5th, 7th, 9th and 11th. However, if the root is omitted, a commonly used barbershop substitution for the 11th chord—sometimes called the sus4 chord—is left. This chord is the *minor 7th* whose root is a 5th above the harmonic pillar, in this case a Dmin7. This choice sounds much smoother, primarily because the tenor note remains straight across on the F rather than move up to the F# on the second chord.

Figure 14.18

Examples of non-pillar chord harmonization, 11th chord extension yielding a minor-minor 7th a fifth above the harmonic pillar.

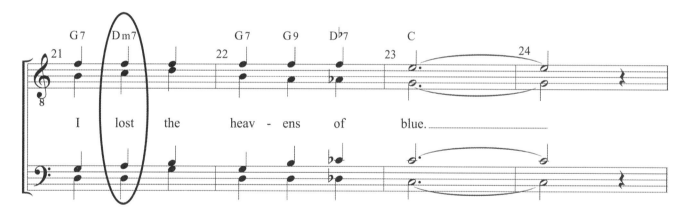

The Dmin7 has two notes in common with the G7 chord—the Bass D and the Tenor F—making the Dmin7 a commonly used chord as an extension of the G7 harmonic pillar. It sounds very similar to the G9 chord we ended up using on the second circled note.

Following these rules and using your musical instincts, you'll be able to write a harmonization that is singable and sounds natural. That is a significant achievement, so don't worry about embellishments now. And when considering the various options, take the time to listen to each and decide if it is a pleasing choice in context. Just because one of the options includes the circled melody note doesn't mean it is a good choice. On the other hand, sometimes there will be more than one option that sounds good, and then it is up to you to choose based on your personal preference.

The harmonic pillars do not have to be exactly what the published sheet music used. Sometimes there are multiple chord options that all feel natural, in which case it is personal preference. In other cases, there may be a progression of chords that appear to work in that they accommodate most of the melody notes, but it just doesn't sound like the song, and this makes the listener uncomfortable.

In the Scottish Folk Song, "Annie Laurie," the bridge repeats the same sequence of melody notes, implying the following harmony (I–V7–I):

Figure 14.19

Excerpt from "Annie Laurie," words and music by William Douglas. Arranged by Steve Tramack with traditional chord pillars.

The melody notes would also imply the following harmonization (I–III7–vi), which, when used the second time, leads to the approach in Figure 14.20, providing more variety while still feeling comfortable to the ear.

Figure 14.20

Excerpt from "Annie Laurie," arrangement by Steve Tramack with alternate chord pillars.

You'll find some additional examples in Chapter 16 of *Arranging Barbershop Vol. 2*, Harmonic Rhythm.

Case Study

The following case study looks at the development of the barbershop arrangement, fleshing out the steps outlined above. Once you have identified the harmonic pillars, write out the melody in the lead part and add in the names of the chords at the points where the pillars change.

Figure 14.21

Melody of "When I Lost You," by Irving Berlin with identified harmonic pillars.

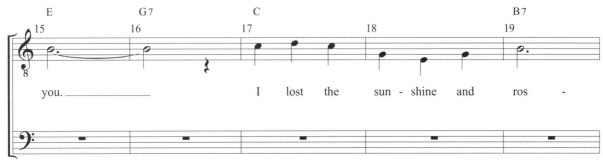

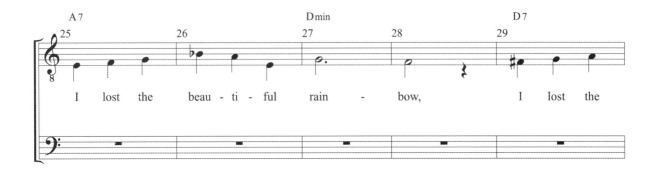

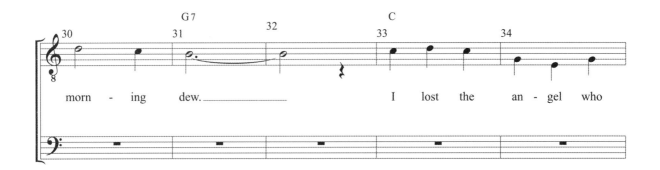

When I Lost You

3

Next, identify non-chord tones. For now, if the melody note is part of the chord you have identified as the harmonic pillar, you will use that chord. When you advance beyond writing harmonizations to full-blown arrangements with use of embellishments to create interest and development in the musical performance, you may well choose an alternate chord, but that will come later.

Figure 14.22

"When I Lost You," by Irving Berlin. Melody with harmonic pillars and identified non-chord tones.

WHEN I LOST YOU

Words and Music by
IRVING BERLIN

Arrangement by
STEVEN ARMSTRONG

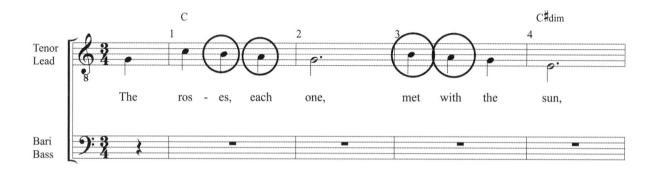

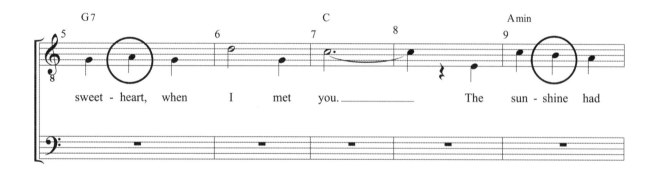

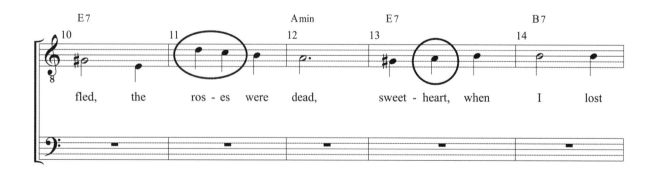

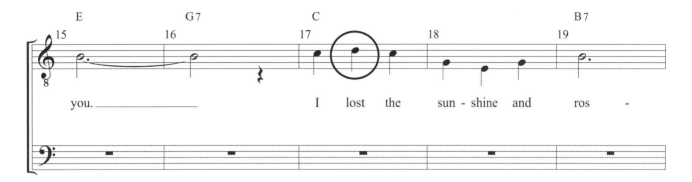

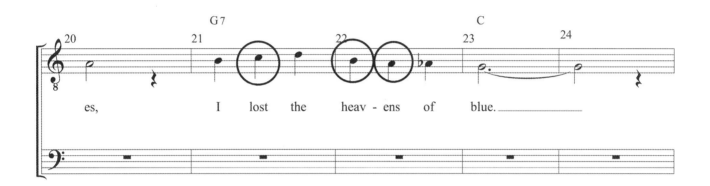

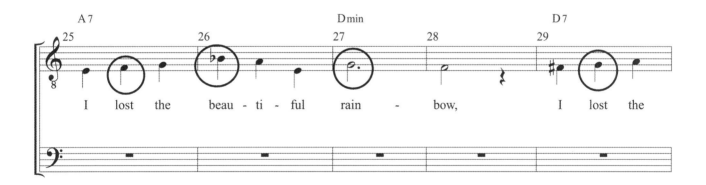

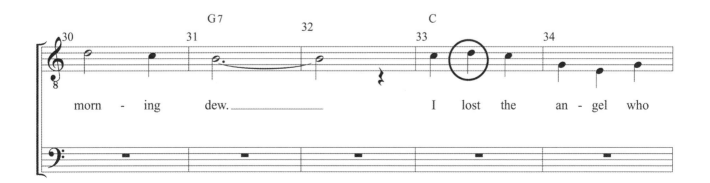

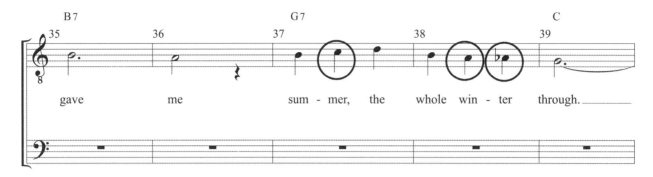

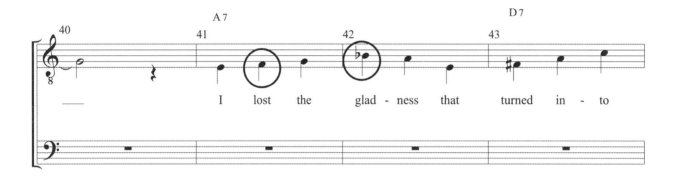

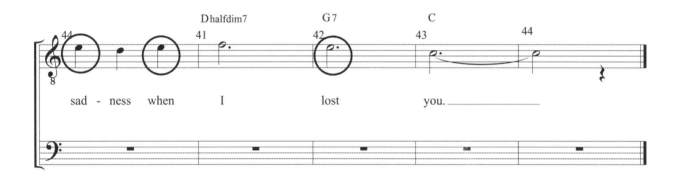

Next, write in the bass notes for any melody notes that are part of the harmonic pillar.

> Keep in mind that for triads, the bass is usually on the root. With seventh chords, the bass is either on the root or fifth. The bass note on the root or fifth is considered a strong voicing and is easier for barbershoppers to tune.

Strive for a smooth, easy-to-sing line. If a choice exists of changing the note when the measure changes or within the measure, it is usually best to have the note change at the beginning. This adds strength to the listener's perception of the harmonic rhythm.

Figure 14.23

"When I Lost You," by Irving Berlin with lead and bass harmonization of melody notes within the harmonic pillars.

WHEN I LOST YOU

Words and Music by
IRVING BERLIN

Arrangement by
STEVEN ARMSTRONG

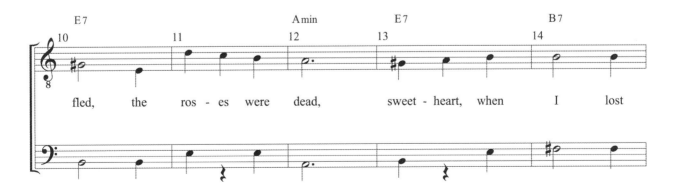

When I Lost You

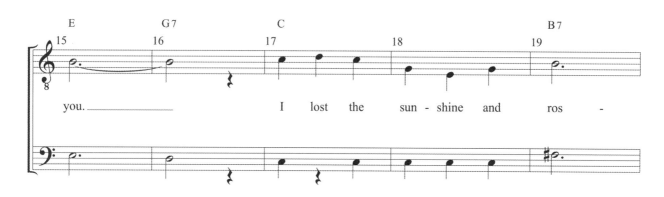

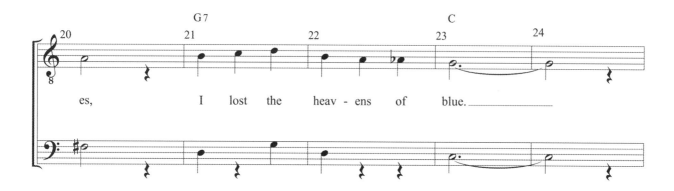

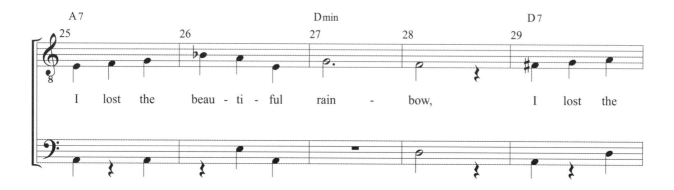

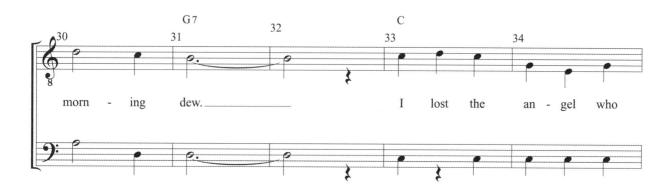

When I Lost You

_3_

gave me sum - mer, the whole win - ter through.

I lost the glad - ness that turned in - to

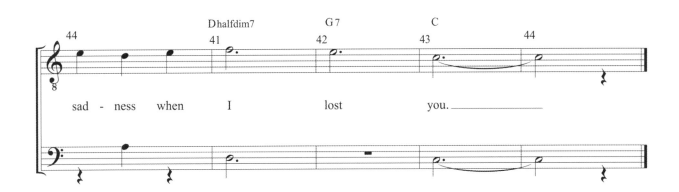

sad - ness when I lost you.

Harmonize the Tenor Line

Next, write in the tenor part, filling in one of the remaining parts of the chord. Again, being sure to write smooth, easy-to-sing lines.

Figure 14.24

"When I Lost You," by Irving Berlin. Lead, bass, and tenor harmonizations of melody notes within the harmonic pillars.

Note that most of the contiguous tenor notes are either a repeated note, or intervals of a third or less. Things were going well until measure 11, as shown in Figure 14.25. At this point, the only two available tenor notes are a G#, which would make an awkward jump of a tritone, or B, which would mean taking the tenor below the lead.

Figure 14.25

"When I Lost You," by Irving Berlin. Tenor harmonization challenge.

The problem can be solved if we adjust what we had written in the bass line and put the bass on the B—the fifth—instead of E. That will allow us to put the tenor on an E, making a nice smooth line.

Figure 14.26

"When I Lost You," by Irving Berlin. Lead, bass, and tenor harmonizations of melody notes within the harmonic pillars.

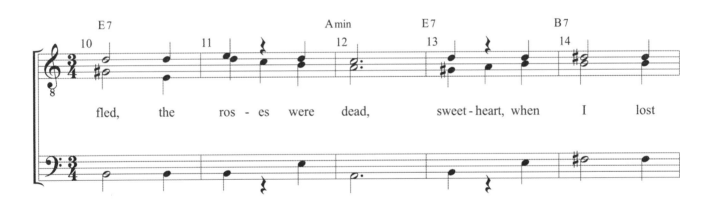

We run into the same sort of problem in measure 43, as shown in Figure 14.27. We could put the tenor on a C for the first two quarter notes, but then it would require a tritone jump up to an F# on beat three or taking the tenor below the lead on that chord. If we change the bass note on beat one to be an A, we can again make for a smoother tenor line.

Figure 14.27

"When I Lost You" by Irving Berlin. Lead, bass, and tenor harmonizations of melody notes within the harmonic pillars.

Harmonize the Baritone Line

Now it is time to complete the chord by adding the baritone part. Be careful that you don't inadvertently double notes of a four-part chord, which means leaving one of the notes out. The barbershop baritone is used to having lines that jump around a little, but we still want to avoid difficult-to-sing lines.

Figure 14.28

"When I Lost You" arranged by Steve Armstrong with four-part harmonizations of melody notes within the harmonic pillars.

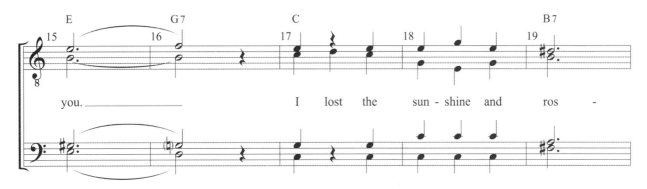

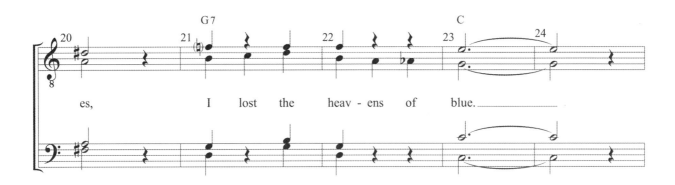

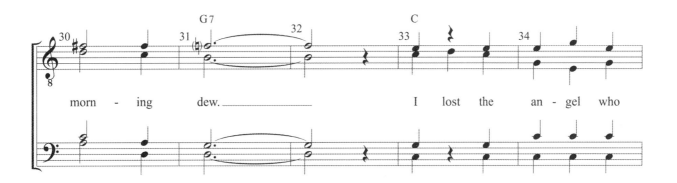

We made it almost all the way through without running into any problems, but when we come to measure 43, as shown in Figure 14.28, the only remaining note is a C. The low C would sound too muddy, and the higher C makes for an interval of a 6th. This could be sung by a baritone, but it is worth looking to see if there is an option that leads to a smoother line. Because this is leading into a higher melody line and, in fact, the climax of the melody, we might want to consider higher voicings here.

A natural spot to do this would be at measure 41, as shown in Figure 14.29, so instead of the tenor and baritone coming down from their previous notes they may go up a little. If we do that, we end up with this, which is a nice smooth line for everybody.

Figure 14.29

"When I Lost You" arranged by Steve Armstrong with modified harmonizations of melody notes within the harmonic pillars.

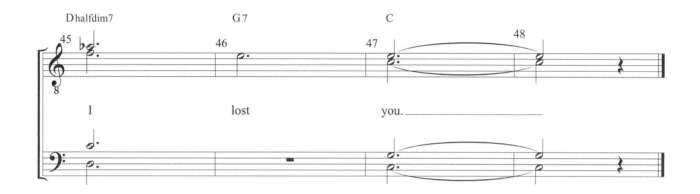

Harmonize Non-Chord Tones

The next step is to determine how to harmonize these non-pillar chord notes. For each note, consider the following options. It is best to play each one on a keyboard or plug them into your music notation software and play it back so you can hear what it sounds like. As a reminder, the options are shown in Table 14.5

Table 14.5

Chord choices for non-pillar chord notes.

Option Number	Chord Type	Distance of Root From Harmonic Pillar
1	Extended chord (add 6th, 7th, or 9th)	On
2	Barbershop 7th	5th above
3	Barbershop 7th	5th below
4	Barbershop 7th	Semitone below
5	Barbershop 7th	Semitone above
6	Barbershop 7th	Tritone
7	Diminished 7th	On

Let's look at some of the non-pillar notes in our example and consider the options. Because measures 1 and 3 each have two non-pillar notes, let's start by looking at measure 5—we'll come back to measures 1 and 3—and consider each of the seven options above. The harmonic pillar is a G7, and the melody note is an A.

- Can we add this note into the harmonic pillar?
  ***Yes*, we could use a G9**
- Can we use the barbershop 7th chord whose root is a 5th above the root of the harmonic pillar?
  ***Yes*, we could use a D7**
- Can we use the barbershop 7th chord whose root is a 5th below the root of the harmonic pillar?
  No, the melody note A is not in a C7 chord
- Can we use the barbershop 7th chord whose root is a semitone below the root of the harmonic pillar?
  No, the melody note A is not in an F#7 chord
- Can we use the barbershop 7th chord whose root is a semitone above the root of the harmonic pillar?
  No, the melody note A is not in an A♭7 chord
- Can we use the barbershop 7th chord whose root is a tritone away from the root of the harmonic pillar?
  No, the melody note A is not in a C#7 chord
- Can we use the diminished 7th chord that shares the same root as the harmonic pillar?
  No, the melody note A is not in a G dim 7 chord

So, we have two options to consider:

Figure 14.30

"When I Lost You" with the extended chord for harmonizing the non-chord tone.

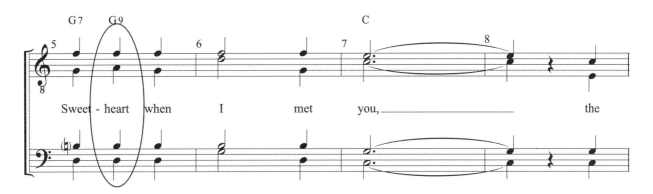

Figure 14.31

"When I Lost You" with a barbershop 7th chord whose root is a fifth above the harmonic pillar for harmonizing the non-chord tone.

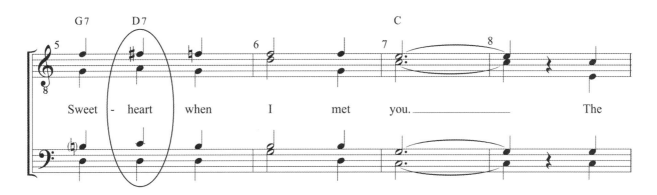

Either could work, but the first option, shown in Figure 14.30, just feels a little smoother. Let's go with that.

Next let's look at measure 9 and again consider each of the seven options from Table 14.5. The harmonic pillar is an A min, and the melody note is a B.

- Can this note be added into the harmonic pillar?
  No, B can't be added to A min and make a chord in the barbershop chord vocabulary
- Can we use the barbershop 7th chord whose root is a 5th above the root of the harmonic pillar?
  Yes, we could use an E7
- Can we use the barbershop 7th chord whose root is a 5th below the root of the harmonic pillar?
  No, the melody note B is not in a D7 chord
- Can we use the barbershop 7th chord whose root is a semitone below the root of the harmonic pillar?
  No, the melody note B is not in a G#7 chord
- Can we use the barbershop 7th chord whose root is a semitone above the root of the harmonic pillar?
  No, the melody note B is not in an B♭7 chord
- Can we use the barbershop 7th chord whose root is a tritone away from the root of the harmonic pillar?
  No, the melody note B is not in an E♭7 chord
- Can we use the diminished 7th chord that shares the same root as the harmonic pillar?
  No, the melody note B is not in an A dim 7 chord

We only have one choice, but thankfully this one sounds really good and works well.

Figure 14.32

"When I Lost You" with option 2 from Table 14.5 for harmonizing the non-chord tone.

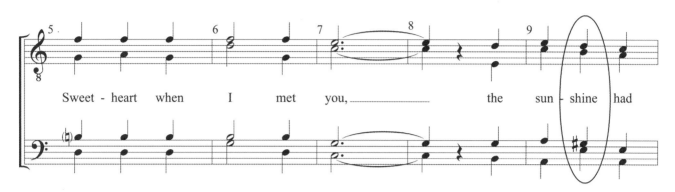

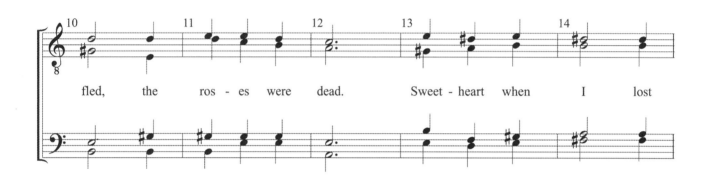

Let's look at another example, in Figure 14.33, measure 13.

Figure 14.33

"When I Lost You" with identified harmonic pillars.

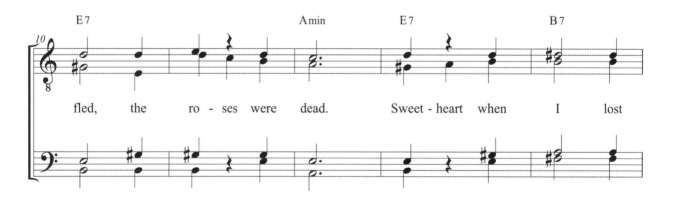

The harmonic pillar is an E7 chord, and the melody note, on "sweet*heart*" in the second beat of measure 13, is an A. Let's look at the seven options from Table 14.5, and what the chord would look like:

- Can this note be added into the harmonic pillar?
  No, A can't be added to E7 and make a chord in the barbershop chord vocabulary
- Can we use the barbershop 7th chord whose root is a 5th above the root of the harmonic pillar?
  Yes, we could use a B7.

This feels natural as well.

Figure 14.34

"When I Lost You" with option 2 for harmonizing the non-chord tone.

A variation on this theme, which also would work well, would be to use the minor 7th chord (min/min7) whose root is a 5th above the root of the harmonic pillar. In this option, the tenor stays on the D for all three notes in the measure, and the minor seventh seems more appropriate to the lyrical subtext of "sweetheart when I lost you."

Figure 14.35

"When I Lost You" with a modified option 2 for harmonizing the non-chord tone.

- Can we use the barbershop 7th chord whose root is a 5th below the root of the harmonic pillar?
  Yes, the melody note A is the root of the A7 chord.

This sounds a bit awkward, though the progression works:

Figure 14.36

"When I Lost You" with option 3 for harmonizing the non-chord tone.

Sweet - heart   when

- • Can we use the barbershop 7th chord whose root is a semitone below the root of the harmonic pillar?
  No, the melody note A is not in an E♭7 chord
- • Can we use the barbershop 7th chord whose root is a semitone above the root of the harmonic pillar?
  Yes, the melody note A is in an F7 chord.

This is an interesting option, though the voice leading for the bass and baritone may be tricky:

Figure 14.37

"When I Lost You" with option 5 for harmonizing the non-chord tone. Note this uses the rootless F9 chord.

Sweet - heart   when

- • Can we use the barbershop 7th chord whose root is a tritone away from the root of the harmonic pillar?
  No, the melody note A is not in an A#7 chord.
- • Can we use the diminished 7th chord that shares the same root as the harmonic pillar?
  No, the melody note A is not in an E dim 7 chord.

Which option should you choose? Several factors are at play. Which option best conveys the subtext of the musical line? Which tug at the listener's ear less or more than others, which should weigh into your decision. Which is easiest to sing, particularly considering this is on a weak beat in the measure, in the middle of a phrase? All these factors play a role in determining what's right for this chart.

Time to try some for yourself! What options would be available in the incomplete measures? From the available options, what do you choose?

Figure 14.38

"When I Lost You" worksheet for practicing harmonization.

WHEN I LOST YOU

Words and Music by
IRVING BERLIN

Arrangement by
STEVEN ARMSTRONG

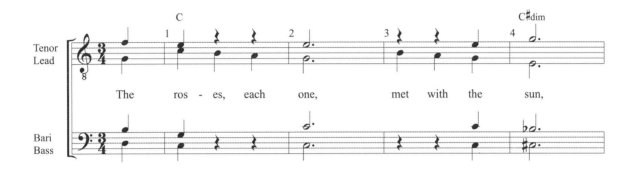

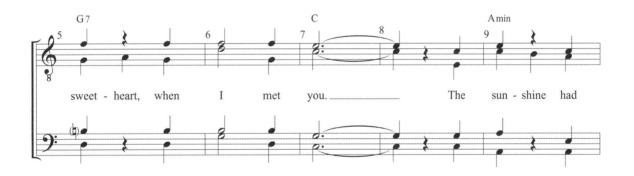

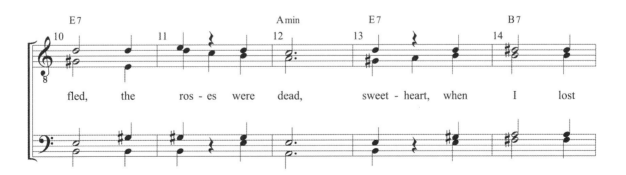

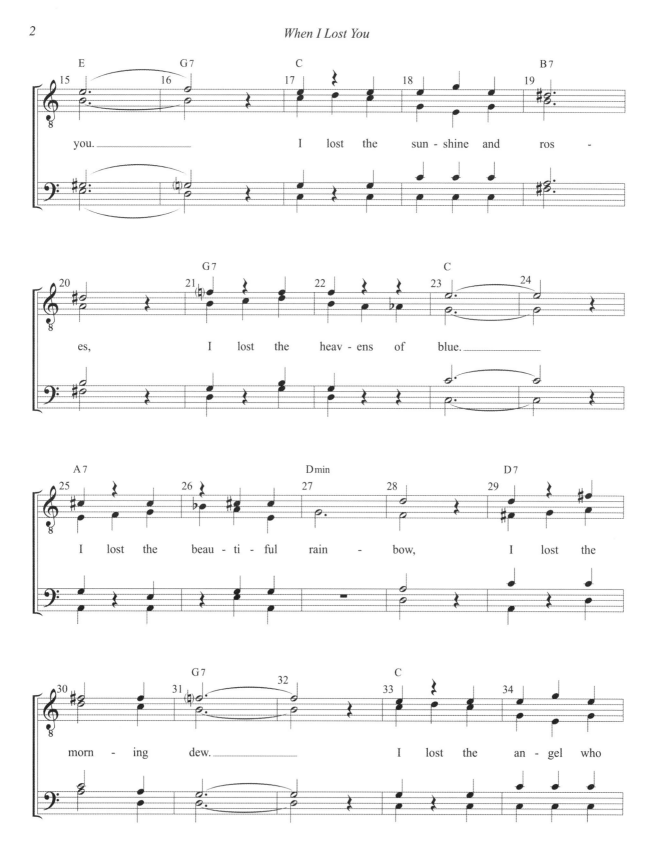

When I Lost You

Let's now look at a completed version of the chart.

Figure 14.39

"When I Lost You," completed arrangement from the Harmony University Beginning Arranging Class, 2019.

WHEN I LOST YOU

Words and Music by
IRVING BERLIN

Arrangement by
STEVEN ARMSTRONG

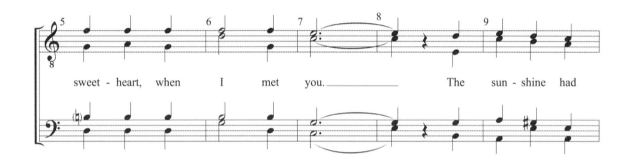

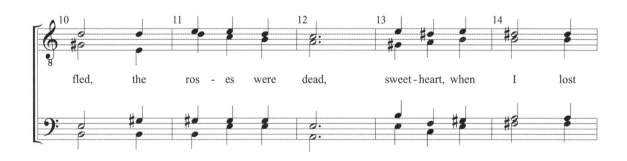

2   *When I Lost You*

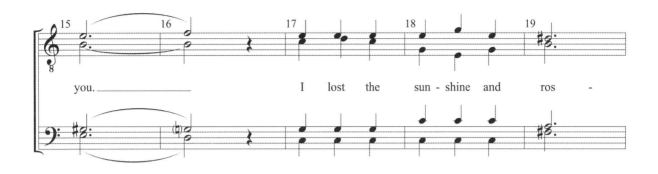

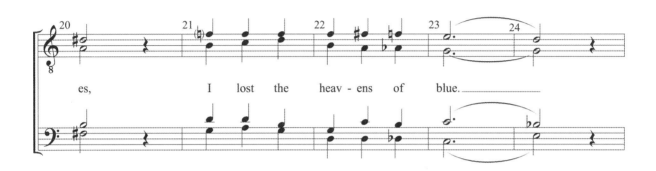

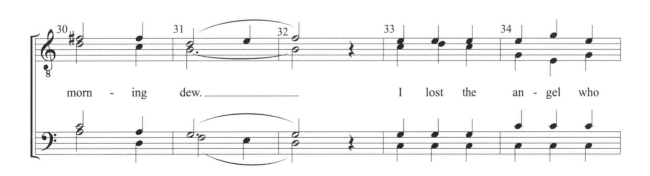

When I Lost You

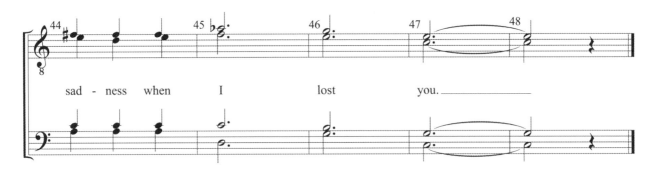

Conclusion

Harmonizing a melody in the barbershop style is both an art and a science. There are seven steps to follow when writing a harmonization: 1) melody and lyrics, 2) identify harmonic pillars, 3) identify non-pillar melody notes, 4) bass harmony, 5) tenor harmony, 6) baritone harmony, and 7) identify potential harmonies for non-pillar notes.

Considering the harmonic rhythm—the rate of change of the harmony—and the harmonic pillars—the prevailing harmony which designates the mileposts for the harmonic rhythm—is an important first step. These harmonic pillars are often found above the staff in printed sheet music and can be further validated by the melody notes within that measure.

Once the harmonic pillars are identified, the next step is identifying which melody notes fall outside that pillar. The harmonization process involves identifying and considering choices for harmonizing those non-chord tones while maintaining good voice leading and pleasing harmonic flow. This chapter reviewed these rules starting with Table 14.1.

Starting with the bass harmony and establishing strong voicing—root position and second inversion chords wherever possible—creates a solid foundation for the barbershop style. Baritone and tenor harmonies are often dictated by a combination of identifying the remaining notes in complete chords and voicing leading considerations.

Chapter 15.
Fundamentals of Arranging: Additional Considerations

By Kevin Keller and Steve Tramack

Chapter 14 covered many of the key concepts associated with the fundamentals of arranging, including:

- A system for laying out the melody line and basic structure of the arrangement. More information can be found on this topic in *Arranging Barbershop Vol. 1* in Chapters 10 and 12.
- An approach for harmonizing melody notes included in the prevailing harmonic pillar for the measure. This started with laying down the foundational bass notes, preferring roots and fifths of the prevailing harmony, followed by the tenor and baritone parts, paying attention to voice leading.
- A system for harmonizing non-chord tones and some examples of trial and error to determine the best options.

There are a few additional considerations one might have when creating a basic barbershop arrangement. The remainder of Part A of this volume will provide the arranger with more insight into additional considerations for when first creating a foundational arrangement. This chapter will address choosing a key for the arrangement, identifying suitable melodies, chord vocabulary best practices, and an introduction to embellishments.

Subsequent chapters will dive deeper into additional considerations. Chapter 16 will discuss harmonic rhythm. Chapter 17 provides considerations for rhythm and meter. Chapter 18 will provide arrangers with advice to avoid common mistakes.

This chapter, combined with the lessons learned in Chapter 14—Laying out and harmonizing a melody, basic structure of an arrangement, and a system for harmonizing non-chord tones—and Chapters 16–18 constitute the fundamentals of arranging.

Choosing the Correct Key for an Arrangement

One of the first challenges that all arrangers face is deciding the key of the song. First, consider the range of the melody with respect to the typical range of the lead singer. Although not necessary, it is often helpful to evaluate whether the melody is a *sol-to-sol* melody or a *do-to-do* melody.

 Sol-to-sol and do-to-do refer to scale degrees five and one, respectively, as part of the solmization of a musical scale, of which solfege is the most common. See the glossary for more information.

Sol-to-sol melodies will feature notes almost evenly distributed above and below the tonic. Common barbershop examples include "My Wild Irish Rose," "Down our Way," and "The Story of the Rose." These melodies are easier to arrange in the barbershop style because the lead part never gets too low or too high in the range.

Note the example of a sol-to-sol melody in Figure 15.1. As a sol-to-sol melody in B♭, we'd expect to see all of the melody notes in "Down Our Way" to be between F and F. This is indeed the case; in fact, "Down Our Way" is more of a sol-to-mi melody, with all the lead's notes falling between F and D.

Figure 15.1

"Down Our Way" words and music by Al Stedman and Fred Hughes. Arranged by Barbershop Harmony Society.

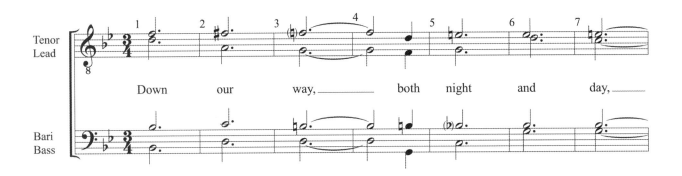

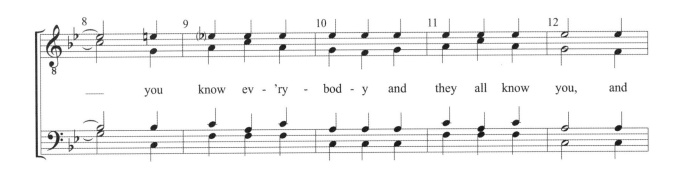

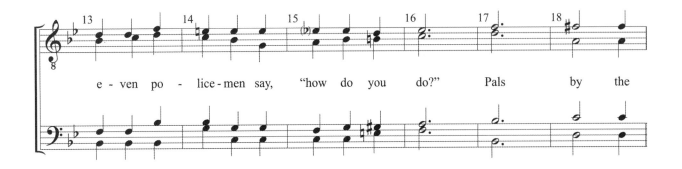

 For TTBB voices, typically these songs will be arranged in the keys of G to D♭. For SSAA voices, typically these songs will be arranged from D to A♭. The key will usually depend on how high the melody goes.

Do-to-do melodies will feature notes mainly within a full octave, relative to the key signature. Commonly known songs include "Sunny Side of the Street" and "Get Happy (Forget Your Troubles)." If the melody goes to the lower octave of the key at the end of a section, it's a do–to–do melody.

Note the following example, "Sunny Side of the Street." In the key of C, the melody both spends time at the low octave, and traverses up an octave and a third to an E in an arpeggiated passage at the beginning of each A section. These melodies are still possible to arrange in the style, but you'll have to consider transferring the melody from time to time to avoid the chords getting muddy.

Figure 15.2

"Sunny Side of the Street," words and music by Jimmy McHugh and Dorothy Fields.

 For TTBB voices, typically these songs will be arranged in the keys of E♭ to F. For SSAA voices, typically these songs will be arranged in the keys of B♭ to C. For SATB and other mixed range ensembles, this will vary depending on the voices in the group.

All these ranges are subject to inspection of the melody. Sometimes there is just one troublesome spot in the melody in a certain key but the rest of it works magnificently. If the arranger will find a solution for that one spot, the rest of the song will sing comfortably.

Suitable Features of the Melody for Barbershop

If you ask barbershoppers if a song is suitable for barbershop or not, they can probably answer yes or no when they hear it, but they may not be able to tell you why. There are actually several aspects to a melody that can indicate its adaptability to the style.

Characteristics of a Melody that Will Favor Barbershop:

- **Implied barbershop harmonies.** Can you hear stylistic chord progressions and implied harmonies right away? If your ear hears it, trust your ear!
- **Melodically simple.** The simpler the melody, the better the barbershop will be. This doesn't mean that the arrangement must be simple, but if the melody is simple, the application of chords will go easier.
- **Singable.** It's not that a song with a complex melody can't be arranged, but if it is difficult to sing, it will be harder for performers to be successful delivering the melody and even the harmonies.
- **Small intervals.** Leads will execute *conjunct* melodies with small intervals—half steps and whole steps—extremely well. *Disjunct* melodies, with larger steps or leaps, will be difficult to sing smoothly, and that can interrupt the ability for the performers to be accurate.

 Conjunct and disjunct refer to melodic motion. Conjunct motion moves in smaller steps—chromatic or scale degree—while disjunct motion refers to interval leaps of greater than a major second. A combination of melodic contour and type of motion can imply degree and types of emotion conveyed by the melody.

- **Rhythmically simple.** Songs in simple meters such as 2/4, 3/4 and 4/4 create a rhythmic foundation for a singable melody. Melodies featuring lots of syncopation and offbeat passages, particularly when coupled with accidentals, create challenges for the melody singer.
- **Not too rangy.** Songs that barbershop well tend to have a range of notes between an octave and an octave and a third, called a tenth.
- **Non-angular melody.** Melodies that frequently and quickly make disjunct leaps present challenges. "Georgia on My Mind" and "Keep Your Sunny Side Up" have melodies that ascend and descend rapidly. Certainly, these can be arranged in the barbershop style, but can be harder to execute. Know the ensemble for whom you arrange.

Figure 15.3

"Sunny Side Up," words and music by B.G. De Sylva, Lew Brown, and Ray Henderson.

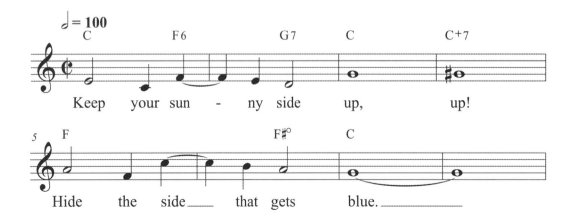

- **Few Accidentals**. Accidentals—sharps, flats, natural signs—alter the note from the scale tones. These can create opportunities for fun harmonies, but lead singers may struggle. Half-step intervals might be the exception. Non-diatonic, chromatically-altered melody notes can signify significant musical events, being different and unexpected gifts from the composer, but can also create challenges to sing accurately. The chorus of "Sweet Adeline" is full of accidentals in the melody and works well in the style, but it is still not too difficult to sing accurately.

Figure 15.4

"Sweet Adeline," words and music by Richard H. Gerard and Harry Armstrong. Arranged by Barbershop Harmony Society.

Another example of a melody that both features melodic accidentals and large, descending octave leaps is "Stormy Weather." Aaron Dale's arrangement makes for great barbershop, but it's certainly not for the faint of heart. Singing this melody effectively requires a great deal of skill from the lead singer.

Figure 15.5

"Stormy Weather," words and music by Ted Koehler and Harold Arlen. Arranged by Aaron Dale.

In summary, it's important to know your ensemble's strengths and weaknesses, even when it comes to accuracy of a delivered melody or rhythm. Matching the capabilities of the ensemble with the characteristics of a melody is a good first step to creating a great barbershop arrangement.

Chord Vocabulary Best Practices

Modern barbershop arrangers have the advantage of learning what works best in the style from the previous generations of arrangers. Today, arrangers with an understanding of chord inversions, doubling, major or minor triads, seventh chords, and voice leading stand to create arrangements that are pleasing to hear and pleasing to sing and are unquestionably stylistic. Here are some basic principles related to chords in the barbershop style:

Chord Inversions

Chord inversions are recognized by the chord member sung by the bass.

- Root Position: bass is on the root of the chord
- First Inversion: bass is on the third of the chord
- Second Inversion: bass is on the fifth of the chord
- Third Inversion: bass is on the seventh of the chord

In barbershop, chords are most frequently voiced in root position or second inversion. The inherent consonance potential of the harmony is aided by *homorhythmic texture* and chords with the bass singing the root or the fifth.

 Homorhythmic texture, as it pertains to barbershop, refers to all voices singing the same word or part of a word, also called a *phoneme*, at the same time.

Basic harmonizations should feature predominantly strongly voiced, root position or second inversion chords. In developing an arrangement further, one can explore other voicings to create a specific effect or impact. When properly balanced, the bass on the third of the chord will have an ethereal sound. However, basses with stronger voices tend to overbalance and sing the first inversion seventh chord out of tune (sharp), and the non-bass voice parts will often under-balance either the root or fifth of the chord. This leads to a less sonorous, out-of-tune chord, which is why it's used sparingly, if at all.

 Particularly for those arrangers who are new to the barbershop style, the recommendation is to avoid first and third inversion seventh chords unless used in a swipe.

The bass on the seventh of the chord can happen on a *scissor embellishment*.

Scissor embellishments refer to contrary motion of two harmony parts. In the classical world, this concept is known as contrapuntal motion. Specifically with a scissors embellishment, the two lines meet in the middle—usually an octave apart—of the embellishment.

Note the scissors embellishments between the tenor and bass in measure 36, and the lead and bass in measures 38–39—though not meeting in the middle—in "Bright Was the Night."

Figure 15.6

"Bright Was the Night" scissors embellishments. Traditional words and music. Arranged by David Wright.

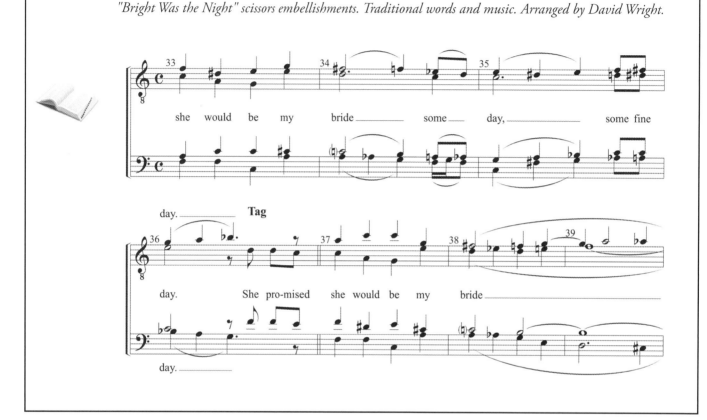

"If I Had My Way," shown in Figure 15.7, leverages both a first inversion seventh chord—seen on the second beat of the second measure of the excerpt—and the third inversion seventh chord—on the first beat of the third measure of the excerpt—to great effect, creating a sense of both instability and intimacy. For proper tuning and balance, the bass needs to be aware of the lead on "tomorROW" and the baritone on "bring."

Figure 15.7

"If I Had My Way," words and music by Lou Klein and James Kendis. Arranged by David Harrington.

Doubling

The tenor, lead, and baritone rarely ever double—singing the same note an octave apart—each other. The exception would be where the bass takes the third of the chord in a major triad. Figure 15.8 shows an exception when the lead and tenor are intentionally doubled in measure 3 to create a sense of loneliness and distance.

Figure 15.8

"If I Had My Way," verse by David and Holly Harrington.

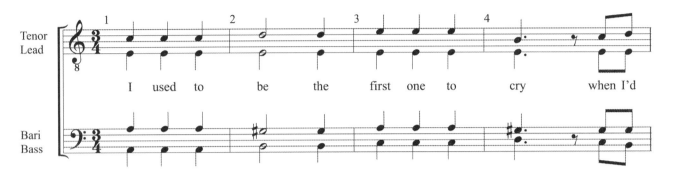

Doubling can and will occur with the bass, either on the same note or an octave, sometimes two, apart. Note the first measure of "If I Had My Way" in Figure 15.8, with the bass and baritone being an octave apart.

Major or Minor Triads

The bass should sing the root of the chord unless there is a valid reason otherwise. Sometimes arranging the bass to sing the fifth of the chord makes sense for either voice leading or a specific musical impact moment, but the best practice involves arranging the bass on the root of triads.

Seventh Chords (any)

What role does the lead note have?

- If the lead is singing the root, put the bass on the fifth of the chord.

- If the lead is singing the fifth, put the bass on the root of the chord.

- If the lead is singing a different note, often the bass will sing the root of the chord, but sometimes the fifth. This is often found based on the voice leading of the bass part. An example of this can be found in measure 52 of the Barbershop Harmony Society arrangement of "Sweet and Lovely," as shown in Figure 15.9.

Figure 15.9

"Sweet and Lovely," words and music by Norman Starks. Arranged by Mac Huff.

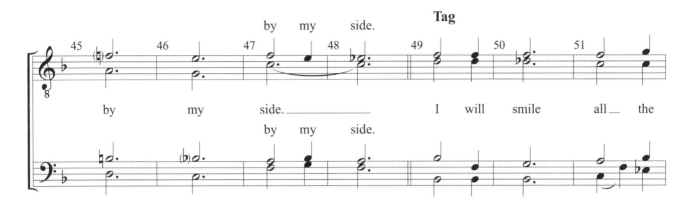

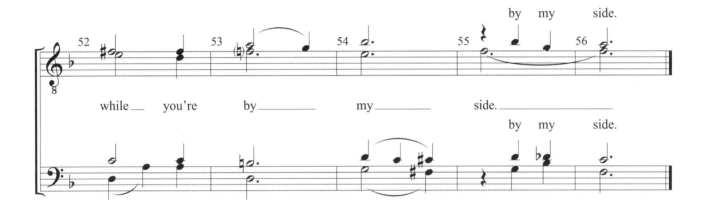

Baritone and Tenor Harmonization

After you've arranged the foundational bass part, add the tenor and baritone lines next.

- **Tenor**: Attempt to move stepwise as much as possible. The smoother the tenor line, the better. Lots of jumps will be problematic. Songs that barbershop extremely well will have the tenor part repeating the same note. When they move, they will move in half-step intervals. Further consider the following ranges when arranging the tenor part:

  - Low voices: keep the tenor at a C4 or above
  - High voices: keep the tenor at a F4 or above

- **Baritone**: If the chord is missing the root or fifth, first consider the baritone to take that missing note. Even though the baritone might be the leftover part, if the baritone is unsingable, look to the bass and tenor notes to find a different solution.
- **Voice Leading**: Ideally every part should be smooth, moving in small intervals and not jumping around a lot. Each part could be sung melodically. When that happens, it will be singable by the group. Go back through your efforts. Identify large intervals. Is there a way to smooth these out? The bass is the possible exception in barbershop music and choral music in general. That singer is most likely to have the most leaps and it's perfectly okay.

Use of Embellishments in Uptunes vs Ballads

Note: this topic is covered in more depth in Chapters 23 and 29 of Arranging Barbershop Vol. 2.

The use of embellishments in barbershop is vital. Because our art form is a cappella, there is no piano or orchestra or band to fill in behind sustained melody notes. The arranger carefully crafts embellishments to create forward motion and sustained interest in the music.

Swipes and *echoes* are the two most common embellishments arrangers use. There are multiple considerations as to whether to use a swipe or an echo. If the lyrics are the prevailing thematic element, consider using echoes to embellish the lyric, supporting what was just sung or foreshadowing what's coming next. If the melody or harmony are of particular importance in a given phrase, consider a swipe to create additional musical tension, excitement, and motion.

Embellishments often serve as rhythmic propellants, adding lyrical reinforcement to the phrase, or, occasionally, lyrical foreshadowing. How arrangers apply embellishments can vary depending upon a variety of factors, but one important distinction is whether the song is an *uptune*, with its constant, driving tempo, or a *ballad*, which often gets a rubato treatment.

Uptunes

There are a number of reasons why an arranger should use echoes in uptunes. First, the choice of words or word parts an arranger applies in echoes can reinforce the meter. Echoes can also reinforce the rhythm of the phrase. Echoes let both singers and their audience know when one phrase ends and another phrase starts.

Keep the amount of words in an echo to a minimum, and strive to use either the original lyrics or rhyming or related words. If you can use the same rhythms from the preceding phrase, so much the better.

Comparatively, swipes used in uptunes are more likely to be rushed. Use them only if you must. Do use the same word or word part as what the melody is sustaining.

Ballads

For ballads, arrangers can use either swipes or echoes. However, unlike uptunes, embellishments can slow down the momentum of the song. This may be something you want. If you need to put on the brakes, adding chords will naturally slow down the song. Figure 15.10 shows an effective use of an embellishment in measure 38 that gives a natural rallentando.

Figure 15.10

"Bright Was the Night" swipes that serve as a natural rallentando. Arranged by David Wright.

If you need an embellishment to transition from one section to the next and the urgency is building, minimize the number of chords. Figure 15.11 shows an effective use of an embellishment in measures 35–36 that adds urgency while using few chords.

Figure 15.11

"Bright Was the Night" building urgency coming into the tag. Arranged by David Wright.

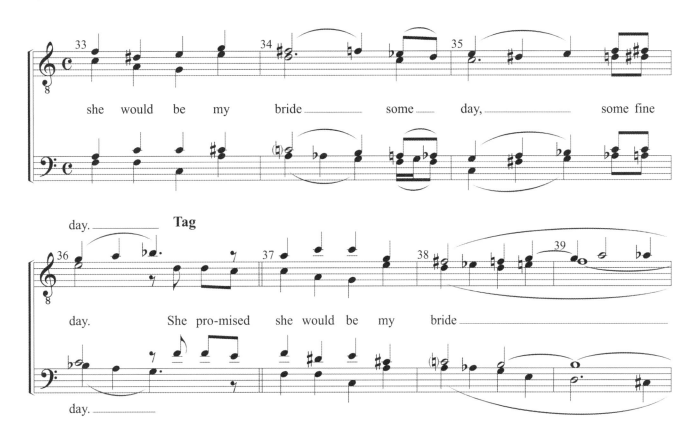

Last, the words used for echoes in a ballad can sound trite after a while, so be judicious in their use. Figure 15.12 displays a tasteful and supportive use of an echo in a ballad.

Figure 15.12

"Not While I'm Around" use of echoes to reinforce key lyrics. Words and music by Stephen Sondheim. Arranged by Steve Tramack.

No One Is Alone / Not While I'm Around Medley   *3*

General Rules for Embellishments

Consider the following suggestions for whether the phrase might need an embellishment:

- If the sustained melody note is longer than one measure
- If the song is in 3/4 and the sustained note is a dotted half
- If the song is in 4/4 or cut time and the sustained note is a whole note, depending upon the section of the song

Always consider the audience, the source material, and the ensemble performing the song in your choice of embellishments.

Conclusion

When first arranging a song, there are several considerations beyond simply how to harmonize the melody. Many of the topics in this chapter will be covered in depth in subsequent chapters in this book. It all starts with the melody. From there, factors such as the key, chord voicing and vocabulary, and key musical events come into focus. Another key consideration is how you intend the song to be performed: uptune or ballad, in tempo or ad lib. These will directly influence embellishment choices, which also allow the song to sound like barbershop. The harmonic rhythm, a concept covered in Chapter 16, further provides insight to the tempo the composer intended the song to be performed.

Chapter 16.
Harmonic Rhythm

By Tom Gentry

The term harmonic rhythm is used to describe the frequency of harmonic changes. It is the rate of chord change in relation to time. A passage in common time with a stream of sixteenth notes and chord changes every measure has a slow harmonic rhythm and a fast surface or musical rhythm (sixteen notes per chord change), while a piece with a trickle of half notes and chord changes twice a measure has a fast harmonic rhythm and a slow surface rhythm (one note per chord change).[8]

An understanding and perception of the primary harmonic rhythm of a song is necessary for successful barbershop arranging. If you have not mapped out the harmonic pillars associated with the harmonic rhythm of the song, you may find yourself using chords that do not fit, or stuck in a harmonic sequence that does not fit the original intent of the song.

For many pianists who play by ear, choosing the right chord at the right time is a learned skill. They may from time to time embellish the harmony implied by the melody, but the essential chord changes are always made in the right places.

Barbershop ear singers who sense what chord is coming next—we would call such people good *woodshedders*—also have this perception.

 Woodshedding is a term commonly used by jazz and barbershop musicians and means to rehearse a difficult passage repeatedly until it is performed with ease, without the benefit of notated music. The metaphor of a woodshed refers to any private or remote location, away from a main house or other listeners.

But whether we are talking about lounge piano players, ace woodshedders, or barbershop arrangers, all of them need to be aware that harmonic changes are required, though others certainly can be added to increase interest or artistry.

Because required harmonic changes are chord root changes, the perception of these primary pillars is, once again, essential to the arranger. Observe the chord changes in the following example, "Roses at Twilight."

Figure 16.1

"Roses at Twilight," words and music by Herbert B. Marple and Ben Black. Includes identified harmonic pillars.

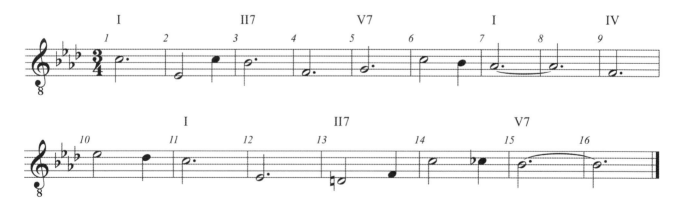

---

8   Wikipedia.com, accessed January 2023.

The harmony implied by the melody requires these root changes at these spots. Of course, there is considerably more harmonic variety that can be introduced. For example, a VI7 chord in measure 12 allows us to introduce another barbershop seventh, providing a more satisfying trip around the circle of fifths.

Different chords will be needed to harmonize *non-chord tones*. This topic was covered in detail in Chapter 14 of this book, and is further covered in *Arranging Barbershop Vol. 4*, but a few words of explanation are in order here.

 A non-chord tone (*NCT*) is a melody note outside the primary chord of a given measure or block of measures. For example, if the primary harmony in a particular spot is C major triad, any melody note other than C, E, or G is an NCT. Sometimes these notes, especially if they are diatonic, can be harmonized by using another chord with the same root; in this example, C6, Cmaj7, or C9. When an NCT is chromatic, though, matters can become more interesting, requiring a different root, offering the arranger opportunities for interest and variety. In either case, even though an NCT may require a chord with a different root than the prevailing harmony, the harmonic pillar remains the same.

Let's now look at the nicely symmetrical harmonic rhythm in the first two phrases of "Roses at Twilight," with each chord lasting for two measures.

Figure 16.2

"Roses at Twilight," with identified harmonic pillars.

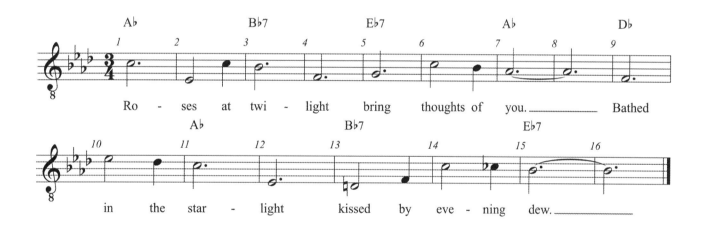

That is by no means the case with all songs, however. For example, in Figure 16.3, notice that each chord in "Five Foot Two" lasts for one measure, except for the VI7 (C7) chord starting in measure 3, which lasts for two measures.

Figure 16.3

"Five Foot Two," arrangement by Joe Liles, with identified harmonic pillars. Note the slowed harmonic rhythm in measures 3–4.

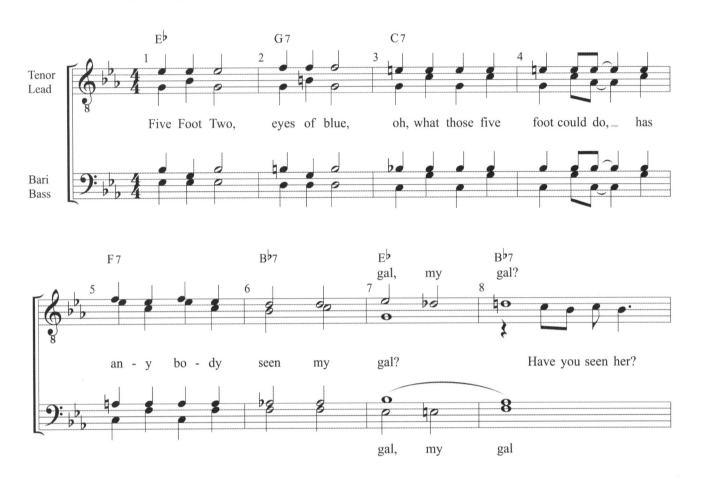

We see that the frequency of primary root changes is not necessarily consistent. Also, in many songs the rate of chord change accelerates toward the end of some phrases—especially in the final cadence—thus generating an increase in interest, emotional intensity, or excitement. Look at the last two phrases of "Roses at Twilight."

Figure 16.4

"Roses at Twilight," with identified harmonic pillars. in the final cadence the chord changes every measure rather than every two measures.

Primary harmonic changes usually occur on strong beats of measures. In 2/4 and 3/4, important chord changes generally take place on the downbeat, while in 4/4 time, changes usually occur on the first and third beats.

Note the chord changes in the following example; whenever you have a choice, make chord changes on accented beats.

Figure 16.5

First harmonic rhythm change example. Written and arranged by Tom Gentry.

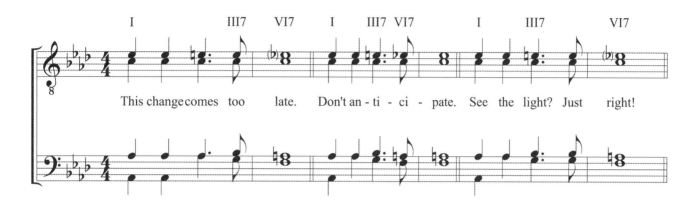

If it is necessary to change the harmony on a weak beat, change the harmony on the next strong beat if possible, as is shown in Figure 16.6:

Figure 16.6

Second harmonic rhythm change example. Written and arranged by Tom Gentry.

If it becomes necessary to change the harmony on the second half of a beat, change on the start of the next beat if possible:

Figure 16.7

Third harmonic rhythm change example. Written and arranged by Tom Gentry.

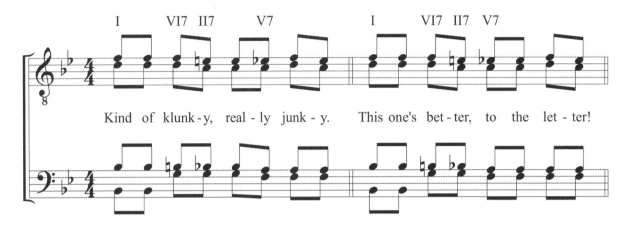

Syncopation

Although the harmonic rhythm normally calls for change on strong beats, when we encounter syncopated rhythm, the accent is displaced. *Syncopation* is defined as "a momentary contradiction of the prevailing meter or pulse. This may take the form of a temporary transformation of the fundamental character of the meter, e.g., from duple to triple or from 3/4 to 6/8, or it may be simply the contradiction of the regular succession of strong and weak beats within a measure or a group of measures whose metrical context nevertheless remains clearly defined by some part of the musical texture that does not itself participate in the syncopation."[9] Some jazz vernacular may call this a push beat, which one could say quickly in a session "push that beat 3."

Figure 16.8

Syncopation example.

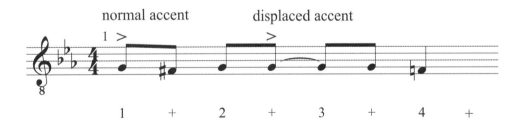

Note that in syncopation the strong accents shift to an earlier beat. The harmony may shift too, as in the example in Figure 16.9.

---

9   Randall, Don Michael. (1999). *The Harvard Concise Dictionary of Music and Musicians.* Page 652. The Belknap Press of Harvard University Press.

Figure 16.9

Syncopation examples. Written and arranged by Tom Gentry.

In summary, the frequency of chord (root) change is harmonic rhythm. The appropriate use of additional chord changes beyond the minimum required by the harmonic rhythm can add interest and artistry to an arrangement.

One other important factor to the barbershop arranger is the kind of chord progressions generated by the harmonic rhythm of the melody. The most stylistic barbershop songs are those in which the melody suggests root movement on the circle of fifths. These natural, ear-singing progressions are what we look for, particularly at the beginning of our arranging journey.

How to Determine the Harmonic Rhythm

You may say, "How do I go about determining the harmonic rhythm of a song I want to arrange?" Here are some factors that can help you in mapping out the harmonic highway:

- Your ears
- The chord symbols in a piano-vocal sheet
- The piano part in a piano-vocal sheet
- The melody notes that often imply certain pillar chords from measure to measure
- The circle of fifths

Your ears are the most important factor in determining the harmonic pillars. How natural does a certain chord or chord progression sound in a given spot? Do things go smoothly, or could there be a more natural-sounding harmonic progression? If you cannot hear whether a chord does or does not sound right, music theory can help a great deal. Arranging is more a Sudoku puzzle than guesswork. It can be more a craft than a creative process, particularly when determining prevailing harmonic pillars. With more experience, however, many arrangers begin to simply anticipate and hear the harmonic patterns. The following are examples of typical harmonic rhythm changes.

Figure 16.10

"When I Lost You" pillar chord changes every two measures.

Figure 16.11

"Five Foot Two" pillar chord changes on nearly every measure.

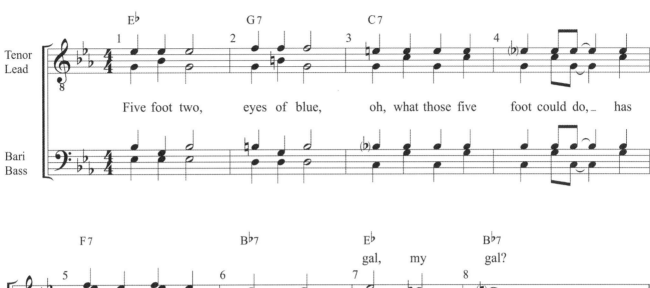

Figure 16.12

"A Nightingale Sang in Berkleley Square," words and music by Manning Sherman. Pillar chord changes every two beats.

Sheet Music

Sheet music often contains chord symbols above the staff. These helpful chord symbols are intended for guitar, ukulele, or piano players to quickly identify the pillar harmony in a song. When starting your arranging journey, seek to utilize sheet music that contains the chord symbols, as they will accelerate your process. Many websites contain several if not dozens of simplified arrangements that contain the chord symbols. That said, sometimes these symbols need to be taken as suggestions, not necessarily the only option. For example, an Am chord in the key of C might sound better to barbershop ears as an A7. Or perhaps what is notated as a Dmin or F chord would sound just fine as a D7, thus strengthening the barbershop character of your arrangement. Do be careful, though, not to force a dominant seventh chord into the musical line. For example, Figure 16.12 features the original harmonization of "In the Still of the Nite (I'll Remember)" by the Five Satins.

Figure 16.13

"In the Still of the Nite (I'll Remember)," words and music by Fred Parris.

This progression is common in songs from the 1950s Doo-wop era: I–vi–IV–V7–I. To make this feel more like a typical barbershop chord progression, one might be tempted to substitute a D7 in measures 6 and 10 to replace the Dmin. Further, to inject some additional circle movement, the last quarter of measure 7 and 11 could be harmonized with a G7 instead of remaining on the B♭ pillar. Listening to the example in Figure 16.13, the character of the piece is noticeably altered, simply with the introduction of the major-minor seventh chord and the alteration of the harmonic rhythm.

Figure 16.14

"In the Still of the Night" with the VI7 instead of vi in measure 6 and 10.

Harmonizing Using Original Sheet Music

Here is a comparison of the original sheet music of "Always" and Don Gray's arrangement of that song. Don chose the key of G for TTBB barbershop, raising it a whole step for the sake of the lead tessitura, but the key of F is used here for ease of comparison with the original sheet music.

Here is a measure-by-measure comparison, with the original sheet music on the left and Don Gray's arrangement on the right.

Note: for figures 16.15 through 16.32, all examples assume the key of F—even if no key signature is shown at the beginning of the measure.

Figure 16.15

"Always" measures 1 and 2 comparison. Words and music by Irving Berlin. Arranged by Don Gray.

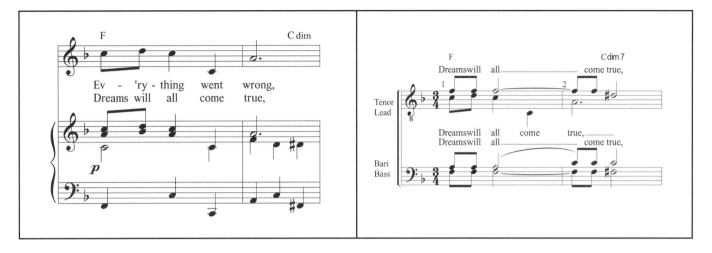

Measure 1: As one would expect, the arrangement begins with the tonic F major triad.

Measure 2: Mr. Gray sticks with sheet music's harmonization, holding off on the diminished seventh past the first beat of the measure.

Figure 16.16

"Always" measures 3 and 4 comparison. Arranged by Don Gray.

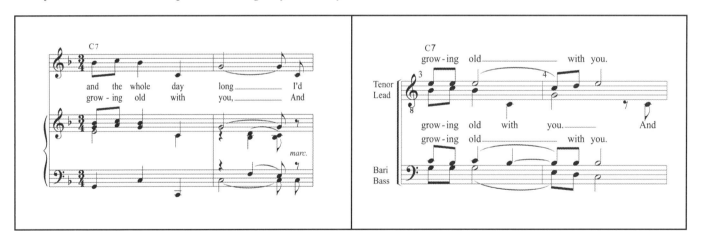

Measures 3–4: Both versions also agree that C7 is the harmonic pillar here.

Figure 16.17

"Always" measures 5 and 6 comparison. Arranged by Don Gray.

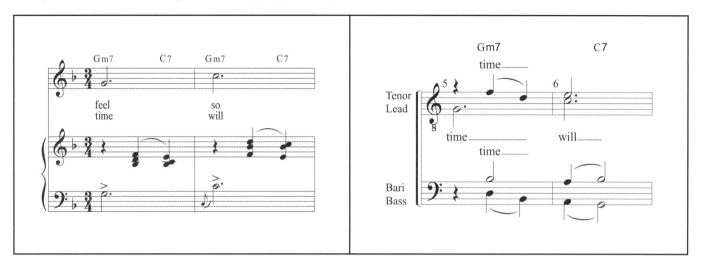

Measure 5: Sure, sticking with C7 in this measure would have worked, but isn't it more interesting to go *retrograde* in the circle of fifths and use Gm7 instead?

 Retrograde progressions refers to moving backwards around the circle of fifths, with root movement of ascending fifths rather than descending fifths.

Both versions use this approach, but now we have some divergence. Mr. Gray wisely avoids returning to C7, which the sheet suggests, at the end of the measure.

Measure 6: Even more sensible is making this measure C7. Gm7 just does not fit well with the C melody note, as the measure 11 chords are not part of the traditional barbershop vocabulary, so the sheet is to be cheerfully ignored here.

Figure 16.18

"Always," arranged by Don Gray. Measures 7 and 8 comparison.

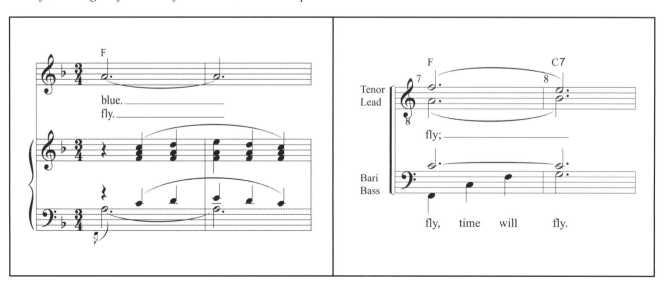

Measure 7: There is no missing the return to F in this spot.

Measure 8: Yes, the basic harmony is still F, but swiping the melody up to allow for a C7 is good writing—especially because measures 9–10 will be F as well, and we could use some variety. But we cannot blame the sheet for sticking with Berlin's melody, of course. Don's arranging choices in measures 6–8 nicely set up the lyric "fly," particularly with the line and contour of the bass embellishment.

Figure 16.19

"Always," arranged by Don Gray. Measures 13 and 14 comparison.

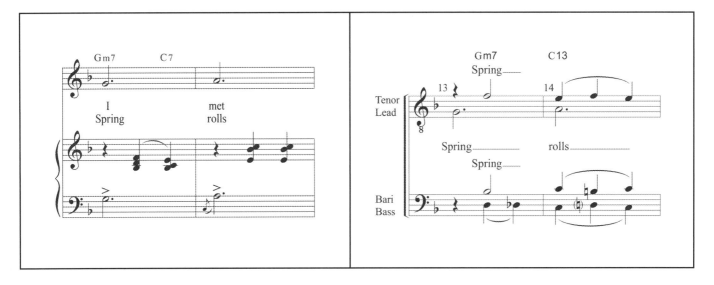

Measure 13: We do not need to anticipate the pillar change in the third beat of the measure. The choice in Mr. Gray's arrangement, moving from the Gm7 to the C13, works fine.

Figure 16.20

"Always," arranged by Don Gray. Measures 15 and 16 comparison.

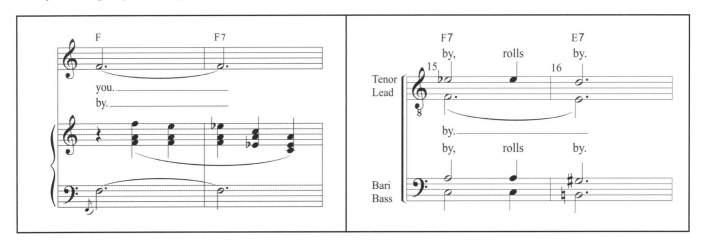

Measure 16: Here, Gray strays from the sheet music, moving the melody down by half step and substituting the F7 for an E7 that leads us in smooth, circle fashion to the Am in measure 17. If we stayed faithful to the original sheet music, we could get to Am, perhaps a little more dramatically, but the E7 allows smoother voice leading for the singers and an easier harmonic transition. Note this does change the melody line briefly.

Figure 16.21

"Always," arranged by Don Gray. Measures 17 and 18 comparison.

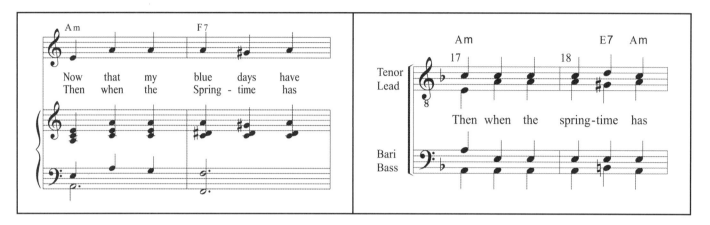

Measure 18: Here again, either E7 or F7 will do the trick. A small difference is that now no melody alteration is needed.

Figure 16.22

"Always," arranged by Don Gray. Measures 19 and 20 comparison.

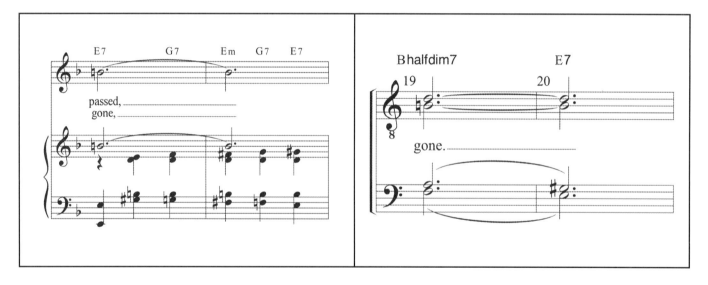

Measures 19–20: These two measures are E7 at heart. The arranger here opted for simplicity. Don's use of B half-dim7 in measure 19 is fitting to the lyric "linger."

Figure 16.23

"Always," arranged by Don Gray. Measure 21 comparison.

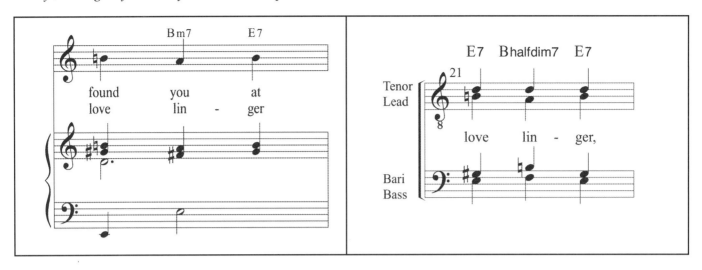

Measure 22: Observe the subtle difference here. The sheet goes with the slightly brighter sounding Bm7 on the second beat, whereas Don again employs the more melancholy B half-dim7. Which do you prefer?

Figure 16.24

"Always," arranged by Don Gray.

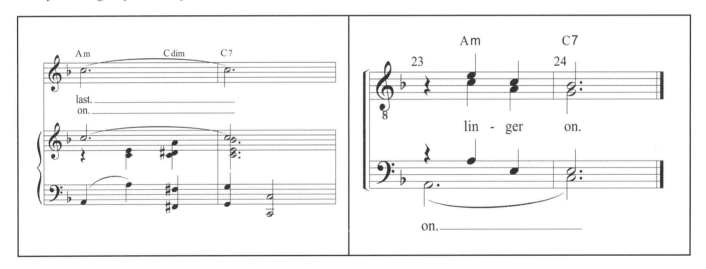

Measure 23: The C dim on beat three in the sheet is a nice touch. And what Don does in measures 23–24 is effective construction. You have good choices here.

Harmonizing From the Original Sheet Music Using a Piano Part

Moving on, even if the piano-vocal sheet you have does not include any chord symbols, it does have a piano part. So if the notes in a given spot are, for example, G, B, D and F, odds are great that the chord in that harmonic block is G7.

Let's look at the "Always" sheet from this point of view, pretending there are no chord symbols. Just a couple of brief examples should give you the idea.

Figure 16.25

"Always," words and music by Irving Berlin.

Measure 1: Sure, your ears will tell you the chord here is F, but isn't it reassuring to see a whole slew of Fs, As and Cs in the piano part?

Measure 3: Likewise, when we see C, E, G and B♭, C7 comes readily to mind.

Figure 16.26

"Always," words and music by Irving Berlin.

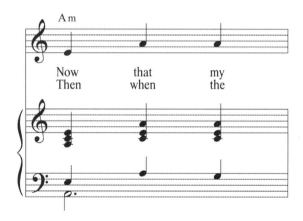

Not much doubt here that we are talking Amin, is there?

These are some obvious examples where the melody notes in a given measure map easily to a given harmonic pillar and the stated piano chords. Do keep in mind that many individual piano chords may need to be adapted, such as demonstrated in the following three examples:

Figure 16.27

"Always," words and music by Irving Berlin.

Measure 14: With the melody on A, we barbershoppers would tend to not include the dissonant B♭ in the chord harmonization, doubling the root as a C6 instead.

Figure 16.28

"Always," words and music by Irving Berlin.

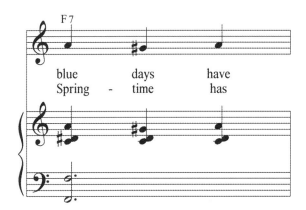

Because the context here is not Fmin7, we would likely put an F °7 on the second beat.

Figure 16.29

"Always," words and music by Irving Berlin.

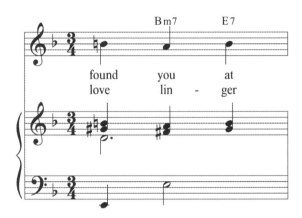

Implied Harmony

We need a chord on the second beat that is part of the barbershop vocabulary, and it will not have an E in it.

The melody notes of your song can be quite a help in determining the harmony. This is known as implied harmony. Implied harmony is taking the melodic notes in a measure and using them to construct harmony. For example, if in the melody line, you see C, E and G, then harmonizing using C major is a good bet.

Let's look at "Always" and determine the difference between implied harmony and melodic embellishment.

Figure 16.30

"Always," words and music by Irving Berlin.

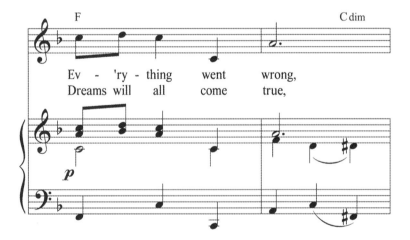

The prevailing harmony in the first measure is F. Sure, there is D in there, but given its brief use and on an offbeat, we will analyze this as a melodic embellishment.

Figure 16.31

"Always," words and music by Irving Berlin.

Other than the brief embellishment on count two of the second bar, this section is clearly outlining C7

Figure 16.32

"Always," words and music by Irving Berlin.

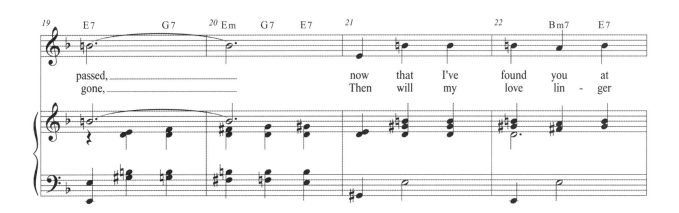

Measures 19–22: Even without a G♯ in the melody, don't you still figure that E7—or at least E-something—is the prime suspect? Even without chord symbols, we might be able to divine the tonicization of another key, given the presence of E on several key moments, we can correctly identify E as the root here.

Because the songs that best fit the barbershop style have plenty of circle of fifths chord progressions, your knowledge of the circle can aid you in setting the harmonic pillars. Are you pretty sure that a given measure is V7? Try II7 or perhaps ii or ii7 for the previous measure. If, in the key of C, you believe a certain pillar is E7, then try A7 or Amin or Amin7 for the next chord.

As a general rule, knowing where we are going in the circle helps us more than knowing where we have been. Let's apply this principle to the 1892 tune "After the Ball," arguably America's first mass hit, the first song to sell over a million copies of sheet music.

How do these harmonic pillars strike your barbershop ears?

Figure 16.33

"After the Ball," words and music by Earnest R. Ball. Note the harmonic pillars.

Yes, those are the pillars according to the original piano-vocal sheet. How can we provide some variety? Let's see if the circle of fifths can help us do just that.

Figure 16.34

"After the Ball" harmonic pillars.

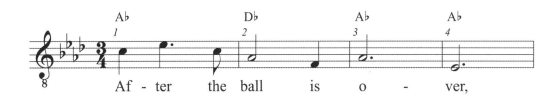

Measure 2: It feels like time to move already, and going back to A♭ in measure 3 seems right. So what will get us there? E♭7 usually does that job, but the melody notes, A♭ and E♭, would seem to indicate another chord. So let's try D♭, making use of the only clockwise progression on the circle; any other clockwise movement is called a retrogression. And sure enough, IV–I works here.

Measure 4: Because measure 5 could also be harmonized as an A♭, we typically would prefer some harmonic variety rather than three consecutive measures of tonic. One option is to use the usual chord that gets us back home in measures 4 or 5, the E♭7.

Figure 16.35

"After the Ball" harmonic pillars.

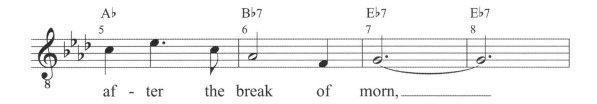

Measure 6: Time to add more circle flavor, so what will get us to the E♭7 in 7? A B♭7 will make it happen.

Figure 16.36

"After the Ball" harmonic pillars.

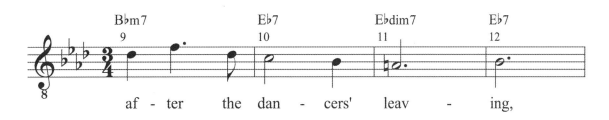

Measure 9: We want to break up this run of E♭7, and a retrogression to the B♭m7 works just fine to give us some variety and get us back to E♭7 in measure 10.

Measure 11: Note that the circle is of no help to us here. Because our chord in measure 12 is E♭7, a B♭ chord might come to mind. However, the major seventh dictated by the A♭ melody note might provide the wrong character for that moment in the arrangement. But the E♭ diminished seventh works well, as would a D7. Note that sometimes the striking sound of a dominant seventh may draw too much undo attention to itself. Hence, the E♭dim7

 This situation, where you have the choice between a diminished chord or a seventh rooted one-half step down from where you are going, will often come up in your arranging. Try them both and see which you prefer.

Measure 16: True, we have just had quite a substantial E♭7 block, but we still want some movement, so using E♭7 here will provide that, as well getting us back to the tonic in measure 17.

Figure 16.37

"After the Ball" harmonic pillars.

Measure 18: This is the same pattern as measure 2, and thus deserves the same consideration. Unless there's a good reason from a development perspective to do otherwise, a good choice—particularly in a song with such elegant simplicity— would be to make the same harmonization choices here in measure 18.

Measure 20: The tonic works well here, but a C half-dim7 would have a typical barbershop flavor. And, of course, we are going to F7 in 21, which is where a C chord leads us in the circle.

Figure 16.38

"After the Ball" harmonic pillars.

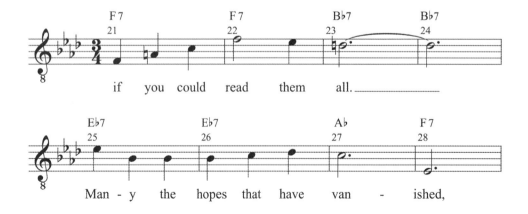

Measure 28: The tonic A♭ works here, but because we are headed for a B♭7 in 29, consider how an F7 propels this sound and moves along the circle of fifths.

Figure 16.39

"After the Ball" harmonic pillars.

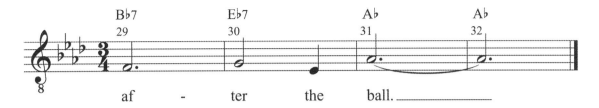

A word of caution: keep in mind that chords can progress in many different ways, even in solid barbershop songs. For example, chords can progress by half steps, so III7 could take you to IV rather than VI7, as it would if following the circle of fifths. Note the example in Figure 16.40.

Figure 16.40

"You Were Only Fooling," words and music by Larry Fotine, Ben Gordon, and Billy Faber. Arranged by Steve Tramack.

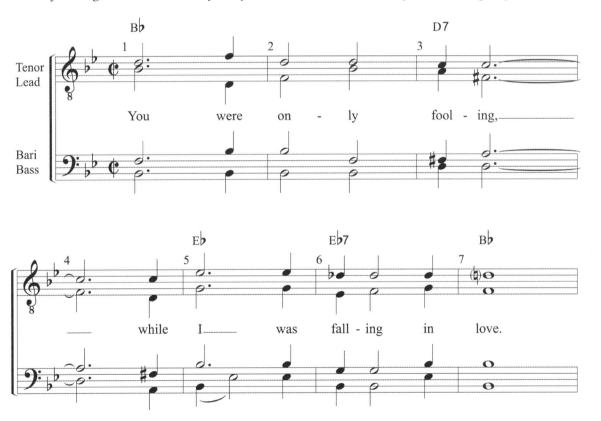

Conclusion

When in doubt, use the original harmonies, and deviate when your ear pulls you in another direction. Experiment with circle of fifths choices that match the harmonic rhythm of the song when looking for variety. Sing each part, ensuring the voice leading feels natural, and as you become more experienced arranging in the style, learn to trust your ear.

Chapter 17.
Common Mistakes of Beginning Arrangers

By Clay Hine

Barbershop music theory and barbershop arranging are unique. While the general techniques and practices are common to any type of vocal arranging, people who have broader experience in music theory and arranging, but are new to arranging for barbershop ensembles, often discover a few concepts that are unique to barbershop along the way. We hesitate to call these rules—some of our best barbershop arrangers have found ways to help our genre evolve by learning the rules and then discovering ways to break them—but there are some concepts that define barbershop music, and conversely, some common mistakes that are only mistakes because they can result in unwanted musical distractions.

To demonstrate some of these distractions, what follows are the arrangements of two old songs: "Mandy Lee" and "Roses at Twilight." Both songs sound like barbershop; when you play or sing through the melody line, you can hear barbershop chords around it. If you were to write an actual contest arrangement, you might want to include more opportunities for development, and add a verse or intro, a repeat of a chorus, or other material. To keep this exercise simple, these are short, and done very much in a basic *barberpole cat* style. Additionally, each arrangement includes some specific elements that don't necessarily break standing general rules of vocal arranging but still create distractions in the barbershop style.

The barberpole cats or "polecats" are standard songs from the early 1900s arranged in the barbershop style with relative simplicity in a comfortable vocal range. They were introduced as common repertoire to encourage quartet activity at chapter meetings and regional events.

Common Traps: Complete Chords

The distractions built into "Mandy Lee" focus on the chords and voicings. Below is the sheet music with an accompanying vocal recording of the music, as written. Following that is an analysis of the distractions that are inherent in this arrangement, along with another arrangement that eliminates these distractions. As you'll see below, one of the key tenets of the barbershop style is the *complete chord*.

In barbershop, most four-part chords are complete, with all chord members present. Triads are a noticeable exception and require a doubling, usually the root. Chords with more than four distinct notes, e.g., barbershop ninth, will be incomplete but with four distinct notes present, i.e., a root or fifth omitted.

Exceptions might include brief passing lead notes where the harmony parts are singing a background neutral syllable. However, when all four parts are singing the same lyrics at the same time, it can be distracting to hear incomplete or "empty" chords. Sometimes these can be written into the chart, and sometimes these empty chords are just created by a performer singing wrong notes. Both examples are included in the weird chart and analysis which follows.

Figure 17.1

"Mandy Lee," words and music by Thurland Chattaway with missing/wrong notes and strange voicings.

Figure 17.2

"Mandy Lee" with identified distractions.

Measure 2: A descending bass line that continues through "love you 'deed I do" might be a choice we'd make in a choral arrangement, but "I" creates a double on the C (octave between bass and lead) that's distracting. In this case, the arranger could replace the bass C with an F to create a complete F7 chord.

Measure 3: Triads built on chords other than the tonic are certainly used in barbershop, and even in this case, a triad built on II on the first beat ("do") adds a great barbershop feel. However, when it continues through the whole measure, and especially when the II triad dips a ½ step to accommodate the melody's ½ step dip, it sounds empty.

Measure 5: The tenor voice leading is smooth with the tenor singing an E♭ on "like," but it creates a chord that sounds empty. This chord is a v°, and while we do see diminished triads in barbershop, we most often see them substituted with fully diminished 7th chords.

Figure 17.3

"Mandy Lee" with identified distractions.

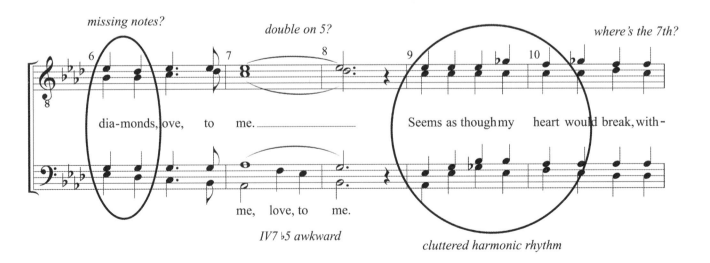

Measure 6: The V triad on "dia-" can work if it moves towards a V7, as it eventually does, except that the 2nd chord on "-monds" sounds like a mistake. In fact, the tenor follows the bass motion, which is a mistake you might hear in a performance. In this case, we see a V7 with doubled 7th and no root.

Measures 9–10: There are a lot of different chords here. There's nothing inherently wrong about this in an arrangement that features ringing chords as a harmonic theme, but in this case, the chords don't all necessarily easily lead from one to the next, and the listener is distracted by the quick chord changes and resulting cluttered harmonic rhythm.

Figure 17.4

"Mandy Lee" with identified distractions.

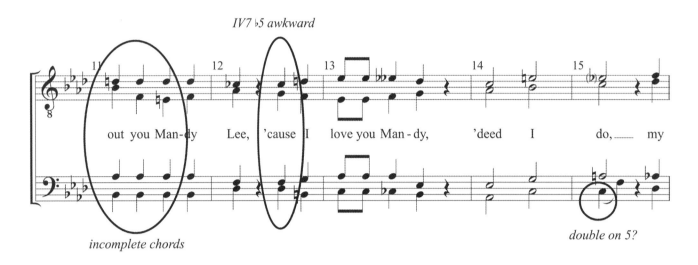

Measure 11: The voice leading is smooth in going from "with" in measure 10 to "out" in measure 11, but it results in an incomplete—and distracting—II7 chord. The lead ½ step dip on "Man-" creates a dissonant and distracting II7♭5 that could be remedied by writing a ♭II7 or even a II°7.

Measure 12: In standard choral arranging, we may not change the harmony parts from "Lee" to accommodate the ½ step lead dip on "cause," but in barbershop arranging, the chord sounds dissonant or empty as written. Note that this is the same distracting chord that we see in measure 11, a dominant 7th with ♭5.

Measures 11–13: The chord progression and voicings here are something we may not see in standard choral arranging—especially the way the II7–IV7–VII7 chords unfold in measure 12—as well as the bass voicing. However, this is an engaging barbershop progression and is an example of arranging that is somewhat unique to barbershop.

Measure 15: What's written is good voice leading and adds a nice bass swipe, but it also creates an empty VI7 chord that doubles the 5th and is missing a root on "do."

Figure 17.5

"Mandy Lee" with identified distractions.

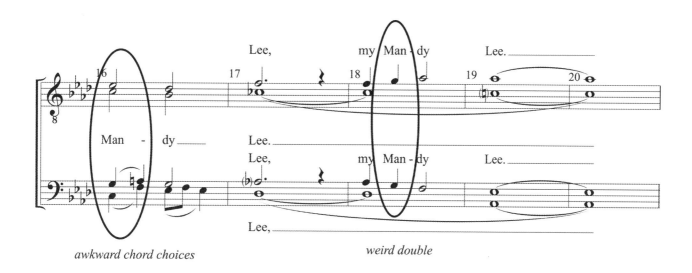

Measure 16: This exhibits nice voice leading and all good chords on "my Man-." In fact, the chord progression is iii–VI7, which follows the circle of 5ths. However, as in measures 9 and 10, it feels cluttered and awkward in the context of the current harmonic rhythm.

Measure 18: The melodic bari/tenor movement, which we'd call a *scissor* because the parts are moving opposite one another, creates both a double and an unusual chord on "Man-," the combination of which is distracting.

Bottom Line: Voice leading is important, as are using complete and appropriate chords. In looking at the relative importance of these elements, the inclusion of complete chords gets more priority than in other styles of arranging. To wrap this up, Figure 17.6 features an arrangement where these issues are addressed.

Figure 17.6

"Mandy Lee" with distractions addressed.

MANDY LEE
(1899)

Words and Music by
THURLAND CHATTAWAY

Arrangement by
C. HINE

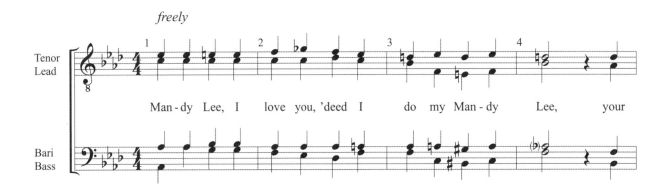

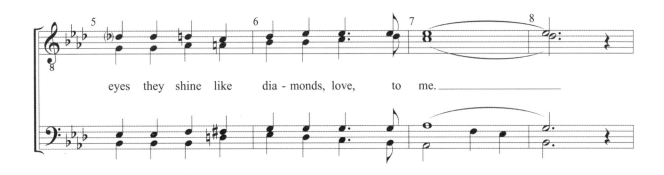

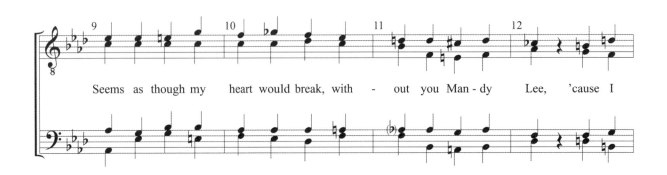

2

Mandy Lee

Common Traps: Harmonic Rhythm

Harmonic rhythm, the rate that chords change, is a subtle but important part of a barbershop arrangement. Because part of the uniqueness of a barbershop performance is the reliance on the occurrence and solidity of barbershop chords, it follows that how these chords flow and change is also somewhat unique to barbershop. This arrangement highlights how harmonic rhythm choices that don't have a natural flow might be distracting.

Figure 17.7

"Roses at Twilight," words and music by Ben Black and Herbert B. Marple with strange harmonic rhythm choices.

ROSES AT TWILIGHT
(1918)

with weird harmonic rhythms

Music by HERBERT B. MARPLE
Arrangement by CLAY HINE

Words by
BEN BLACK

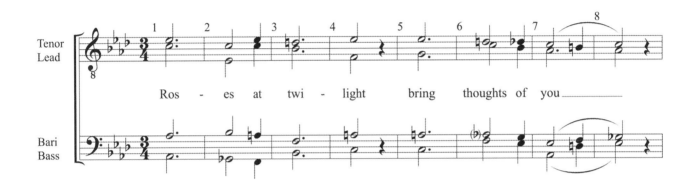

2

Roses at Twilight

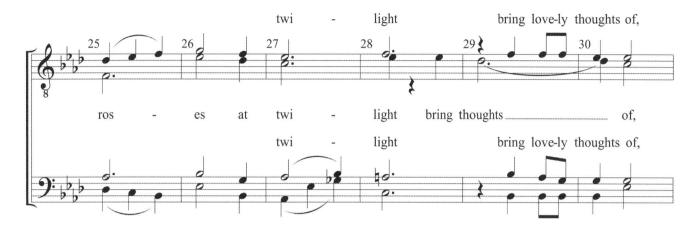

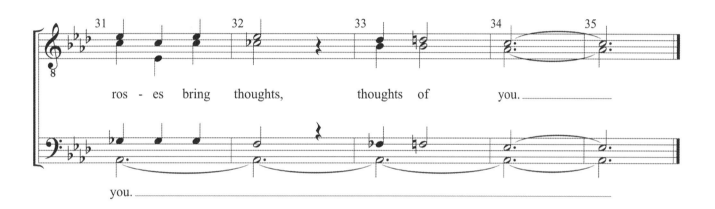

Figure 17.8

"Roses at Twilight" with identified distractions.

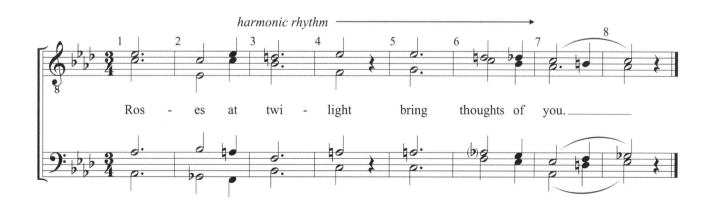

Measures 2–6: These measures feature awkward harmonic rhythm.

Figure 17.9

"Roses at Twilight" with identified distractions.

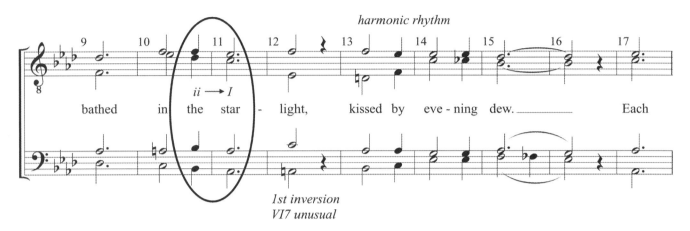

Measures 10–11: This is subtle, but the ii–I on "the star-" is awkward, as it neither follows the circle of fifths nor acts as what might be considered a pleasing substitution.

Measures 12–13: "Star-light" is an example of good voice leading using good barbershop chord progressions (I–VI7), but results in a weak, first inversion voicing on "light" that is distracting.

Measures 13–14: Another example of awkward harmonic rhythm.

Figure 17.10

"Roses at Twilight" with identified distractions.

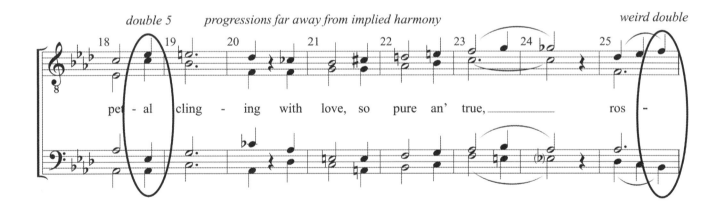

Measure 18: This is an example of a distracting voicing. While we do sometimes see the fifth doubled on a triad in barbershop, we rarely, if ever, double the fifth on a root position triad.

Measures 19–22: This is a chord issue that is less about harmonic rhythm than about using chords that are so far away from what's implied that, coupled with awkward chord motion, i.e. "love" resolving to "so" and "pure" resolving to "true." The result is awkward and distracting.

Measure 25: Doubling the fifth on the last chord in this measure may be good voice leading, but the resulting chord is missing a third, and as a result, sounds empty and distracting.

Figure 17.11

"Roses at Twilight" with identified distractions.

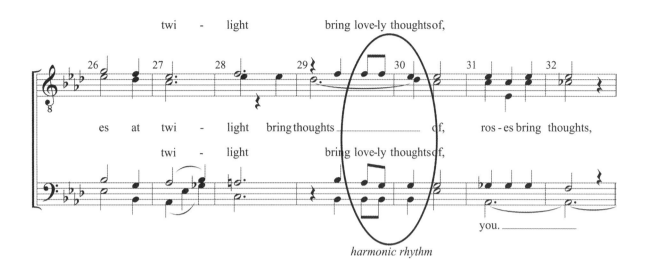

Measure 29–30: This is an awkward harmonic rhythm specifically because measure 29 sounds like ii moving to ii7, then moving to V7 in measure 30. While a typical barbershop circle of 5ths chord progression, the V9 (no root) on the last chord of measure 29 ("-ly") sounds like we got to V one chord too soon, which is distracting.

Figure 17.12

"Roses at Twilight" with identified distractions.

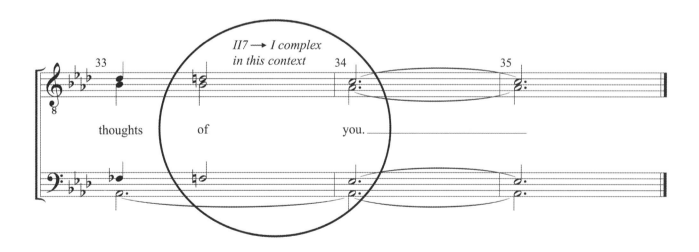

Measure 33: II7–I is an unusual chord progression in barbershop. Still, we see it sometimes, and in the right context can add a surprising but satisfying feel to the musical flow. However, in this case where the chord progressions throughout the song imply more traditional barbershop progressions, e.g., predominantly circles of fifths, this sounds out of context.

Here's a version of the song with a more typical, implied harmonic rhythm.

Figure 17.13

"Roses at Twilight" with distractions addressed. Arranged by Clay Hine.

ROSES AT TWILIGHT

(1918)

more normal voicing

Words by
BEN BLACK

Music by HERBERT B. MARPLE
Arrangement by CLAY HINE

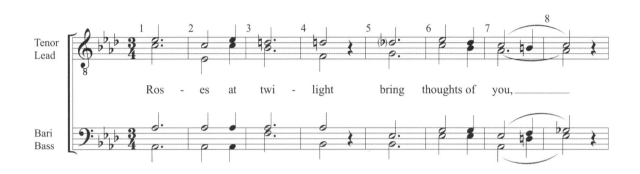

Ros - es at twi - light bring thoughts of you,_____

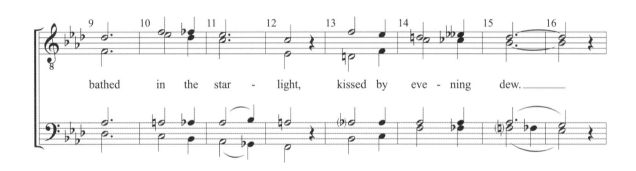

bathed in the star - light, kissed by eve - ning dew._____

Each pet - al cling - ing with love, so pure an' true,_____

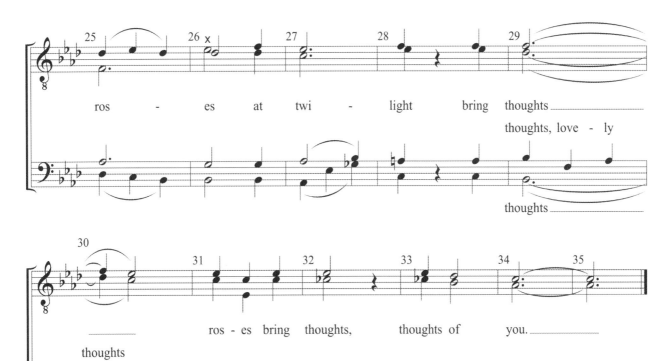

The Bottom Line

The chord vocabulary is an important part of a barbershop arrangement, as is how the chords support the flow of the music. Make thoughtful choices that imply either an even flow, or, if you choose to make chord choices that pull focus away from this flow, do so with a specific, musical purpose.

Chapter 18.
Basic Rhythmic and Meter Considerations

By Tom Gentry

Introduction

In *Arranging Barbershop Vol. 1*, Chapter 2: "Definition of the Barbershop Style," we explored how musical parameters such as lyrics, melody, harmony, form, and embellishments contributed to the style. Not mentioned in this chapter, but also important, are two more aspects of the style: *rhythm* and *meter*. Let's start with rhythm.

Rhythm

A more detailed discussion of this subject, as it affects arranging, will be found in Chapter 25 of *Arranging Barbershop Vol. 2*. Here, though, we will deal with the rhythmic considerations of the song in relation to creating a basic barbershop arrangement.

In the simpler, slower times when barbershop quartet singing flourished—from the turn of the last century into the 1920s—popular songs were typically intended to be sung. Folks provided much of their own entertainment back then, gathering around the parlor piano to sing the hits of the day. Countless classic barbershop songs, which feature simple rhythms easily rendered by the average singer, are typical of this era.

With the advent of phonographs and radios and the growing popularity of movies, entertainment increasingly became a spectating enterprise and less of a participatory activity. Songs written after 1930 reflected this increased sophistication, featuring more complex rhythmic patterns including syncopation, triplets and swing grooves that developed around the more layered and textured sounds of the dance band. These rhythmic devices are often found in arrangements more typical of the 2000s and beyond.

Songs that leave room for the characteristic embellishing devices, which are detailed in Chapter 23, often adapt well to the style. Consider the example in Figure 18.1.

Figure 18.1

"Little Patch of Heaven," words and music by Glenn Slater and Alan Menken. Arranged by Aaron Dale..

Figure 18.2

"Love Me," words and music by Jerry Lieber and Mike Stoller. Arranged by Aaron Dale.

We would be remiss not to include a few words on freestyle ballads here. There is quite an art to interpreting such pieces effectively, and barbershop singers are among the very best in the musical world at doing so. The concept of *rubato* comes into play here. To be more expressive, the performer stretches certain beats, measures or phrases, and compacts others. Of course, this needs to be accomplished in an artistic, non-distracting fashion, while clearly maintaining the underlying meter of the song. Otherwise, the listener is likely to experience a sense of unease. Note the example in Figure 18.3 where the written rhythm is fairly simple, the texture is *homorhythmic* and the embellishments limited. This allows for the performer's interpretation of the music.

 Homorhythmic texture refers to all voice parts singing the same words at the same time.

Figure 18.3

"Not While I'm Around," words and music by Stephen Sondheim. Arranged by Steve Tramack.

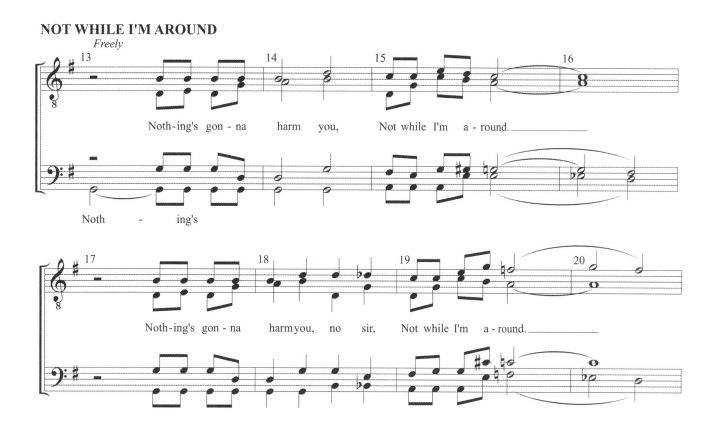

Meter

The subject of meter is also important in any musical style. The meter of barbershop songs is usually simple rather than compound. We generally sing songs in 4/4 (common time), 2/2 (cut time), 3/4, or 2/4 time. Occasionally we sing compound meters like 6/8 or 12/8, but usually we perform songs in simple *duple* (two beats per measure), *triple* (three beats per measure), or quadruple (four beats per measure) meter.

Songs with constantly changing meters are not typical of the barbershop style. Songs with complex rhythms found in the jazz world such as 5/4 are also atypical, though not unheard of. Arrangements having one meter in the verse and another in the chorus can provide interest and variety, as does employing a different meter in a particular segment of a song for an embellishing effect.

Sometimes songs that didn't necessarily fit naturally into a given meter were adapted to conform to the fashion of the day. In the heyday of the *foxtrot*, for example, a song that might more naturally be a 3/4 time waltz tended to end up in 4/4 so people could dance to it in lively fashion.

 The foxtrot is a smooth, progressive dance known for its continuous flowing dance movements. The dance itself is similar to the look of a 3/4 waltz, but the rhythm is in 4/4 time. It developed in the 1910s and was most popular in the 1930s when the Barbershop Harmony Society was founded.

Have a look at the 1922 song, "Who's Sorry Now?" in the two different meters.

Figure 18.4

"Who's Sorry Now?," words and music by Ted Snyder, Bert Kalmar, and Harry Ruby. Shown in 3/4 time and 4/4 time.

In the barbershop world a song with sentimental lyrics that was written as a 2/4 march can sometimes be performed effectively as a freestyle ballad in common time. Figure 18.5 features the beginning of the verse to the World War I song, "I May Be Gone for a Long, Long Time" in both meters.

Figure 18.5

"I May Be Gone for a Long, Long Time," words and music by Albert Von Tilzer and Lew Brown. Shown in a 2/4 march time and common time.

Conclusion

Rhythm and meter are two important considerations when developing a barbershop arrangement. The intended treatment of the arrangement—free form, rubato, strict meter, subdivision of beats and tempo—will drive arranging choices. Embellishments are closely linked to rhythm, providing the means of propelling rhythm through the song. This is particularly true when the melody demands orchestration. Meter considerations also come into play when choosing a song to arrange in the style and when looking for development opportunities. Part B and Part C of the book will cover rhythmic concepts in more detail.

Part B.
Developing an Arrangement

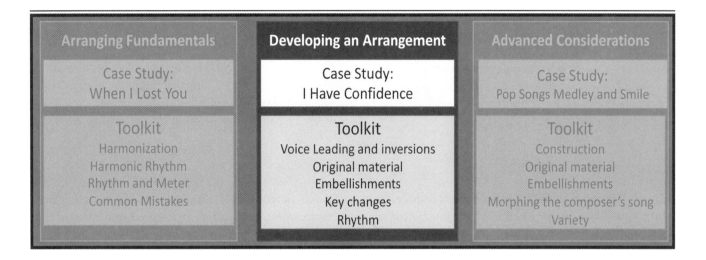

Part B, *Developing an Arrangement,* builds from the foundational skills from Part A. This part focuses on the skills and approaches to develop an arrangement with embellishments, development of themes (rhythm, melody, lyrics, harmony), textures, intros, and tags.

Chapter 19: Developing an Arrangement Overview

Steve Tramack provides an executive summary of some of the core considerations included in this part of the book, including a step-by-step case study of Intermediate Arranging in action, along with several deep-dive chapters covering key topics for arrangers looking to build their skills.

Chapter 20: "I Have Confidence Case" Study

Step-by-Step Case Study: Steve Armstrong walks through the process of developing an arrangement, building on the base harmonization concepts to consider aspects such as form, embellishments, alternate harmonizations, and developing common types of original material.

Chapter 21: Voice Leading and Inversions

Building on the concepts in the arranging case study, this deep dive chapter explores a broader range of harmonic options. Adam Scott covers topics such as chord vocabulary, voice leading and chord inversions, voicings, and substitution options.

Chapter 22: Original Material (Intros, Tags, and Interludes)

Introductions and tags are the most common examples of original material in the barbershop arranging style and often are an arranger's entrée into beginning arranging. Kevin Keller explores considerations and approaches for writing effective introductions and tags, providing several iconic examples.

Chapter 23: Embellishments

Whereas Part A primarily focused on basic harmonization, Part B, aimed at experienced arrangers, focuses on development to create interest and contrast. In addition to harmonic development and form/construction considerations, embellishments are a set of key tools at the arranger's disposal to build texture, interest, variety, and unique perspective on the music. Steve Tramack provides an in-depth view into the foundational set of embellishments in the style.

Chapter 24: Key Changes

Worthy of their own chapter, key change embellishments serve multiple purposes in an arrangement. Key changes can be used to provide interest in a multi-verse and chorus construction, set up melody passing in a reprise, and serve as a climactic music event. While David Wright expands on the concepts of embellishments and key changes in the advanced arranging section in Part C of *Arranging Barbershop*, Vol. 2, he provides an overview of the most common, fundamental key changes here in Part B.

Chapter 25: Rhythm

The concept of rhythm in arranging for barbershop encompasses several elements: meter, tempo, beat, subdivision accent, groove, and rhythmic embellishments. Aaron Dale introduces key concepts related to rhythm in barbershop arranging in this chapter, further expanding on the concepts in the Advanced Arranging part of this section.

Chapter 26: Additional Considerations

Leveraging embellishments, textures, form and construction, and different harmonic choices, an arranger has a multitude of choices for developing a foundational arrangement. In addition to the deep dive concepts reviewed in this chapter, Steve Tramack and Aaron Dale provide additional insight into methods and approaches for developing an arrangement.

Chapter 19.
Developing an Arrangement Overview

By Steve Tramack

In Part A, we focused on the core set of skills required to successfully harmonize a melody in the barbershop style. We discussed in detail the various options for harmonizing non-chord tones and a strategy for part-by-part harmonization. Key concepts such as harmonic rhythm and the impact of rhythm and embellishment when dictated by sustained melody notes provides the foundation for creating an arrangement that both sounds like barbershop and will be enjoyable to sing.

Part B of this book focuses on the next step in the arranging journey—developing an arrangement. While part A focused on the arranger finding their footing on the path, this part involves making more creative choices. What should the overall structure of this arrangement be? Should I consider developing original material, such as an introduction or a tag? How should the arrangement vary from section of form to section of form, e.g., A1 to A2? While this content is targeted at arrangers who have some experience in the barbershop style, both newer and more experienced arrangers will likely benefit from the approaches and considerations outlined in this section.

What are the prerequisites required to be successful in this first stage of your arranging journey?

- Deep understanding of the theory of barbershop harmony, as covered in Chapter 5 of *Arranging Barbershop Vol. 1.* Understanding chord qualities, inversions, and how to complete triads and seventh chords in four-part voicings are essential skills. Understanding of voice leading and chord progressions—particularly tritone resolution tendencies—will aid in your arranging development journey.
- Deep understanding of the definition of the barbershop style, as covered in Chapter 5 of *Arranging Barbershop Vol. 1.* When starting to stray off the beaten path in any journey, it's important to understand what kind of landscape one will need to traverse to be successful and what tools one might need. Finding deeper understanding of how different elements of the style build upon the foundation of harmonizing a melody is essential.
- Skill and experience in harmonizing a melody, as covered in Chapter 14 of *Arranging Barbershop Vol. 2.* Oftentimes, new arrangers want to immediately dive into embellishments, key changes, chord vocabularies, and inversions that are leveraged by experienced arrangers in songs sung by top-level ensembles. As the saying goes, "You have to know the rules before you break them." Starting with a solid foundation of harmonizing a melody with strong-voiced chords mapped to the harmonic rhythm of the song is key to the success of any arrangement.
- Understanding the importance of harmonic rhythm, as covered in Chapters 16 and 17 of *Arranging Barbershop Vol. 2.* In particular, review the examples in Chapter 17, which are accessible through www.halleonard.com/mylibrary, to gain an understanding of the impact of harmonic rhythm choices in the listen-ability of an arrangement.

Enjoy the journey!

Chapter 20.
"I Have Confidence" Case Study

By Steve Armstrong

Developing Through Embellishments

In this chapter we build on the concepts of the previous chapter and go beyond writing a basic harmonization using embellishments to create a complete arrangement. Whereas the method in the previous chapter might have felt formulaic and mechanical, it builds a foundation upon which we can make creative choices and sometimes break the rules we just established. In all cases our artistic judges as musicians will serve as our guide. At the end of the day, as early society leader Hal Staab said, "If it sounds good, it is!"

One of the primary ways an arranger provides interest and variety in music is by using *embellishments*.

> Embellishments are different types of ornamentation to a melody found in many styles of music. Their prevalent use in the barbershop style are as characteristic as the barbershop seventh itself.

Embellishments provide the performer the opportunity to reinforce key thematic aspects, e.g., lyrics generate anticipation and musical tension and express their unique character. Embellishments provide the arranger the opportunity to develop themes and create a sense of long line development throughout the entire musical journey. Embellishments allow the arranger to inform the performer about the purpose of the music, building on the composer's and lyricist's intentions.

We can group embellishments into a few categories:

- Harmonic, e.g., swipes, key changes
- Rhythmic, e.g., pickups, bell chords, propellants
- Lyrical, e.g., echoes, patter
- Melodic, e.g., melody passing, unison
- Texture, e.g., backtime, solo, duets, call and response, neutral syllable

For a more in-depth exploration of embellishment, visit the following chapters:

- Chapter 22 provides an in-depth exploration of added material such as intros, tags, and interludes. This added material is used to complete the end-to-end journey of the music.
- Chapter 23 explores examples of some of the foundational embellishments used in the style and where embellishments are used in support of each other and the development of the music, e.g., swipes or echoes that lead to a key change.
- Chapter 24 focuses on some of the most typical key changes in the style.

Let's now explore an example of moving beyond the basic harmonization to developing an arrangement with the following case study.

Case Study

The song we will use in our case study is "I Have Confidence" from *The Sound Of Music*. This was selected because it works well in the barbershop style, and there are no well-known arrangements of it. Also, it has some challenges that we will need to work through so it will be an interesting exercise.

This was first done as part of the Intermediate Arranging Class at Harmony University in 2019 and was arranged for a specific group. It is important to know the characteristics of the group the arrangement is being written for as that will guide you in the choices you make. In this case, it is for a male chorus that typically scores in the mid B range. They don't want the leads to be much higher than an F, and the basses are best kept at A♭ or higher but can handle an occasional G.

The Song

Figure 20.1 shows the sheet music for voice and piano.

Figure 20.1

"I Have Confidence," words and music by Richard Rodgers. Vocal and piano score.

I Have Confidence

Lyrics and Music by
RICHARD RODGERS

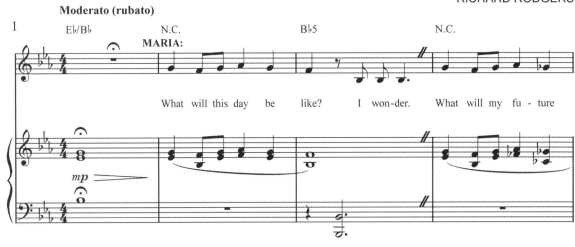

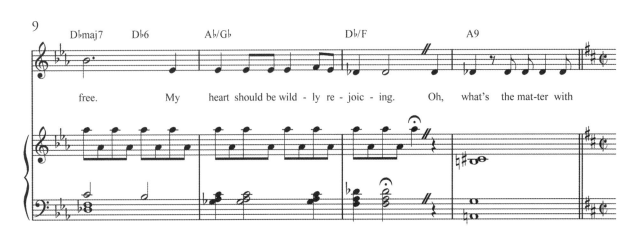

Form and Structure Considerations

Some general observations about the song:

Verse

This is a lengthy stop and start section that serves the show well as the character is being introspective and trying to build up the courage to declare what follows. Also, some of these lyrics are very specific to the scenario of the show and don't work well as a stand-alone vehicle, particularly when sung by a men's chorus. It is wonderful music, and we would want to use some of it. Ultimately, it seems like if we use measures 14–29, measures 34–39, and measures 48–49, we would be able to retain much of what is great and have the right degree of setup for the conviction of the choruses.

In particular, measures 48–49 musically feel like the storyteller is turning a corner and actually gaining confidence with each change in harmony, as it is a rising sequence. Here, we can change the lyrics to "I must find the courage I lack, so," and it connects us well from what precedes it. Now our verse lyrics will be:

> *I've always longed for adventure to do the things I've never dared*
>
> *Now here I'm facing adventure, then why am I so scared?*
>
> *Oh I must stop these doubts, all these worries. If I don't I just know I'll turn back.*
>
> *I must dream of the things I am seeking, I must find the courage I lack.*

Roadmap

Now that we've settled on the verse, what will the rest of the roadmap be? Once the first chorus starts in measure 50 it works very well just to follow the roadmap of the piano score. We have one full chorus, measures 50–99, followed by a two-measure interlude that gives us a key change up a half step. We may or may not need these two measures. This key change is a significant part of the growing excitement of the song. Then we have a second full chorus, measures 102 to the end, that includes a wonderful surprise key change up a tone coming out of the bridge. It features a reflective repeat of measures 142–145 used to heighten the satisfaction of the conclusion as well as use of augmentation—doubling the length of the melody notes—in measures 154–157.

Lyrics

The lyrics now mostly work as-is except for the first bridge. Those lyrics are too specifically tied to the character becoming a nanny rather than pursuing her own dream.

Key

The first chorus on the piano score is in D, and after 2 key changes, it ends in F. It would be great to start in G so the basses can sing the tonic an octave below the melody note the many times that is called for, but that will just put the lead line too high too much of the time. A good compromise is to start the first chorus in F and figure out creative solutions that do not put the basses on the low F. When we get to the end in A♭, transfer the melody over to the tenors for the last two notes. They can do a post with the bottom 3 parts doing something rhythmically to continue to build excitement to the final chord. Looking back at the music we selected from the verse, this means we will do the first 8 measures in F, transition to E♭ for measures 9–15 and then transition back to F over measures 16 and 17.

On the following pages, you will find the roadmap we've settled on in the keys that we've selected. The harmonic pillars are also indicated, and these are mostly the same as those found in the piano score, but there are some instances when we've gone with different harmonies.

Figure 20.2

"I Have Confidence" melodic roadmap with harmonic pillars.

Challenges

Measures 1–4: the sustained pedal is a feature that we wish to retain but we can make it a little less dissonant by using F in measure 2 instead of Fmaj7 and C7 (V7) in measure 4 instead of continuing the pedal and having C/F.

Figure 20.3

"I Have Confidence" with identified harmonic pillars, measures 1–7.

Measures 15–17: We'll figure out something here that has the sense of growing conviction without being quite so dissonant.

Figure 20.4

"I Have Confidence" with identified harmonic pillars, measures 12–19.

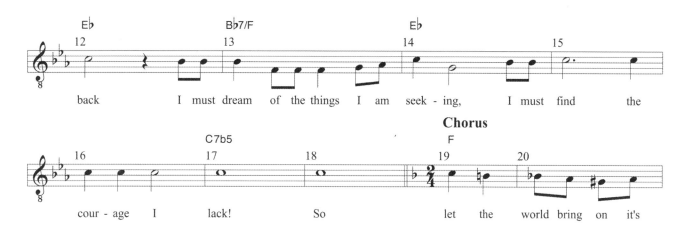

Measures 20–21: Again, we'll use the more consonant C7 (V7) rather than C/F.

Figure 20.5

"I Have Confidence" with identified harmonic pillars, measures 20–21.

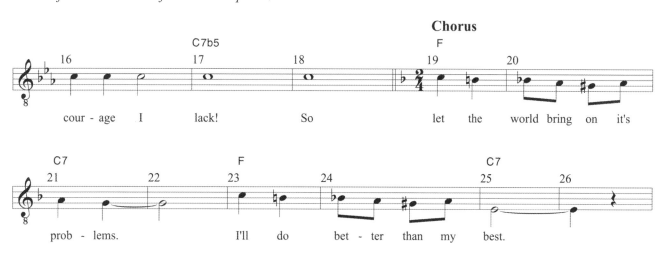

Measure 31: We'll use G7 (II7) here rather than G7/C.

Figure 20.6

"I Have Confidence" with identified harmonic pillars, measures 30–31.

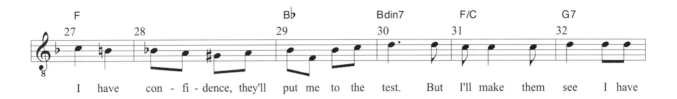

Measures 36–37: The piano score uses an augmented triad to harmonize this melody note.

Figure 20.7

"I Have Confidence" with the piano score, measures 36–37.

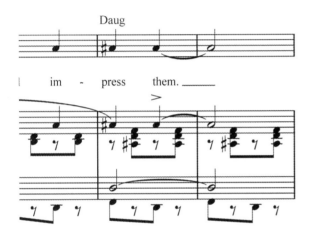

Two of the notes in that triad are found in A7 (III7) and this works well in between harmonic pillars of B♭ (IV).

Figure 20.8

"I Have Confidence" with identified harmonic pillars, measures 35–37.

Measures 40–41: We'll go straight to D7 here (VI7) rather than have the dissonance of the suspension in measure 40.

Figure 20.9

"I Have Confidence," with identified harmonic pillars, measures 40–41.

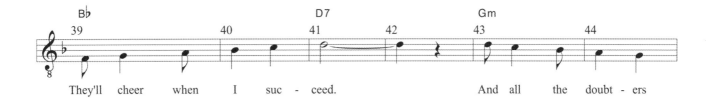

Basic Harmonization

Next, we would go through the steps of writing a basic harmonization by looking at the options to harmonize each non-chord tone. This was outlined in detail in the previous chapter so we won't repeat all of that here, but the result would be a harmonization as seen in Figure 20.10. We'll show one full chorus here as the harmonization choices would repeat. Discussion of choices will follow.

Figure 20.10

"I Have Confidence," with basic harmonization. Arranged by Steve Armstrong.

One of the first things we might notice about this melody is the descending chromatic passage in the first two measures that happens repeatedly, e.g., measures 18–19, 22–23, and 26–27.

Figure 20.11

"I Have Confidence," with descending chromatic melody. Arranged by Steve Armstrong.

The choice that we used in measures 18–19 can be mostly arrived at by using the system for harmonization from Chapter 14 of *Arranging Barbershop*, Vol. 2, but the first chord in measure 19 isn't really one of the choices in the system. This works because of the smooth voice leading with the top 3 parts descending while the bass repeats the same pitch. It is a variation of a stock barbershop progression that you can hear in your head by imagining the last four chords of "My Wild Irish Rose" while the lead is holding "Rose" (I7–Idim7–ivm6–I).

Figure 20.12

"My Wild Irish Rose," with standard barbershop progression.

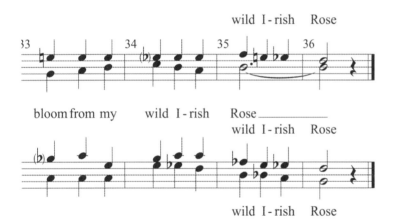

In this case, in measures 18–19 we could use I without the 7th for the word "let," then Idim7 for "the," iv6 for "world," and back to the tonic for "bring." If we wanted to, we could have the baritone continue to descend to an "F" on "bring" doubling the bass note instead of doubling the lead note, and we might have made that choice initially, but as we continue to work through that measure, we can see that the baritone part would then have a difficult jump from F to B♮ so we went with the A instead.

Of course, the melody continues to descend, so we'll use Idim7 again for "on" and finally back to I for "it's." Because these notes go by much more quickly than the tag of "My Wild Irish Rose," it might be better to simplify the tenor part by using a D natural instead of a D♭ on the word "world." That would still have most of the feeling of descending through these chords due to the lead and baritone movement, but it would be much easier to sing. These are the sorts of choices that arrangers find themselves having to make—what sounds great on my computer versus what can human singers perform accurately. In this case, we'll go with the D natural to make it a more singable line, which is especially true when we consider what measures 26–27 would look like with a D♭ on "con."

Figure 20.13

"I Have Confidence," with alternate harmonization at measures 26–27. Arranged by Steve Armstrong.

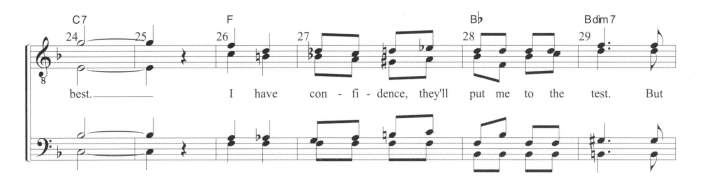

Let's talk more about the unusual choice here of having the baritone double the lead note on the third of the chord on "bring," as shown in Figure 20.11. We almost always double the root of a triad, sometimes the fifth and very rarely the third. This is entirely done to make the voice-leading a little smoother for the baritone part. With the bass-repeated F acting as a *pedal* in these measures, the baritones would either move down and double with the basses or move up and double with the leads.

 A pedal is any sustained note, often in the bass, while other harmonies change in the other parts. Earlier we referred to the most common pedal in barbershop, a post or hanger, in which a note is held without interruption. However, a pedal can also be re-articulated in lyrics on the same note, as demonstrated here.

In the first choice, they would have a very awkward tritone interval that would need to be sung very quickly (F to B). It would be difficult for them to sing this well, and this doubled third will go by so quickly that it won't be noticed at all.

Figure 20.14

"I Have Confidence," with the baritone doubling the third in measure 19. Arranged by Steve Armstrong.

Moving on, we started off using the same pattern for measures 22–23, but on "than" we moved the bass to a D and the tenor up to an F. That allows us to leave all the harmony parts on the same note for "my," and that turns this into a G9 chord when the leads move back up to the A. This creates a simple variation on the pattern and creates a bit of a II7–V7–I progression at the end of the first eight measure phrase.

Figure 20.15

"I Have Confidence," with a circle of fifths progression. Arranged by Steve Armstrong.

This pattern comes up again in measures 27–28, and we basically repeat the pattern of measures 22–23 except that, because we are moving to a B♭ chord in measure 28 (IV), we can add the seventh to the I chord on the word "they'll." That gives a nice pull to the IV chord.

Figure 20.16

"I Have Confidence," with a I7–IV progression. Arranged by Steve Armstrong.

Note that in measure 33, shown in Figure 20.17, the melody ends up on a low tonic. With many groups we would put the bass an octave lower here, but because the group we are writing for doesn't want the bass note to go below a G, we'll just have the bass double with the leads in the same octave. We don't sit on this note for very long, so this is fine.

Figure 20.17

"I Have Confidence," handling a low tonic in the melody. Arranged by Steve Armstrong.

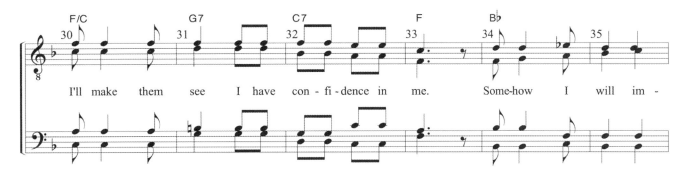

Please also note the choices made in measures 39–40. This is another progression that will sound familiar to you; we hear this progression frequently in the barbershop style.

Figure 20.18

"I Have Confidence." Arranged by Steve Armstrong.

Using our system to harmonize we know that we could use an F7 chord for the last beat of measure 39. The chord we've used, Aø7, has all the same notes as an F9 chord, so it is very similar to an F7 and by using this voicing we start a circle of fifths progression with the Aø7. Also, by moving to the D triad first, we derive two benefits. First, there is strength created while arriving there as the bass and lead move to the D from different directions, called *contrary motion*. Secondly, it allows us to create a little bit of interest on this held note by swiping to the D7 chord in measure 41.

Our harmonic pillar for measures 42–43 was Gmin.

Figure 20.19

"I Have Confidence," with contrary motion. Arranged by Steve Armstrong.

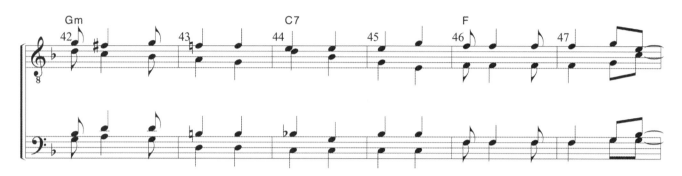

We could certainly do this, but when we examine the melody notes we see that the B♭ appears in measure 42, requiring us to use the minor triad. However, the notes in measure 43 could just as easily work with a B natural in the harmony. So, we can treat measure 43 as if the harmonic pillar is G7 which has a stronger pull through the circle of 5ths. This gives us a nice progression starting with the last note of measure 39 of III∅7–VI–VI7–ii–II7–V7–I.

Figure 20.20

"I Have Confidence," with a circle of fifths progression. Arranged by Steve Armstrong.

That move from a minor triad to a dominant 7th chord works nicely because it increases the desire for resolution. Moving in the opposite direction (i.e., II7 to ii) is almost always unsatisfying.

One last thing to comment on is the use of the unison, with the tenor an octave higher, at measure 46. This is another situation where the melody is on the low tonic, and we can't put the bass an octave below for this ensemble. Doing that would also require work to not have the bass line be too jumpy.

Figure 20.21

"I Have Confidence," with a low tonic in the melody in measure 46. Arranged by Steve Armstrong.

Development Within a Chorus

Musically, and in the original lyric, this moment seems emphatic or defiant, and the use of the unison reinforces that feeling as it is such a stark contrast to the four-part texture we have used up to this moment. When we write the new lyrics for this moment, we'll need to remember to capture that same sense lyrically.

So, our harmonization is complete, and it feels natural and satisfying, but if we were to perform it this way (with new lyrics, of course), the result would still feel unsatisfying musically. This is because it is a rhythmic song, but we have all these long notes at the ends of the phrases where nothing is happening rhythmically. To elevate this from a harmonization to an arrangement, we need to use embellishments to make it more interesting. Look at the changes in the version below:

Figure 20.22

"I Have Confidence," with additional development via embellishments. Arranged by Steve Armstrong.

I Have Confidence

Words and Music by RICHARD RODGERS

Chorus 2

4

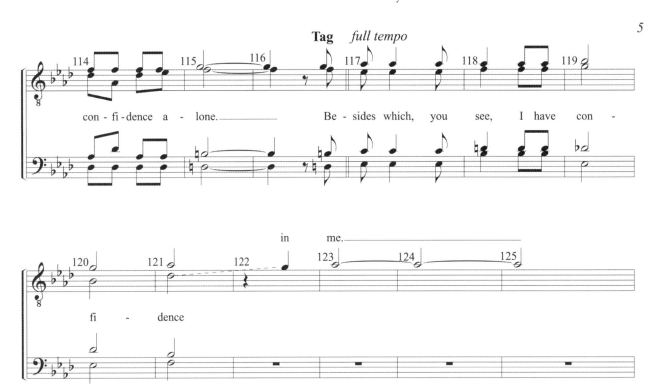

5

Let's look at the embellishments that were added in Chorus 1. At the end of the first four-measure phrase, measures 20–21, we create rhythmic interest by having the bass and tenor move on quarter notes in contrary motion.

Figure 20.23

"I Have Confidence," with rhythmic interest in measures 20–21. Arranged by Steve Armstrong.

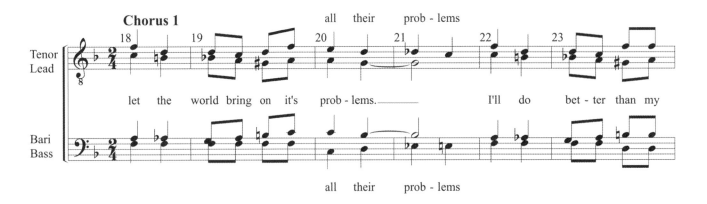

This is what we call a *scissors* move. This often consists of three chords, with the first and third chords often the same. The middle chord of scissors motion often doubles on an octave or unison as the parts swap notes in the chord. The contrary motion as the two parts converge and swap resembles the shape of scissors. This sort of embellishment—with the moving parts on a swipe or on lyrics—is very common in barbershop arranging and often used to create some motion while the melody is on a longer note. In this case, we start with a V7 chord in root position, the next chord sees the tenor and bass double on the D that makes this a ii chord in second inversion, then we have a ♭VII7 chord in root position and finally back to V7 but in first inversion. This works because of the two notes that are in common for all these chords, i.e. the G and B♭ sustained by the lead and baritone.

Then, at the end of the next four-measure phrase we chose to not have any rhythm interest. This creates contrast with the first choice but also gives the listener a chance to rest and the satisfaction that comes with that.

Figure 20.24

"I Have Confidence," with a contrasting homorhythmic texture. Arranged by Steve Armstrong.

In measures 36–37, we again create *rhythmic interest* simply by letting the lead sing the original rhythm but having the harmony parts delay moving to the second syllable, creating a *backtime* effect. This also helps both the performer and the listener to hear the major pulses more easily in the music and not lose where the downbeats are.

 Backtime is a device that lengthens syllables or words in harmony parts while the melody is delivered at its original pace. This technique may omit or use alternate words while reinforcing strong beats to support the melody.

Figure 20.25

"I Have Confidence," with rhythmic interest in measures 36–37. Arranged by Steve Armstrong.

In measures 40–41 we use another standard barbershop embellishment: a *swipe*. We start with the VI triad and then move the 5th of the chord up to the 6th and then the 7th, with the bass taking over the 5th on the last move.

This is just like the sequence halfway through "My Wild Irish Rose" on the word "rose," followed by the baritone echo "my rose."

Figure 20.26

"My Wild Irish Rose" example

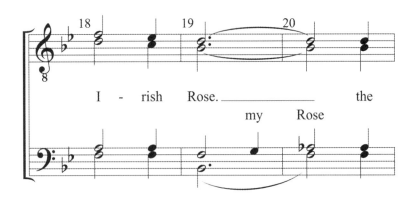

In that case the first chord is a I triad, then the baritone moves from the fifth to the sixth and finally the seventh. Note that the sixth used can either be the major sixth above the root, like in "My Wild Irish Rose," or the minor sixth above the root, like in "I Have Confidence." You will typically use the note that resides in the key you are currently in as that sounds more natural. Technically, you could describe the chord that we used on the second beat of measure 40 as a D augmented triad that is misspelled.

In measures 46–47 the melody is on repeated low Do (F).

Figure 20.27

"I Have Confidence," with low melody in measures 46–47. Arranged by Steve Armstrong.

Our harmonic pillar here is F. If we tried to harmonize this measure with an F major chord, we'd have to put the bass on low F and then get it back up to the G a ninth above that for the next measure, or double the lead note or put the bass above the lead that is always difficult to make work from a tuning and balance perspective. We could substitute a D minor chord for measure 46 and a G7 chord for measure 47, which would give us a little circle progression, but instead we have decided to use a unison here with the tenor an octave above.

Figure 20.28

"I Have Confidence," with an alternate approach in measures 46–47.

The original lyric was "they will look up to me!" The music feels declarative, so this is a good solution. We'll just have to remember to capture that sense in the new lyrics when we write them.

In measures 50–57 we come back to the first A section and, to create variety, we handle these phrase endings a little differently than the first time.

Figure 20.29

."I Have Confidence," with harmonic variety in measures 50–57. Arranged by Steve Armstrong.

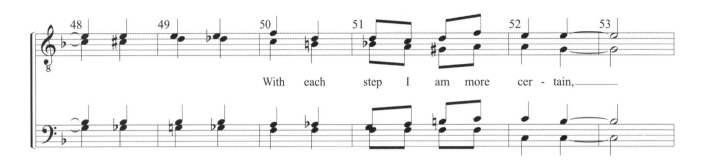

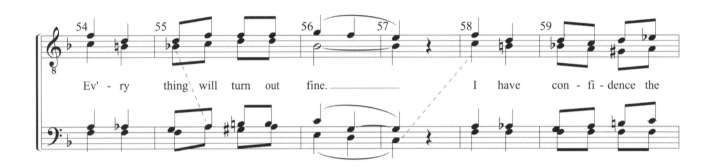

In measures 52–53 we allow the long notes to provide a moment of rest because there is none at the end of the bridge, and then we create rhythm interest with a swipe in measures 56–57. Note that we also briefly transfer the melody to the bass starting in measure 55. This not only creates interest, but it solves the problem of how to create a swipe or echo around a sustained low melody note.

For similar reasons, we transfer the melody to the bass again in measures 64–68.

Figure 20.30

"I Have Confidence," with bass melody transfer in measures 64–68. Arranged by Steve Armstrong.

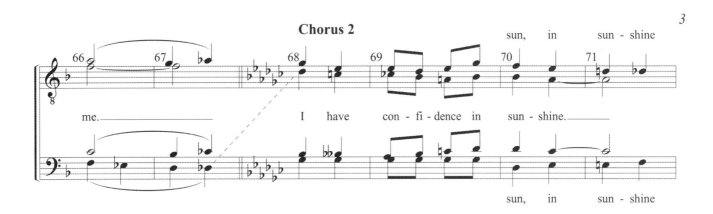

This is done partly because if the leads go to the low tonic, we either must double it on the same pitch—as we did in measure 33—or we must put the basses on the low F, and we need to avoid that voicing for this group. So, we give the melody to the bass, then have a four-chord swipe to carry us through the key change, and all the voices can stay higher making the excitement of the half-step lift even greater.

Development from Chorus to Chorus

Now let's look at Chorus 2. In measures 70–71, 74–75, 86–87, 90–91 and 96–97 we decided to use the same approach as we did in Chorus 1.

Figure 20.31

"I Have Confidence," chorus 2. Arranged by Steve Armstrong.

4

Remember, we are writing this for a chorus that scores in the mid-B range in BHS contests, circa 2023. Groups scoring in this B-level range frequently demonstrate a good mastery of the musical elements. The music is generally well suited to the performers. The theme of the song is well communicated, but there may be moments where technique becomes apparent. The harmony is generally consonant, with chords clearly distinguishable, and the embellishments tastefully support the song. The performance generally reflects understanding of, and sensitivity to, the music with high musicality in its best moments. The musical elements are generally executed accurately.

There is already variety because the composer has given us different lyrics for Chorus 2. Also, the composer has built in a wonderful key change in measures 98–100.

Figure 20.32

"I Have Confidence," with the composer's key change. Arranged by Steve Armstrong.

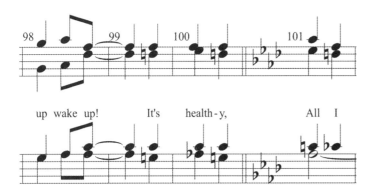

The arrangement will not feel like it is lacking if these moments are treated the same. On the other hand, if we made them only slightly different, many performers would have difficulty remembering which treatment happens on which chorus, and in performance we will likely get a messy mix of the two approaches. As arrangers, if we make it different, we really need to make it different so they can remember it.

One of the spots that will be only slightly different, but is worth it for the impact is the key change in measures 98–100. What makes this so effective is the element of surprise. However, because this song has been heard for over 55 years, most people won't be surprised but instead satisfied to hear it where they expected it. The chord sequence in measures 98–99 are the same as in 48–49.

Figure 20.33

"I Have Confidence," with the same chord sequences in measure 48–49 and 98–99. Arranged by Steve Armstrong.

In the first chorus, the last chord of that sequence is ♭II7 which acts as a substitute for V7 and resolves down to I. In the second chorus, everything is the same up to that point but then the ♭II7 chord acts as a VII7 chord and resolves up to the new I. This works beautifully and is so much fun to sing and hear, but the performers will want to make sure they drill this enough to remember the difference or there will be some interesting sounds in measure 100.

With the added excitement injected by that key change, it is time to add some new ideas. In measures 100–103 we will take advantage of the fact that our harmonization of these measures will have the bass repeat the same note. This time we'll just have the bass sustain that note as a pedal while the top three parts sing the lyrics then have the bass catch up on the words in measures 102–103.

Figure 20.34

"I Have Confidence," with additional development after the key change. Arranged by Steve Armstrong.

We'll employ the same scissors move as we've used before, but instead of quarter notes echoing the lyrics, we'll use some eighth notes to have more motion and fit the lyrics in. We could have the tenors continue the same lyric pattern as the leads and baritones and sing a three-note swipe on "to" in order to contribute their half of the scissors move, but instead we'll add strength to these delayed bass lyrics by having the tenor abandon their original lyric line right before the word "to" and join in with the basses on their lyrics.

In measures 106–107 we have a lower sustained melody note. At this point, the energy is high, and it will be easier for our performers to keep it there if we can avoid moving everybody into a lower tessitura.

Figure 20.35

"I Have Confidence," maintaining energy. Arranged by Steve Armstrong.

Measures 106–107 represent an appropriate time to alter the melody slightly going up to a D♭ instead of down to a G. This melodic alteration allows the harmony parts to stay higher, and we can fill in these measures rhythmically with a standard barbershop swipe.

When we get to measures 110–111, we have added a tempo marking to slow down and then sing measures 112–116 freely.

Figure 20.36

"I Have Confidence," with the ritard in measures 111–112. Arranged by Steve Armstrong.

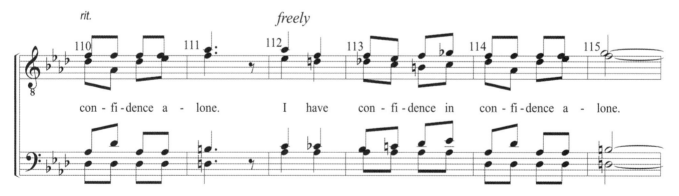

This is imitating the performance from the movie where, you'll no doubt recall, it appears like doubts are creeping in one more time and then emphatically pushed away with the return to tempo at measure 117. We can add to the sense of growing determination in measures 115–116 by substituting a more consonant sounding VII7 chord in place of the diminished seventh just by changing the tenor note. The change is small but makes a dramatic difference.

Figure 20.37

"I Have Confidence," heading into the tag. Arranged by Steve Armstrong.

Original Material

This completes the two choruses with the tag still left to write, plus some lyrics in chorus 1. We will also need to arrange the verse, but we are starting to see an arrangement emerge from our work.

Now let's address the passage where the original lyrics don't work out of the context of the musical. Arrangers often need to write lyrics for intros or new verses, or for interludes or sometimes, for a repeated portion of a song where you wish for the story to continue to develop rather than just restating what was already said.

For example, you might have a song where the chorus is in AABA form. Musically it feels right to repeat the BA for further development, but the last A section concludes the story. You could go back and restate it, or you could expand on the conclusion, or it might feel best to move the last A section lyrics to the repeat and write new lyrics in the middle to keep building to the lyrical conclusion. So, the new form would be AAB(AB)A where the sections in parentheses have new lyrics written by the arranger.

In any event, sometimes you already have music you are writing lyrics for, and sometimes you are writing new music as well. When we already have the music, it is much better if we use the same number of syllables as the music originally had. In other words, don't cheat by splitting a quarter note into 2 eighth notes! We also want to follow the original rhyme scheme so let's take a look. The original lyrics were:

Somehow I will impress them

I will be firm but kind

And all those children, Heaven bless them,

They will look up to me and mind me.

Figure 20.38

"I Have Confidence," with alternate lyrics. Arranged by Steve Armstrong.

There are rhymes at the end of lines one and three on "press them" and "bless them" and the end of line two on "kind" that rhymes with the second last syllable in line four on "mind". This exact pattern is used again when the bridge is repeated, so it clearly is intentional, and we should adhere to it.

Next, determine what lyrical message is desired. In our example, the storyteller is expressing a growing determination to succeed no matter what the world throws at them. There are references to "them" and "they," which in the original context would have meant the children Maria was going to care for, but in this context refers generically to the people in the world that would doubt the singer's ability to succeed.

Let's continue to develop defiance and conviction. Some people have a gift with words and at this point could just rattle off some lines that are very elegant and work perfectly, with the right number of syllables and rhymes where we want them. If that is not your gift, you could try writing down a list of words that might be useful. Then you can use a thesaurus to find similar words you could consider. It is also very helpful to use a rhyming dictionary. You can easily find a thesaurus and a rhyming dictionary free online.

express them	*repress them*
bless them	*dispossess them*
possess them	*caress them*
suppress them	*transgress them*
oppress them	*depress them*

Let's start with our first rhyme of "press them." A quick search finds:

Many of these spark ideas of how they could be used. We could end up with something like this:

> *Somehow I will impress them*
>
> -------
>
> *And all my doubts, I will suppress them,*
>
> ------

This works, but that line is a little inelegant. We may want to look at some rhymes for just the last syllable, which isn't ideal but may end in a better outcome. A quick search finds among the list the word "mayhem," which is unusual and provocative, and combined with the idea of doubt we can get this line:

> *Somehow I will impress them*
>
> -------
>
> *And all the doubters causing mayhem,*
>
> ------

Let's go with that as it seems more interesting. Now for the other lines. What are some other words that fit this message?

What does the storyteller want to do?

> *show them, prove to them, lead them, etc.*
>
> *prevail, win, overcome, achieve, succeed, etc.*

You could search for synonyms and rhymes for each of these and likely these words will start to spark some ideas. You may end up with two or three partial lyrics that follow completely different paths but have potential. Don't be afraid to abandon ideas and try new ones. It is likely that eventually one will come along that you'll be pleased with. This may take longer than any other part of the process.

In the end, it turns out that we had a rhyme in the words listed—the second syllable of "succeed" and—the first syllable of "lead them," which is exactly what we need. We can expand on that idea and end up with this:

Somehow I will impress them

They'll cheer when I succeed

And all the doubters causing mayhem,

Soon they will look to me to lead them.

You may come up with lyrics you like even better, but these will work, and they express just what we need in the story.

Writing a Tag

Now we need to write a tag. One of the key things to consider here is that this tag exists as the end of a song/arrangement, so it should function in a way that it provides a satisfying conclusion. If you were writing a stand-alone tag, you might make other choices as it would no longer have that function.

The original songwriter helps us get started by elongating the notes in the melody starting in measure 121 and slightly modifying the melody to climb to the high tonic instead of the low tonic as it did in measures 65–67. We can hand off the melody from the leads to the tenors for the last 2 notes to keep the parts in ranges they can sing well. We also can change the rhythm in measure 124 to be a quarter rest followed by a quarter note to give our singers a chance to breathe. This is a very important consideration and easy to forget when we are constantly hearing the computer play the arrangement back to us.

Figure 20.39

"I Have Confidence," tag. Arranged by Steve Armstrong.

Completing the Verse

We're almost done but we haven't yet arranged the verse. We have already sorted out what measures we will use and their keys and have included all of that information in the road map, but now we must go back and arrange it. By the way, it is not unusual to arrange these segments out of sequence. In fact, it is often helpful to do the verse or intro last when you have a complete picture of what it is leading into.

We know that the tempo will start at the beginning of Chorus I, which is also where the storyteller has arrived at the conclusion that they will succeed no matter what comes their way! The lyrics in the verse are less confident and show the internal struggle this person has experienced. We can support that uncertainty using texture. We'll start with only the leads on the words and then have the baritones and tenors join in on words in the second half of measure 2. The basses will stay on an "oo" right up until measure 4, which has the added advantage of being able to use the pedal tone that was featured in the original.

We can bring the voicings up in measure 6 to support the excitement of the possible adventures ahead and then bring them right back down again with the confession of being frightened by all of this. Our first tricky spot here is how to get from the key of F to the key of E♭. We are on a C7 in measure 8 and want to get to a B♭7 in measure 9. We know that one of the chords we can use to harmonize non-chord tones is the diminished 7th chord built on the same root. Well, it just so happens that the diminished 7th chord built on B♭—remember we are moving towards a B♭7 chord—has almost the same notes as C7. The only difference is that the C is replaced with a C#; of course we're taking liberties with the spelling here, but it is the sound of the chord that is most important. That scissors move in measure 8 creates interest but it also gets us into the first inversion of C7. From there the tenor can make a quick move up to C# on "I" and then the harmony parts all move up one semitone to "must" while the lead stays on the say note. This is a very smooth transition to V7 of the new key.

A couple more comments about this transition. We changed the melody note on the pickup, we left a word out—"Oh I" became "I"—and we moved the melody to the bass. Let's talk about each of these.

- The bass melody creates a little more interest, and it solves the problem of how we would harmonize the E♭ in measure 10. The melody does not return to the low tonic, so this is the only occurrence we need to worry about in the verse. It turns out the melody is almost entirely on 5ths and roots, so we still have strong voicings.
- When we added in the scissors move, it felt a little cluttered lyrically plus our singers need to breathe somewhere. Removing the word "Oh" gives us a spot for a breath, and it no longer feels too busy.
- We generally try to stick to the original melody, but we can often change a pickup note without having any impact on the overall character of the melody, especially if it is during a transition as it is here.

Here is what our verse looks like so far:

Figure 20.40

"I Have Confidence" verse. Arranged by Steve Armstrong.

Continuing with the end of the verse, we can again reinforce the excitement of the "dreams" by utilizing higher voicings in measures 13 and 14. We then come to measures 15 to 18 where the original score has this sense of climbing musically to reinforce the determination welling up inside the storyteller just before it bursts out in the chorus. Creating that musical effect but staying within our chord vocabulary would be ideal. We often see echoes like this:

Figure 20.41

Typical barbershop echoes. Arranged by Steve Armstrong.

Having the three harmony parts climbing is exactly the feel we want, and if you look at measures 17–18 below, that is exactly the same as the last three chords in the example above. However, we want this effect to be longer, so if we use a different voicing for the first time through the pattern, the bass can start on the D in measure 15 and climb in semitones all the way to measure 18. The baritone ends up singing the same pattern twice and the tenor climbs in measures 15–16, then jumps down and climbs again in measures 17–18 but the effect is created! And as it turns out, that first chord in measure 15—a D half diminished 7th or F minor 6th that moves through the diminished 7th to get to C7—could also be considered a B♭9 chord in first inversion. Because we are starting this passage in the key of E♭, it feels like V9 at the start. We build conviction through the climb and when we get to the chorus, we're now in F!

Figure 20.42

"I Have Confidence," end of verse key change into the chorus. Arranged by Steve Armstrong.

Conclusion

We now have a completed arrangement, and it turned out well. Our verse not only supports the emotional uncertainty of the storyteller while they build up their courage but also moves through a couple of nifty key changes along the way. Our first chorus has the rhythmic drive that characterizes the song. We have lyrics that work outside of the original context of the musical. We exploit the feeling of becoming more and more emboldened by lifting the key a semitone and then a whole tone. We have a momentary relapse just before the tag and then we end with conviction. It seems like this would be a fun chart to sing!

Figure 20.44

"I Have Confidence," completed arrangement. Arranged by Steve Armstrong.

4

6

Chapter 21.
Voice Leading

By Adam Scott and Rafi Hasib

Barbershop arranging is a learned skill. Evidence for this abounds. Whereas in the previous century of barbershop there were a small handful of arrangers—a sort of inner circle—the 2023 Barbershop Harmony Society International contest cycle saw arrangements from 60 different arrangers! More arrangers mean a rich variety for barbershop both in skill and genre of song choices. But how does one become a skilled arranger? Beyond song choice, a solid knowledge of mechanics is an absolute must. At the heart of that skill set is voice leading.

Voice leading is the treatment of the harmony parts both vertically, i.e., how they line up in the chord, and horizontally, i.e., their own individual line as a melodic line. To understand how they work together, it is important to first understand each dimension separately. Having a functional understanding of music theory concepts related to the barbershop style, documented in *Arranging Barbershop*, Vol 1, is a prerequisite to the content in this chapter which follows.

Chord Voicing

Across the four voice parts, the voicing of a given chord may be described as any of the following:

- **Closed**: When the interval between highest and lowest voices is an octave or less
- **Open**: When the interval between the highest and lowest voices spans over an octave, such as a 10th (octave plus a third)
- **Homogeneous**: When the intervals between adjacent voices are similarly sized
- **Spread**: When this interval between the highest and lowest voices approaches or exceeds two octaves
- **Divorced**: When an outer voice is separated from its neighbor voice by more than on octave, usually from the trio by more than a fifth, i.e., divorced bass, divorced tenor

A barbershop melody may be harmonized with a constant change between open and close voicing. Homogeneous voicings are often easier to tune and balance, whereas spread voicing is typically reserved for special effect or to highlight particular voices. For examples, the bass or tenor are often divorced when taking over the melody or during a feature as part of a tag.

Chord Inversions

As a close-harmony style, barbershop relies on chords that are quick and easy to tune vertically. Though the melody implies the harmony, the arranger ultimately chooses the chords and which chord members go to which parts. The choice of chord inversion can not only produce desired effects or moods, but it can also help the ensemble's tuning and balance.

- The barbershop style primarily uses strongly voiced chords, with the lowest voice—almost always the bass—singing the root or fifth, with overall chord root position or second inversion, respectively. Other inversions may occur, but less frequently on strong or emphatic beats.
- Triads consist of only three unique tones, distributed among the four parts. They usually occur in the root position, i.e., root in the bass, with the root doubled in another voice. In rare cases, when the major or minor triad appears in first inversion, i.e., third in the bass, the root or fifth may be doubled.
- Seventh chords, and other chords with at least four notes, often occur in root and second inversion. Third inversion, i.e., seventh in the bass, may also occur, usually during a swipe.
- Ninth chords have five notes—including the seventh and ninth—spread across four voices. To retain the dominant sound, they omit the root or fifth, placing it in second inversion or root position, respectively.

- Sixth chords typically appear in root position as incomplete with the root doubled at the octave in lieu of the fifth. An example would be C–E–A–C. In rare cases, it may include the complete chord—Add6—with both the fifth and sixth. An example would be C–E–G–A. The minor sixth chord—minor triad with the added sixth—should have all four notes present. An example would be C–Eb–G–A.

Principles of Voice Leading

Voice leading refers to the ease with which a voice part progresses from one note to the next. Much of the basic approaches come from the common practice era of European music, from roughly 1650 to 1900, covering the Classical and Romantic periods. A college curriculum often reinforces the conventions of the time through four-part Bach chorale harmonization, treating a soprano melody with alto, tenor, and bass harmonies. The barbershop style retains several of these conventions for smooth voice leading, noting that the melody primarily occurs in the second highest voice. Having melody in an inside voice has strong implications for the other voice parts.

Retain Four Parts

Barbershop is a four-part harmony style with frequent use of four-part chords. Even with triads, a given chord should strive for four distinct tones, including octaves, unless used for effect, e.g., parts peeling off from unison or doubling to a four-part chord. When harmonizing a melody or shifting harmonies within a chord, this may require other voices to change notes to accommodate the harmony. This notion differs from the common practice in other styles where smooth voice leading and independence of voices often supersedes the need for complete, four-part chords.

Reinforce the Role of Each Voice

In most barbershop settings, each voice part serves a particular function with respect to the vocal line. As the arrangement develops, individual role may change—particularly when the melody passes around—but the fundamental roles remain throughout.

The lead typically sings the melody, which drives the message of the song and implies the harmonies. The part is often determined by the source material and informs the other parts. Unlike in classical music, the melody is usually sung by an inner voice.

The bass sings below the lead to provide the foundational harmony with strongly voiced chords. As the bass often drives the harmony and rhythm, it serves as a secondary melody when the lead sustains a note. Occasionally, the melody transfers from the lead to the bass to accommodate a lower range.

The tenor sings above the lead on the highest harmony. Because our ears are naturally drawn to the highest voice, as they would to a soprano singing melody in a classical setting, great care should be taken to ensure a smooth tenor line that doesn't pull the focus from the lead. To accommodate the lead line with smoother voice leading, the tenor may incidentally dip below an ascending lead line rather than remain consistently above the lead.

The baritone sings the remaining inner harmony, often singing above and below the lead to complete the chord. Unlike a classical inner voice, e.g., alto or tenor, this voice's range overlaps with the other inner voice and is not expected to remain solely below the lead. When the melody dips low enough, this often requires the baritone to sing above the lead. Because its function is primarily to ensure four distinct notes and complete the chord based on the others' notes, the baritone line is often the least musically intuitive—ironically, making it quite predictable.

Regardless of chord voicings, the arrangement should ensure a clear and distinguishable melody. The arranger's choice of harmony can offer each part a relatively melodic line with smooth voice leading that are both pleasant to sing and hear, all while guiding the technical and artistic treatment by the performers. The following are guidelines which both adhere to standard music theory conventions and make for great barbershop arrangements.

Move Upper Voices the Shortest Distance Possible

When a chord contains one or more *common tones* reused in the following chord, these notes should remain and be retained in their respective parts. The remaining parts should move by step, if possible, or the smallest interval.

 Avoiding large leaps makes for more singable parts above the bass.

The exception to this is that the bass prefers roots and fifths to create strongly voiced chords. As the foundation for the harmony, this voice part has characteristic leaps to notes that make it easier for the other voices to tune their notes. However, the arranger should still take great care to retain notes in this voice part for a smooth vocal line where possible.

Avoid Awkward Intervals

In providing each voice the most melodic line possible, it is valuable to avoid awkward intervals:

*   Large skips in the tenor and baritone part
*   Skips to chromatically altered pitch
*   Skips to the seventh of the chord
*   Skips of diminished or augmented intervals

Although these are preferred, these are not rules, and the desire for particular harmonic progressions or effects, e.g., a spread chord, may outweigh accommodating easier voice leading.

Avoid Parallel Fifths Between Outer Voices

Common practice music restricts the use of parallel octaves and fifths between voices to promote independent voices. In contrast, the barbershop style favors the harmonic effects and convergence to the overtone series of a single voice, relaxing the rules of parallels. Though parallel octaves are rare, parallel fifths may occur—particularly between the bass and baritone—though one should avoid them between the bass and tenor, as consecutive fifths in outside voices have a rather harsh quality. Again, such parallel intervals may occur in areas that favor the effect or chord progression over the strict voice leading. Other parallel intervals, i.e. thirds, sixths, and tenths, are quite common, often providing a natural harmonization to the melody, though it is rare to have multiple consecutive chords in parallel harmony across all voices.

Let Tempo Drive the Voice Leading

In uptunes or up-tempo songs, a fast tempo may demand voices to frequently accommodate the melody. As a result, voice leading takes priority over preferred chord voicings, often discouraging harmonic variety. It is common for the underlying pillar chords to change less frequently, allowing voices to intuitively move to between complete, four-part chords. To accommodate this, avoid large and frequent skips with difficult intervals, such as tritones, sixths, and sevenths.

In contrast, in a ballad, optimal chord voicing and harmonic variety may take greater priority over voice leading, with more frequent changes in the underlying chords. The slower tempo allows for more complex harmony, including larger skips and more difficult intervals, particularly in swipes.

This will be further explored when discussing harmonic rhythm. For now, let's put these ideas into practice.

Harmonizing a Melody

In the context of an arrangement, one might think of barbershop voice leading as a kind of musical Sudoku puzzle. Fill in parts in as you work—with a few principles as guideposts—and remember these are not hard and fast laws. Here are the basics, with an example to help illustrate the steps.

Fill in Your Melody

This may seem obvious but put down your melody first. Two things go into consideration. One, the key you pick will have a ripple effect. Start too high/low and you'll paint yourself into a corner. It's a good idea to put down a good chunk of your melody—a verse or chorus—and see if you agree with where the tessitura, or comfortable resting range, sits. Two, in the event your melody line rises too high, this is a good opportunity to plan for melody transfers to the tenor line. In like manner, if a few notes are too low, passing them off to the bass is a natural fix. If you find yourself constantly transferring the melody, you likely have chosen a key that is fighting against you.

Keep in mind that when a melody has a large jump, the harmony parts may not have to jump the same amount or in the same direction, because the baritone and tenor will fill in notes around and can accommodate occasional voice crossing by the lead. As you place the melody and predict the chords to harmonize, you will get an idea of where the neighboring voices will fit in.

Fill in the Bass

Why bass next? Basses are the foundation. Your bass singer is going to be the nimblest singer of your group, often leaping greater distances than the other singers. This singer is going to be placed on roots and fifths most often. If you are in doubt, try analyzing any polecat. You'd be hard-pressed to find moments when the bass is not on a root or fifth.

When basses are on the third or seventh of the chord, they have the tendency to overbalance their note in the chord. This is exacerbated in a chorus setting. Basses may also sing major thirds too sharp.

Figure 21.1

Lead and bass harmonization of "When You Wore a Tulip," words and music by Jack Mahoney and Percy Weinrich. Arranged by Adam Scott.

In this chorus of "When You Wore a Tulip," we see that the bass is very often singing the root or the fifth, depending on the chord member sung by the lead. This often leads to stepwise and jumps as we transition between chords. Remember that the bass can and is expected to handle jumps to strong members of chords.

Let's look at a couple of spots in particular:

- In measure 13, "blessing," the bass moves from singing the root to singing the fifth but moves like this are only executed because the root of the chord was taken over by the lead.
- In the cadential moment in measures 7 and 15, effort was made to prolong the cadence by embellishing it stepwise. These moves will make more sense when the baritone and tenor are added back in.

Add the Remaining Voice Parts in Tandem

For voice leading purposes, you may find it beneficial to give deference to the tenor over the baritone. The ear will naturally pick up on the voice leading of highest voice over an inner, overlapping voice that shares the lead's range.

This may sometimes be difficult to manage, particularly with a jumpy melodic line, e.g., "Over the Rainbow." If you find yourself stuck, consider jumping ahead to cadential moments and working backwards. If you know where you need to land, you can often reverse engineer yourself out of tough situations, which can guide the middle phrases.

Let's build on the bass harmonization of "When You Wore a Tulip" from the last example to fill in the tenor and baritone. Before you look at complete harmonization in Figure 21.2, analyze the previous excerpt. What choices would you make for the remaining harmony parts? Why?

Now let's look at one way to harmonize this passage. Notice we say, "one way," not "the way." There are several small changes one could make to this passage. Indeed, an arranger might incorporate some of these decisions later in the song.

Figure 21.2

Four-part harmonization of "When You Wore a Tulip." Arranged by Adam Scott.

Notice how the smooth the tenor voice leading is, rarely jumping more than a third. The baritone also retains as smooth voice leading as possible, usually jumping to accommodate the lead. Now, could we have made other choices? What about this one in measure 7?

Figure 21.3

Alternate harmonization for measure 7 of "When You Wore a Tulip." Arranged by Adam Scott.

The voice leading changes a little. Instead of the bass moving stepwise, as in Figure 21.2, now the bass has been altered for a more standard root movement. A more solid choice harmonically, perhaps. Does that one move affect the piece as a whole? No. Such changes might affect the piece in minor ways, but subtle changes like this would likely go largely unnoticed.

Let's see what happens when we start making more changes.

Figure 21.4

Alternate harmonization of "When You Wore a Tulip." Arranged by Adam Scott.

There are subtle changes in this right from bar one, all while still keeping the idea of smooth stepwise voice leading in mind. Instead of an innocuous V9 or even a Iadd6 chord, we use the VII7 (A7) chord. Being so far removed from the key, it demands a little more attention. Is it wrong? Again, no. It is simply a different choice. When the arranger makes more changes like this, it begins to stick out to the listener. However, drawing attention to these small changes may distract from other elements of the song. If a song is lyrically treated and the arranger makes more harmonic and textural changes, it may distract from the message of the song. That leads us to our next point.

Additional Considerations

What Effect Does Tempo Have on the Chord Choice?

One important element to consider is the impact of tempo when choosing chords. Consider the example in Figure 21.2 where the arranger chose to leave the E♭ as the pillar chord and treat the D natural in the lead as an unimportant E♭maj7 chord on the last chord of measure 9. The version in Figure 21.4 harmonized that note. This made a D7 out of that one eighth note. Does it work? Yes. Is it realistic? Perhaps not. To make the chord work we had to move the bass melodically up a tritone. It also forces the bass to either move back a tritone, which would be two awkward intervals, but we had to double the fifth, joining the baritone on the B♭. Is that something that a bass singer could execute? Yes. Probably.

This is a lot of harmonic work for a short-term gain. The faster the tempo of the piece, the tougher these types of quick movements will be to execute.

Impact of Non-Chord Tones

Harmonizing notes that don't fit in the pillar chord or prevailing harmony of the measure can be challenging. Often these are neighboring chords or chords that force us out of the chord we'd prefer to hear. Let's return to the example song. The ending to the song has the melody and chords like so:

Figure 21.5

Ending of "When You Wore a Tulip." Arranged by Adam Scott.

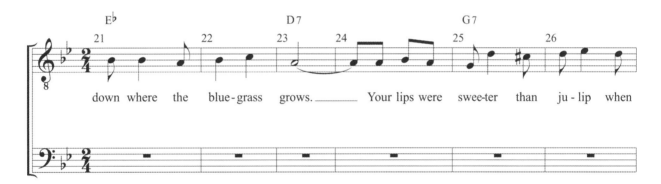

Right away we're presented with a few problems. Though the first section was not without a few tricky elements, this second half presents some melodic notes that don't fit in the measures. Some are obvious, like the C# in the G7 chord. Take a moment and analyze the excerpt and circle the notes that don't fit in the prevailing harmony. When you're satisfied, continue below.

Figure 21.6

Identifying non-chord tones in the ending of "When You Wore a Tulip." Arranged by Adam Scott.

Some of these asterisks are obvious. Your ear will likely disapprove of the B natural in bar 27 whose chord C7 contains a B♭. It will sound like an obvious mistake. How do we reconcile these pitches? The example in Figure 21.7 will serve as an aid to provide examples of ways to harmonize in several standard ways.

Figure 21.7

Harmonization of the ending of "When You Wore a Tulip." Arranged by Adam Scott.

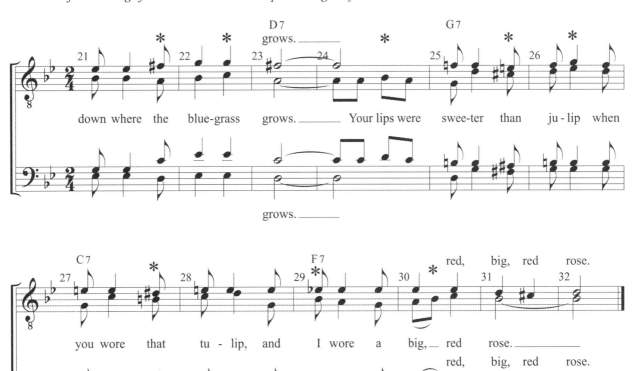

Let's examine these chord choices one at a time.

First, the D7 in bar 21 seems at first blush to be an odd choice. Though the D7 employed in Figure 21.4 above was problematic, using it here works better for the following reasons:

- The bass is only moving by half steps, as is the lead, meaning the voice leading for two parts is less obtrusive.
- The D7 here hints at the strong D7 harmonic move in 23 on "grows."
- While we could keep the bass on the Eb and have a fully diminished chord here—a fully viable choice—this one serves the ear best knowing we're starting up a sequence of harmonic events (the circle progression from D7–G7–C7–F7–Bb, from III7 back to I).

Second, the C in "grass" in bar 22 is examined as an Eb add6. Though we could return to the D7, doing so here would produce a strong harmonic moment on a weaker beat that feels more like a misstep to the ear. Instead, in retaining the Eb root, we preserve the pattern of pillar harmonic structures change at the rate of one chord change every two measures.

Third, the "lips" chord in bar 24. We could use a few chords here. This choice maintains the flavor of D7, though augmented flavor of the Bb is best harmonized by the bari doubling the root rather than staying on the fifth. Carried out to its full analysis the Bb is technically a Vb13 (D–F#–A–C–E–G–Bb).

Next, let's look at both non-chord tones in the G7 area. In bar 25, we dipped down chromatically for an F#7 chord. Why not employ the same treatment to the E♭ and use an A♭7—a half-step up from the pillar chord? For two major reasons:

- The dominant seventh is harmonically rich and, when used on weak beats, outside the harmonic rhythm, or outside the pillar harmony of a measure, tends to attract a lot of attention.
- The E♭ again or V♭13 naturally occurs in the key signature whereas the C# was a chromatic addition to the melodic line. The E♭ will feel more natural in this key.

Our next two asterisks will employ the same logic: the C7 bar with the B natural in the melody in measure 27 becomes a quick neighboring B7, while the D natural in bar 28 in the context of C7 becomes the 9th, i.e. rootless C9.

Last, let's consider the B♭ at the start of our F7 in measure 29 and the handling of the non-chord tone on the melodic swipe. This seems almost like the composer's fault—right at the natural V7 we get an incidental B♭ in the melody. The easiest way around this is a quick retrograde progression to the Cm7 with the baritone similar motion swipe. The voice leading for the lead and baritone, the common tones for the bass and baritone, and the chord a fifth away from the pillar, make this feel natural.

Summary

Let's review the general guidelines for voice leading:

1. Retain four parts
2. Reinforce the role of each voice
3. Move upper voices the shortest distance possible
4. Avoid awkward intervals, including parallel fifths between outer voices
5. Let tempo drive the voice leading
6. Consider the impact of non-chord tones

Again, these guidelines help inform the arranging choices as you place the melody in a suitable range, add in the bass with primarily roots and fifths, and fill the remaining parts in tandem, working backwards as needed.

Chapter 22.
Original Material: Intros, Tags, and Verses

By Kevin Keller

Original Material

One way in which an arranger develops a complete musical journey is through the creation of original material. This is most often the case with introductions, tags, and original verses—important components of arrangements within the style. A key challenge with creating original material is making it sound cohesive with the composer's and lyricist's work. This chapter explores several successful examples of and approaches to creating original material.

Introductions

Arrangers are faced many times with writing new material to start the arrangement, including:

- No verse exists, and it needs a verse.
- A verse exists but it isn't very good, or it doesn't express the emotions you wish.
- It is abrupt to just start with the first phrase of the chorus.

There are different philosophies on when you generate the introduction. For intermediate arrangers, likely it is best to arrange everything else and figure out how to go backwards such that the introduction supports the rest of the arrangement. Creating the introduction first may dictate how the arrangement goes, as choices made drive future choices.

Definitions

For this chapter, we will use these terms throughout.

- **Intro**: One or two phrases long that lead us quickly into the chorus; can be lyrical or instrumental
- **Verse**: Provides some lyrical background information that brings us to the present-day storyline
- **Chorus**: The primary material of the arrangement

Decisions

There are some decisions that are to be made:

Decision 1: Do you need an intro or a verse? There are some arrangements that have both, but it doesn't happen all that often. When just starting to explore the creation of original material, choose an intro or a verse but not both.

Decision 2: If you are doing an intro, is it lyrical or instrumental?

Decision 3: At the end of the intro/verse, is the music climbing to the sky or becoming intimate?

Instrumental Intros

These are becoming more and more popular in today's barbershop, circa 2023. They are effective when the initial lyrics of the chorus are generally strong enough to convey to the audience where we are in the storyline, and additional background information is not needed to frame the song. Without the aid of lyrics, neutral syllables and chords should create a mood that draws the listener toward the performer. Whatever is arranged needs to allow the performer to understand and create a musical arc. For example, there can be a sense of the chords rising and then falling, or the same set of chords are repeated twice with different dynamics in the two sets of chords.

Come What May

This arrangement includes a simple four bar introduction with "doo" on staggered notes to create a bell chord effect. Note the three harmony parts rising from measures 1–3 and then resolving back in measure 4. This gives the performer the ability to create a musical line and coming back down in measure 4 draws the audience to the lyric.[10]

Figure 22.1

An instrumental intro for "Come What May," words and music by Kevin Gilbert and David Baerwald. Arranged by Kevin Keller.

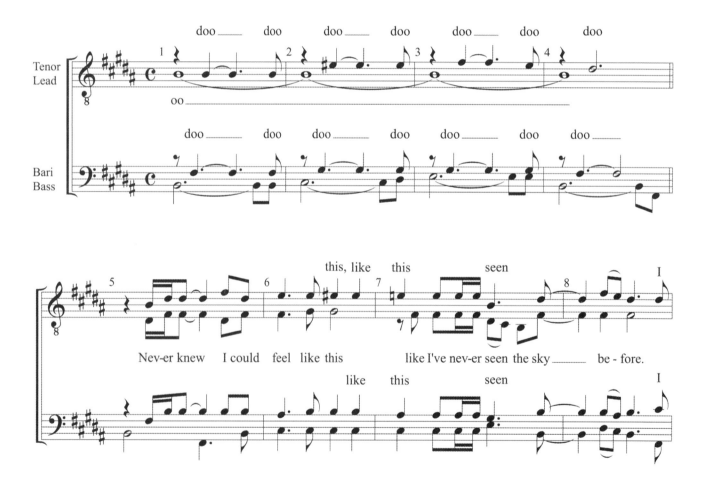

---

10   Barbershop Harmony Society. (2017, Aug 18). *After Hours - Come What May [from Moulin Rouge!]* [Video]. YouTube. https://youtu.be/VsAb54zJRcI

If You Go Away

The immediate bari/bass octave is strong and foreboding. The tenor/lead descent and the notes chosen draw the listener in forecasting the sentiment of the song. David's treatment creates an element of suspense that can be quite powerful for the performer to leverage.[11]

Figure 22.2

Instrumental intro for "If You Go Away," words and music by By Rod Mckuen and Jacques Brel. Arranged by David Wright.

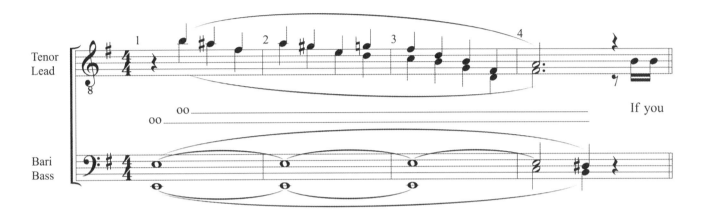

I Love a Parade

Jay effectively creates a trumpet fanfare that gets things going quickly into the first song of a parade medley, "I Love a Parade." In addition, with the syllables it is quite percussive, which will help establish a martial feel and also provide vocal contrast to the likely smoother "Oh, I love a parade." The quartet or chorus can start off strongly with the unison start and then crescendo through the intro to the chorus.

Figure 22.3

Instrumental intro for "I Love a Parade," words and music by Ted Koehler and Harold Arlen. Arranged by Jay Giallombardo.

---

11   Barbershop Harmony Society. (2019, Oct 7). *Zero8 - If You Go Away* [Video]. YouTube. https://youtu.be/vTTzu8Q2DsE

The Next Ten Minutes

Note the bass line moving downwards. This will draw the listener's ear. In measure 4 the bass rises from A to B.[12]

Figure 22.4

Instrumental intro for "The Next Ten Minutes," words and music by Jason Robert Brown. Introduction written and arranged by Theo Hicks.

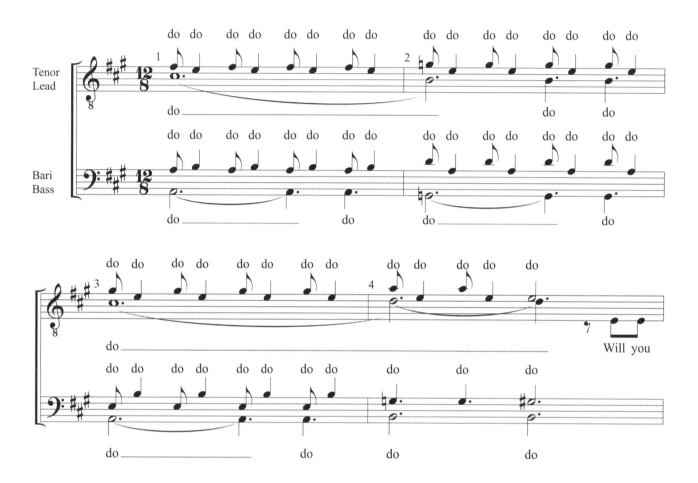

In all cases shown, there is a sense of musical arc even though the introductions were relatively short—4 measures.

---

12   Barbershop Harmony Society. (2018, Jul 13). *After Hours - The Next Ten Minutes [from The Last Five Years]* [Video]. YouTube. https://youtu.be/WgwuDAvLxNE

Lyrical Intros

The goal of the intro is to lead us to the chorus or verse as quickly as possible. Not much needs to be said, but without an intro, it could be quite abrupt. Think about what you want the intro to say, and say it as economically as you can.

The Sunshine of Your Smile

This intro was arranged to establish the subtext of the song: a love story about the person that brings sunshine, joy, and meaning into the singer's life. If Tom had elected to start with the verse, "Shadows may fall upon the land and sea," the subtext of the song would not have been immediately evident. This lets the audience know that, even though there may be hard times, the story has a happy ending.[13]

Figure 22.5

Lyrical intro for "The Sunshine of Your Smile." Written and arranged by Tom Gentry.

---

13   Barbershop Archive. (2020, Jun 21). *Power Play & Frontier - The Sunshine of Your Smile* [Video]. YouTube. https://youtu.be/p08WnYBXMN4

Ring-A-Ding-Ding

This intro shows a common trick that arrangers will employ: borrowing a thematic element from the song. It could be melody, lyric, harmony, or rhythm. Anthony borrows all of these from the song and makes some tweaks to get the song kicked off in four measures.[14]

Figure 22.6

Intro for "Ring-a-Ding-Ding!" Words and music by Sammy Cahn and James Van Heusen. Arranged by Anthony Bartholomew.

Redhead

This is an example of a chart that has both an intro and a verse. The overall goal is to start off strong and then tell the story. The intro first grabs the audience's attention in measure two with the big swipe upward. It also sets up and contrasts with the verse, which starts in a low register following a key change. Without the intro, it may have been more challenging for the performer—and confusing for the audience—to start the uptune with a verse in a low register.[15]

Figure 22.7

Intro for "Redhead," words and music by Dorothy Fields and Albert Hague. Arranged by Jim Clancy.

15   Nicole Adams. (Mar 1, 2017). *Vocal Majority International Champs 1997 [Video]*. YouTube. https://youtu.be/CASDGXLtxdI?si=JqPidAyGnmoCpUeU&t=304

Lyrical Verses

You've arrived at this point because there is more backstory to be established than will fit into a short intro. The song doesn't have a verse, or the verse that is there doesn't convey the right backstory. Now you must write something new. For most of us, this is the biggest challenge in barbershop arranging. Compared with writing lyrics, chords are easy!

Most of the songs we arrange come from the Great American Songbook. They are quite predictable in their form. The chorus typically has a simple form like AABA, ABAC, or ABCA. Audiences like familiarity, returning to something they've heard before. Composers realize this. Furthermore, songs from this era tell the story in the body of the chorus. The verse—if one exists—serves to bring the audience up to speed on who the characters are, how the characters are placed together, and then some element of suspense or conflict that requires resolution. The chorus is how the characters resolve the conflict. The verse is typically past tense while the chorus is often present tense. The story unfolds before our eyes.

If you must go down this path—and sometimes you must—then consider the following:

1. What is your story of the chorus? What is its emotional arc? How does your story end?

2. What information needs to be shared upfront with the audience, so they recognize how you got to the place where the conflict or suspense needs to be resolved?

Consider the start of stories. "Once upon a time…" We learn about the characters involved, how they are placed together in a timeline, and what has happened requiring resolution. We want to learn what happens next. That's the role of the chorus. "Once upon a time" should be as efficient and economical as possible.

Another way to consider it is that you can walk up to the microphone and share the backstory with the audience. What would you tell them? You certainly wouldn't tell them what happened because then there's no reason to sing. You only tell them enough to whet their appetite.

Anything Goes

Now that you've established what information needs to be shared, do you have a lyrical hook? In "Anything Goes," I used "The more things change, the more they stay the same" as the setup to the story. [16]

Figure 22.8

Verse for "Anything Goes," words and music by Cole Porter. Intro written and arranged by Kevin Keller.

That hook drives decisions ahead and behind it. Sometimes you get lucky in finding a hook. Other times those hooks don't come to you, but it makes it easier when you can create one.

Write phrases attempting to convey the information that needs to be shared. Don't worry about rhyming words yet. You'll go through many attempts until you find phrases you like.

16   Barbershop Harmony Society. (2019, Aug 30). *Alexandria Harmonizers - Anything Goes* [Video]. YouTube. https://youtu.be/okUtCTl7W3M

I Can't Give You Anything But Love

In David Harrington's arrangement of "I Can't Give You Anything But Love," David creates two sets of original material. As opposed to the original verse which speaks of being broke, he creates the character that is in love and is bewildered as to how to give a birthday gift worthy of their love. We arrive at the chorus of "I can't give you anything but love" quite successfully. Most arrangers would consider doing a chorus and a half of that song. But David cleverly goes back to the original set of characters and further develops their story line to where not only is the character stating how worthy this other person is of their love, but now becomes undying love with asking "If you'll agree to marry me." Clever use of rhymes throughout the original material written in a similar language to the Fields/McHugh song.[17]

Figure 22.9

Original verse for "I Can't Give You Anything But Love," written and arranged by David Harrington.

Auld Lang Syne

It's been so grand with you my friend / But soon now, our time will end

But we'll have the mem'ries of times we knew / The mem'ries of friends like you

These original lyrics employ a simple rhyme scheme—friend/end, knew/you—and establish a clear backstory: close friends have been together but are soon leaving each other. These are special relationships.[18]

Figure 22.10

Original verse for "Auld Lang Syne," traditional. Written and arranged by Clay Hine.

The element of suspense is in the arranging detail. Clay extends it two measures, and the chords slowly lower to an intimate level.

---

18   TalkinShop. (2011, Aug 3). *Platinum - 1999 International Quartet Final* [Video]. YouTube. https://youtu.be/-kHwxfs7xdk?t=197

Cruella De Vil

There's a wicked woman so despicable it's sad; /

She's heart-less, cold, and pitiless, she's evil and mad; /

And when she's about, you better look out /

I wanna tell you she's bad

Here, David pays more attention to rhymes on sad/mad/bad but also rhymes in phrase 3 with "about" and "look out." The rhythms are quite similar between phrases 1 and 2.

Figure 22.11

Original verse for "Cruella De Vil," words and music by Mel Levin. Verse written and arranged by David Wright.

David extends the last phrase an additional two measures to give Tim Waurick, Vocal Spectrum's tenor, a long post and create excitement as well as elevate the chords to a thrilling musical climax.[19]

---

19   Barbershop Archive. (2019, Feb 4). *Vocal Spectrum: Cruella De Vil* [Video]. YouTube. https://youtu.be/YU9rUXf11zQ

Jeannie with the Light Brown Hair

Of all the tales that you will hear as thru this life you go /

There's none so sad or teary as a lover's tale of woe /

So listen to this poet's song, its words so full of pain /

The emptiness of love gone wrong, the love I loved in vain

Figure 22.12

"Jeannie With the Light Brown Hair," words and music by Stephen Foster. Verse written and arranged by Ed Waesche.

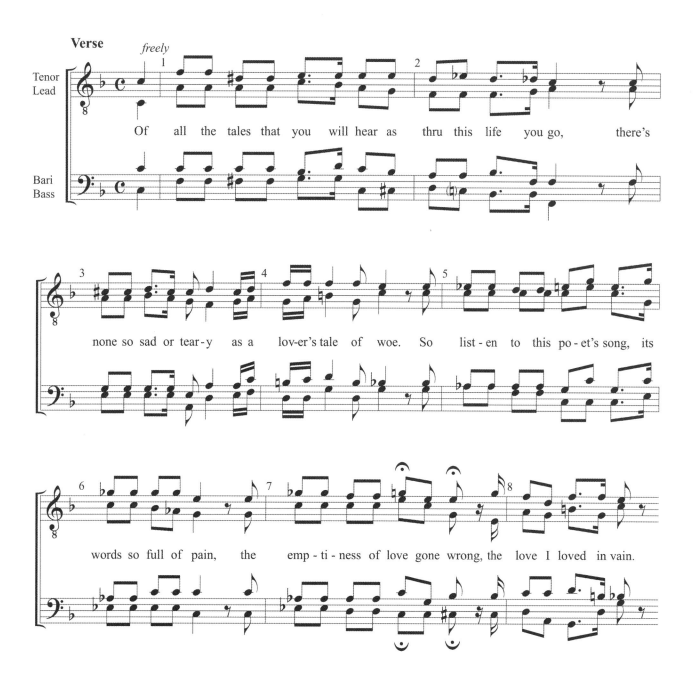

The twist is right at the end. Ed uses second person to tell the audience, "Listen to this sad story of love lost," and in the last clause share that it is about the performer's love lost. Now we are drawn in.[20] In terms of rhyming, there are simple rhymes of go/woe and pain/vain, as well as song/wrong and hear/tear(y).

Note the matching number of six syllables in "its words so full of pain" and "the love I loved in vain." The first halves of those phrases each contain eight syllables. The rhythms are slightly different, but these are some of the secrets of good lyric writing.

Tags

Let's not beat around the bush. The tag is the most important section of the song! Not every tag will rise to the status of a "classic tag" and be iconic, but all tags must be the perfect ending to the song and arrangement. The culture of barbershop singing cherishes and worships tags. Unlike many other genres of music that can simply fade away or allow the audience to take over applauding, the barbershop style creates constant musical tension and release. The tag puts the final statement on the chart. It can't simply be song over, but must be the perfect vocal, musical, and emotional expression of the song and arrangement.

There is no science or formula to writing tags. It's an artistic process involving a lot of trial and error, but there are some guiding principles we can explore to improve our own efforts. We will now review examples of tags that contain most or all of these principles:

Compelling

When we reflect upon tags that we teach each other, why do we pick certain tags to teach? Because there is something compelling about the tag. Typically, it has some sort of hook to it. It could be a single chord, it could be the lyrics, it could be a particular sequence of chords, or some sort of surprise. If you can find a hook, super! It doesn't stop your tag from being a successful way to close out a song if people aren't singing it later. But if you can imagine teaching your tag successfully out of context and inspiring others to do the same, then likely you've done well.

What is compelling about your tag? If you can find something that is compelling about the tag, simply arrange the rest of the chords so nothing competes with the hook. It's the rare tag that has more than one hook.

Organic

The tag must be written in the same style as the rest of the arrangement. If you are married to the tag but the rest of the arrangement doesn't sound like the tag, you have two simple choices. Rearrange the song to fit the tag or save your tag idea for another arrangement.

Succinct

Prior to 1993, tags were rather limited in their development due mainly to the issue of time penalties in contests but also balance. The length of a tag should be balanced with the rest of the arrangement. With time penalties removed in 1993, arrangers began exploring more development opportunities throughout the song. With these new extensions some tags became codas!

For now, recognize that most classic tags are still relatively short. David Wright likes to say that a tag to be taught by rote should be 20 chords or less, although some of our iconic tags can be a bit longer than that. It's a good practice to incorporate at this stage of your development. Don't confuse length with degree of success.

- Short does not mean simple
- Long does not mean complex

---

20   Barbershop Harmony Society. (2018, Sep 13). *Second Edition - Jeanie with the Light Brown Hair*. YouTube. https://youtu.be/p9PGxnY9rE0

Emotional Conclusion

In Chapter 14 of *Arranging Barbershop Vol. 2*, we put very simple chords and extensions onto our song and declared victory. At an intermediate level, we need to start focusing on the emotional trip you want your arrangement to take. The tag must be more intimate, or more triumphant than all of what preceded it. The enemy of tag writing is being ambiguous. Make it clear to the performer and thus the audience; confusion is never a good approach! Never cop out on writing the tag. If you do, the performer will rewrite what you give them, guaranteed!

Let's get into some specific case examples of great tags to great arrangements. They might not be classic tags but they're perfect endings to their associated arrangement.

Always

In Don Gray/Mark Hale's arrangement made popular by Michigan Jake, we see the beautiful tenor note emerging above the rest and then an intimate "Always" voiced by the lower three voices. Emotionally, there is nothing more to say but "Always." You've said everything that needs to be said and said it elegantly. The voicings preceding the tag are high and dramatic and have been coming down steadily. There's a little peel off to allow it to softly build and then fade away on the last two chords.[21]

---

21 TalkinShop. (Aug 3, 2011). *Michigan Jake - 1999 International Quartet Semifinal [Video]*. YouTube. https://youtu.be/qgj0efUXeCU?si=kaMDQ40IA4UXQrDA&t=10

Figure 22.13

Tag for "Always," words and music by Irving Berlin. Arranged by Mark Hale.

If I Only Had a Brain

In Clay Hine's arrangement made famous by Four Voices, a simple transfer of the melody to the highest voice, either lead or tenor, creates a more vulnerable sound. This sound has not been used before in the arrangement, giving it a feeling of, "we're finishing the song" with a final emotional statement that ends up much more intimate than what just preceded it.[22]

Figure 22.14

Tag of "If I Only Had a Brain," words and music by Yip Harburg and Harold Arlen. Arranged by Clay Hine.

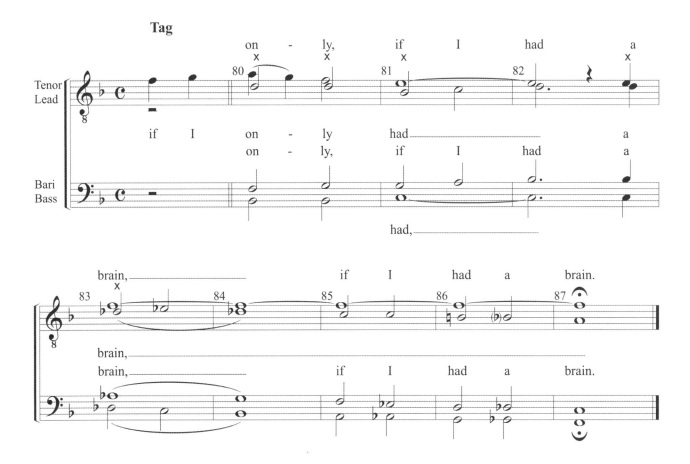

22   Nathan Johnston. (2019, Jul 19). *Four Voices-If I Only Had a Brain* [Video]. YouTube. https://youtu.be/p9PGxnY9rE0

Bright Was the Night

This is one of the classics for sure! Construction-wise, it is quite straightforward. It follows an old tradition of tag writing where, after the chorus, the arranger closes out the arrangement with the last part of the chorus. Prior to David Wright's arrangement for the Gas House Gang, this song was associated with *chord worshiping*.

 Chord worshiping is a colloquialism in barbershop circles for ignoring the musical line and sustaining the chords for the sake of enjoying the harmony.

David converted it to a lyric-centric ballad. In the tag, David extends "bride" a bit more to pay homage to its chord worshiping heritage. The final chords end up elevated, celebrating how wonderful and triumphant that night was.[23]

Figure 22.15

Tag of "Bright Was The Night," traditional. Arranged by David Wright.

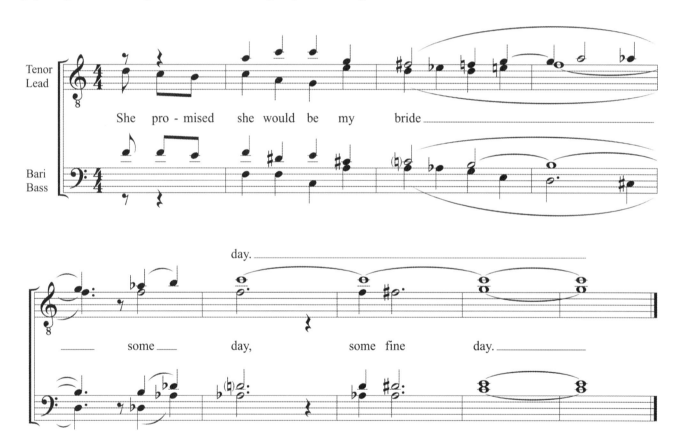

23   Barbershop Harmony Society. (2018, Sep 14). *The Gas House Gang - Bright Was the Night* [Video]. YouTube. https://youtu.be/k-q3Opw3DDw

Tag Comes First

There are times where the tag comes first in the arrangement process. It can be that you hear the tag and write it, or the tag exists, and you construct an arrangement to accompany the tag. In either case, all the musical choices made in the chart must bring the listener to hear the tag logically. The rest of the chart must reflect the same writing in the tag.

Veni Veni Emanuel

The American Contemporary Christian Music group First Call did an arrangement of "Veni, Veni, Emmanuel" in the mid-1980s. One of the interesting hooks in the original song is the shift between major and minor. I loved the modal change at the end of the song First Call did, ending on VI of the key with a dramatic melody note. I started with a barbershop interpretation of that tag they sang. In the first echo, it ends in a minor triad and then the second echo it resolves into a major triad. It then back to a minor feel on "Em-ma-nu-el," ultimately leading to the post by the lead on VI and doing what barbershoppers love to do best—ring chords.

Figure 22.16

Tag of "Veni Veni Emanuel." Traditional. Arranged by Kevin Keller.

Cheer Up, Charlie

Brent Graham's classic tag had been around for years, and Vocal Spectrum loved singing the tag so much that they asked their coach Jim Henry to do an arrangement for them and use the tag. Jim contacted Brent for permission to use the tag; the tag was previously standalone. Jim writes the rest of the chart in a style that naturally leads into Brent's gorgeous tag.[24]

Figure 22.17

Tag of "Cheer Up, Charlie," arranged by Brent Graham.

Featured Singer

If you're lucky, the group you are arranging for has some sort of strength they want to leverage. Perhaps the bass can sing really low. The tenor or lead or bari can post a really high note. Perhaps the singers have unusual ranges. And so on. If the tag can support that, go for it. And even if they can't quite do it today, if you write it, they may rise to the occasion.

24   terfone16. (Apr 20, 2011). *Cheer Up Charlie - Vocal Spectrum [Video]*. YouTube. https://youtu.be/
F4IGwqdL32c?si=QWczdnqfnkIxI3UN

Put On A Happy Face

The first song After Hours asked me to arrange was this one. Their original lead, Ben Harding, could sing an F# full out for 28 seconds. They wanted a 28 second F# post for the tag. I wrote the tag and timed it out for 28 seconds. Then the entire chart was constructed to get the quartet into the Key of F# (G♭) by the end. It started in the key of G.[25]

Figure 22.18

"Put On A Happy Face" words and music by Lee Adams and Charles Strouse. Arranged by Kevin Keller.

25   Barbershop Harmony Society. (2019, Sep 13). *After Hours - Put on a Happy Face* [Video]. YouTube. https://youtu.be/ l8H5oN6FnK0

Cruella De Vil

Tim Waurick, tenor of Vocal Spectrum and learning track maker supreme, is the postmaster general. David Wright continues to pile on and on about how terrible Cruella is. However, the audience really isn't hearing the words. They are marveling at the post. Meanwhile, David is increasing the rhythmic drive with the percussive nature of the words in its triplet form that hasn't been explored before. And then when it should be over, it's not. What is key is that the tag is constantly developing musically underneath. It has highs and lows throughout. Definitely advanced arranging but there is a vision behind the madness!

Figure 22.19

"Cruella De Vil" arranged by David Wright.

Rhythmic Extension

One of the important changes after 1993 was that arrangers took more care to not break the rhythmic drive of the chart. The rhythmic theme(s) extend into the tag rather than stopping and singing chords. This can be a powerful device to continue sustaining ideas into the tag. The previous two tags, "Put on a Happy Face" and "Cruella De Vil," show continued rhythmic propulsion through the posts. Let's look at a few more rhythmic tags.

Love Me

Aaron Dale is simply one of the best at the use of subdivided triplets throughout his driving tempo songs. Because it is so firmly ingrained in our minds, he continues after the lead post "Love Me," triplet on "baby, oh" and then a simple set of chords on "Love Me." The juxtaposition is the economy of the final "Love Me" vs. everything that came before it.[26]

Figure 22.20

"Love Me" words and music by Jerry Lieber and Mike Stoller. Arranged by Aaron Dale.

---

26   OCTenor2. (2008, Aug 24). *OC Times - Love Me* [Video]. YouTube. https://youtu.be/l8H5oN6FnK0

Mardi Gras March

In 1981 Ed Waesche created undoubtedly the most electrifying chart barbershop had heard with his Mardi Gras March for the Louisville Thoroughbreds, who won their 5th international chorus gold medal and set a new standard for excitement in the style. From the opening stanza there was one driving tempo throughout the entire song. In his original tag you can see he has the chorus interrupting the tempo. Driving tempo creates a kinesthetic response in the audience's body, and arrangers should and do continue to extend that as long as possible. However, the tag was a bit too brief, and so he extended it a few measures with rests. The performer took out the rests and condensed it a bit to make it fit their performance vision.[27]

Figure 22.21

"Mardi Gras March" words and music by Paul Francis Webster and Sammy Fain. Arranged by Ed Waesche.

---

27   Jeff Myers. (2016, Aug 14). *The Thoroughbreds Mardi Gras March. 1981 International Chorus Championship* [Video]. YouTube. https://youtu.be/6T-CfkF0CyA

I Can't Give You Anything But Love, Baby

David Harrington updated his 1990 era chart for Ringmasters. Prior to the tag there are many Beatles' references to songs of love. The tenor, Jakob, can post forever, which gives David the opportunity to reference another song with love in the title— the Queen song "Crazy Little Thing Called Love." What is truly brilliant is the choice of song matching the key words of "thing" and "love." This rhythmic tune keeps the tag driving right to the end.[28]

Figure 22.22

"I Can't Give You Anything But Love" words and music by Dorothy Fields and Jimmy McHugh. Arranged by David Harrington.

28   Barbershop Harmony Society. (2020, Jul 4). *Ringmasters - I Can't Give You Anything But Love* [Video]. YouTube. https://youtu.be/yj2iY3BSPWs

Arranging New Renditions of Iconic Tags

Unlike "Cheer Up, Charlie," where Vocal Spectrum wanted to keep the iconic tag, some arrangers will re-envision a song that happens to have an iconic tag. It's critical that the tag come naturally from the music that preceded it and support the emotional and musical vision of the song. It can and has been done!

Sunshine of Your Smile

In arranging this song for Power Play, Tom Gentry wanted to keep the trajectory of the love and joy as high as possible. Notice in the iconic version of "sunshine of" the chords go low. In fact, throughout the original arrangement there are dramatic highs and lows. Tom smooths out those high and low spots and finds a higher tag that doesn't get the quartet trapped in lower ranges.[29]

Figure 22.23

"The Sunshine of Your Smile" tag, arranged by Bill Diekema.

29   Barbershop Harmony Society. (Jun 29, 2020). *Instant Classic - Sunshine of Your Smile [Video]*. YouTube. https://youtu.be/ DobHLEzq4OY?si=xYvsJ3RZleYR7vsp

Figure 22.24

"The Sunshine of Your Smile" tag, arranged by Tom Gentry.

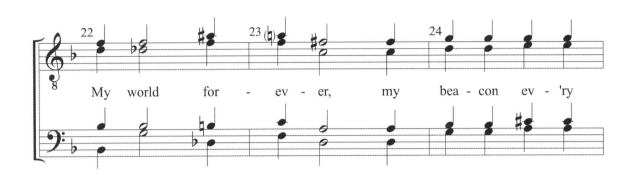

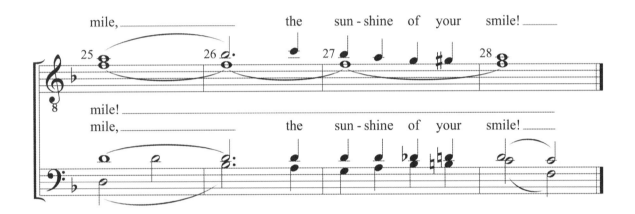

Brother, Can You Spare a Dime?

In 1960, the Nighthawks sang this immortal tag and electrified the audience. It cries of angst and literally peels paint! One of the great all-time tags.[30]

Figure 22.25

"Brother, Can You Spare A Dime" tag. Words and music by E.Y. "Yip" Harburg and Jay Gorney. Arranged by Greg Backwell.

In 2001 Steve Armstrong rearranged the song for Toronto Northern Lights. After you reach out one final time, there is despair in receiving the response of no help. The song must end low because misery sets back in. Steve returns to the minor triad and a low bass punctuation on dime to reinforce it.[31]

---

30 Spaguy62. (Feb 3, 2012). *Buddy, Can You Spare a Dime (Live) - The Nighthawks Barbershop Quartet SPEBSQSA BHS [Audio].* YouTube. https://youtu.be/ofZtJy_LRl8?si=XX1vR4bBmhpIlIpY

31 TalkinShop. (2020, May 16). *Toronto Northern Lights - Brother, Can You Spare a Dime?* [Video]. YouTube. https://youtu.be/txJKmwtT3rA

Figure 22.26

"Brother, Can You Spare A Dime," arranged by Steve Armstrong.

How Do You Get Out Of This?

Occasionally the arrangement is so well developed that you may wonder how to conclude the song. Let's hope that you are finding such successes in your arrangements that you encounter this dilemma.

The key is to somehow find a way to slow down the momentum of the song to put an exclamation point on it. There are different ways to go about doing this.

Girls Medley

One of the greatest arrangements of all time was Ed Waesche's Three Girls Medley as sung by the Bluegrass Student Union. Ed marries up "Margie," "No No Nora," and "Rosie" in a rollicking medley of songs that accelerates and thrills the audience. Once the three songs are over, now what? The tag starts where he originally started: "I never thought that I would fall in love with you, I never thought that you would fall for me." He then brings all three girls together quickly and efficiently and ends with "You're the One I Love!." It perfectly bookends the intro.

Figure 22.27

"Girls Medley" tag. Written and arranged by Ed Waesche.

Pass Me the Jazz

Jeremy Johnson did a phenomenal job of taking the Real Group's five-part jazz version of this song, embracing all the character of the piece and working it into the barbershop style. Arrangers commonly use this sort of simple tag emblematic of a big band/traditional New Orleans Jazz band type of ending.[32]

Figure 22.28

"Pass Me the Jazz" words and music by Anders Edenroth. Arranged by Jeremy Johnson.

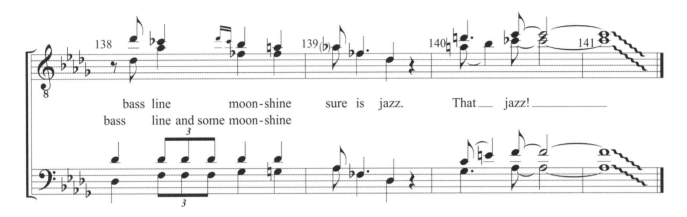

32   Barbershop Harmony Society. (2016, Jul 27). *Lemon Squeezy - Pass Me the Jazz* [Video]. YouTube. https://youtu.be/es_TYo7K3yo

Louise

David Wright wrote this highly developed piece, but what do you do when so much momentum has been built? Diffuse the momentum by ending where you started the chorus. A simple statement—"I hear your name in the breeze, Louise"—at an intimate level.[33]

Figure 22.29

"Louise" words and music by Leo Robin and Richard A. Whiting. Arranged by David Wright.

---

33 Barbershop Harmony Society. (2017, Jun 22). *Michigan Jake - Louise (2000 International)* [Video]. YouTube. https://youtu.be/GdnIIPzyK2M

Tag

In closing, there is no formula for writing tags. Pick up great charts and examine them for a formula; you won't find one. Some are short, some are long. Some have a lot of syllables, some have a few. Some have posts, some don't. The common element is that the tag is a logical musical and emotional conclusion to the journey that the arrangement took. To misquote David Wright, "A tag has the perfect number of notes. Not one less and not one more."[34] It needs to state as economically as possible the feelings of the conclusion of the story. If you can use fewer notes and words, do so. Make the music more intimate or more joyous than it's been during its entire journey. Spend the time to make the tag right.

---

34   He said that in reference to an entire chart, but it works here, too

Chapter 23.
Embellishments

By Steve Tramack

Overview

Composers often leave spaces at the end of phrases. There may be several beats or perhaps even more than a measure. In these spaces, the melody either sustains the final note of the phrase or releases altogether, allowing the accompaniment to fill. Much of the magic in music occurs in these spaces; this is where the performer, the band, and the arranger develop the music. In barbershop, the arranger's added material falls under the category of *embellishments*.

Embellishments, or ornamentation, are common in other forms of music. Embellishments are usually associated with the harmony and rhythm that ornament that line and provide interest and variety. Call and response-style songs sung by Frank Sinatra and the Count Basie Band, such as "Learnin' the Blues," feature both embellishments by the Basie Band— replying to Sinatra's phrases—and development of the texture using different instruments and delivery styles. Within the barbershop style, we embrace the use of embellishments as a crucial element of the style nearly to the same extent as the barbershop seventh chord.

Purpose of Embellishments

An embellishment can serve several purposes in an arrangement:

- Enhance the *musical theme*, e.g., lyric, melody, rhythm, harmony, and parody. Embellishments can serve to either:
    - *Reinforce* a key thematic idea, amplifying that idea; or
    - *Foreshadow* the next thematic idea, thereby bridging phrases, thoughts, or themes.
- Establish and reinforce *rhythmic* delivery aspects, e.g., tempo changes, pulse, groove, and meter.
- Create a *textural theme* for a given section of form based on types of embellishments, tessitura, sense of motion, harmonic changes, etc.
- Create *variety and interest* for both the listener and performer. A suitably embellished arrangement can assist the performer in their development of the long line of a musical journey. These contrasting devices help to reinforce the key messages and focus of unified textures.
- Create *word painting* effects, providing an onomatopoeic effect for a given lyric or phrase.

Motion

Embellishments create a sense of motion and direction in the musical line, aiding in the development and creation of textures. The rules of motion in barbershop arranging are closely related to counterpoint musical styles and adhere to the concept of *contrapuntal motion* from classical music theory.[35] There are four types of contrapuntal motion:

1. Parallel motion is a rarely used device that features two lines moving in the same direction, maintaining the same interval, e.g., perfect fifth. This type of motion is typically discouraged in classical counterpoint theory, though we do see examples in the barbershop style, especially in descending chromatic and dominant seventh lines.

---

35   Taken from https://en.wikipedia.org/wiki/Contrapuntal_motion in January, 2023

2. Similar motion is a frequently-used device that features musical lines moving in the same direction, with the interval between them changing. We see this often in swipes featuring higher inversions of the baritone and tenor line swapping functions in the chord (3rd/7th), or bass and baritone or lead swapping functions (root/fifth) with ascending motion.

3. Oblique motion is an occasionally-used device that features movement of one or more lines while others remain on the same pitch. While not as frequent as similar and contrary motion in barbershop, we do see examples of oblique motion, e.g., pyramid and blossom effects.

4. Contrary motion is a frequently-used device that involves two lines moving in opposite directions. This is the motion perhaps used most often in barbershop embellishments, often called scissoring. We'll see several examples of contrary motion in this chapter.

Type of Embellishments

In this section of the book, we'll discuss some of the most useful embellishments to start creating a more interesting journey. Further exploration of embellishments can be found in other deep-dive chapters in this section: original material, rhythmic development, and key changes. More advanced, complex examples and techniques can be found in Chapter 29, Advanced Arranging Topics, of *Arranging Barbershop Vol. 2*.

In this chapter, embellishments are grouped into multiple categories. Here are the areas mostly closely associated with developing an arrangement that we'll cover in detail:

- Harmonic
  - Swipes
  - Glissandos
  - Pedal tones, commonly referred to as *posts*
  - Bell chords
  - Phrase painting through motion
- Lyrical
  - Echoes
  - Patter
- Melodic
  - Melody passing
  - Unison/octaves
- Textural
  - Solos/duets/trios
  - Half-time
  - Back time
  - Call and response
  - Scat
  - Neutral syllables

Embellishments serve multiple purposes within the musical line. Further, in advanced arranging examples, we see *stacking* of embellishments, where multiple embellishments are used in support of each other and the development of the music.

Harmonic

Swipes

Swipes are one of the most common embellishments used to develop arrangements in the barbershop style. While movements from chord-to-chord or note-to-note on the same syllable—*melismas*—are found in other styles, they're elevated to their own art form in barbershop.

Although they appear in all different types of delivery, swipes are especially effective in rubato and free form ballads, as well as slower-tempo meter delivery. Swipes are often found at the end of a phrase—the *cadence*—though they can be used to add harmonic interest any time a melody note is sustained for more than a couple of beats.

The most common types of swipes are:

- Harmonic holding patterns
- Change of inversions
- Circle progressions

Harmonic Holding Patterns

These swipes serve to create motion and build anticipation, starting and ending on the same chord with some frequently used progressions in between.

A common example features movement from I–IV7–I with the melody starting and ending on the chordal root, as seen in measure 4 of Figure 23.1.

Figure 23.1

Harmonic holding pattern swipe, from "Girls Medley," arranged by Ed Waesche.

We see the retrograde version of the harmonic holding pattern swipe in measure 16 in Figure 23.2, going from V7–II7–V7.

Figure 23.2

Retrograde swipe, from "Wait 'Til the Sun Shines, Nellie," words and music by Andrew B. Sterling and Harry Von Tilzer. Arranged by Buzz Haeger.

A popular way of increasing the tension on the dominant (V7) when the melody is on the root of the chord (V) is to have the harmony parts dip a half step, creating a Vdim7, and move back to the V7. Figure 23.3 shows an example in measure 12.

Figure 23.3

Harmonic holding pattern swipe from "Give Me a Night in June." Words and music by Cliff Friend. Arranged by Mark Hale.

Scissors

Scissors are swipes where two parts move in contrary directions, often converging in the middle on unison or an octave. This embellishment is frequently used by arrangers to create motion within a given harmonic pillar. Take this classic example from the tag of "Wait 'Til the Sun Shines, Nellie," which uses two successive scissor embellishments between the bass and tenor.

Figure 23.4

Scissors swipe in "Wait 'Til the Sun Shines, Nellie," arranged by Buzz Haeger.

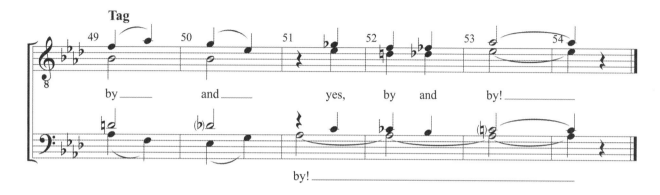

Scissors frequently involve the fifth and seventh of the chord swapping parts, often doubling on the sixth in the middle. Measure 14 of Figure 23.5 creates wonderful tension with the full-step rub between the chordal root (baritone) and seventh (bass), scissoring with the tenor. This kind of swipe happens most often with the melody on the root or third of the chord in order to remain on the same note during the swipe.

Figure 23.5

Scissors swipe in "Brother, Can You Spare a Dime?" Words and music by E.Y. "Yip" Harburg and Jay Gorney. Arranged by Steve Armstrong.

This example from "Bill Grogan's Goat" adds one more wrinkle: a dim7 in measure 23, in a dominant seventh, inversion-changing swipe.[36]

Figure 23.6

Scissors swipe with an added wrinkle in "Bill Grogan's Goat." Words and music by John Feierabend. Arranged by Clay Hine.

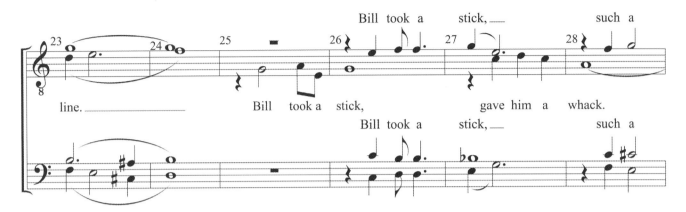

The following is yet another example from "Louise," arranged by David Wright, which uses a scissor effect to word paint: note the tenor emulating a sigh on the lyric in measure 28.[37]

Figure 23.7

Scissors swipe from "Louise." Words and music by Leo Robin and Richard A. Whiting. Arranged by David Wright.

36   Barbershop Harmony Society. (2019, Oct 11). *Category 4 - Bill Grogan's Goat* [Video]. YouTube. https://youtu.be/Wuzuky-2Gok
37   Barbershop Harmony Society. (2017, Jun 22). *Michigan Jake - Louise (2000 International)* [Video]. YouTube. https://youtu.be/GdnIIPzyK2M

Same Chord, Different Inversion

A common swipe involves moving from one dominant seventh chord to a higher inversion, creating a sense of excitement and anticipation. This often involves an inside voice, such as the lead in measure 48 in Figure 23.8, swiping up to the tenor note, and the tenor swiping up to an octave above the starting baritone/lead note.[38]

Figure 23.8

Higher inversion swipe from "I Want You, I Need You, I Love You." Words and music by Rick Nielsen. Arranged by Aaron Dale.

Another example of this would be moving from a *hanging 7th* voicing, with or without a chord in between, such as this I7–v7–I7 instance in measure 4 in Figure 23.9.[39] [40]

The *hanging 7th* voicing is popular in barbershop arrangements. This second inversion chord features the root in the highest note of the chord, often sung by the tenor or the lead. The seventh of the chord is positioned a major second below the root, with the third a tritone below the seventh. This is the chord found in the first beat in measure 4 of Figure 23.9, with the tenor on the root and the baritone on the seventh.

---

38   Barbershop Harmony Society. (2019, Oct 8). *City Limits - I Want You, I Need You, I Love You (Elvis Presley cover)* [Video]. YouTube. https://youtu.be/eSXxwY6fIYE

39   Previously, this second inversion, with the root in the top voice and the flat 7th a full step from the root, was called a *Chinese 7th* due to the major second interval of the root and seventh sounding like the beginning of "Chopsticks." However, being sensitive to societal norms, we'll refer to this as a *hanging 7th* for the purpose of this book.

40   Jared Wolf. (2020, May 17). *The Allies - Sweetheart of Sigma Chi* [Video]. YouTube. https://youtu.be/hfV-u3AczMw

Figure 23.9

Higher inversion from hanging 7th in "Sweetheart of Sigma Chi." Words and music by Byron Stokes and F. Dudleigh Vernor. Arranged by Steve Tramack.

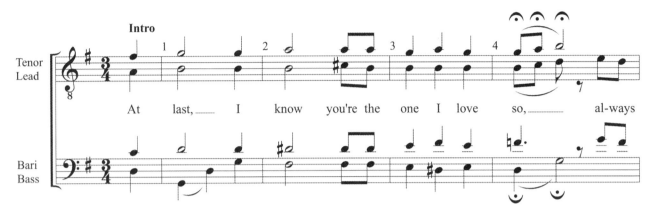

This embellishment can also feature a dominant 9th moving to a higher inversion, as in measure 73 in the example from "Not While I'm Around" in Figure 23.10.[41]

Figure 23.10

Dominant 9th higher inversion swipe in "Not While I'm Around." Words and music by Stephen Sondheim. Arranged by Steve Tramack.

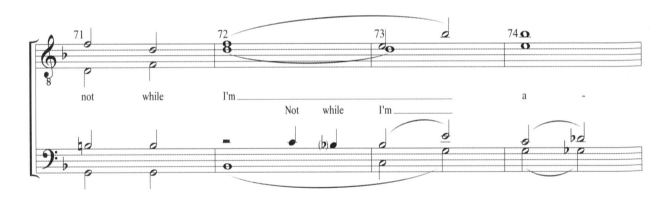

The example in Figure 23.11 in measure 17 moves from a more stable root position II7 to an unstable first inversion, employing *similar* motion from II7—v7—II7, requiring the lead to move from the fifth to the root, and then leading to a second inversion II7 chord on the next beat. Note the bass voice leading through this swipe.[42]

41 Barbershop Harmony Society. (2019, Oct 15). *After Hours - Not While I'm Around [from Sweeney Todd]* [Video]. YouTube. https://youtu.be/lEIT8s5LSWg
42 Barbershop Harmony Society. (2016, Jan 22). *Alexandria Harmonizers - Someone Like You (International 2015)* [Video]. YouTube. https://youtu.be/MLvqGGdID68

Figure 23.11

Similar motion higher inversion swipe in "Someone Like You." Words and music by Frank Wildhorn and Leslie Bricusse. Arranged by Steve Tramack.

Another example occurs at measure 51–52 of the same arrangement. This leverages the same type of progression and voice leading—in a higher tessitura—to create a musical climax.

Figure 23.12

Climactic higher inversion swipes in "Someone Like You," arranged by Steve Tramack.

Circle Progressions: Triad to Seventh

Swipes are often used to move from a triad to the seventh within a measure, in order to facilitate a circle of fifths progression. A popular variant of this is the bass (root) and baritone (5th) swiping to the 5th and 7th of the chord, respectively, as the V—V7 in measure 4 of Figure 23.13.

Figure 23.13

Triad to seventh swipe in "Sunshine of Your Smile," arranged by Tom Gentry.

The example in Figure 23.14, from measure 10 of "Bright Was the Night," uses a swipe from III to III7. The bass moves from root to fifth and tenor from fifth to seventh, providing textbook voice leading to the vi in measure 11.[43]

Figure 23.14

Swipe for voice leading example in "Bright Was the Night." Words and music by Glenn Howard. Arranged by David Wright.

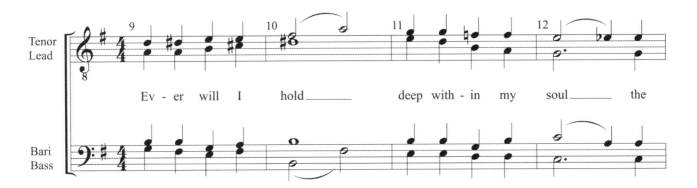

Another popular variation, as shown in Figure 23.15, involves the baritone moving from the fifth to the seventh of the chord stepwise through the sixth, with the melody on root or third of the pillar harmony. This often also features the bass moving from the root to the fifth, such as the VI–VI6–VI7 progression in measure 7. This precedes and progresses to the II7 pillar in measure 8.

---

43   Barbershop Harmony Society. (2018, Sep 14). *The Gas House Gang - Bright Was the Night* [Video]. YouTube. https://youtu.be/k-q3Opw3DDw?t=25

Figure 23.15

"Sunshine of Your Smile," arranged by Tom Gentry.

Moving from I to VI7 often will go through iiiø7 with the melody typically remaining on the third or fifth of the chord. Note this example in measure 5 from "Beautiful Dreamer."[44]

Figure 23.16

"Beautiful Dreamer" progression from I to VI7. Words and music by Stephen Foster. Arranged by David Wright.

Here's another example, from "When I Lost You," using the voice leading of the bass line to facilitate the circle movement from VI7 to ii in measures 27–28.

44   Barbershop Harmony Society. (2019, Sep 12). *The Allies - Beautiful Dreamer* [Video]. YouTube. https://youtu.be/JNK4-bEbQTo

Figure 23.17

"When I Lost You" progression from VI7 to ii. Words and music by Irving Berlin. Arranged by Steve Tramack.

An alternate version of this swipe moves from V–Vdim7–V7 with melody on the root, such as in measure 16 from "If I Only Had a Brain."[45]

Figure 23.18

"If I Only Had a Brain" swipe from V—V7. Words and music by Yip Harburg and Harold Arlen. Arranged by Clay Hine.

45   Nathan Johnston. (2019, Jul 19). *Four Voices-If I Only Had a Brain* [Video]. YouTube. https://youtu.be/0RuCuV5AS8Y

Circle Progressions: Chord Changes

Retrogression, or moving backwards through the circle of fifths, is also a typical method of embellishment. This is often used where the cadence ends on the tonic in the first beat of the final measure of that phrase rather than V7. In this example from "Brother, Can You Spare a Dime?" the swipe in measure 24 starts on the E♭min (i) and moves to B♭7 (V7).[46]

Figure 23.19

"Brother, Can You Spare a Dime?" Arranged by Steve Armstrong.

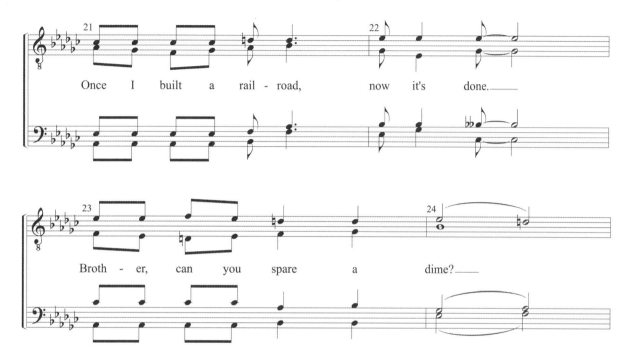

Here's another popular progression from "If I Only Had a Brain" when the melody is on the root or fifth. The progression in measure 22–24 moves from I–V7–I, preceding movement to IV.

Figure 23.20

"If I Only Had a Brain" swipe from I–V7–I7, arranged by Clay Hine.

46   TalkinShop. (2020, May 16). *Toronto Northern Lights - Brother, Can You Spare a Dime?* [Video]. YouTube. https://youtu.be/txJKmwtT3rA

Moving from I–Vdim7–V7, with the melody on the 5th, is a common swipe for creating both motion and tension, which is then released when returning inevitably to the tonic. Here's a classic example in measure 39 from "Sweet Adeline."

Figure 23.21

"Sweet Adeline." Words and music by Richard H. Gerard and Harry Armstrong. Arranged by Jay Giallombardo.

As an advanced example, here's a beautifully ornamented version of this swipe in measure 20 from "If I Give My Heart to You," using the Iadd9 as part of a wonderful line for the baritone.[47]

Figure 23.22

"If I Give My Heart to You." Words and music by Jimmie Crane, Jimmy Brewster, and Al Jacobs. Arranged by Jim Clancy.

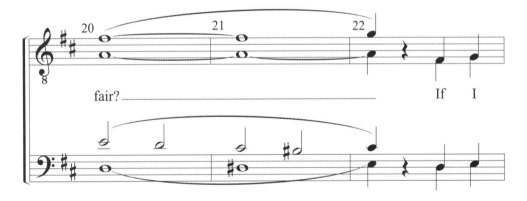

One of the more common swipes ties together circle movement from either the dominant or minor seventh chord based on the second degree of the scale (II7 or ii7) to ii⌀7, to the dominant (V7), with the melody on the second or fourth/sharp-fourth degree of the scale.[48] We see this in measures 15–16 of "Not While I'm Around."[49]

---

47   Barbershop Harmony Society. (2018, Oct 4). *Pathfinder Chorus - If I Give My Heart to You* [Video]. YouTube. https://youtu.be/tMSxg8Si9ks

48   If the melody is on the sharp-fourth degree of the scale, it will move as part of the swipe when progressing to the dominant seventh.

49   Barbershop Harmony Society. (2019, Oct 15). *After Hours - Not While I'm Around [from Sweeney Todd]* [Video]. YouTube. https://youtu.be/lEIT8s5LSWg

Figure 23.23

"Not While I'm Around," arranged by Steve Tramack.

Using a higher inversion, coupled with a common tone substitution for the ii7, leads us to a more dramatic ♭VII–ii°7–V7 variation in measures 19–20.

Figure 23.24

"Not While I'm Around," arranged by Steve Tramack.

Circle Progressions: Tritone Substitutions

Tritone substitution swipes are a useful swipe for creating motion without changing the resolution. For example, the first beat in measure 74 of "Not While I'm Around" is a V7 (C7) in the second inversion (5–1–3–7), which naturally resolves to the F, the tonic, in measure 75. The swipe on beat 3 of the measure features the bass moving down a half step to the G♭ and the baritone moving up a half step to the D♭. This creates a ♭II7 chord, with the lead and tenor remaining on the same notes, but swapping 3rd/7th functions from chord to chord. This swipe provides a sense of motion, variety, and anticipation, without changing the resolution.

Figure 23.25

"Not While I'm Around," arranged by Steve Tramack.

Swipes Master Class

"Bright Was the Night," as performed by The Gas House Gang, is truly a master class in how to utilize swipes. This is true throughout the arrangement—but particularly in the last 11 measures—creating excitement, anticipation, and variety.[50]

Figure 23.26

"Bright Was the Night," arranged by David Wright.

50   Barbershop Harmony Society. (2018, Sep 14). *The Gas House Gang - Bright Was the Night* [Video]. YouTube. https://youtu.be/tMSxg8Si9ks

Glissandos

Glissandos are a more intense sibling of swipes. Whereas swipes provide a variety of options for how a performer can interpret the delivery, particularly in a free form ballad approach, a glissando (*gliss* for short) explicitly states "perform as a continuous glide from one pitch to another." This can help the performer create tension, anticipation, and energy in key musical events. Like other dramatic arranging devices, glissandos have an impact on the flavor of the chart. Think of them like a powerful spice used in cooking: in the right place and the right amount, they bring the dish to life. Used in the wrong proportion or the wrong place, they overpower the dish. The following are examples where glissandos are appropriately used for impact.

Feature One Voice Part

In "Cuddle Up a Little Closer," a gliss is used to highlight the bass line in the tag, with an arpeggio feel setting up the exposed pedal tone around which the tag is built.[51] The bass for whom this was arranged created impact with the gliss and the exposed post, generating even more anticipation leading to the climactic final chord.[52]

Figure 23.27

"Cuddle Up a Little Closer." Words and music by Karl Hoschna and Otto Harbach. Arranged by Clay Hine.

---

51 Barbershop Harmony Society. (2023, Mar 3) *The Ladies - Cuddle Up a Little Closer, Lovey Mine [from Three Twins]* {Video}. YouTube. https://youtu.be/6MvRIHhxKFs

52 Arranged for the 2000 Barbershop Harmony Society quartet champions, Platinum. Bass Kevin Miles was also known for his work in the Walt Disney World a cappella ensemble "Voices of Liberty," and was the "Voice of Walt Disney World," having done the voiceover for several Park announcements.

Bridge the Interval Leap

In "Redhead," the gliss is used to highlight the leaps for the bass clef while creating additional excitement, impact, and tension associated with the dominant ninth and the 9–1 resolution from the lead part.

Figure 23.28

"Redhead," Words and music by Dorothy Fields and Albert Hague. Arranged by Jim Clancy.

Word Painting

Glissandos are also effective at aiding in word painting, particularly when thinking of lyrics such as "sigh" or, in the case of "I Want You, I Need You, I Love You," "dreamin'."[53]

Figure 23.29

"I Want You, I Need You, I Love You," arranged by Aaron Dale.

53   bhsstud5565. (Aug 26, 2008). *OC Times - I Want You, I Need You, I Love You [Video]*. YouTube. https://youtu.be/uX0eScR4NC8?si=HWRnnQ_wSpZaUdSq

Pedal Tones (Posts)

This popular embellishment is found frequently in tags and at key transition points in an arrangement, e.g., introductions, transitions from verse to chorus, etc. Posts feature a single voice sustaining a note while the other voices change chords—either via swipes or echoes—around the sustained note. In other forms of music, the pedal tone frequently lies in the bass line and includes dissonance to add tension. In barbershop arranging, the chords around the post almost always feature only consonant, complete chords. Here are examples of posts in each voice part.

Lead Post

Measures 1–4 of "Seventy Six Trombones" features a lead post reinforced with the octave pickup measure to the pedal tone. David Wright uses echoes to establish the 6/8 meter of the arrangement.[54]

Figure 23.30

"Seventy Six Trombones," Words and music by Meredith Willson. Arranged by David Wright.

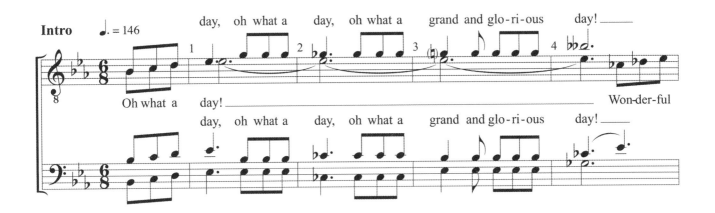

Here's an example featuring a combination of swipes and echoes in the tag of "The Sunshine of Your Smile."

Figure 23.31

"The Sunshine of Your Smile." Words and music by Lilian Ray. Arranged by Tom Gentry.

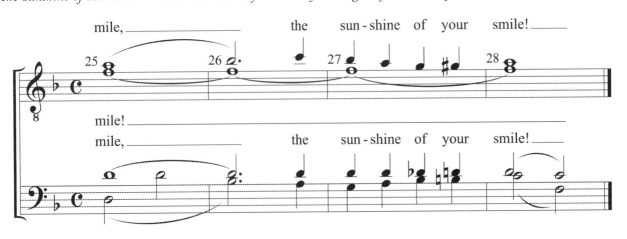

54 Barbershop Harmony Society. (2009, Jul 22). *Ambassadors of Harmomy - Seventy-Six Trombones [from The Music Man]* [Video]. YouTube. https://youtu.be/QmDGntpZC3I

Sometimes, a lead post will begin with the lead part taking the highest voice in the chord, with the tenor crossing over the lead post at some point during the post as excitement and anticipation builds. Here's an example from "I Want You, I Need You, I Love You," which enhances the build toward the climax of the song.

Figure 23.32

"I Want You, I Need You, I Love You," arranged by Aaron Dale.

Bass Post

Bass pedal tones share affinities with other styles of music and are effective ways of changing the texture of a phrase. Bass posts are often found at the end of verses and introductions, allowing for a foundation to build ascending chords with increasingly higher tessitura from the treble trio. Note the growing excitement from the voicing above the post in measure 8–11 in "Anything Goes."[55]

Figure 23.33

"Anything Goes." Words and music by Cole Porter. Arranged by Kevin Keller.

55   Barbershop Harmony Society. (2019, Aug 30). *Alexandria Harmonizers - Anything Goes* [Video]. YouTube. https://youtu.be/okUtCTl7W3M

Tenor Post

Tenor pedals are typically used for climactic events and textural change, posting on the root of the initial pillar. In "Louise," the tenor post in measure 60 emerges from the homorhythmic texture right after a key change at the new I pillar chord.[56] This foreshadows the tenor posts in the tag of the song, preparing the listener for the tenor voice playing that role at key moments.

Figure 23.34

"Louise" tenor post, arranged by David Wright.

56   Barbershop Harmony Society. (2017, Jun 22). *Michigan Jake - Louise (2000 International)* [Video]. YouTube. https://youtu.be/GdnIIPzyK2M

Baritone Post

You might be thinking, "isn't a baritone post the same as a lead pedal? They're both inside voices." In some cases, the baritone may be the voice that is best suited for a given post in a tag based on range or timbre. In these cases, the baritone is simply filling the role of the lead. Here's an example from "Astonishing," where the baritone is best suited to post the A♭ in the tag. The lead, who sang the A♭ in measure 85, passes the post to the baritone in measure 86 and then assumes the baritone harmony part role for the remainder of the tag.[57]

Figure 23.35

"Astonishing" baritone post. Words and music by Mindi Dickstein and Jason Howland. Arranged by Steve Tramack.

A baritone post is an effective change of pace when exchanging the post from the lead to the baritone, when associated with a temporary modulation to another key. This creates a different texture and degree of interest. It could also be used as part of a circle progress, as is the case in "Put Your Arms Around Me, Honey," where the baritone takes a one-measure post on the V7 pillar in measure 76.[58] The baritone then passes the post to the lead at the return to the tonic in measure 77.

Figure 23.36

"Put Your Arms Around Me" baritone post. Words and music by Albert Von Tilzer and Junie McCree. Arranged by Aaron Dale.

57   Steve Tramack. (2015, Nov 12) *Taken 4 Granite - Sutton Foster (NYC) Montage* [Video]. YouTube. https://youtu.be/T-dST7W0lGY?t=175
58   Barbershop Harmony Society. (2009, Jan 9). *Max Q - 2007 International Quartet Champions* [Video]. YouTube. https://youtu.be/kwxEHFVHkAM

The post-passing doesn't stop here; the lead passes the post to the tenor, with a key change from F to C in the process.

Figure 23.37

"Put Your Arms Around Me," arranged by Aaron Dale.

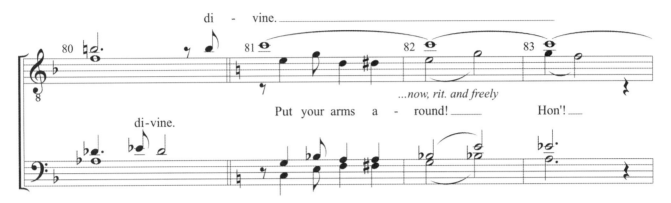

Bell Chords

Bell chords are an arranging device where the individual notes of the chord are sung in sequence. These are often arpeggiated from lowest to highest, from highest to lowest, also called a *cascade*, or as a connected sequence of the two, called a *pyramid*. While popular in barbershop arranging, bell chords can be found in other styles of music including traditional jazz and even pop rock. Think of the "magnifico" sequence from Queen's "Bohemian Rhapsody."

Here's an example of an ascending arpeggio in measure 55–56 of "Looking at the World Through Rose Colored Glasses."[59]

Figure 23.38

"Looking at the World through Rose Colored Glasses" bell chord. Words and music by Thomas Naile and Jimmy Steiger. Arranged by David Wright.

59   Barbershop Harmony Society. (2016, Aug 30). *Take 4 - (Looking at the World Thru) Rose Colored Glasses (live at Harmony University 2016)* [Video]. YouTube. https://youtu.be/98wWxlJJX94

Here's a classic example of descending, cascading bell chords in the tag of "Who'll Take My Place." Note the descending feel in the harmony parts while the lead note remains the same in each case. The arpeggiated chords are I7–dim7–iv6–I. This familiar progression could have also been accomplished with swipes or echoes, but the bell chords elevate this tag to an iconic status.

Figure 23.39

"Who'll Take My Place When I'm Gone" bell chord. Words and music by Raymond Klage and Billy Fazioli. Arranged by Greg Lyne

Here's a *pyramid* effect—ascending and descending arpeggios—in "Girls Medley." Note how the effect is used as a precursor to a key change into another song in the medley. The embellishment is used effectively to signal the end of one song and transition into another.

Figure 23.40

"No No Nora" bell chord into key change. Words and music by Gus Kahn and Ernie Erdman. Arranged by Ed Waesche.

The bell chord concept can also be used with a word or short phrase, providing a layered entry and opportunity to feature each voice part. Here's an example using the title of the song "Louise" at the end of the chorus, leading into a second bridge.

Figure 23.41

"Louise" bell chord, arranged by David Wright

Here's another example featuring the title of the song and using the melodic hook in the baritone line and the beginning of the tenor echo. This also sets up a featured musical event: the lead solo leading into the final chord, which is taken right from the original orchestration of the song.

Figure 23.42

"Someone Like You" bell chord, arranged by Steve Tramack.

Phrase Painting

Arrangers can create harmonic motion effects using combinations of contrary, parallel, similar, and oblique motion. We've explored contrary motion effects—scissors—in the swipes portion of this section. Let's look at examples of three additional types of motion effects used to create phrase-level impacts: blossoming and cascading.

Blossoming

A *blossom* effect leverages contrary motion to create the illusion of the harmony expanding from a smaller to larger spread in voicing. In the case of the introduction to "If I Give My Heart to You," this begins with a duet a third apart.

Figure 23.43

"If I Give My Heart to You." Words and music by Jimmie Crane, Jimmy Brewster, and Al Jacobs. Arranged by Jim Clancy.

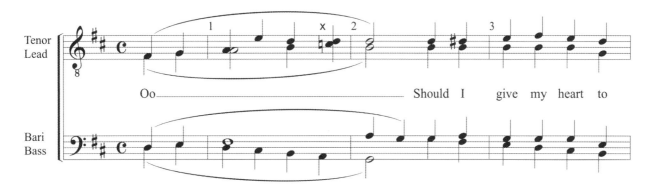

Another example of blossoming leverages oblique motion, building chords from a unison pitch. This frequently involves a bass pedal tone or a repeated bass note while singing lyrics, with the other voice parts moving upwards in steps or leaps. Here's an example of oblique motion blossoming from a popular tag, "Old Dominion Line."

Figure 23.44

"Old Dominion Line" tag, arranged by Earl Moon.

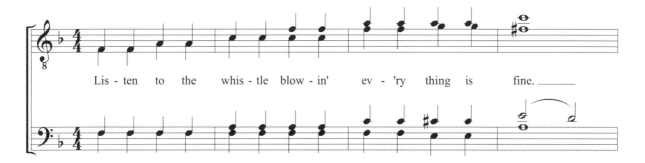

Cascading

A *cascade* effect also leverages oblique motion, with the upper voice—typically the tenor—sustaining a pitch while the other voice parts move downward in steps or leaps. Here's an example that blends a bell chord-style delayed entry with a cascade effect from "The Marx Brothers Opener."[60]

Figure 23.45

"Marx Brothers Opener" words, music and arrangement by Jay Giallombardo.

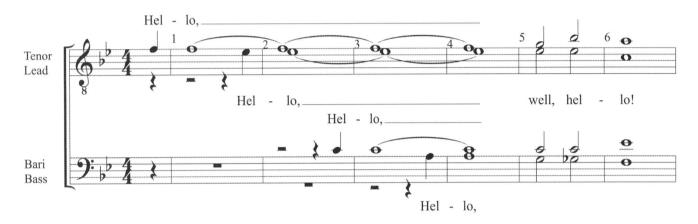

The tag of "Louise" starts with a tenor pickup note and is followed by a succession of chords from the three lower voice parts that descend through the end of the phrase.

Figure 23.46

"Louise" cascade, arranged by David Wright.

Lyrical

As lyrics are a primary musical theme for conveying the intent of music in the barbershop style, it only makes sense to use lyrical embellishments for developing an arrangement. We'll focus on *echoes* and the multitude of functions and approaches an arranger can take when using this embellishment. We'll also look at *patter*, a specific type of lyric-based texture.

---

60   Barbershop Harmony Society. (2016, Feb 24). *The New Tradition - The Marx Brothers Opener (1994 Show of Champions)* [Video]. YouTube. https://youtu.be/a-MFesEOnRs

Echoes

Echoes and swipes are the most common embellishments used to develop barbershop arrangements. Whereas swipes are particularly effective in highlighting motion via harmony in rubato or free form delivery, echoes provide the same motion and harmonic impact in strict meter delivery. Echoes oftentimes provide better opportunities for synchronization and maintaining tempo, meter, and rhythmic pulse points.

The primary functions of echoes are to:

- Reinforce, repeat, or amplify the preceding lyrics or subtext via different adjectives and perspectives
- Foreshadow or transition to the next set of lyrics or subtext
- Provide rhythmic development

Effective echoes can serve different purposes in helping the arranger develop the musical story line. *Repeated lyrics* help to reinforce the concept just conveyed in the preceding phrase. *Rhyming lyrics* can expand on the concept while maintaining the same intent. Altogether *new lyrics* can help to foreshadow the next musical thought or introduce a new spin on the previous phrase.

Like swipes, echoes also pair with harmonic aspects of contrapuntal motion to create different types of impact. Let's look at how echoes are paired with contrary, similar, and parallel motion in the following examples.

Scissors (Contrary Motion)

Contrary motion tends to add musical tension, with the feeling of the moving lines both being aware of and in opposition to each other. Blossoming contrary motion often indicates a crescendo, or emotions that are escalating and being outwardly expressed. Here's an example of an echo from "Girls Medley." Measure 90 sees blossoming contrary motion between the tenor and bass lines to continue motion while maintaining the same V7 harmonic pillar.

Figure 23.47

"My Blushing Rosie." Words and music by Edgar Smith and John Stromberg. Arranged by Ed Waesche.

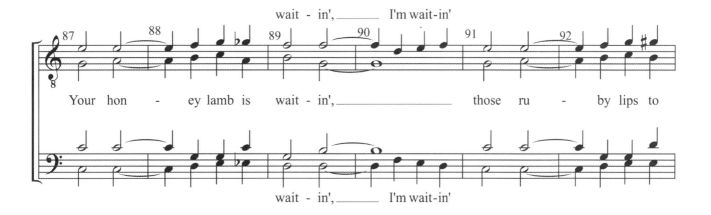

Collapsing contrary motion tends to indicate a decrescendo, or a more intimate delivery. Another example of collapsing contrary motion in an echo, this time featuring a bass/baritone duet to lead from V7 to I, can also be found in "Girls Medley."

Figure 23.48

"My Blushing Rosie," arranged by Ed Waesche.

Here's another from "Liar Medley" using a pickup, a weak beat syncopated onset and high tessitura bass/tenor scissors. This creates a great deal of excitement and motion while maintaining the same II7 pillar.[61]

Figure 23.49

"How Could You Believe Me." Words and music by Burton Lane and Ana Jay Lerner. Arranged by Renee Craig.

Measure 13 shows an example of an echo with contrary motion between the lead and bass from "Redhead." Although all four parts are singing the lyrics, it is considered an echo because it is device added by the arranger that is not found in the original composition. Note the tenor changes function from the seventh in the first beat to the root of a hanging seventh second inversion in the third beat. This also help to create a sense of destination and excitement for the phrase.[62]

61   Barbershop Harmony Society. (2017, Nov 2). *Keepsake - How Could You Believe Me/It's a Sin to Tell a Lie Medley* [Video]. YouTube. https://youtu.be/vJrkY6tQSIM

62   Nicole Adams. (Mar 1, 2017). *Vocal Majority International Champs 1997 [Video]*. YouTube. https://youtu.be/ CASDGXLtxdI?si=JqPidAyGnmoCpUeU&t=304

Figure 23.50

"Redhead," arranged by Jim Clancy.

Similar and Parallel Motion Echoes

Similar motion is motion in the same direction with the intervals between the voice parts changing from first to last chord. Parallel motion is motion by two or more lines in the same direction, keeping the same interval between them from chord to chord. Parallel motion is often discouraged in traditional music theory and is only used in special circumstances in barbershop. Descending chromatic movement from I7–VI7 is one example where parallel motion is embraced in the barbershop style. Ascending similar or parallel motion creates a sense of escalating tension or growth, heading toward a climactic moment. Descending similar or parallel motion is often leveraged when departing from a climactic moment or heading toward one of the valleys in the chart.

Note the motion of the bass and tenor lines in the following example from "For the Life of Me." The motion in measure 11 is similar with the bass ascending a whole step and the tenor a half step. The motion in the echo in measure 12 is parallel for all three harmony parts and helps to reinforce the subtext of the line, "three stories high."[63]

Figure 23.51

"For the Life of Me" similar and parallel motion. Words and music by Jeanine Tesori and Richard Scanlon. Arranged by Steve Tramack.

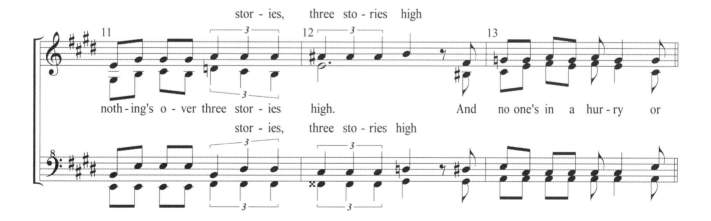

---

63   Steve Tramack. (2015, Nov 12) *Taken 4 Granite - Sutton Foster (NYC) Montage* [Video]. YouTube. https://youtu.be/T-dST7W0lGY?t=175

Here's an example of parallel motion from "Cuddle Up a Little Closer," using chromatic descending dominant seventh chords to move from I7 to VI7 in measure 45. The motion creates a sense of passage of time and provides a reset between the second and third choruses of the song.[64]

Figure 23.52

"Cuddle Up a Little Closer" parallel motion, arranged by Clay Hine.

Here's an advanced example of both similar motion swipe from all harmony parts—measure 38—and a contrary motion echo—measure 42—between the bass and tenor from "Louise."[65]

64   Barbershop Harmony Society. (2023, Mar 3) *The Ladies - Cuddle Up a Little Closer, Lovey Mine [from Three Twins]* {Video}. YouTube. https://youtu.be/6MvRIHhxKFs

65   Barbershop Harmony Society. (2017, Jun 22). *Michigan Jake - Louise (2000 International)* [Video]. YouTube. https://youtu.be/ GdnIIPzyK2M

Figure 23.53

"Louise," arranged by David Wright.

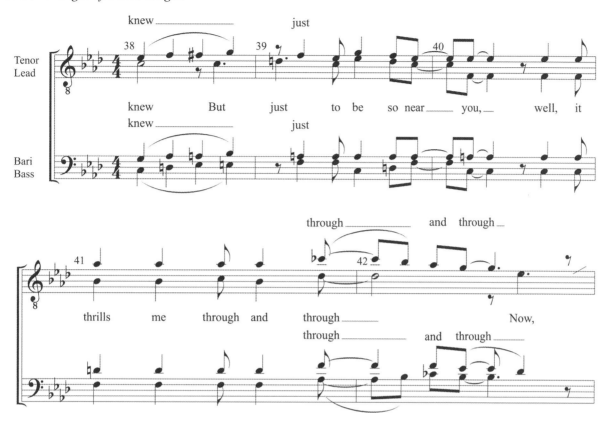

Same Chord, Different Inversion / Voicing

Here's an example from "I Want You, I Need You, I Love You," which uses a bass arpeggio echo to generate excitement on a sustained IV pillar in measure 33. The arpeggio also serves to tie together the bass voice leading before and after measure 33.

Figure 23.54

"I Want You, I Need You, I Love You" bass arpeggio. Arranged by Aaron Dale.

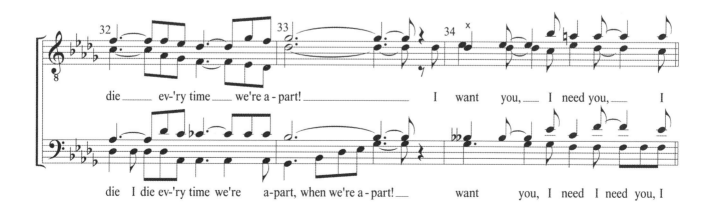

Text and Subtext

Echoes can serve to reinforce the subtext of the lyrics, providing both additional context and depth, as is found in "Mean to Me." The bridge provides several excellent examples of this, adhering to the existing rhythmic scheme in measures 34. 36 and 37, and breaking it when serving as a downbeat and bridge to the next thought in measures 38–39.[66]

Figure 23.55

"Mean to Me" echoes. Words and music by Fred E. Ahlert and Roy Turk. Arranged by David Wright.

66   Barbershop Harmony Society. (Oct 11, 2022). *Fleet Street - Mean to Me (Annette Hanshaw cover) [Video]*. YouTube. https://youtu. be/XHPTKvyg0jI?si=p7akwPi3HUucaOuQ

In the tag, the echoes do an outstanding job of reinforcing the alternate subtexts for the same text—"mean to me"—serving as an excellent recap of the singer's core struggle at the heart of the song in measures 51–53.

Figure 23.56

"Mean to Me" tag, arranged by David Wright.

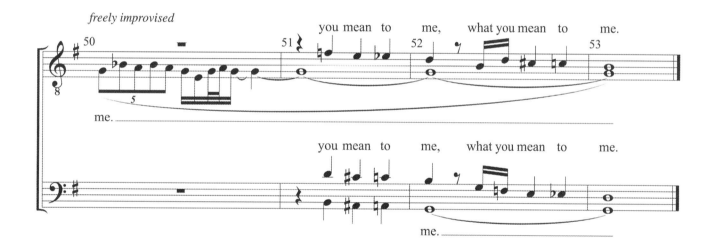

Rhythmic Reinforcement

Oftentimes, echoes are used to help deliver and reinforce the rhythmic subtext of a song, particularly where, in the original composition, a band would provide that needed fill and rhythmic drive. In the bridge of "Love Me," we see numerous examples of how echoes reinforce and drive the rhythm, using enhancing echoes that express the depth of feeling and emotion behind the lyric.[67]

Figure 23.57

"Love Me" rhythmic subtext. Words and music by Jerry Stoller and Mike Lieber. Arranged by Aaron Dale.

In the second bridge, lyrics are effectively used to deliver the triplet subdivision feel of the 12/8 meter.

67   OCTenor2. (2008, Aug 24). *OC Times - Love Me* [Video]. YouTube. https://youtu.be/qrvai9qHvEA

Figure 23.58

"Love Me" rhythmic subtext. Arranged by Aaron Dale.

Patter

Patter songs are characterized by moderate-to-fast tempos, with a rapid succession of rhythmic patterns, where each note is attached to a syllable of text. Patter songs have their roots in comic opera, such as the works of Gilbert and Sullivan. This technique is sometimes used in arranging in the barbershop style to create an alternate chorus, sung by the melody over the harmony parts singing the original chorus timing, such as with "Down Our Way."

Figure 23.59

"Down Our Way" with patter lyrics. Words and music by Al Stedman, Fred Hughes. Arranged by Floyd Connett.

Gee, but I wish that I could **wan**-der through the fields of
clo-ver and the new-mown **hay**, and go
strol-ling down a dusty **coun**-try road a-mid the
beau-ti-ful flow-ers that bloom in **May**, and on
Sat-ur-day night you go a-**court**-in' with your girl-y
neath a bright and sil-v'ry **moon**, and on the
way to church on Sun-day **morn**-ing peo-ple say,
"How do you **do?"** I'd love to

sit once more and spin a **yarn** with all the boys down
at the corn-er gro-c'ry **store.** I can
al-most see the good luck **horse**-shoe hang-in' up a-
bove the vil-lage smith-y's **door**. And that
old gang of **mine**, they sang
"Sweet A-de-**line,"**
How'd you like to come a-**long** with me and wan-der
Down our **Way, Down** our **Way.**

Patter lyrics by John (Jiggs) Ward

These patter lyrics can be sung by the lead section while the rest of the chorus (or quartet) sings their written parts softly in the background. Syllables in bold face type represent the beginning of each measure. The melody line follows closely that of the melody line of the chorus.

Patter is also used as an embellishing technique, providing background lyrics delivered against the melody in a rhythmic fashion highlighting beat subdivision. Such is the case with the eighth note patter reinforcing the 12/8 meter of "I Want You, I Need You, I Love You."[68]

---

68   Barbershop Harmony Society. (Oct 8, 2019). *City Limits - I Want You, I Need You, I Love You (Elvis Presley cover) [Video]*. YouTube. https://youtu.be/eSXxwY6fIYE?si=r3Hi5ix48ejtTqHi

Figure 23.60

"I Want You, I Need You, I Love You" patter. Arranged by Aaron Dale.

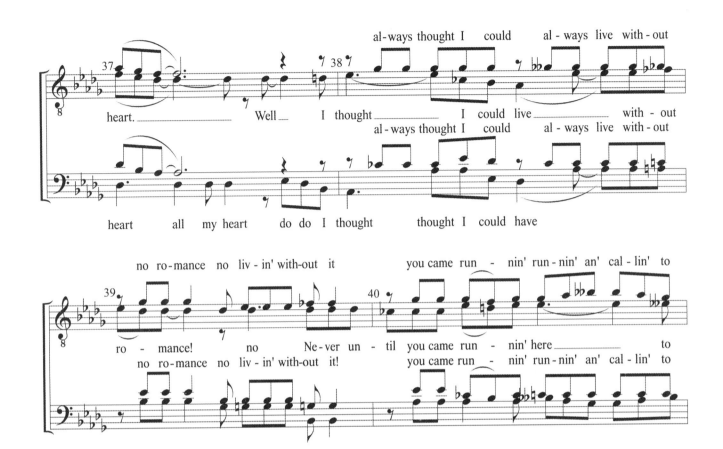

Rhythmic

The concept of rhythmic thematic development, like key changes, tags, and introductions, is so important that it warrants its own chapter. You'll find more information on rhythm concepts in Chapter 25. In this chapter we'll focus on the three more common approaches to rhythm-based embellishments:

1. Reinforcing *beats*, particularly the downbeat of a measure
2. Reinforcing *subdivision* of the beat
3. Reinforcing *syncopation*

Reinforcing Beats

Let's look at some of the most common ways rhythmic embellishments help to reinforce the downbeat, particularly at the beginning of a measure.

Pick-Ups / Lead-Ins

A common compositional technique to highlight the melody and lyric—as well as provide rhythmic interest—is the concept of a *phantom downbeat*. This is where the expected melody note, and often the entire chord, is delayed from the downbeat to a weaker beat, typically the second beat or the syncopated "and of 1."[69] The challenge becomes that if there are too many phantom downbeats in succession, the second beat can begin to feel like the downbeat, thus disrupting the sense of meter and pulse in the song. A common arranging device is to use pickups by one or more parts on the downbeat to maintain the sense of beat 1. This is most effective when the part(s) performing the downbeat pickup are also singing the tonic of the prevailing harmony, to provide both a sense of vertically-tuned and horizontally-timed home. This often leads to the bass part singing the pickup, such as in measure 9 of "Brother Can You Spare a Dime."[70]

---

69   When counting a duple subdivision of four beats in a measure, one would say "one and two and three and four." The half-beat preceding the second beat of the measure would be referred to as the "and of one."
70   TalkinShop. (2020, May 16). *Toronto Northern Lights - Brother, Can You Spare a Dime?* [Video]. YouTube. https://youtu.be/txJKmwtT3rA

Figure 23.61

"Brother Can You Spare a Dime" bass pickup. Arranged by Steve Armstrong.

Here's an example in "NYC" from the musical *Annie* where there are three measures of melodic phantom downbeats in a row. The arrangement plays off of the lyrics "three," "two," and "one" in measures 21–23 to dictate how many parts sing the pickup on the downbeat, including modifying the lead part timing on the final pickup. In measures 26–27, we see an echo that begins in the preceding measure, leading into the pickup on the downbeat in measure 27.

Figure 23.62

"NYC," words and music by Charles Strouse and Martin Charnin. Arranged by Steve Tramack.

Walking Bass Line

A common method of reinforcing the groove and syncopation is by providing a walking bass line—similar to what an upright bass fiddle would play in a big band orchestrated version—juxtaposed with the melody singing the syncopated line. The baritone and tenor often join one of those textures. This rhythmic treatment is frequently used in swing songs. In "I Want You, I Need You, I Love You," we see examples of both bass against the treble trio in measure 23 and a two-by-two texture with lead/baritone and bass/tenor together in measure 24.

Figure 23.63

"I Want You, I Need You, I Love You" walking bass line rhythmic texture, Arranged by Aaron Dale.

Downbeat Versus Offbeat

Related to the walking bass line, this effect can be used more broadly by the harmony parts, functioning similar to a band backing the soloist. This reinforces and highlights the syncopation in the melody while providing a sense of grounding to the beat. This type of approach doesn't typically work well with faster tempos, creating too much distraction. However, it can be particularly effective in a slow swing number—around 60 bpm—such as "Mean to Me."

Figure 23.64

"Mean to Me" use of downbeat and syncopation. Arranged by David Wright.

Note the effective use of bass reinforcement of subdivision and pickup in measures 49 and 50.

Bass Propellants

Propellants are covered in more detail in *Arranging Barbershop Vol. 2* Chapter 25, *Rhythm*. Perhaps the most common rhythmic propellant found in the style involves the bass line voicing a lyric or neutral syllable on a strong beat, similar to that of an upright bass or line in an accompanied version of the song. Here's an example of the walking bass line feel adding the rhythmic propellants transitioning into the bridge of "Looking at the World Through Rose Colored Glasses" using "bm bm bm" in measures 33, 34, and 36.

Figure 23.65

"Looking at the World Through Rose Colored Glasses" bass propellants. Words and music by Thomas Naile and Jimmy Steiger. Arranged by David Wright.

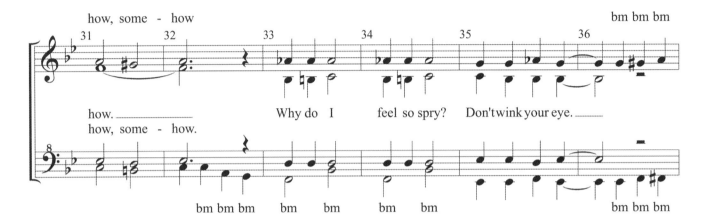

Reinforcing Syncopation

Delayed Entry

Delayed entry is another example of a rhythmic propellant, using one or more voice parts to emphasize a push beat based on when they enter. Here's an example from "Louise," with:

- The baritone entering in measure 39 on beat two
- The tenor entering on beat three
- The bass entering on the syncopated three-and, highlighting the groove in the piece as well as setting up the offbeat passage to follow

Figure 23.66

"Louise," arranged by David Wright.

Reinforcing Subdivision

Here's an example once again from "Love Me," this time showing how the echo lyrics reinforce the triplet subdivision feel. In this case, the arranger explicitly writes the eighth note triplets into the harmony parts.

Figure 23.67

"Love Me," arranged by Aaron Dale.

Texture

Musical texture is defined as how the tempo, melodic, and harmonic materials are combined in a musical composition, determining the overall quality of the sound in a piece. The texture is often described in regard to the *density,* or thickness, and *range,* or width, between the lowest and highest pitches, both in relative terms and, more specifically, according to the number of voice parts and the relationship between these voices. A piece's texture may be changed by the number and character of parts singing at once, the timbre of the voices singing these parts, and the harmony, tempo, and rhythms used.[71]

The most common texture in barbershop arranging is *homorhythmic,* which refers to multiple voices with similar rhythmic material in all parts. However, other *homophonic*—melody plus accompaniment—textures are leveraged in the style to create interest and contrast. Embellishments are one of the key tools to develop textures as an arrangement progresses. This process will be explored further in Chapter 29, Advanced Arranging Concept. Here are a few of the most common non-homorhythmic textures found in the style.

71   Wikipedia, referencing Benward, Bruce, and Marilyn Nadine Saker (2003). Music: In Theory and Practice, seventh edition, vol. 1. Boston: McGraw-Hill. ISBN 978-0-07-294262-0.

Solos, Duets, and Trios

The use of solos, duets, and trios—either alone or featured within a four-part texture—is a common embellishment for creating focus and development. A classic example of this is in the verse of "Sweet Adeline," which starts with the lead solo, adding additional parts phrase by phrase.[72] The introduction of the four-part texture features a blossom effect.

Figure 23.68

"Sweet Adeline" textural development. Words and music by Richard H. Gerard and Harry Armstrong. Arranged by SPEBSQSA.

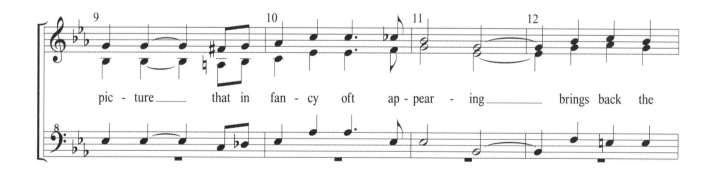

72   Sweet Adelines International. (2018, Oct 19). *ClassRing, Quartet Finals, 2018* [Video]. YouTube. https://youtu.be/iAwSkvYDPkM?t=259

Often times, duets are used to highlight a phrase with one duet and then provide an echo with the other duet. Here's an example in measures 19 and 20 from the Barry Manilow song, "All the Time."[73]

Figure 23.69

"All the Time" echoes. Words and music by Barry Manilow and Marty Panzer. Arranged by Steve Tramack.

73 Barbershop Harmony Society. (2022, Oct 11). *Throwback - All the Time (Barry Manilow cover)* [Video]. YouTube. https://youtu.be/Q9kgWfv10Nw

Here's another example of using lyrics and neutral syllables to provide the sense of a true duet. This duet from "It Had to Be You" uses similar motion featuring the lead and baritone in measures 22 and 23 against a backdrop of block chords.[74]

Figure 23.70

"It Had to Be You," arranged by Steve Tramack.

74   Barbershop Harmony Society. (2022, Oct 12). *Sweet & Sour - It Had to be You (Isham Jones Orchestra cover)* [Video]. YouTube.
https://youtu.be/rpjsImkFmsM?si=YN88V6cBUI2zbE3T

Call and Response

Call and response is a compositional technique that functions as a musical conversation. In barbershop arrangements, the *call* is typically performed by the melody, which is answered by the *response* from the harmony parts. Much like barbershop, call and response has its roots in traditional African music, and is popular in gospel, as well as standards. Several iconic examples are found in the barbershop style.

"Bill Grogan's Goat" is a popular call and response song.[75] In this updated arrangement, the first two calls follow the traditional format of the lead issuing the call and the harmony parts following with the echoed response. The next two call and response couplets start to layer textures, featuring a pair of duets followed by a trio/solo approach.

Figure 23.71

"Bill Grogan's Goat" call and response examples. Words and music by John Feierabend. Arranged by Clay Hine.

One of the most iconic call and response songs sung in the barbershop style is "Bright Was the Night." David Wright's arrangement follows a similar approach to "Bill Grogan's Goat." This starts with the lead call and harmony part responses in measures 20–21 followed by a pair of duets in measures 22–24.[76]

---

75 Barbershop Harmony Society. (2019, Oct 11). *Category 4 - Bill Grogan's Goat* [Video]. YouTube. https://youtu.be/Wuzuky-2Gok

76 Barbershop Harmony Society. (2018, Sep 14). *The Gas House Gang - Bright Was the Night* [Video]. YouTube. https://youtu.be/Wuzuky-2Gok

Figure 23.72

"Bright Was the Night" call and response. Arranged by David Wright.

"Seventy Six Trombones" features a great example of using call and response techniques similar to solo performers and orchestras.[77] The leads and basses take turns calling as would Frank Sinatra, and the other three parts respond as would the Count Basie Band. The calls tend to foreshadow and the responses reinforce.

---

77   Barbershop Harmony Society. (2009, Jul 22). *Ambassadors of Harmony - Seventy-Six Trombones [from The Music Man]* [Video]. YouTube. https://youtu.be/QmDGntpZC3I

Figure 23.73

"Seventy-Six Trombones" call and response. Words and music by Meredith Willson. Arranged by David Wright.

Backtime

The Glossary of Barbershop Terms defines *backtime* as "an arranging device that lengthens the duration of syllables or words in the harmony parts as they support the melody." The melody is delivered in its original form and timing, while the harmony parts omit words or deliver alternate words, most often providing reinforcement of key lyrics, typically on strong beats to reinforce pulses/meter.

Here's an example from "A Handful of Stars," using backtime to additionally reinforce the rhythmic sense of the beating hearts while supporting key lyrics.

Figure 23.74

"A Handful of Stars," Words and music by Ted Shapiro and Jack Lawrence. Arranged by Steve Tramack.

Here's an example from "Anything Goes" where the bass has the melody in measures 65–68 in the second chorus. The harmony parts use extended backtime in a similar fashion to neutral syllable block chords with an added call and response, changing functions between the trio's call and the bass' response to create further interest.[78]

78　Barbershop Harmony Society. (2019, Aug 30). *Alexandria Harmonizers - Anything Goes* [Video]. YouTube. https://youtu.be/okUtCTl7W3M

Figure 23.75

"Anything Goes," Words and music by Cole Porter. Arranged by Kevin Keller.

Half Time

If backtime effects feature the original melody, with a sense of stretching time from the harmony parts, *half time* has the sense of stretching time for the melody, doubling the number of measures required to complete the affected section. This can be accomplished by simply doubling the time associated with each melody note, as is the case in "California, Here I Come." Note in the first chorus that each syllable in the lyric "California" has two beats, indicated in the meter by half notes.[79]

Figure 23.76

"California, Here I Come," Words and music Bud DeSylva, Joseph Meyer, and Al Jolson. Arranged by David Wright.

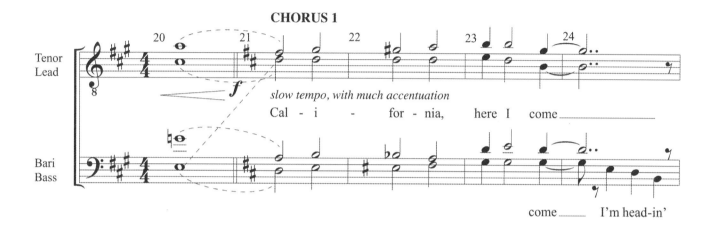

79 Barbershop Harmony Society. (Oct 7, 2019). *Voices of California - California, Here I Come [from Bombo]* [Video]. YouTube. https://youtu.be/Fsmh-xmkLAA?si=nuce6okqvzibdZD3

Whereas, in the second chorus, starting at measure 91, each syllable has a whole note associated with it. The arrangement leverages a patter to provide the sense of motion, even though time from a meter perspective has been cut in half.

Figure 23.77

"California, Here I Come" half time effect. Arranged by David Wright.

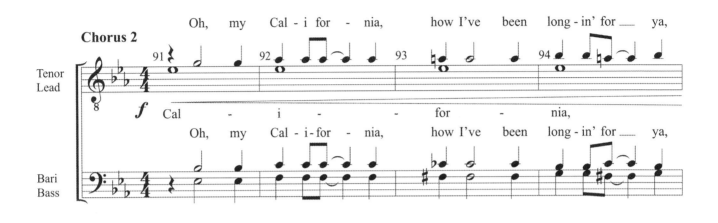

In "Looking at the World Through Rose Colored Glasses," the half time is created in the second B section through a combination of added material and stretching held lead notes at the ends of phrases.[80] Here's the first B section which spans eight measures.

Figure 23.78

"Looking at the World Through Rose Colored Glasses" first B section. Arranged by David Wright.

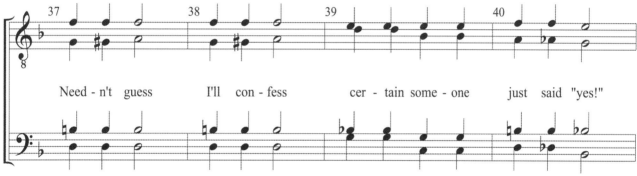

80   Barbershop Harmony Society. (2016, Aug 30). *Take 4 - (Looking at the World Thru) Rose Colored Glasses (live at Harmony University 2016)* [Video]. YouTube. https://youtu.be/98wWxlJJX94

Here's the sixteen-measure second bridge.

Figure 23.79

"Looking at the World Through Rose Colored Glasses" second B section. Arranged by David Wright.

Neutral Syllables

A common way to texturally develop an arrangement and feature a single voice is through the use of neutral syllables, e.g., "oo." In "A Handful of Stars," the first bridge leverages a homorhythmic texture in measures 25–26.

Figure 23.80

"A Handful of Stars" homorhythmic texture. Arranged by Steve Tramack.

In the second bridge, the texture changes to melody-over-neutral-syllable ("oo"). Notice the pillar chords are the same between the two sections.

Figure 23.81

"A Handful of Stars" solo over neutral syllable. Arranged by Steve Tramack.

In "Come What May," the rhythmic neutral syllable approach is used to create an instrumental texture, simulating the introduction from the original artist's version of the song.[81]

Figure 23.82

"Come What May" faux-instrumental introduction. Words and music by Kevin Gilbert and David Baerwald. Arranged by Kevin Keller.

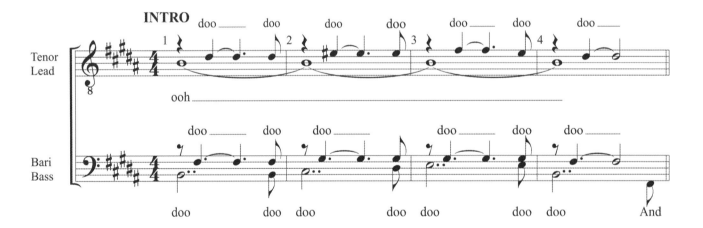

81   Barbershop Harmony Society. (2017, Aug 18). *After Hours - Come What May [from Moulin Rouge!]* [Video]. YouTube. https://youtu.be/VsAb54zJRcI

Advanced Techniques: Scat and Instrumental

As we've seen the inclusion of songs from the Great American Songbook, Broadway, and jazz standards into the barbershop style, we've seen the evolution of handling of instrumental transitional material. This often is found as transition material between verses and choruses, or serving as introductions or interludes. Particularly in rhythmic-themed interpretations of the source material, leveraging short sections of scat or instrumental emulation often helps to retain the feel of the original song.

Based on a Michael Bublé version of the song "For Once in My Life," the arrangement leverages the big band feel and basic melodic motif in the introduction.[82] Scat lyrics with a combination of swing eighths and rests create an immediate sense of a rhythmically-fueled approach to this song.

Figure 23.83

"For Once in My Life" scat introduction. Words and music by Cy Coleman and Robert Wells. Arranged by Steve Tramack.

---

82 Michael Bublé. (2014, Nov 8). *For Once in My Life* [Audio]. YouTube. https://youtu.be/grI20umvWzY

In an arrangement of "It Had to Be You," inspired by another Michael Bublé performance—this time a duet with Barbra Streisand—the transition between the verse and the chorus also serves to move from a free form lyric delivery into a swing groove.[83] This instrumental interlude serves a storytelling function, bridging from past to present. The walking bass line offset against the treble trio's syncopation further emphasizes the groove, which is thematically developed in the arrangement.

Figure 23.84

"It Had to Be You" scat transition from verse to chorus. Words and music by Isham Jones and Gus Kahn. Arranged by Steve Tramack.

83   Barbershop Harmony Society. (2022, Oct 12). *Sweet & Sour - It Had to Be You (Isham Jones Orchestra cover)* [Video]. YouTube. https://youtu.be/rpjsImkFmsM?si=YN88V6cBUI2zbE3T

In "Seventy Six Trombones," where instruments are referenced throughout the song in the lyrics, embellishments that simulate instruments provide opportunities for the performer to bring the song to life.[84] Note the trumpet's "ta-ket-ta tah" call and response fanfare to bridge the first and second choruses in David Wright's arrangement.

Figure 23.85

"Seventy-Six Trombones" fanfare. Arranged by David Wright.

84   Barbershop Harmony Society. (2009, Jul 22). *Ambassadors of Harmony - Seventy-Six Trombones [from The Music Man]* [Video]. YouTube. https://youtu.be/QmDGntpZC3I

Melodic

We don't often think of the melody of a song as an embellishment. Embellishments support the song's melody and lyrics. However, creative treatment of the melody can address range issues and create interest. Harmonic devices such as unison and octaves can bring attention to a particular melody note, word, or phrase.

Melodic Transfers

Melodic transfers are popular arranging devices, used to introduce variety and interest at a bridge, reprise or second chorus. Such is the case with "Always," where the arranger uses an implied circle of fifths key change from A♭ to D♭. This allows for transitioning the melody to the bass for four measures before passing the melody back to the lead.[85]

Figure 23.86

"Always" key change and melody passing to the bass. Words and music by Irving Berlin. Arranged by Don Gray and Mark Hale.

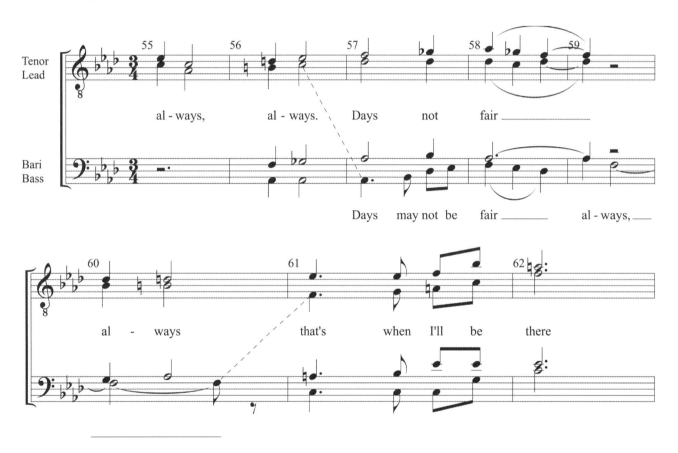

Passing the melody to the bass and then to either the baritone or tenor can provide both performance opportunities and different textures. Taking advantage of the different timbre, range and musical delivery approaches between the voice parts allows the arranger to create interest above and beyond the original compositional material. In "All the Time," the arranger features the bass and baritone on the melody for contrast before passing the melody back to the lead. The tertian key change, which is covered in more depth in Chapter 29, *Advanced Arranging Concepts*, provides a better range for the bass melody, and a semitone key lift from the II7 of the new key becomes the dominant of the original key, providing a sense of

85   TalkinShop. (Aug 3, 2011). *Michigan Jake - 1999 International Quartet Semifinal [Video].* YouTube. https://youtu.be/
qgj0efUXeCU?si=kaMDQ40IA4UXQrDA&t=10

lift upon returning to the original key. Also note the bass solitary echo in measure 27, which is then sustained through the other motion of the baritone and tenor echoes and ensuing swipes. The bass echo draws the listener's attention to the bass line and prepares them for the transition of the melody to that part.[86]

Figure 23.87

"All the Time" melody passing to the bass and baritone leveraging a tertian key change. Arranged by Steve Tramack.

86   Barbershop Harmony Society. (2022, Oct 11). *Throwback - All the Time (Barry Manilow cover)* [Video]. YouTube. https://youtu.be/Q9kgWfv10Nw

Some melodies are rangy, spanning more than an octave and a third. In these cases, passing the melody to an outside voice part provides the opportunity to keep a song in a comfortable key. Such is the case with "Up a Lazy River."[87]

Figure 23.88

"(Up a) Lazy River." Words and music by Hoagy Carmichael and Sidney Arodin. Arranged by Clay Hine.

Unison/Octaves

Unison or octaves within an arrangement can create a powerful impact. It acts as a focusing or unifying agent, highlighting a key word, thought, or transitional moment in the chart. Unisons and octaves can help support large melodic leaps where trying to harmonize the chord would create awkward voice-leading or place voices outside their comfort zones.

In "Louise," the octave on "you" in measure 40 supports the melodic leap and reinforces the concept of "only you," which appears later in the arrangement. It creates a sense of anticipation that springs into the next phrase from both a tessitura and syncopation perspective.

87   Barbershop Harmony Society. (2018, Oct 5). *Category 4 - Lazy River* [Video]. YouTube. https://youtu.be/ctbtz8tj5sE

Figure 23.89

"Louise," arranged by David Wright.

In "Someone Like You," an octave is used at the melodic climax in measure 54 to focus the listener on this key moment of the arrangement and provide a break in texture that signals a departure from the climax. This effect is reinforced by the cascading echo with the harmony parts falling below the sustained melody note.[88]

Figure 23.90

"Someone Like You," arranged by Steve Tramack.

88   Barbershop Harmony Society. (Jan 22, 2016). *Alexandria Harmonizers - Someone Like You (International 2015)* [Video]. YouTube. https://youtu.be/MLvqGGdID68?si=vUF732ZRpWnA6ast

Voices Left Hanging

Arrangements sometimes require a transition between dynamic levels, sections of form, or dramatically different textures. One approach to doing so is leaving a single voice sustaining while the other parts release. This draws focus to the hanging voice and the lyrics at that moment.

This example from "Put Your Arms Around Me, Honey" leaves the lead voice hanging at the end of the intro in measures 22–23.[89] This helps to blunt the momentum established through the high tessitura, exciting chords, strong voicing, and passing posts. The lead voice hold-over creates a clear break for the transition into the chorus. The layered introduction of voices further creates a sense of ramping energy.

Figure 23.91

"Put Your Arms Around Me." Words and music by Albert Von Tilzer and Junie McCree. Arranged by Aaron Dale.

89   Barbershop Harmony Society. (2009, Jan 9). *Max Q - 2007 International Quartet Champions* [Video]. YouTube. https://youtu.be/ kwxEHFVHkAM

Embellishment Stacking

The following are advanced technique examples of *embellishment stacking*, or leveraging different types of embellishments and motion to develop key moments of an arrangement.

In "Louise," we see a combination of textures and embellishment techniques to create a unique texture for the bridge of this fantastic arrangement.[90] Note the use of the following embellishments:

- Tenor post
- Lead/bass duet with ascending similar motion
- Bass downbeat against treble trio syncopation

Figure 23.92

"Louise," arranged by David Wright.

---

90   Barbershop Harmony Society. (2017, Jun 22). *Michigan Jake - Louise (2000 International)* [Video]. YouTube. https://youtu.be/GdnIIPzyK2M

In the reprise of the bridge in Figure 23.93, we see a similar rhythmic approach, but this time with a sense of rising and falling pyramid motion. This leads to a jazz release at "joy" and further rhythmic accents to create a decidedly different texture for the same section of form.

Figure 23.93

"Louise," arranged by David Wright.

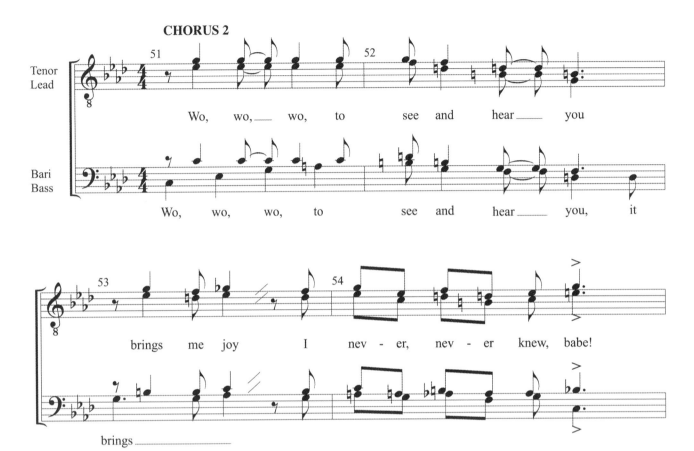

In the following example from "It Had to Be You," a similar motion ascending swipe, leading to an echo with a contrary motion swipe, creates anticipation and energy at the end of the verse, leading into a key change along with the melody passing from the baritone to the lead.

Figure 23.94

"It Had to Be You," arranged by Steve Tramack.

In the same arrangement, the second A section of the chorus uses delayed-entry bass rhythmic syncopations as well as a duet echo with contrary motion. This leads to a climactic moment at the melodic peak at the pickup to measure 45.

Figure 23.95

"It Had to Be You," arranged by Steve Tramack.

Tag and Conclusion

Just like every great barbershop song, we need a tag to make this chapter in our arranging journey feel complete. Embellishments are a critical element in developing the base harmonization and make an arrangement feel well-rooted in the barbershop style. Tags often feature high-impact embellishments set to leave a lasting impression in the audience's mind. One great way to practice your craft as an arranger is to write more tags that allow you to focus on one or more of the kind of embellishments provided in this chapter. Here's a great tag written by Brian Beck from the song "I'm Sorry I Made You Cry."[91] This leverages a swipe that feels like a cascade due to its high unison starting point. It actually turns out to be a blossom effect, exposing a lead post and a scissors echo with contrary motion leading to the climactic conclusion. This is a wonderful example of how embellishments create iconic, memorable musical events and aid in the long-line development of an arrangement.

Figure 23.96

"I'm Sorry I Made You Cry" tag. Words and music by N.J. Ciesi. Arranged by Brian Beck.

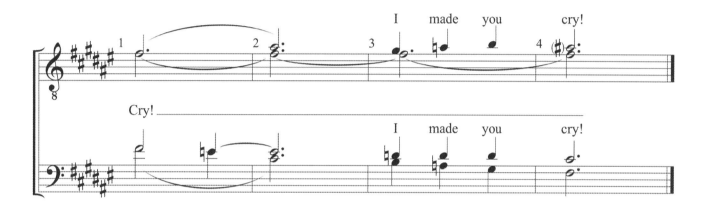

91   Barbershop Harmony Society. (2020, Dec 16). *Side Street Ramblers - I'm Sorry I Made You Cry* [Video]. YouTube. https://youtu.be/zqsKVUV32xc

Chapter 24.
An Introduction to Key Changes

By David Wright

Introduction

Why have key changes? Most arrangements have at least one key change. Quite often the arranger makes this choice in order to create musical interest. Sometimes a key change that raises the key is just the perfect spark to heighten the intensity at a critical moment and it may lift the tessitura into a better place for an exciting ending. Key changes are often needed in the transition from one song to another in a medley. Sometimes a key change enables the transition of the melody from lead to bass—or vice versa—for a brief segment of the song. As a general rule, key changes should be placed at a strong structural point of the song.

We will discuss and exemplify four types of basic key changes below. Each of these types, excepting one example at the end, is modulated, e.g., achieved by using a chord leading to the new key. In these examples the modulation chord is the dominant seventh rooted a fourth below the note class of the new key, leading to the tonic triad of the new key. These examples go from a major key to another major key. More types of key changes, including the involvement of minor keys and advanced techniques for writing them, appear in Chapter 29, *Advanced Arranging Concepts*. The reader is advised to understand and master the more basic types in this section before proceeding there.

Half-Step Key Lift

The most basic key change is one that raises the key by a half-step by means of the modulation chord that is the dominant of the new key, which is ♭VI of the old key. Thus a song in C evokes A♭7 to modulate to the key of D♭. Here is such an example from "Wait 'Til the Sun Shines, Nellie."

Figure 24.1

"Wait 'Til the Sun Shines, Nellie" half-step lift. Words and music by Harry Von Tilzer and Andrew B. Sterling. Arranged by Buzz Haeger.

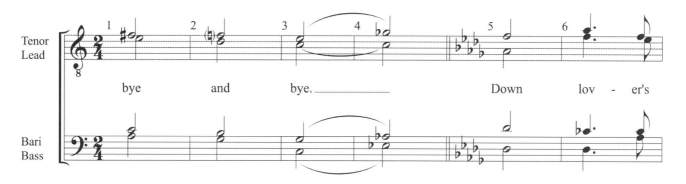

Full-Step Key Lift

Very similar to this is the key change that lifts the key a full step, in which case VI7 serves as the modulation chord. This is a bit more dramatic, and the arranger must take care that there is head room for the full step elevation without pushing the range constraints of the singers. The following examples show how this can be accomplished to get from one song to another. Here's another version of the "Wait 'Til the Sun Shines, Nellie" key change, which moves directly from I to VI7, serving as the dominant of the new key.[92]

Figure 24.2

"Wait 'Til the Sun Shines, Nellie" full-step lift. Words and music by Harry Von Tilzer and Andrew B. Sterling. Key change by Alan Gordon.

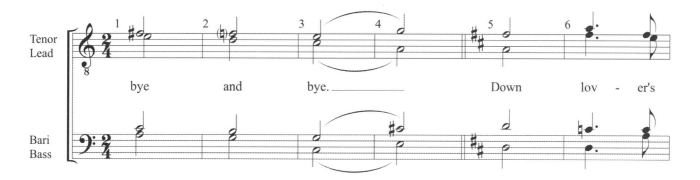

Up a Fourth Key Change

A totally different modulated key change, also very common, raises the key by the interval of a fourth, or five semitones. Here the modulation chord is just the tonic seventh chord, or I7, of the old key. Thus a song in C uses C7 to modulate to F. Because this changes the tonal center significantly, this key change is often used in a medley, say to go from a sol-to-sol song in C to a do-to-do song in F. Here are three examples. Figure 24.3 also uses the triplet to help establish the new time signature, shifting from Cut Time to 3/4.

---

92   Barbershop Harmony Society. (2020, Nov 25). *Gotcha! - Wait 'Till the Sun Shines, Nellie* [Video]. YouTube. https://youtu.be/8tqn0KIwTL8

Figure 24.3

"The Bowery" by Percy Gaunt and Charles H Hoyt. Arranged by SPEBSQSA.

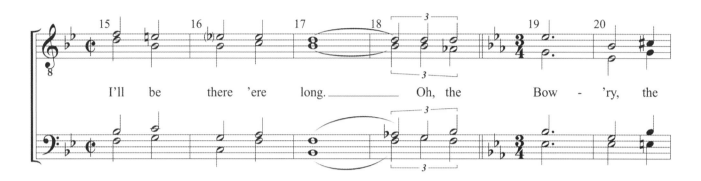

This is perhaps the most basic movement from I to the modulation chord (I7):

Figure 24.4

"We Sing That They Shall Speak / Keep the Whole World Singing," words and music by Clarence Burgess. Arranged by SPEBSQSA.

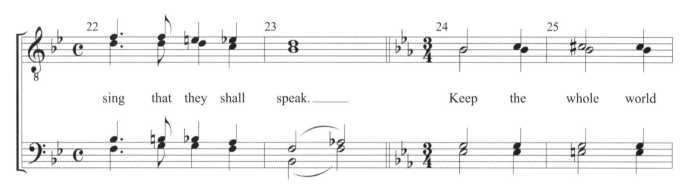

It often is used to transfer the melody from lead to bass or vice versa, as in the following example from "I Got Rhythm."[93]

---

93   Barbershop Harmony Society. (2016, Aug 15). *Forefront - I Got Rhythm* [Video]. YouTube. https://youtu.be/3frH41TZcaU

Figure 24.5

"I Got Rhythm." Words and music by George Gershwin. Arranged by David Wright.

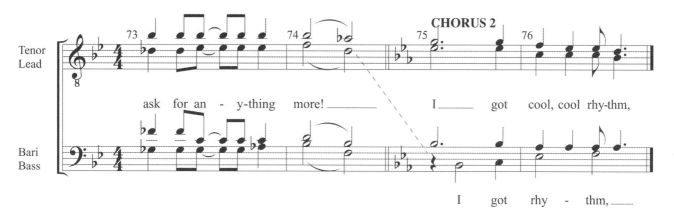

This example from "Always" uses the I–dim7–I7 progression in the original key to lead to the new implied key of D♭ with the bass melody.

Figure 24.6

"Always," Words and music by Irving Berlin. Arranged by Mark Hale and Don Gray.

Up a Fifth Key Change

Finally, we mention the "opposite" of the previous version—namely the key change that lifts the key a fifth or down a fourth. This may be used in several instances:

- Revert to the original key after the previous type of key change has been employed
- Place the song in the appropriate key for a melody change
- Move to another song in a medley.

The modulation chord here is II7.

Figure 24.7

Up a fifth key change. Arranged by SPEBSQSA.

And here we touch on a topic that is pursued further in Chapter 29, *Advanced Arranging Concepts*, by saying that this key change is sometimes affected with no modulation chord. Here's an example from "Lida Rose" where the arrangement goes directly to the new key with a bass melody.

Figure 24.8

"Lida Rose" by Meredith Wilson. Arranged by Tom Gentry.

Conclusion

Key changes are frequently found in barbershop arrangements with the purpose of creating interest and developing the song. Key changes don't need to be exotic to create excitement; a well-placed half-step or full-step key lift can facilitate a climactic musical event. To facilitate melodic transfers to an outside voice—bass or tenor—consider up-a-fourth or up-a-fifth key lifts. Further exploration of key changes can be found in Chapter 29 of *Arranging Barbershop Vol. 2.*

Chapter 25.
Rhythmic Development

By Aaron Dale

Introduction

Rhythm is utilized in the barbershop style generally as it is in all music. Patterns of sounds and silences are woven throughout a song along with other musical elements to create a desired sound, feeling, mood, or groove. Why would you consider using new or modified rhythmic patterns that differ from the original composition?

- To help generate contrast and unity
- To create tension and release
- To build and sustain forward motion
- To create grooves representative of different styles of music, e.g., country, rock n roll, blues.
- To simulate a well-known groove or pattern from a recording of the original song

Patterns in Downbeat Songs

Downbeat songs are driven by strong pulses on nearly every strong beat, versus the weak, or unaccented, beat. In a standard meter of 4/4 that could include each beat 1-2-3-4, or every other beat emphasizing 1 and 3. Many *straight* groove songs with straight eighth notes not swung are driven by downbeats with syncopation.

 Beats can be subdivided in two ways: duple or triple. *Triplet* subdivision divides each beat in three. It is most often associated with swing music and is counted as "1-and-a-2-and-a-3-and-a-4-and-a." *Duple* subdivision divides each beat in half, meaning two eighth notes for every quarter note. It is counted as "1-and-2-and-3-and-4-and."

In the following examples, the notated downbeat patterns drive the song phrase to phrase. All voice parts help create the downbeats but not always at the same time.

Downbeat-Driven

In the arrangement of "Get Me to the Church On Time," downbeats are driven by a strong *march* feel.[94] The half note is the dominant marching pulse, and quarter/half durations are the main driving durations.

Figure 25.1

"Get Me to the Church on Time," Words and music by Frederick Lowe and Alan Jay Lerner. Arranged by Aaron Dale.

94 Barbershop Harmony Society. (2016, Apr 11). *Brothers in Harmony - Get Me to the Church on Time (International 2015)* [Video]. YouTube. https://youtu.be/0to1fyuh0iA

Downbeat Latin

"Sway" features strong downbeats on 1 and 4.[95] The tenor, lead and baritone sing with the bass, creating syncopation on the and of 2. This rhythmic pattern is repeated in the bass and sometimes in the other parts on echoes. Syncopated offbeats are placed between the strong downbeats.

Figure 25.2

"Sway," words and music by Luis Demetrio, Pablo Beltrán Ruiz, and Norman Gimbel. Arranged by Aaron Dale.

95   OCTenor2. (2008, Aug 24). *OC Times - Save the Last Dance/Sway Medley* [Video]. YouTube. https://youtu.be/NVWE39OniDo

Notice how in Figure 25.3 the same rhythmic pattern using syncopation on the and of 2 and the and of 3 is repeated in measures 68–69. Then, measures 72–76 features patterns with syncopation on the and of 4 alternating with measures ending with strong downbeats on 3 and 4. The measures with strong downbeats help to highlight the offbeat Latin rhythmic syncopation.

Figure 25.3

"Sway," words and music by Luis Demetrio, Pablo Beltrán Ruiz, and Norman Gimbel. Arranged by Aaron Dale.

Rock

In this passage from "Fun, Fun, Fun," notice again the strong downbeats on 1 and 3. In addition, the dotted quarter/eighth bass pattern under the top three parts sets up the listener to perceive the backbeat of the non-stressed beats 2 and 4. This is similar to what you might hear from a rock snare drum. Middle beats are syncopated between bass and other parts.

Figure 25.4

"Fun, Fun, Fun," words and music by Brian Wilson and Mike Love. Arranged by Aaron Dale.

Patterns in Swing Songs

Swing songs are driven by patterns and groove with prominent *backbeat*. Syncopated swing rhythms are intertwined with strong downbeats for strength and stability.

 *Backbeat* refers to rhythmic pulses that accentuate the second and fourth beats in a measure. Almost as importantly, the strong beats—first and third—are deemphasized unless the downbeat is pulsed to specifically establish a sense of structure. This is common in jazz and rock music. Coupled with triplet subdivision, backbeat forms the foundation for swing and shuffle grooves.

Swing notation can be different based on the tempo and style of the original song. Medium to fast swing songs are often notated in duple meters of 4/4 or 2/4 with standard eighth notes, but a swing articulation mark is notated in the score. This swing marking tells singers that two eighth notes back-to-back should instead be performed as a quarter note followed by an eighth note within a quarter-note triplet.

Swing! ♫ = ♩♪

This tells the performer to simulate a 12/8 meter in performance while the notation remains simpler in 4/4. Performers make a mental shift to audibly change the notated rhythms, creating a groove of 3 eighth notes per beat instead of 2.

Slower swing songs often feature many literal triplets with three eighth notes back-to-back and are typically notated using a 12/8 time signature. It might not always be the best choice, but it could be a quicker and cleaner notation process compared to using 4/4 and adding a triplet symbol over every eighth note triplet.

Swing songs could also be notated in 4/4 with dotted eighth/ sixteenth notes. That notation creates a natural swing / bouncy rhythm but the swing symbol is still used. This is notated as follows but it is less common.

Swing! ♪.♫ ♪.♫ = ♩♪ ♩♪

Successful swing rhythms will include the placement of obvious downbeats to help maintain stability for the performer and listener. For most swing songs, not every phrase can or should just sit on the backbeat or upbeat.

Rockabilly / Quick Swing / Shuffle

"Rock This Town" is still downbeat driven, but a strong swing backbeat is felt.[96] The beat is officially swing as each beat could be divided into three eighth notes. This may also be notated as *shuffle*, which features both downbeat-driven pulse and swing subdivision. See the off beats generated by neutral "dat" syllables and bass driving the down beat with swung eighth notes throughout.

Figure 25.5

"Rock This Town," words and music by Brian Setzer. Arranged by Aaron Dale.

* Word *well* drawn out over two syllables

96   Barbershop Harmony Society. (2018, Oct 5). *Studio 4 - Rock This Town* [Video]. YouTube. https://youtu.be/sytu4HB-1vU

Slow Swing / Blues / 12/8 Meter

These swing songs have strong downbeats, but you can more easily notice the subdivision of each beat into three eighth notes. The backbeat is stronger on beat 2 and 4. Figure 25.6 shows notation in 4/4 but with swing articulation noted at the beginning of the arrangement. Triplets are notated with a 3 over the top of the eighth notes.

Figure 25.6

"Love Me" notated in 4/4. Words and music by Jerry Leiber and Mike Stoller. Arranged by Aaron Dale.

And here's the same passage but notated in 12/8. The triplets are built into the 12/8 time signature.

Figure 25.7

"Love Me" notated in 12/8. Arranged by Aaron Dale.

Medium Swing

Medium tempo swing songs will feature a more emphasized backbeat of 2 and 4 due to the more laid-back *moderato* tempo (108–120 BPM). This allows for more variation of pushing or jumping the beat, while still allowing the downbeat to be recognized. You can still identify the subdivision of each beat into three eighth notes.

The following from "You Took Advantage of Me" example shows various places where the melody lands on either the 2nd or 3rd eighth note in a group of three.[97] This pushes or jumps the beat but still allows the downbeat to be noticed when it comes back often.

97   Barbershop Harmony Society. (2015, Sep 1). *The Crush - You Took Advantage of Me (International 2015)* [Video]. YouTube. https://youtu.be/n3hOn3A_1RU

Figure 25.8

"You Took Advantage of Me." Words and music by Richard Rodgers and Lorenz Hart. Arranged by Aaron Dale.

Propellants

In the context of the barbershop style, propellants can be heard anywhere in a song. They frequently occur at the end of a phrase. They are essentially specifically designed rhythmic patterns sung typically by one part and inserted to provide a boost of forward motion. They are most commonly found in the bass part.

Why and when would you consider using a variety of rhythmic propellants throughout an arrangement? To accomplish the following:

- Help move and connect phrases throughout the song
- Provide a downbeat when the melody does not land on the downbeat
- Help generate contrast and unity
- Create tension and release
- Build and sustain forward motion
- Provide solo opportunities
- Create artistically planned breath points

Here the bass sings "and" on beat 4 making a solid downbeat that provides stability as the top three parts breathe and move forward with the offbeat of "and."

Figure 25.9

"You Took Advantage of Me" bass propellant. Arranged by Aaron Dale.

In "Yona from Arizona," shown in Figure 25.10, the bass swipes on beat two then sings a downbeat on "na" on beat three to move the song forward.[98]

---

98   Barbershop Harmony Society (208, Dec 13). *Masters of Harmony - 2008 International Barbershop Chorus Champions* [Video]. YouTube. https://youtu.be/O6IJWTXzgVs?t=298

Figure 25.10

"Yona from Arizona." Traditional. Arranged by Aaron Dale.

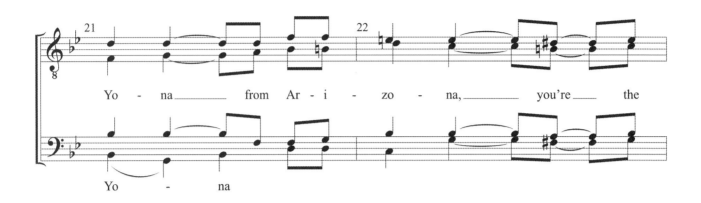

In Figure 25.11, the bass propellant on the echoes in measures 3 and 5 push the shuffle swing feel into the next measure.[99]

Figure 25.11

"Good Luck Charm" propellants. Words and music by Aaron Schroeder and Wally Gold. Arranged by Aaron Dale.

99 bhsstud5565. (Aug 26, 2008). *OC Times - Good Luck Charm* [Video]. YouTube. https://youtu.be/
LzetDk6a3Z8?si=FlzgMYTMQ42tzQ6F

The next three examples are from "Seize the Day," arranged for The Westminster Chorus as part of their 2015 International Chorus championship in the Barbershop Harmony Society.[100] Figure 25.12 features bass propellents under the top three parts. This moves the passage along with more rhythmic drive even though the tempo is generally slow.

Figure 25.12

"Seize the Day." Words and music by Alan Menken and Jack Feldman. Arranged by Aaron Dale.

The swipes in measures 78–79 are used as moderate rhythmic propellants to continue the pulse through the end of the phrase.

Figure 25.13

"Seize the Day" swipes used as rhythmic propellants. Arranged by Aaron Dale.

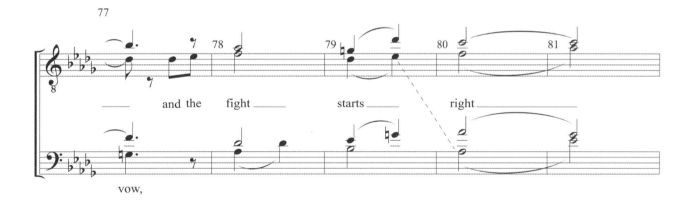

100 Barbershop Harmony Society (2015, Jul 17). *Westminster Chorus - Seize the Day [from Newsies]* [Video]. YouTube. https://youtu.be/2EZ3k10Hpp4

Melody notes sometimes are sustained during faster tempo song. In the original works, this is usually a place where the orchestration maintains the tempo and rhythmic drive of the song with instrumental fills. In "Seize the Day," I used fast bass rhythmic patterns to propel the end of this phrase. This is indeed a case where the passage is arranged with voices holding a long chord at this cadence point, which were instruments in the original version. The bass creates forward motion under the held chords.

Figure 25.14

"Seize the Day" bass motion under sustained chords. Arranged by Aaron Dale.

The next three examples are from "Georgia May," originally arranged for the 2009 Barbershop Harmony Society International Quartet Champions, *Crossroads*. Bass Jim Henry is an exceedingly musical singer with a dominating bass voice that lends itself well to bass propellants.[101] Figure 25.15 features a typical rhythmic texture in the barbershop style. The bass sings notes on downbeats while the top parts are syncopated. The bass downbeats propel the song forward and are often sung with a bit more pulse to establish the strong beats among the syncopation of the other parts. In measure 5, the bass breathes and sings a syncopated pickup to propel into measure 6.

 This syncopated pickup approach seen in measure 5 is an advanced arranging trick. This allows both a more singable line for a quartet singer as well as providing additional rhythmic interest and development.

101 Barbershop Harmony Society. (Mar 30, 2019). *The Newfangled Four - Georgia May* [Video]. YouTube. https://youtu.be/1D0nAgQZjhg?si=KLLGu3lDzEokom52

Figure 25.15

"Georgia May," words and music by Paul Denniker and Andy Razaf. Arranged by Aaron Dale.

Figure 25.16 includes examples from "Georgia May," demonstrating bass downbeat and syncopated pickups to move the song forward. Note the rests for each voice part, allowing breaths while accentuating the rhythmic subtext.

Figure 25.16

"Georgia May," arranged by Aaron Dale.

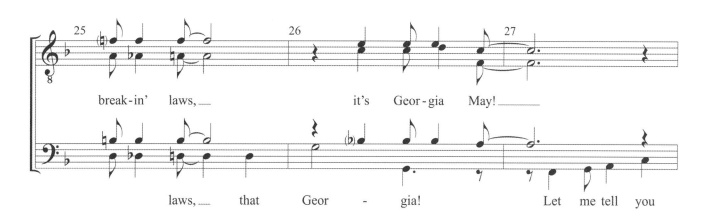

Here the top three parts land on the downbeat in measure 63 on the lyrics "oh yeah." This keeps the forward motion while the bass breathes mid-phrase.

Figure 25.17

"Georgia May." Arranged by Aaron Dale.

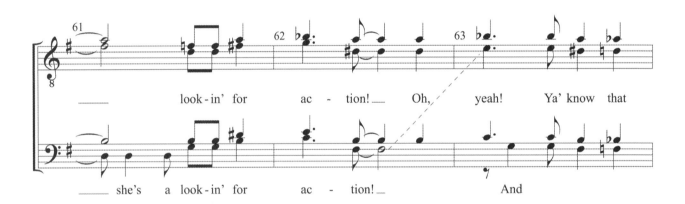

Here's one final example from "From Now On" of how to address instrumental interludes in a barbershop arrangement.[102] The example in Figure 25.18 leverages bass propellants in measures 49–52, with neutral syllables simulating percussion and bass guitars. Measures 57–60 use original lyrics that reinforce the previous phrase's lyrics and thoughts. These propellants provide motion under long sustained chords indicative of strings or woodwinds. This helps to bring the gap in a transitional portion of the arrangement.

102 Barbershop Harmony Society. (2019, Oct 15). *Westminster Chorus - From Now On/Come Alive Medley [from The Greatest Showman]* [Video]. YouTube. https://youtu.be/bLwblLkxQDw

Figure 25.18

"From Now On," Words and music by Benj Pasek and Justin Paul. Arranged by Aaron Dale.

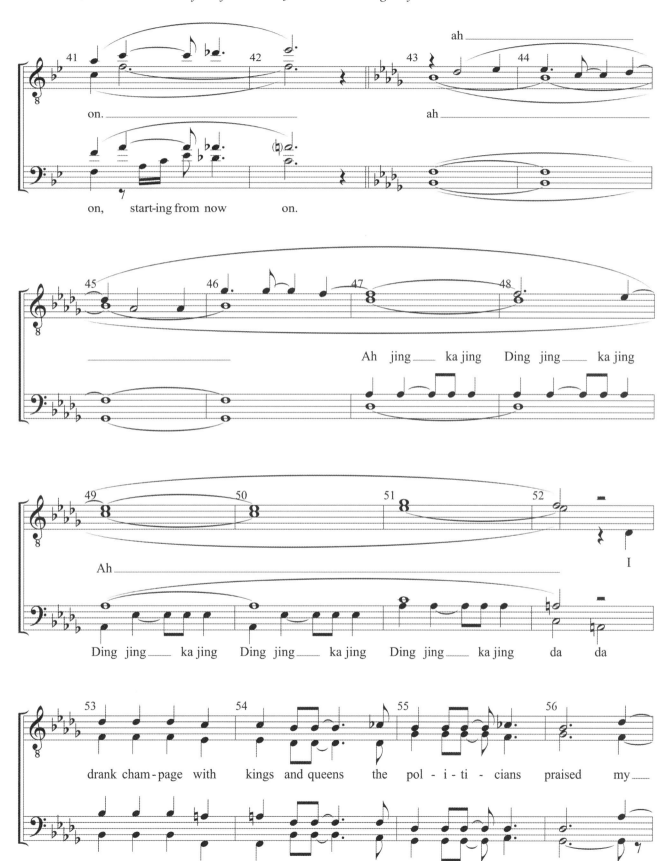

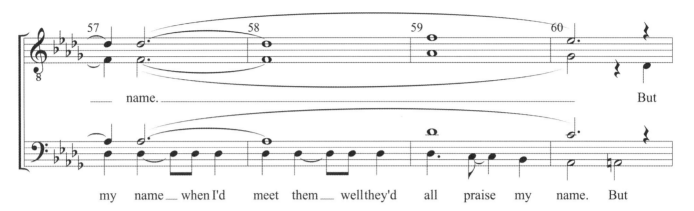

Conclusion

In this chapter, we've explored how rhythm can be used in the development of music. Rhythmic development is important to help achieve the following:

- Generate contrast and unity
- Create tension and release
- Build and sustain forward motion
- Create grooves representative of different styles of music, e.g., country, rock n roll, blues.
- Simulate a well-known groove or pattern from a recording of the original song

This is especially important in songs where rhythm is a primary musical theme. Understanding groove, rhythmic patterns in different styles of music, the use of downbeats and synchronization, and propellants are important in this journey. Chapter 31 of *Arranging Barbershop Vol. 2* goes into even more depth of advanced rhythmic development concepts.

Chapter 26.
Additional Development Considerations

By Aaron Dale

Introduction

Much of the science, art, and magic of arranging comes from development choices made during the creative and editing process. Development comes in many forms:

- **Melodic.** Use of higher inversions, passing the melody to different voice parts, and changes to the melody as the song progresses are just a few ways in which the melodic motifs can be used to develop the arrangement.
- **Harmonic.** Use of different harmonizations, different inversions, and higher or lower tessitura can contribute to key musical events.
- **Rhythmic.** Use of varying rhythmic patterns that emphasize offbeats and syncopation, stretching and shrinking patterns, and use of subdivision are a few areas we'll explore.
- **Textural.** One of the most important development techniques is exploring different textures, which refers to how different voice parts combine to create the sound of the phrase. Barbershop primarily features a homorhythmic texture where all voices are singing the same words and rhythms at the same time. Arrangers creates interest via duets, three-against-one, walking bass lines, and other patterns to create a satisfying musical journey.
- **Compositional.** The structure of the arrangement is another important factor in developing the arrangement. This may involve repeated sections such as bridges and half choruses and the introduction of original material such as introductions, interludes, and tags.

Development choices are also driven by the ensemble for whom you're arranging, the type of ensemble, and even the intended venue or event for the performance.

Let's Start at the End

You have to know where you're going to know how to proceed getting there. The arranger and performer should start with the end in mind, painting as vivid a picture as possible for how the audience will feel after the final chord. With that vision in mind, ask yourself: do your choices create the desired length, form, feeling, and mood? For example, Figure 26.1 features the introduction and first half of the chorus from "Strike Up the Band."[103] The elements of rudimentary percussion in the bass line, coupled with lyrics like "step it up, kick it up," provide an overall feeling of rhythmic energy that makes you want to dance.

---

103 Barbershop Harmony Society. (2009, Jan 23). *Westminster Chorus - Strike Up The Band/Everybody Step Medley* [Video]. YouTube. https://youtu.be/cDgZ-_5GMeg

Figure 26.1

"Strike Up the Band," words and music by George and Ira Gershwin. Arranged by Aaron Dale.

This drive and excitement leads directly into the second song in the medley, "Everybody Step." The feeling of joy, movement and excitement permeates the arrangement. Let's look at the core musical parameters that will allow us to design and develop an arrangement that allows us to release our vision.

Considerations of Core Musical Elements

One of the best places to start our development journey should be to consider what's provided by the composer and lyricist. The melody, harmony, lyrics, and rhythm of a song naturally include aspects of development that can serve as a foundation for the arranging blueprint.

Melody

Long after a performance, the audience may not remember the lyrics or the specific rhythmic patterns, but they may indeed remember the melody. If a song easily becomes an earworm, the melody is a prime source for development. In order for the song and arrangement to be successful in the barbershop style, the melody needs to be suitable to the intended performer. It needs to be recognizable and understandable throughout. If you question these aspects as you're notating the arrangement, it's likely that there will be challenges for the performance and audience.

If the challenge is one of range, melodic transfers—as covered in Chapter 23—to the bass or tenor can help. This can create additional challenges, as it may be difficult for the audience to follow the melody line as it moves from the lead singer. Some of this onus is on the performer who must be sensitive to when the melody moves from the lead. Both the receiving part—who needs to sing with melodic interpretation and vocal presence—and the lead singers—who must assue more of a background role—need to cooperate in these instances.

Knowing who you're arranging for is important; can the intended harmony singer carry the melody for that portion of the transfer? Key changes are often used as a development device, which can also present challenges for the melody singer. Will the melody still be singable in a different key by the lead singer, or will this necessitate transfer to another voice part?

A more advanced development technique involves melodic alteration. This is most often found in later sections of form to provide interest and contrast. This is a common technique used by pop and jazz performers, often with songs featured in our style. You may even find a recorded example of this kind of melodic modification that is well-known enough that audiences consider it the written melody.

Harmony

Harmony—chord vocabulary, progressions, voicings, inversions—is core to the barbershop style and should be considered throughout the arranging process. When contemplating harmonic choices, there are many factors to consider:

- The composer's original composition
- Popular recordings of the song
- The chord choices implied by the melody
- Characteristic chord progressions by harmonic pillar in the barbershop style

Listen to multiple available recordings of the song you're arranging. These may present different options for chord progressions, chord vocabulary, and harmonic rhythm. This is particularly important if there is a single, iconic version of a song. By following the harmonizations, rhythmic patters and structure of that iconic recording, your arrangement will map to the version that the audience hears in the head—a positive thing.

Harmony is also closely tied to texture choices. Harmonic choices will sound different depending on whether you have four parts singing the same words at the same time on each chord, have fewer than four parts singing, or have different textures at the same time, e.g., solo lyrics over neutral syllable block chords from the harmony parts.

Rhythm

The topic of rhythm is covered in Chapters 25 and 31 of this book. Two things to keep in mind related to rhythmic development: the composer's original intent and the singability for the performer. If you choose to alter the rhythmic patterns from the original composition, do so in the spirit of helping the performer successfully execute the arrangement.

Here's the initial rhythmic pattern played by the bass and lead guitars in the introduction of Kenny Loggins' "Footloose."

Figure 26.2

"Footloose," words and music by Dean Pitchford and Kenny Loggins,

Here's the arrangement simulating these rhythmic licks.[104]

Figure 26.3

"Footloose," arranged by Aaron Dale.

You may also make different artistic choices to create contrast that converges back to unity. Focus also on establishing and developing an overall sense of groove to maximize the impact on the audience.

104 Barbershop Harmony Society. (Mar 1, 2016). *Kentucky Vocal Union - Footloose (Kenny Loggins cover)* [Video]. YouTube. https:// youtu.be/_2oCPyUdCUs?si=dLc9tPf1tPOzQiw_

Compositional Considerations

Particularly when creating a new vision for a piece of music, you as the arranger have many tools at your disposal to develop a journey that fits your vision and creates an impact on the audience. Simply organizing the core compositional elements—verse, chorus, bridge, tag, etc.—creates a natural sense of development. Within a given section of form, exploring how the voices layer together to create different textures creates further interest and contrast. Bringing together multiple songs into a medley allows for potentially an even more interesting and varied journey.

Organization and Balance

One of the first considerations when planning an arrangement is the intended length of the piece. If the original composition is eight minutes with lots of important material—think Billy Joel's "Scenes from an Italian Restaurant"—it would be an injustice to cut it down to two minutes. The length will not determine everything you do with other musical elements, but it provides a framework for development. Some organizations such as Sweet Adelines, as of 2023, have time limits on their contest performances. Other ensembles may envision this song in a given spot in a show package, which might also drive a desired length based on the song's function.

Doing some planning before you start arranging will help in this process. There are lots of great thoughts and tools, such as the blueprint spreadsheet, included in *Arranging Barbershop Vol. 1*, Chapter 12. Think about the expected tempo and create a map of the form. Chart sections and measures for the introduction, verse(s), chorus(es), bridges or interludes, and the tag. Seek out audio or video recordings and assemble them into the structure of your blueprint. It's always a good idea to sing through passages yourself, checking for both singability and a sense of balance.

Once you have your blueprint, notate or sketch out a skeleton of the groove, section by section. Think of patterns and sequences of rhythm you've heard in other songs, and use iconic recordings of this song for inspiration. Perhaps start with the bass part, and then alternate with the harmony parts, going back and forth in the pattern. Once you have a basic groove sketched out, consider whether you need to simplify or embellish. Don't settle on something that doesn't quite work. How do you want the audience to feel? The groove you choose can trigger emotions from the audience. This can be beneficial for the performer as they engage the audience in real time.

Source Material

The best place to start when arranging a new song is with some existing source material. Sheet Music Direct has literally millions of arrangements available for purchase and download.[105] Find a piano and vocal score if available. If there is a recorded version of the song that will serve as foundational inspiration, look for a version of the sheet music that matches that performance.

Note the original recording of "Little Patch of Heaven" from the Disney film, *Home on the Range*.[106] Here's an excerpt from the sheet music of the k. d. lang performance from the movie.

---

105 www.sheetmusicdirect.com
106 Reykjavik1992. (2011, Apr 21). *Little Patch of Heaven* [Audio]. YouTube. https://youtu.be/gnqBunt6Xlo

Figure 26.4

"Little Patch of Heaven," words and music by Glenn Slater and Alan Menkin.

Compare that with the arrangement as sung by Crossroads, 2009 BHS International Quartet Champion, as seen in Figure 26.5.[107] Note similar bass and harmonic patterns and harmonies.

Figure 26.5

"Little Patch of Heaven," words and music by Glenn Slater and Alan Menkin. Arranged by Aaron Dale.

on a lit - tle patch o' heav - en a - way out

west, way ___ out west.

Verse 2

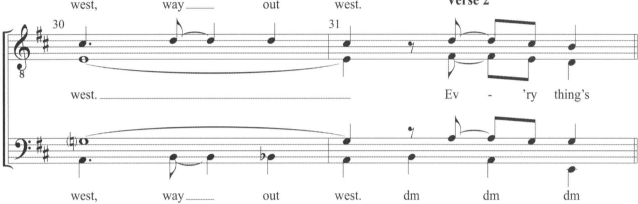

west. ___

Ev - 'ry thing's

west, way ___ out west.   dm   dm   dm

Single Songs Versus Medleys

Most single song arrangements in the barbershop style are in the 2:00 to 4:00 minute range, though there certainly are examples of songs with lengthy forms that are much longer. *Medley* or *montage* arrangements can be the same but can be much longer.

 Both medleys and montages feature several songs. For the purposes of this book, *medleys* are defined as having a recapitulation of the first song. *Montages* do not, often featuring one song after another with little or no connecting material.

Oftentimes, the medley will focus on one song, with one or more sections from an additional song or songs inserted for contrast and development. It's usually a quick tie-in to the main theme, serving as a bridge. Parts of that song may be used as added material or embellishments in the intro or tag as a further tie-in.

In the following example, the theme of the medley is music loosely categorized as Funk.[108] The anchor song is "Uptown Funk" which sets up the energetic dance and rhythmic funk feel usually equated with the Godfather of Soul, James Brown. James Brown's "I Got You (I Feel Good)" is then featured, along with other funk songs for contrast and variety.

---

108 Barbershop Harmony Society. (Jul 10, 2016). *Vocal FX – Funk Medley* [Video]. YouTube. https://youtu.be/ zrdE15auxlQ?si=FMaQz1cB0X2oer7f

Figure 26.6

"Uptown Funk," words and music by By Charles Wilson, Rudolph Taylor, Philip Lawrence, Jeff Bhasker, Devon Gallaspy, Mark Ronson, Nicholaus Williams, Bruno Mars, Robert Wilson, Ronnie Wilson, and Lonnie Simmons. "I Got You (I Feel Good)," words and music by James Brown. Arranged by Aaron Dale.

The reprise, featured in Figure 26.7, utilizes portions of "Uptown Funk" and lyrics that reference other songs from the medley.

Figure 26.7

Reprise of "Funk Medley." Original material developed and arranged by Aaron Dale.

Non-Homorhythmic or Neutral Syllable Introductions

Over the past several years, neutral syllable introductions have become a popular way of establishing a mood set at the beginning of your development journey. Used to emulate an instrumental introduction as you would find in most original versions of the song, neutral syllables can help establish mood and create an emotional fabric: various open vowels can emulate strings, scat syllables can emulate big band horns, and "ch" or "ng" can approximate rock guitar lines.

Here's an example of a sweeping orchestral introduction for a dramatic treatment of "If You Go Away."[109]

Figure 26.8

"If You Go Away," words and music by Rod Mckuen and Jacques Brel. Arranged by David Wright.

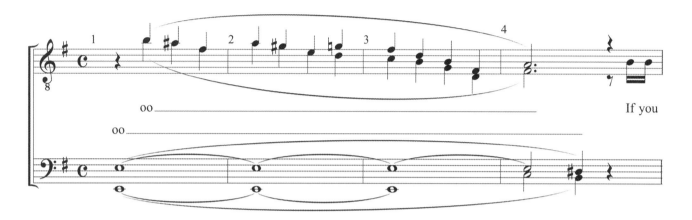

The following example emulates the horn section at the beginning of Michael Bublé's recording of "For Once in My Life."[110]

109 Barbershop Harmony Society. (2019, Oct 7). *Zero8 - If You Go Away [Video]*. YouTube. https://youtu.be/vTTzu8Q2DsE
110 Michael Bublé. (2014, Nov 8). *For Once in My Life* [Audio]. YouTube. https://youtu.be/grI20umvWzY

Figure 26.9

"For Once in My Life" introduction. Words and music by Cy Coleman and Robert Wells. Arranged by Steve Tramack.

Neutral syllable passages are often found in interludes and reprise choruses, much as they would in a popular version of the song. Consider the reprise half chorus from the same arrangement of "For Once in My Life." In the Bublé version, the band plays the entire section of form. Because this arrangement is intended for use in a barbershop contest, the band section is interwoven with lyrics in a *trading fours* structure. See Chapter 31 for more details on rhythmic development techniques.

Figure 26.10

"For Once in My Life" reprise. Words and music by Cy Coleman and Robert Wells. Arranged by Steve Tramack.

In a Barbershop competition setting, where aspects of the style are more carefully considered and evaluated, the amount of acceptable neutral syllable content may be limited. Barbershop is a homorhythmic, lyrical style at its core. Using sections of neutral syllables as a contrasting device can work if appropriate for the length of the arrangement and converges to *homorhythmic* texture quickly.

Texture

Textural choices are important in creating a sense of contrast and interest in the listener's ear, even when the composer's building blocks remain constant.

Texture refers to the different layers within the music that are combined to create the overall sound. There are three important terms related to musical textures in the barbershop style to understand:

Homophonic literally means same-sounding. This is the texture most closely associated with voice parts primarily singing the same syllables, with one voice part acting as melody and the others accompanying.

Homorhythmic means all parts singing the same rhythms. This is the sensation experienced when all four parts sing the same syllables at the same time. Barbershop textures are primarily homorhythmic.

Sections of an arrangement featuring different rhythms, e.g., baritone/tenor backtime and bass on neutral syllables emulating a bass guitar and drums, are still considered homophonic. These would be classified as non-homorhythmic or *polyrhythmic*. Successful barbershop arrangements typically feature passages of polyrhythmic textures that converged back to homorhythm.

Using neutral syllables to emulate instruments is a common method of developing contrasting textures. The most often is the case with the bass emulating a bass guitar, providing either a walking bass line against syncopated melody and harmony parts, or syncopation against more simplistic rhythms from the treble trio. These textures are frequently found in songs featuring rhythmic thematic elements.

Note the bass line syncopation against the lead in Figure 26.11 in measures 5–7 and the downbeat-driven instrumentation in measure 14. Note also how the texture converges back to homorhythm in measures 8–13 right as the lyrics feature the title of the song.

Figure 26.11

"You Took Advantage of Me," words and music by Lorenz Hart and Richard Rodgers. Arranged by Aaron Dale.

Ensemble Considerations

Chorus Versus Quartet Arrangements

Arrangements intended for choruses often feature slightly different development techniques than those intended for just four voices. A chorus can stagger breathe, allowing for longer phrases. Choruses also design larger productions including staging, use of props, and choreography. This can make it difficult for featured dancers or actors to fully contribute vocally. A quartet may not be able to convey that same sense of performance grandeur as would a chorus. Understanding the performance plan for the song ahead of time can and should affect your arranging decisions.

Take, for example, "Man in the Mirror."[111] The opening phrases were built for mood setting by a chorus.

---

111 Barbershop Harmony Society, (2019, Mar 27). *Kentucky Vocal Union - Man in the Mirror (Michael Jackson cover)* [Video]. YouTube. https://youtu.be/FD3M3UMDhh4

Figure 26.12

"Man in the Mirror," words and music by Siedah Garrett and Glen Ballard. Arranged by Aaron Dale.

The song selection with something like "Man in the Mirror" comes into play. Introspective, metaphorical lyrics are typically more difficult to convey without the aid of staging and choreography for a chorus to present.

Embellishment choices will differ between chorus and quartet, as embellishments designed for high level quartets don't easily transfer to most choruses. Skilled quartet singers are able to execute a degree of rhythmic complexity that is difficult for a chorus section comprised of multiple singers with different skill levels. Focus on simplifying embellishments when arranging for a chorus—even one at the same overall level of skill as the quartet.

Similarly to a quartet of singers with unique strengths, chorus arrangements can and should be tailored to fit the strengths of a given chorus. The bass section of Toronto Northern Lights in the early 2000s was outstanding: amazing depth and clarity of tone. Steve Armstrong took advantage of this when arranging the final impact moment in the tag of "Brother, Can You Spare a Dime," allowing the treble trio to establish the final chord before the basses entered on the low octave.

Figure 26.13

"Brother, Can You Spare a Dime?" tag, arranged by Steve Armstrong to take advantage of the Toronto Northern Lights bass section.

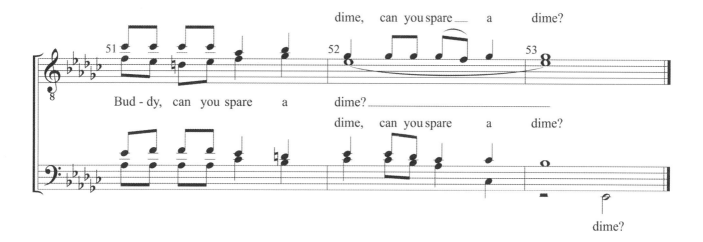

Similarly, chorus arrangements allow for longer held chords and phrases. A quartet version of the same arrangement would need to consider passing the sustained post or other devices driven by the limitations of a given singer.

Arranging for a Specific Group

It is best to arrange for a specific group—even if that ensemble isn't going to sing the song and simply serves as a blueprint for making choices in the arrangement. Find out as much as possible about the group's strengths and weaknesses to fit their voices. This concept is covered in depth in *Arranging Barbershop Vol 1,* Chapter 12. Here are a few sample questions as a starting point:

1. What's the intended use?
2. Is there a reference performance(s) of the song that you'd like to capture? Are specific elements of a performance(s) that you would like to capture?
3. What's your vision for the song?
4. Ensemble info:
    a. Ideal, or sweet spot, ranges for each part.
    b. Absolute limits for each part and any contingencies, e.g. the bass can sing down to a low E♭ as long as he doesn't stay there for a full measure.
    c. What should we avoid for each member of the quartet / section of the chorus?
    d. What type of texture fits the ensemble best, e.g., homorhythmic, syncopated with bass on downbeats, embellished, etc.
5. Think about when the ensemble is singing at its best:
    a. What is the best voicing and vowel(s)?
    b. What is the best chord, e.g. E♭ major triad, 1–5–1–3 voicing, bari on 5?
    c. Typically, which voicing is best: bari above or below the lead?
    d. How does the tenor do on fifths and roots, where the timbre and volume need to match the lead/bari?
    e. How does the bass do singing downbeats against syncopation?
6. Which voices can be featured?
    a. Who can post, and on what notes / vowels? For how long at the end of a song?
7. Anything else I should know?

Intended Use: Contest Versus Show

As of this writing in 2023, each barbershop organization had slightly different guidelines as to what was acceptable for use in contest. The Barbershop Harmony Society's Contest and Judging Rules provide both guidelines for what constitutes good barbershop, as well as specific rules related to elements of the style.[112] Global organizations who hold contests such as Harmony, Inc., BinG! (Barbershop in Germany), BABS (British Association of Barbershop Singers), LABBS (Ladies Association of British Barbershop Singers), IABS (Irish Association of Barbershop Singers), Holland Harmony, BIBA (Barbershop of IBeria Association), SNOBS (Society of Nordic Barbershop Singing), BHA (Barbershop Australia), and BHNZ (Barbershop New Zealand) all follow BHS contest rules. Sweet Adelines International have different rules related to what constitutes an acceptable arrangement.[113] While the rules are similar to BHS, there are some important differences, e.g., some organizations have time limits for two-song contest sets.

When writing a contest arrangement, ensure it fits within the guidelines of the competition in which the group would like to participate. Much of this comes down to the choice of chord vocabulary and polyrhythmic textures. If it is only for show, query the group regarding how much they want it to sound like contestable barbershop. If they have no preference, honoring the original song and source inspiration performance is a good starting point. While one may interject their own personal taste and choices, focusing first on making it sound like the original typically leads to success. This includes utilizing recognizable rhythms, melody hooks, and chord progressions from the source recording. This concept applies for both contest and show arrangements.

---

112 https://files.barbershop.org/PDFs/Contests-Judging/CJ_Handbook.ver_14.2_Jul_2022.pdf
113 https://sweetadelines.com

Consider the following arrangement, arranged for Musical Island Boys, the 2014 BHS International Quartet Champions, for use in contest. The song is "Ain't Too Proud to Beg," as sung by The Temptations.[114] The arrangement leverages the form, melody, original harmonizations, original rhythms, and as many of the iconic moments as possible.[115] It also features the musical elements expected in contest, including converging to homorhythmic texture after the first phrase, heading into the title of the song.

Figure 26.14

"Ain't Too Proud to Beg," words and music by Edward Holland Jr. and Norman Whitfield. Arranged by Aaron Dale.

114 The Temptations. (2019, Jul 4). *Ain't Too Proud to Beg* [Audio]. YouTube. https://youtu.be/_ObVQPBD0Uw

115 Barbershop Harmony Society. (2019, Mar 30). *Musical Island Boys - Ain't Too Proud to Beg (Temptations cover)* [Video]. YouTube. https://youtu.be/YZ2h7Qeaxww

Sometimes a show arrangement starts with the core musical elements suitable for a barbershop contest but then strays for the sake of development. Consider the following arrangement of "Come On, Get Happy."[116] It starts off with simple harmonies and texture, as the original would have. It then takes a turn toward vocal jazz in the second half of the arrangement.

Figure 26.15

"Come On, Get Happy," words and music by Danny Janssen and Wes Farrell. Arranged by Aaron Dale.

116 Trevor Bruger. (2009, Jul 21). *Realtime in Australia performing Come on Get Happy* [Video]. YouTube. https://youtu.be/ KNcstXgGOuA

Conclusion

Harmonizing the melody is just the beginning of the arranging process. The arranger can aid in creating an interesting, exciting, emotional, and memorable experience for both performer and audience by exploring various elements within the song.

Part C.
Advanced Considerations

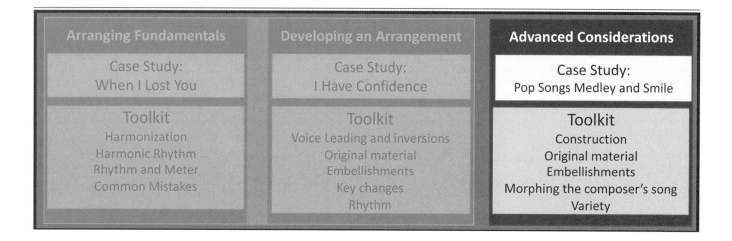

Part C, Advanced Considerations, expands on previous concepts, delving into a variety of challenges and choices that experienced arrangers use to create exciting musical journeys for talented performers. While it might be tempting to jump right into these advanced arranging topics, the content assumes that the reader possesses expertise and experience covered in Part A and Part B in order to gain the maximum benefit of the content in Part C.

Chapter 27. Advanced Arranging Overview

Steve Tramack provides an executive summary of some of the core considerations included in this part of the book, including a step-by-step case study of Intermediate Arranging in action, along with a number of deep-dive chapters covering key topics for arrangers looking to build their skills.

Chapter 28. Arranging for A-level Groups Case Study

Clay Hine provides an in-depth look into arranging for one of the top performing ensembles in the barbershop style, the 2017 BHS International Quartet Champions, Main Street. Clay explores how the personality of the individuals and the ensemble play a major role in determining choices made in the arrangement, while considering inspirations and intended impacts of two very different arrangements. Compared with the other case studies in *Arranging Barbershop Vol. 2*, this is more of a clean-sheet approach required for arranging specifically for a top ensemble.

Chapter 29. Advanced Arranging Topics

David Wright leads a thorough review of challenges facing experienced arrangers and presents options for addressing these challenges. Filled with over a hundred examples coupled with David's observations, this chapter serves as an advanced arranging class unto itself; in fact, this served as the curriculum for David's Advanced Arranging Class at Harmony University.

Chapter 30. Advanced Development Topics

Aaron Dale provides deeper insight into development using some of the key musical building blocks: lyrics, melody, and harmony. While these concepts are covered elsewhere in *Arranging Barbershop Vol. 2*, this chapter explores how choices made by the arranger affect the outcome on the listener. He provides some in-depth guidance on topics such as use of chord vocabulary, voice leading and alternate harmonizations to create a desired mood.

Chapter 31. Advanced Rhythm Topics

In the final chapter of *Arranging Barbershop Vol. 2*, Aaron Dale digs into the topic of rhythmic development as only a master arranger and percussionist can do. The concepts in this chapter build on material from the rest of this book and explore groove, influences from different musical styles, and construction of complex rhythmic textures that sound balanced to the listener. Of particular interest is how Aaron explores finding the balance between the homorhythmic textures indigenous to barbershop and iconic rhythmic hooks from popular music.

Chapter 27.
Advanced Arranging Overview

By Steve Tramack

In Part A, we focused on the core set of skills required to successfully harmonize a melody in the barbershop style. We discussed in detail the various options for harmonizing non-chord tones and a strategy for part-by-part harmonization. Key concepts such as harmonic rhythm and the impact of rhythm and embellishment, when dictated by sustained melody notes, provide the foundation for creating an arrangement that both sounds like barbershop and will be enjoyable to sing.

In Part B, we focused on the next step in the arranging journey—developing an arrangement. This part explored making more creative choices. What should the overall structure of this arrangement be? Should I consider developing original material, such as an introduction or a tag? How should the arrangement vary from section to section and phrase to phrase, e.g., A1 to A2? This part of the book provided a case study in developing an arrangement and provided a rich toolbox of techniques and approaches to provide musical interest and contrast. Part B devotes entire chapters to embellishments, key changes, and rhythmic devices.

Part C is targeted at experienced arrangers looking for new ideas, learning from expert arrangers, and ways to overcome common challenges facing arrangers. Much in the same way as a performer builds skills and enhances techniques to enable artistic performances, this part of *Arranging Barbershop* Vol. 2 assumes deep understanding and expertise in the skills and techniques of arranging. The case study focuses more on the performer's unique attributes than on theoretical aspects, and the advanced arranging techniques chapters assume deep harmonization and development skills.

What are the prerequisites required to be successful in this advanced stage of your arranging journey?

- Deep expertise in the theory of barbershop harmony, as covered in Chapter 5 of *Arranging Barbershop Vol. 1,* including:
  - Understanding of chord qualities, inversions, and how to complete triads and seventh chords in four-part voicings
  - Understanding of voice leading and chord progressions—particularly tritone resolution tendencies
- Deep expertise in the definition of the barbershop style, as covered in Chapter 5 of *Arranging Barbershop Vol. 1*.
- Skill and experience in harmonizing a melody, as covered in Chapter 14 of *Arranging Barbershop Vol. 2*. It is assumed that the reader has extensive experience with harmonizing a melody with strong-voiced chords mapped to the harmonic rhythm of the song is key to the success of any arrangement. Further, the reader understands aspects such as harmonic rhythm, as covered in Chapter 16 and 17 of *Arranging Barbershop* Vol. 2.
- Experience in developing original material, such as introductions, interludes and tags. This is covered in Chapter 22 of *Arranging Barbershop Vol. 2*.
- Deep understanding of development techniques. This includes embellishments in Chapter 23, key changes in Chapter 24, and rhythmic development in Chapter 25 of *Arranging Barbershop Vol. 2*.

Enjoy the journey!

Chapter 28.
Case Study: Arranging for A-Level Groups

By Clay Hine

Overview

Congratulations! If you've read this far, you've probably become a master at barbershop music theory, have a found a few old or new songs gems that you were able to adapt to the barbershop style, and written several arrangements that groups really like singing. And now last year's 2nd place silver medalists from the Barbershop Harmony Society international contest have emailed you and asked you to write an arrangement to help them make the jump to gold! How exciting, scary, and humbling! Now what?

Actually, arranging for A-level groups could mean arranging for the next international quartet champion, but it could also mean arranging for any ensemble who has a good chance of scoring in the A range, an average score of 81 or greater, in a BHS contest.[117] Even more generally, it could mean arranging for any fairly accomplished ensemble, whether they're trying to win a gold medal or just trying to be entertaining at their next performance. Regardless, these groups share similar qualities that might help drive how we write an arrangement for them. The items below are items that we might consider for any arrangement, regardless of the intended ensemble, but they're also aspects we might weigh more heavily when arranging for more accomplished groups.

Singing Level

Here's a factor that might seem obvious: A-level groups usually sing really well. This may mean they have better individual resonance, artistic vocal delivery, in-tune singing, ringing chords—or that they excel at any number of aspects of quality singing. In all cases, this also means that they typically have more of an awareness of and reliance on their vocal strengths and weaknesses. In fact, a key aspect that defines an A-level group is just that: they have awareness of what they do well and what they don't do well, and their success has come with material that aligns with this.

Lower A-level quartets usually have one standout song that suits them well, while higher A-level quartets often possess a repertoire of songs that showcase their strengths. There may be some chords they sing that ring better or are more engaging than other chords due to range, how the individual voices best line-up on chords, voice leading, etc. As the arranger, it's crucial to recognize these vocal qualities and craft arrangements that highlight the ensemble's best features. There are several aspects of this, which we'll explore further.

Character in the Vocal Delivery

Usually, higher level quartets have a combination of a great ensemble sound and one or two voices that really add character to ensemble delivery. It could be a lead with a great lyric delivery, a bass with amazing presence over a certain vocal range, a tenor who has a great full voice or a sweet falsetto, or a bari who's great at helping chords ring when below or above the lead. Even with a chorus, it could be an especially passionate delivery, or a bass section that's really driving and dominant. A great example is Vocal Majority's "Hey Mr. Leader Man/Strike Up the Band."[118] A chorus may also feature an exciting, clear and crisp sound. A great example is Kentucky Vocal Union's "Footloose."[119]

---

117 Visit www.barbershop.org and search for "Contest and Judging Handbook" for more details about what constitutes the various scoring levels in a BHS contest.

118 Barbershop Harmony Society. (1985, July 6). *Vocal Majority: Hey Mr. Leader Man/Strike Up the Band* [Audio]. YouTube. https://www.youtube.com/watch?v=VarDUkx6pBI

119 Barbershop Harmony Society. (2012, July 6). *Kentucky Vocal Union: Footloose* [Video]. YouTube. https://www.youtube.com/watch?v=_2oCPyUdCUs

Maybe the group has a great feel for swing or for singing homorhythmically. Or maybe the group has a great solo feature with three parts doing backtime. Or maybe a hundred other things that vocally allow an ensemble to best connect with their music and with an audience. Maybe they're very aware of this or do it naturally. As an arranger, you'd need to listen to recordings of them and think, "What about this delivery is, or isn't, uniquely engaging?" With that singing ability and vocal character, ensembles at this level have often found or begun to find their unique personality.

Personality

Higher-level groups also usually have a better sense of their ensemble personality, and it could be that they are a higher level group because of this awareness. Maybe their delivery is especially poignant when they sing about their first love, lost love, or the love they haven't found. Or maybe they don't sing touching ballads well, but they excel at easy swing, blues, or straight-eighth uptunes. In the case of a quartet, any of these strengths might come from one or two individuals. For example, if the ensemble is funny, it's usually because each person naturally plays a unique role in this. One individual might be a great joke teller, one might be a great straight man, and maybe the other two are good at creating a setting or just good at laughing, or not laughing, at the comedy. Maybe someone's solo voice gets especially intimate when telling a certain story, e.g., Main Street's "I'll Take You Dreaming."[120] Some groups have a personality that says "we love ringing chords," e.g., Gotcha's "Wait 'Til the Sun Shines, Nellie."[121] With a chorus, the personality often comes from the director or other musical leaders.

Song Choice

The ensemble's personality will also highly influence their song choice. Some higher-level groups will come to you with a specific song in mind, some may just have a type of song they want, and some may not know. They just know they've liked your arranging style. In any of these cases, it'll help you as an arranger to know why. Why choose this specific song, why choose this specific type of song, or what about my style do you like? Every song you arrange should have a story and sense of musical development that tells that story, and any of the embellishments and arranging devices that you find in this book could contribute to that. With a higher-level ensemble, how you do this, how you plan for the song to unfold and develop, and how you plan for the ensemble to connect with this is likely to be an even more significant part of the result. And all of these overlapping elements overlap with vision.

Vision

It's important to align with the group on their vision and your vision for the song. They may have a specific thought on what story motivates a certain song, how a song unfolds, what keeps the story interesting, how a certain section of a song might be delivered really well, or how the song ends. You may have a different idea that may be better, but in any case, the performer's vision—especially when the performer is at an A-level—can be a great resource and great help in your ability to create a setting that allows the ensemble to create a great performance through the arrangement.

Different arrangers have different processes they go through to create an arrangement from start to finish. What matters most is the end result: the performance. I remember Ed Waesche saying that "music doesn't exist on paper." An arrangement is only great when it helps create a great performance. With that, I have my own general process that I use. It varies depending on the song, but it always involves envisioning the ensemble's performance of the song that I'm arranging. I'll visualize as many details as I can imagine, and I'll try to manuscript the arrangement of the performance I'm envisioning.

---

120 Barbershop Harmony Society (2017, July 6). Main Street: I'll Take You Dreaming [Video]. YouTube. https://www.youtube.com/watch?v=0Om5heprR9Y.

121 Barbershop Harmony Society (2004, July 3). Gotcha: Wait 'Til The Sun Shines, Nellie [Video]. YouTube. https://www.youtube.com/watch?v=8tqn0KIwTL8

Bringing it All Together

With all of the items above, you often have more defined tools to work with when arranging for A-level groups, mostly because A-level groups are more aware, consciously or unconsciously, of the aspects of their ensemble that work or don't work especially well. All of the notes above are just suggestions to help find those characteristics of the ensemble that may help create that amazing performance of your chart. You may want to re-read the above through that lens, and then we'll dive into a couple of real-world examples or arrangements that were created with a very specific ensemble and for a very specific setting or impact.

Case Studies

I was fortunate enough to have been able to create several arrangements for Main Street (MS), the BHS 2017 International Quartet Champions. To say it was fun would be a huge understatement. Helping any group at this level create uniquely engaging and memorable performances is extremely rewarding, and having the chance to play a part in that and watch the success of the end result is a pretty special. Looking back through the introduction of this section, the experience I was fortunate to have with Main Street really helps exemplify several of the aspects mentioned in the introduction of this section, and I believe highlights some things to generally consider when arranging for A-level ensembles.

First of all, the members of Main Street are exceptional individual singers. As an ensemble, they sing at a high A-level, and they have a great sense of what works best for them. The tenor and baritone have some wonderful qualities in their vocal delivery. In this ensemble, the tenor and the baritone aren't necessarily big vocal personalities, but they are especially good at blending and helping to glue together the vocal impact of the ensemble. The lead and bass also do this very well, but a lot of the character of the ensemble comes from their delivery. The lead is outstanding at turning this character on and off, so throughout much of his range he can focus on blending or adding character, depending on what's appropriate, e.g., supporting deliveries that are fun/comedic, emotional/dramatic, and intimate/sensitive. The bass is extremely present and can use this to help ring chords, which the ensemble does very well, and to add a great vocal character to the ensemble sound.

Personality is really where this ensemble shines the most uniquely. They actually started with a very clear vision of their personality, which is unusual. Most quartets—even high A-level quartets—need time together to see how the ensemble develops and how the individual voices and personalities work together to have the best impact as an ensemble. Probably because of their backgrounds, this group knew who they wanted to be even before their first rehearsal. With that, much of their successful song selection comes down to aligning the music with their personality.

A lot of what we think of as classic barbershop has very strong roots in Vaudeville and Vaudeville-style performances. Vaudeville performances were heartfelt, silly, straightforward, dorky, charming, goofy, genuine, very accessible, G-rated, and just fun. Barbershop has been through a lot of evolution since then, and today we enjoy the barbershop style through the lens of a lot of different genres of music—jazz, doo-wop, classic rock, disco, country, contemporary rock, classical, musical theater—just about every genre of music can be enjoyed through lens of the barbershop style. Still, there's something about classic vaudeville/barbershop that's uniquely fun. Just watch how much tens of millions of people every year love watching Disney's Dapper Dans. All four members of Main Street had a great deal of performing experience and were eager to bring the love and enjoyment of classic barbershop delivery and style to audiences. They love barbershop and entertaining audiences so much it was just easy for them to take that enjoyment to the stage.

With that, their vision for how songs unfolded always supported that personality, whether the songs were light and fun, silly and endearing, or sweet and poignant. Here are two examples of this. These pieces and end performances couldn't be more different, except that both were developed and arranged with Main Street's voices, ensemble strengths, personality, and overall vision in mind.

Case Study #1: Pop Songs Medley

Like many song ideas, the germ of this idea came from watching another performance. Disney's Dapper Dans had a piece they did in their inimitable style that was a medley of three songs done by contemporary boy bands.[122] MS thought something like this could translate well to their own style of delivery. In fact, they sent me an audio recording of the Dapper Dans performing it, and the audience response was huge as the quartet went from one song to another and the audience recognized that a vaudeville-style barbershop quartet was singing a song by the Backstreet Boys.

Most of the arranging thought process on this song revolved around MS's unique personality. Several factors played into how to bring this concept to life for MS on a barbershop contest stage:

1. The *setup*: We don't get a chance to go through an elaborate verbal setup for a song in a barbershop contest. The rules say we can have some verbal setup, but this was going to take more than a few words, which means it would probably take some original material. And with that, we're creating the story.
2. The *story:* Songs need a journey to feel complete. That doesn't necessarily mean a detailed story, but it does mean that pieces need to feel like they develop and lead the audience through different experiences that connect and build from each other. A collage of songs can be good. A medley of tunes from a Broadway show or a movie can be a fun tribute piece. But a journey gives much more opportunity to connect with and enthrall an audience with your personality. And to help with this journey, we'll need construction.
3. The *construction:* How do we stitch several different songs together so that it all feels like not just one story, but one complete song? It includes the pop songs themselves. Which ones do we use, and why? But let's not forget that has to be barbershop. Not all contemporary songs lend themselves to the barbershop style, so we need to choose songs that will allow for arrangements that don't stray too far from that.

One other big factor with song selection, especially in a piece like this, is that familiar is good. Audiences like the familiar. Many songs have forms like AABA or ABAC. You find when you hear the A section and then hear it again with a different twist, it's satisfying to revisit that material. From a broader perspective, audiences also like to hear familiar songs, especially when your personality is that of a vaudeville-era performer and especially when the impact of the performance comes from the audience recognizing the comedy in the juxtaposition of a vaudeville-style quartet singing contemporary songs. At a barbershop contest, it could be that a lot of audience members aren't familiar enough with contemporary material to get it, and the comedy you're hoping for goes right over their heads.

Again, the ensemble's personality is what drove a lot of this process. I personally don't typically like to share a complete chart until I feel like it's finished, mainly because there are elements of the arrangement that may not have the same impact without seeing the whole piece. This chart was an exception due to its complexity and a need for it to fit them every step of the way for the desired impact. There was a lot of continual collaboration along the way in terms of constructing the song, deciding which pop songs to use, and developing the story. Let's dive in.

Construction

If this piece is more than just a collection of pop songs, how does it fit together in a musical way? In this case, what seemed to be a good formula was:

1. Introduce the song to set up this story (verse)
2. Feature a body song that tells the basic story (chorus)
3. Offer pop songs after the "body" song that show what the story means (around four pop songs)
4. Revisit the body song for development with different lyrics and musical texture (chorus)
5. Add quick snippets of other songs to re-emphasize the point of the story and add more development
6. End with a funny tag that wraps it up, which risks derailing a completely thought-out comedy song

---

122 Walt Disney Company (2013, February 13). *Dapper Dans: Boy Band Medley* [Video]. YouTube. https://www.youtube.com/watch?v=8igP6chM_Ng

Story

"What motivates MS to sing a medley of pop songs?" The answer to that is the story of the song. In this construction, this is the story that the chorus needs to tell. MS loves old songs—that's always been a key part of their personality. At international competitions, we all see how barbershop continues to evolve, and a question MS might ask is, "What if it evolved so much, it got silly?" With that, we could generally find a story that says, "Here's what we might hear one day if barbershop keeps evolving." That's the general framework I started with when I started looking for the chorus of the arrangement. For the chorus, I saw three options:

1. Write an original piece, although something somewhat familiar is usually preferable.
2. Find a piece that already tells a story that would string these tunes together.
3. Find a piece that told part of the story and make lyric changes to round it out.

We landed on number three when MS's baritone suggested a song he found called "These Will Be the Good Old Days (Twenty Years from Now)," which I immediately loved, partially because it was sung by my very first barbershop chorus, Detroit #1, which my dad directed.

I was familiar with it, and although it's not a well-known song, it sounds like a familiar song—very light, fun, and really sounds like barbershop. It had lyrics that told part of the story yet could be altered. And with that, a more detailed story started to emerge: "You've heard MS sing about the good old days, well, this is what the good old days will sound like twenty years from now if we take the evolution of barbershop to its comedic extreme." Before looking at lyric changes to the chorus to tell this story, I jumped back a step to look at what might set up this story.

Setup

The setup starts as soon as the quartet walks on stage. In fact, at an international quartet competition, it starts when the emcee announces them, because the audience knows that MS is next, they know MS, and they already have an expectation for what MS does. For the setup, I assumed they were onstage with these audience expectations and that the verse would start the story from there.

MS is known for tunes about the old days or from the old days. They even sang "Bring Back Those Good Old Days." It seemed aligned with their established personality to have the story start there. Different arrangers have different approaches to writing original material, several of which are detailed in chapters of this book. I usually start with lyrics and rhythm/pacing before composing a melody that supports the flow of the story. I'll write a story and use www.rhymezone.com for words that should rhyme, tell the story in rhythm with a musical flow, and fill in the melody along the way to support that story. I started with that and came up with this first draft, including a rough chart of the chorus with the original lyrics, just to get a feel for how these fit together.

Figure 28.1

First draft of "These Will Be the Good Ol' Days (Twenty Years From Now)."

Chorus

I didn't love this first cut at the verse. It told a story but seemed too long—it's really a setup for a story. But even the story is just a setup to get to the real funny section: pop songs done by a barbershop quartet. Part of telling a story is telling it efficiently. If you can tell the same story in one minute that you can tell in two minutes, you should tell it in one minute. Similarly, with original compositions, if I can set up a story in twenty-eight measures or twelve measures and nothing adds interest in those additional sixteen measures, then the shorter route is probably better. After chewing on this for a couple of days, I cut it up a lot, reshaped a bit, and came up with a shorter—and better—verse.

Figure 28.2

Second draft of the verse for "These Will Be the Good Ol' Days (Twenty Years From Now)."

Story

For my process with this chart—or any chart I do—filling in the story came down to envisioning the performance. With a verse that was too long and involved, it was tough to envision MS launching into the chorus of the song to tell the type of story I'd thought about. With a setup that worked better, I could picture the quartet delivering the verse before moving into the chorus and the story. Then it was easier to picture which original lyrics didn't fit or might better fit the story. For example, "they're on the radio now" in measure 19, changed from "the ones we're living now," would draw more connection to "we're talking about pop songs."[123]

Figure 28.3

Revised lyrics in a later draft of the chorus in "These Will Be the Good Ol' Days (Twenty Years From Now)."

"Now it seems the old songs were sung by Billy Joel" is a reference to Billy Joel songs on the radio now, but it's also a direct reference to how an A-level chorus had sung a Billy Joel song a year before at the previous international contest. The line before that, "We remember when the old songs were the songs our fathers know," came about because I needed a rhyme—or, in this case, an almost rhyme—for "Joel." Sometimes lyrical lines like this are written in reverse. Because the intent of the line comes at the end, it's easier to back into a word like "know" and rhyme with a lyric that's specific, like "Joel."

123 Barbershop Harmony Society. (Oct 20, 2015). *Main Street - Pop Songs Medley (International 2015)* [Video]. YouTube. https://youtu.be/MdTS6-fbNH0?si=xQrGqP9AX1_fpnAb

Figure 28.4

Referencing Billy Joel in "These Will Be the Good Ol' Days (Twenty Years From Now)." Arranged by Clay Hine.

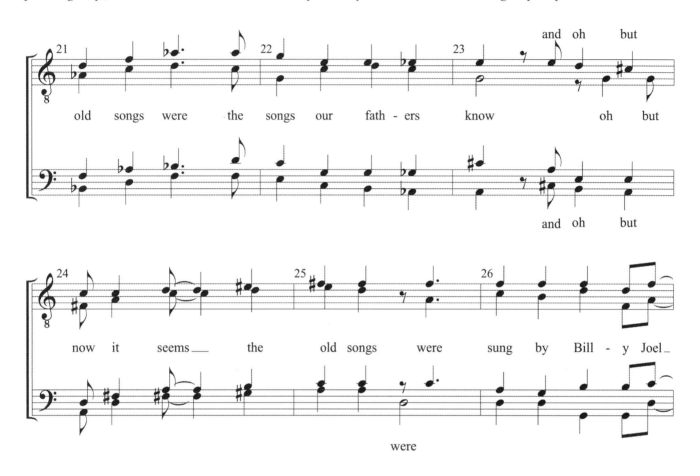

From there, the lyrics tell the rest of the story, taking the listener on a journey to the real reason for the song: "Can't wait to sing the good ol' songs twenty years from now" (original lyrics) and "those songs are that are the hit today our contests will allow" (new lyrics written to rhyme). We're almost there!

Figure 28.5

Choosing rhyming words to further the story in "These Will Be the Good Ol' Days." Arranged by Clay Hine.

Now we just need something that says "And now we'll show you what we mean," which was delivered with "here's a glimpse of what's to come / just remember when we're done / that these will be the good old songs 20 years from now."

Figure 28.6

Choosing words to convey "we'll show you what you mean" in "These Will Be The Good Ol' Days." Arranged by Clay Hine.

The process of creating the verse and chorus was less focused on the arrangement and more on the story and flow of the music. This also helps guide the arrangement itself. In a song where lyrics and their impact is a priority, the arrangement needs to stay out of the way of the song and the performer. There are certainly places where the arrangement can help emphasize strengths of individual singers or the ensemble. For example, the high lead notes at "strange" in measure 9 and the weird key change on this word in measures 9–11 highlight the agility of lead and the quartet in general.

Figure 28.7

Emphasis of "strange" with a strange key change in "These Will Be the Good Ol' Days." Arranged by Clay Hine.

There are many places in the chorus that use embellishments that sound stylistically barbershop. This helps drive the message that "we love barbershop" and takes advantage of MS's great delivery of classic barbershop progressions.

Figure 28.8

Use of embellishments in the chorus of "These Will Be the Good Ol' Days." Arranged by Clay Hine.

I also chose many of the specific rhythms and progressions around them to help emphasize a specific lyric delivery. Again, this is key when the message of the lyrics is a priority.

Figure 28.9

Use of rhythms to emphasize lyric delivery in "These Will Be the Good Ol' Days."

Speaking of lyrics, most of the main chorus lyrics were kept, other than replacing "days" with "songs." For those that knew the song before, there's still a sense of familiarity, but the lyric changes give a slightly different meaning to what was already familiar. The result is that we have a setup, story, and fortunately a few funny lines mixed in to keep the interest going. It took all of this to get to the actual original concept! Again, though, in picturing MS's personality, their vocal delivery, joy in performing, and charm with this type of story make for an engaging experience. And now we're finally at the main feature of the arrangement!

The Pop Songs

Throughout the whole process of developing the first version of the Pop Songs Medley that MS performed in 2015, we had listed more than 25 potential pop song options. These included songs in the original piece that Dapper Dans had done, songs we'd heard on the radio, songs our kids had suggested because they listen to the radio, and songs I found on YouTube when I checked to see which songs had the most hits, many of which were songs we'd never heard of.

Between the two choruses, we needed three to four of these songs. We also needed and a few songs at the tag where we'd just use snippets, such as the main title lyric of the song. There were a few factors that went into narrowing this list down:

- The longer pieces that fit into the middle of the medley needed to be songs that would not only lend themselves to barbershop, but also be easily recognizable when done in this context.
- Ideally, the songs themselves would be recognizable. Again, the challenge here was that many of the people in the audience might not listen to current pop music, and with that, I looked at:
  - Songs that were pop hits at one point, but may not be any more.
  - Songs that much of the younger portion of the crowd audience would enjoy so much that their reaction would make it fun for the portion of the audience that didn't know the songs.
  - Songs that were so fun when done in a dorky barbershop style that they'd be entertaining regardless of their recognizability.

As you can see in the chart, we landed on these pieces for the middle:

- "Oops I Did It Again" (Britney Spears)
- "Bye Bye Bye" (N' Sync)
- "So What" (Pink)
- "Uptown Funk" (Mark Ronson / Bruno Mars)

And these pieces for the end:

- "Poker Face" (Lady Gaga)
- "SexyBack" (Justin Timberlake)
- "Moves Like Jagger" (Maroon 5)
- "All About That Bass" (Meghan Trainor)
- "Gangnam Style" (Psy)
- "Thriller" (Michael Jackson)

Now I'm at the point where it's time to arrange pop songs in the barbershop style! Finally, the reason for doing this whole piece!

What's the first step? That's easy! Download the sheet music to the iconic version of the songs from Sheet Music Direct. This gives me the right notes I don't have to plunk them out myself. More importantly, it helps me easily see the iconic musical feature of the original song. With that, I could listen to the original, think about the key iconic feature, see it on the sheet music, and make sure I captured that in the arrangement so that the result would sound like the original. We don't always do this; in fact, many times we strive to create a new setting of a song. But in this case, what was critical was that the audience both recognize the song and also relate it to the version that made the song famous.

Oops I Did It Again and So What

It turns out that in a lot of driving 4/4 pop songs, the driving downbeat is iconic. You might notice that in the bass line of "Oops I Did It Again" and parts of "So What," which I tried to capture in the barbershop versions.[124]

---

124 Barbershop Harmony Society. (2015, Oct 20). *Main Street - Pop Songs Medley (International 2015)* [Video]. YouTube. https://youtu.be/MdTS6-fbNH0

Figure 28.10

Harmonization of "Oops I Did It Again" in the "Pop Songs Medley." Words and music by By Rami Yacoub and Max Martin. Arranged by Clay Hine.

Figure 28.11

Harmonization of "So What" in the "Pop Songs Medley." Words and music by By Shellback, Alecia Moore and Max Martin. Arranged by Clay Hine.

Pop songs are also often hit because of the vocal character of the singer, so I tried to give appropriate notes to the MS lead to let the character he has in his high range be a key feature. Note "sent from above I'm not that innocent" in measures 51–53 of Figure 28.12.

Figure 28.12

Lead feature voice crossing in "Pop Songs Medley."

Bye Bye Bye

"Bye Bye Bye" sounds a lot like a well-known old barbershop song—"Bye Bye Blues"—so you'll notice I used bell chorus on these words to go into and get out of this song to try to give it a charmingly dorky barbershop feel.

Figure 28.13

Chorus from "Bye Bye Blues." Arranged by Lem Childers.

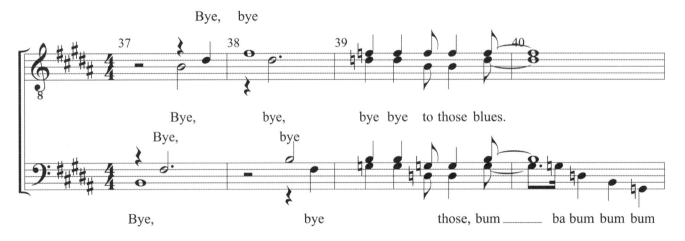

Figure 28.14

Reference to "Bye Bye Blues" leading into "Bye Bye Bye," within the "Pop Songs Medley." Words and music by By Jake Schulze, Kristian Lundin and Andreas Carlsson. Arranged by Clay Hine.

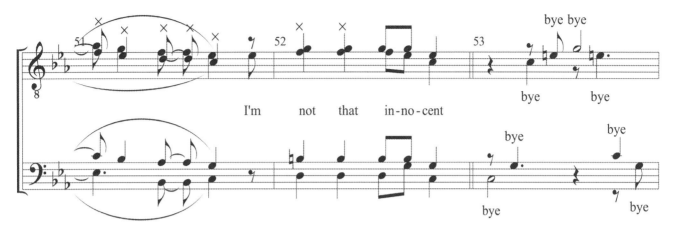

Bye Bye Bye. Words and Music by Kristian Lundin, Jake Schulze and Andreas Carlsson

Uptown Funk

Uptown Funk was interesting because the version I arranged included many of the elements shown earlier. MS very brilliantly went with a different direction, took the "dorky barbershop" concept even farther, and turned this into a dramatic barbershop ballad, complete with a soaring climax.

Figure 28.15

Harmonization of "Uptown Funk" in the "Pop Songs Medley." Words and music by By Charles Wilson, Rudolph Taylor, Philip Lawrence, Jeff Bhasker, Devon Gallaspy, Mark Ronson, Nicholaus Williams, Bruno Mars, Robert Wilson, Ronnie Wilson, and Lonnie Simmons. Arranged by Clay Hine.

Uptown Funk. Words and Music by Mark Ronson, Bruno Mars, Jeff Bhaskar and Philip Lawrence

Second Chorus

After a quick transition, return to the chorus. Because it's the second chorus, it's delivered differently, using:

- A stomp for dramatic effect, which allows more passion after the delivery of the pop songs
- An accelerando to build momentum into a big finish
- Some different lyrics to finish out the story
- A few melody changes to allow for some fun barbershop chords, like measures 117–119, "An' remember where it all began"

Figure 28.16

Treatment of the second chorus of "These Will Be the Good Ol' Days" in the "Pop Songs Medley."

Pop Songs Medley

More Pop Songs

With all of that excitement and sense of driving to a tag, it made sense to insert a few more interruptions in an urgent, slightly frantic way. Both the tension and need for conclusion were heightened by the contrasting, back-and-forth between snippets of articulated pop songs and the long, smooth phrases of the "twenty years from now" lyric. This time it uses:

- "Poker Face," emphasizing the driving downbeat through the bass' presence
- "SexyBack," emphasizing the driving downbeat and lead character
- "Moves Like Jagger," as a recognizable hook
- "All About That Bass," which lyrically fits great in a barbershop song
- "Gangham Style," where the harmony parts emulate rhythmic background. The lead gets to be visually funny, which he does uniquely well
- Finally, "Thriller," which has a timeless appeal as a pop song

Figure 28.17

Interruptions and interpolations in the second the chorus of "Pop Songs Medley."

12

Pop Songs Medley

Pop Songs Medley

harmony parts trail off, Myron stops Tony,
says "wait someone did that last year...", etc

"Thriller" was also relevant as it had recently been done at BHS international, which gave a great reason to motivate a tag. As the last few pieces progressed, the medley gets more frantic, so that by the time Thriller comes around, it feels like "these pop songs are making everyone crazy." With a very few spoken words to break the tension, like "someone's actually already done this in contest," we can change direction and express, "Let's go back to what we do well: sing the old song," which is where this entire adventure started!

Figure 28.18

Spoken words leading to the tag in "Pop Songs Medley."

It's important to note the use of talking to continue the story. It was minimal, intended to transition into the tag and help break the intentional musical franticness. As a musical device, it's appropriate to include intentional, purposeful talking in a chart like this—assuming, of course, there is someone in the ensemble who you can envision delivering these lines appropriately.

As we enter the tag, we call back to a familiar piece from earlier in the chart, "Bye Bye Bye." It is also similar to well-known and well-loved classics: the bell chords of "Bye, Bye Blues," and the "Bye and Bye" in the tag of "Wait 'Til the Sun Shines, Nellie."

Figure 28.19

Tag of "Wait 'Til the Sun Shines, Nellie." Arranged by Buzz Haeger.

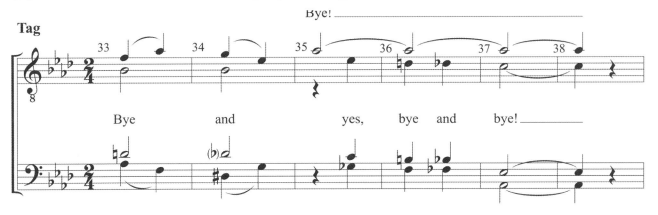

There's then a last echo that wraps up the entire journey with the same message we started the song with, while adding the intent that "no matter what, we'll keep doing our thing." It not only provides a satisfying end cap, but also allows the audience to celebrate MS endearing themselves with comedy, bringing their personality to new styles of songs. In the end, MS will keep doing what we all love most about barbershop.

Figure 28.20

Tag of "Pop Songs Medley." Arranged by Clay Hine.

Additional Revisions

As a final note, this song was also unique in that it was intentionally updated multiple times after the initial performance in 2015, once each for the 2016 and 2017 BHS international competitions.[125][126] MS wanted the chance to deliver the same message with different pop songs, so we again went through many options to find pieces that worked in barbershop and allowed their individual and ensemble strengths to shine. It's actually interesting to see how many pop tunes can generally work in barbershop—at least for 16–24 measures.

Ones that worked especially well included:

- "Livin' La Vida Loca" (Ricky Martin)
- "Play that Funky Music" (Wild Cherry)
- "Superstar" (The Carpenters)

Figure 28.21

Additional songs featured in later versions of "Pop Songs Medley." "Livin' La Vida Loca" words and music by Desmond Child and Robi Rosa. "Superstar" words and music by Leon Russell and Bonnie Sheridan. Arranged by Clay Hine.

2

Superstar. Words and Music by Leon Russell and Bonnie Sheridan

Overall, there were probably 100 different songs we considered over the contest life of this piece. One tune that we kept trying to work in, but never seemed to fit right, was "Single Ladies (Put a Ring on It)." Just for fun, here's what we tried.

Figure 28.22

Segment of "Single Ladies (Put a Ring on It)," scrapped from "Pop Songs Medley." Words and music by Terius Nash, Christopher Stewart, Beyonce Knowles, and Thaddis Harrell. Arranged by Clay Hine.

Single Ladies (Put a Ring on it). Words and Music by Terius Nash, Christopher Stewart, Beyonce Knowles and Thaddius Harrell

Again, this particular piece was very unusual in a lot of ways, but as you arrange for groups with very specific and defined personalities, you might find that there are other unique things that end up being part of the whole process.

Case Study #2: Smile

MS didn't sing a lot of ballads, and the ones they did sing really needed to be especially relevant and personal to them. I think you'll find this to be the case with most A-level groups. Ballads are challenging because in order for them to connect with an audience, especially at a very high level, the performer needs to be vulnerable and share feelings that a lot of us don't easily share. It's difficult to achieve this unless you as a performer can easily connect with the story of the song. This limits the choices of ballads for any group, but even more so for an A-level group. Most high level groups don't sing many ballads, but when they do, the result is often pretty great, because they've chosen material that helps them tell a story that has very special and personal meaning to them.

By 2017, MS had competed at international competition every year since 2011 and had amazing success. Success at that level is incredibly rewarding, and it's also incredibly consuming. It takes a lot of effort, focus, time away from family, and time away from careers, making it hard to sustain for more than a few years. MS had decided after finishing 3rd place in 2015 and 2016, that they'd keep doing performances but wanted to jump off of the contest roller coaster. Then in early 2017, they decided that they'd give international just one more go-around, and they'd really focus on being prepared a little earlier and what they liked most about MS, which was having fun and making people smile. In fact, they wanted to spend five songs showing everyone a bit of zany material, some good singing, some really fun comedy, a few poignant moments, and then in their last song, leave the audience with the message they'd hoped all of these different faces of MS would make clear. To accomplish this, they asked me to arrange "Smile," with an original verse to the start the song that would frame MS's intentions in telling the story.[127]

A wonderful arrangement of Smile already existed, arranged by the great Tom Gentry a few decades ago.[128] Tom's arrangement has been done by many ensembles including BHS international quartet champions The New Tradition,[129] Nightlife,[130] and Ringmasters.[131] The fact that many ensembles of different levels have performed it successfully is really a testament to the quality of this chart. It was also a part of MS's vision because they wanted their performance to be completely fresh and to really have a different motivation and intention than what we'd seen before.

Tom's iconic version comes with a high, loud tag, arranged by The New Tradition's baritone, Bobby Gray Jr. Yet MS wanted it to end softly and intimately and very simply. Would it be better if it were paired with another song in a medley? That could certainly help give it a different message than what people had heard before from this song. So we'd initially looked at doing this in a medley with a new song that was very popular at that time, "Audition" from the movie *La La Land*.

This was a ballad for a really good quartet. It ended up being fairly straightforward in terms of construction: Verse—Chorus—Repeat part of Chorus—Tag. All of the additional information above is to help you understand that there was a lot of personalization that went into filling in all of the details of how this chart developed and helped MS tell the story they wanted to tell with this piece. Again, because an A-level group usually has a really good handle on their own personality, this presents a great opportunity for an arranger to help them bring a message that's meaningful to an audience.

---

127 Due to copyright holder restrictions, we are unable to include sheet music examples of "Smile" within this book. Instead, we've included links to performances referenced, as well as any original material written by the arranger.

128 Barbershop Harmony Society. (2018, Feb 16). *The New Tradition - Clown Medley and Smile (live on the 1988 AIC Show)* [Video]. YouTube. https://youtu.be/Ql8dahHOf6c?t=367

129 Barbershop Harmony Society. (2018, February 16). *The New Tradition: Smile* [Video]. YouTube. https://youtu.be/Ql8dahHOf6c?t=360

130 Rob Menaker. (2013, October 8). *Nightlife: Smile* [Video]. YouTube. https://youtu.be/_ixv8LKnZzM

131 Barbershop Harmony Society. (2020, October 23). *Ringmasters: Smile* [Video]. YouTube. https://youtu.be/4SBxjHyZ4KU

Where I can, I like to arrange from the top to the bottom of a song, and this comes back to the technique where I envision a performance as I arrange. For the "Pop Songs Medley" there were reasons why it was easier to skip around a bit. In this song, I started at the beginning and jumped right into writing the verse. Just like the "Pop Songs Medley," I assumed that the audience knew the quartet, understood their personality, and had expectations based on that, so the verse would start from there and then take the audience on a brief journey to the chorus. The entire intent of the verse was to give context to the chorus, and that's where MS's intention and reason for wanting to deliver this message comes in. All of the exposition about MS, their history, where they were now in their lives, and what the experience with MS had meant to them, was the context. Writing the verse, then, was about putting that story into a concise, poetic, musical pattern. Rhymezone, here I come!

"We've had a great several years together, been awed by great the responses you've given us, enjoyed all of the laughs, worked hard to have fun, and will always remember this" became, "Oh what a time what moments we've shared, our mem'ries together can't be compared."[132]

Figure 28.23

Original verse, written and arranged by Clay Hine.

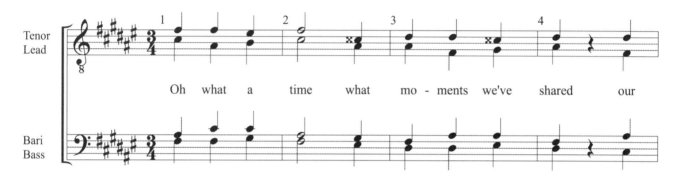

Again, the goal is to find a very concise way of stating their intent, putting it in a musical, slightly rhythmic, context. Worth noting, I did toy with swapping "moments" and "mem'ries," but this seemed to flow a little easier.

Next was the idea of, "We hope you've enjoyed it as much as we have, and through all of the zany material, hopefully good singing, really fun comedy, few poignant moments, we want to leave you with this one thought that sums up the reason we do what we do" became, "We hope that we've brought you a laugh and a song and one simple thought that you'll all take along."

132 Barbershop Harmony Society. (2017, Jul 10). *Main Street - Smile* [Video]. YouTube. https://youtu.be/iPEY2SE1vXk

Figure 28.24

Second part of the original verse, written and arranged by Clay Hine.

This line was more challenging than the first line. I didn't want to just say, "We hope we've made you laugh," because MS did other things besides just comedy. Because "song" seemed like a good metaphor for "joy in the barbershop world," I used that. I was also a little stuck on the rhyme. I wanted to say, "A thought you'll all take with you," or, "A thought you'll remember," but it was tough to get the right rhythmic feel. Although I didn't love "thought that you'll all take along," it seemed to be close enough, and the poetic feel of the line might help compensate for the slightly different phrase.

I wanted the verse to evoke a sense of journey and transition into the chorus, creating an engaging musical experience. There's nothing overly rangy about the music in the verse because the intent was not to be flashy or to showcase any individual singer, but rather to give a sense of the quartet taking a journey together. The chorus begins with a solo and the word "smile," conveying a simple message: we want you to smile. From there, the story would be why it's important to smile, sometimes it's harder to smile, sometimes it seems that you can't smile, and sometimes life looks a little better if you just smile, and sometimes life can look a lot better if you just keep smiling.

Figure 28.25

Ending of the opening verse of "Smile," arranged by Clay Hine.

Lead singer Tony is great at delivering music with a great deal of sensitivity, so it worked well for him to sing the solo on the first line of the chorus, measure 17–18 (0:55–1:04 in the video) to create that sense of complete simplicity. Because this is about their journey as a quartet, I wanted to bring in the other three, but gradually so that there was nothing jarring about this message. That meant bringing in the bari next at measures 19–20 (1:05–1:10), because he sings in the same range as lead and could help expand the intimacy of the lead solo delivery.

The bass entrance at measure 21 (1:11) introduces bass singer Myron in at a natural music cadence where the music has a strong sense of a tonic. With the bass's natural presence and genuineness in delivery, it really helps invite the whole quartet to tell the story together.

The word "smile" occurs in this song about 7,000 times. It's an important word, but it's also important to give this word different treatments to help the journey and musical development. In measure 25 (1:23), I used a higher but less dynamic voicing on "smile," with the chords unfolding into "smile" in measure 27 (1:29).

I thought of the smoothness and character in the bass's voice when I wrote measures 25–27. The "smile" chord in measure 27 is crying for a resolution that we're all waiting for. This lines up with the lyric intent, so that you can effectively say "Smile through your fear and sorrow, smile," and the music can convey a sense of fear and sorrow. But we're not done yet, and it'll be fine, which is what the next lyrics say. After the unfolding feeling in measure 25–27, the chords in measures 29–30 (1:38–1:41) have much more solidity in expressing a sense of hope. This includes the word "sun" which uses a triad with no seventh, to convey the majesty of "seeing the sun," followed by the chords with the raised third on "shinin'" to convey a feeling of hope.

Again, all of this takes advantage of MS's ability to sing easy, ringy chords really well and very joyfully. Then immediately after that in measures 32–33 (1:45–1:53) we have a ½ step key lift at "for you light up for face with gladness" to help the sense that this story is actually turning. It tells the listener, "You were sad, you smiled, and your spirits lifted, and your face started to light up."

This continues through the harmony parts' ascent at "face with gladness" in measure 34 (1:54), descending in contrast in the following measure at "trace of sadness."

Measure 43 (2:14) features an unexpected chord on "smile" to convey a different texture with a dom7 chord. It's followed by a short transfer of the melody to the bass for a different texture. While we could have kept the melody in the lead, this would have created a greater dynamic feel that we weren't quite ready to offer, as we still have more story to tell and urgency to build.

At measures 45–47 (2:18–2:30), it starts to feel like we're building toward a climax, but there's more to tell. The message of the story is that no matter what happens in life, you can get through it and find joy. We still wanted to convey that a lot can happen to get in the way of that, making it harder to have that joy, but it's still there.

There's a back-and-forth feeling that we wanted to communicate, which motivated a fun, unexpected key change in measures 48–49 (2:30–2:41). This happens just as it sounds like the song could be wrapping up, but it's subverted by the first chord in the new key on "smile." The intent was to keep this back-and-forth going.

Right after that we have new lyrics based on earlier words, "although your heart may be breaking apart" (2:39–2:47), featuring a bass melody to enhance the character of the delivery. The chords get higher and more spread. This also takes advantage of tenor singer Roger's character on "part," as I imagined how his vocal delivery would help emphasize the feeling of being apart.

We're now building even more urgency to the message through the lyrics and a sense of motion through the chords in measures 53–57 (2:47–3:03), leading to a solid barbershop chord on "life" that clearly cries for resolution.

And now we're getting to the big climax. Because we wanted a soft tag, it made sense for the very last message to be very simple: that all of this starts with a smile. It also felt like a simple word could be the answer to a huge build in urgency that says "what can we do when life really gets us down." With the lyric "you'll find that life is still worthwhile" it made sense to drive this urgency even more. This happens in measures 61–63 (3:10–3:26), where you'll notice that all voices go higher in their range. We didn't use this ranger earlier in the chart because we wanted urgency to build. When you're considering big, loud, powerful chords, there's nowhere to go from a place where everyone sings loud and tightly together. So we saved this powerful effect for these measures, having teased it earlier and backed off in order to develop and sustain the "back-and-forth" feeling.

The first tag I wrote for this song remained in the key of G. However, as I was writing it, I felt some chord movement that took an unexpected turn, ending up in B♭. It sounded cool to me, but I wondered if it was a bit too gratuitous without following musical guidelines. So I sent them the first tag I'd written.

They liked it, and I had the chance to work with them on their delivery of this shortly after that. We got to the tag, and it was good, but not amazing. We talked about a couple of minor changes, and then I said "okay, here was my first idea, but I was concerned that it was too weird." I played them what quickly became the final version of this tag—the one they won with and the one they now close all of their afterglows with.[133] A good lesson for all arrangers out there from this is: when you're envisioning a performance and manuscripting what you hear, if it's great, trust it, and keep second guessing to a minimum!

Part of why this works is because it goes through some big changes, including a key change, which I think helps emphasize the message of "life has big highs and lows," making the very simple end even more appropriate. And speaking of the end, it was very appropriate to bring back the simple lead solo we started the chorus with, then bring the other parts in with a unison and a slight unfolding to one more interesting chord. We go to a ♭III chord at measure 67, which should sound like one last ray of hope, then one last little lead solo feature. And then end on a straightforward 1—5—1—3 B♭ major chord, which is about the most simple, unpretentious, uncluttered chord that barbershoppers anywhere can sing.

No one voice is featured, no voice is in any part of their range where their quality might draw individual focus. It's just an easy chord that helps with the message "it starts with a smile."

133 Barbershop Harmony Society. (2017, Jul 10). *Main Street - Smile* [Video]. YouTube. https://youtu.be/iPEY2SE1vXk?t=190

Chapter 29.
Advanced Arranging Topics

By David Wright

Overview

Learning by Example

After mastering the basics of arranging in the barbershop style, the next step is to learn advanced techniques that will enable one to create arrangements with the potential of a powerful performance. This requires an expanded toolkit with varied techniques that can be applied to songs of different types. In this section, we will point out numerous such tools and cite examples that utilize them, all of which have led to successful performances.

At this level, the best way to expand one's skill set as an arranger is to study such examples, examining the mechanics to understand why they work. This section provides access to each arrangement cited and a link to a performance of the arrangement, usually video, often sung by the group for which the arrangement was created. It should be noted that performers sometimes make incidental changes to the arrangement and perhaps sing it in a different key, so the recorded example of a chart may not be a perfect representation, but it will be close.

What Song to Arrange

Arrangers sometimes arrange a song because they have an affinity for it or a particular idea about how to frame it. Alternatively, they may agree to arrange a song at the request of the ensemble who will sing it. The former situation may be seen as more desirable in that the arranger has a good vision of the goal. In the latter case the arranger may have to devote some thought to determining a hook for the song that will allow a dynamic performance by that particular group. Of course, a best-case scenario is when both situations apply.

A mark of an excellent arranger, however, is their ability to create a successful arrangement of a song for which they had no special vision before being asked to arrange it. This requires imagination and some musical empathy, as the arranger seeks to understand why someone else might like the song even though they themselves are ambivalent towards it or perhaps don't like it at all. In any case, a necessary condition for the arrangement to succeed is that the arranger eventually comes to understand the song's redeeming features and arrives at a strategy to make it work.

Who Will Sing the Arrangement?

A good arranger is usually in demand and will write arrangements that are commissioned by a quartet or chorus. This is a desirable situation because the arranger is likely familiar or can become familiar with the group's skill level, persona, range constraints, special abilities, etc. The arrangement is then tailored with these things in mind. It may, for example, involve extreme range in one or more parts to spotlight the special talents of one or more of the singers.

But most arrangers, at least some of the time, write arrangements with no designated performer in mind. This may be because the arrangement is for publication or is intended for wide usage by groups at all levels. In this situation, most arrangers will make more conservative choices, staying within the normal ranges for the four parts, avoiding gymnastic voice leading, and utilizing a high percentage of ringing chords in solid voicings.

How to Get Started

Before beginning an arrangement, the arranger should examine the published sheet music of the entire song as written by the composer(s), rather than depending entirely on some recorded version, another arrangement, or the arranger's memory of how the song goes. This should be done even if the arranger intends to morph the song in one way or another. The arranger then needs to decide what if anything needs to be added.

Typically the arrangement will need some kind of introduction and a tag. Certainly, the composer's chorus or main refrain will be the centerpiece of the arrangement. Beyond that, one can consider any other material provided, usually the verse. Some songs have quite recognizable verses that the listener might expect to hear, which would be a strong incentive to use the composer's verse. Many songs have verses that are obscure, not well-written, or not in line with the kind of arrangement envisioned by the arranger; in these cases the arranger may decide to write a verse, crafting it after their vision for the song. If the arrangement will go through the chorus more than once, then an interlude or some transitional material may be required. Sometimes lyrics that are archaic or not in good taste by virtue of changing standards will need to be replaced, and sometimes the arranger will choose to compose alternate lyrics in repeated segments of the song. This needs to be considered in advance, which brings us to the next topic, construction.

Construction

Most arrangers find it helpful to lay out the order of events. Will the song begin with an introduction? Does the composer's verse serve as such? If not, will the verse be used at all, perhaps as an interlude later in the arrangement? Determine if and how many times the chorus will be sung, possibly with a half-chorus meeting the need. The plan may require an interlude, extensions, or other connecting material (see Added Material below). It will be helpful to determine in advance which special effects will be employed. For example, a harmonic half-time effect may require writing additional words, or a melody transferred to another part may require key changes. The plan should identify the general contour and where the song's climactic moment(s) will be.

The planned construction should pinpoint where material needs to be composed. This plan, or parts of it, may well be tentative, with certain decisions deferred until some of the pieces come together. For example, the arranger may delay the decision of whether to include an introduction or verse until the rest of the arrangement nears completion, then decide if it is really needed. In the end, every new turn in a successful arrangement is satisfying, delightful, meaningful, and refreshing, but not necessarily predictable. Surprises should be pleasantly diverting but not shocking, unless shock is for some good reason an intended effect. Ending the arrangement in an appropriate and satisfying way is an absolute must. Here are some possible constructions, with examples:

Chorus—Tag

Sometimes, something very simple like this is all that's needed. Take "Beautiful Dreamer," which packs a great deal of interest into twenty-two measures of music.[134]

---

134 TalkinShop. (2011, Aug 1). *Nightlife - 1995 International Quartet Semifinal* [Video]. YouTube. https://youtu.be/4ZwDa9ALvfQ

Figure 29.1

Chorus-Tag form featuring "Beautiful Dreamer." Words and music by Stephen Foster. Arranged by David Wright.

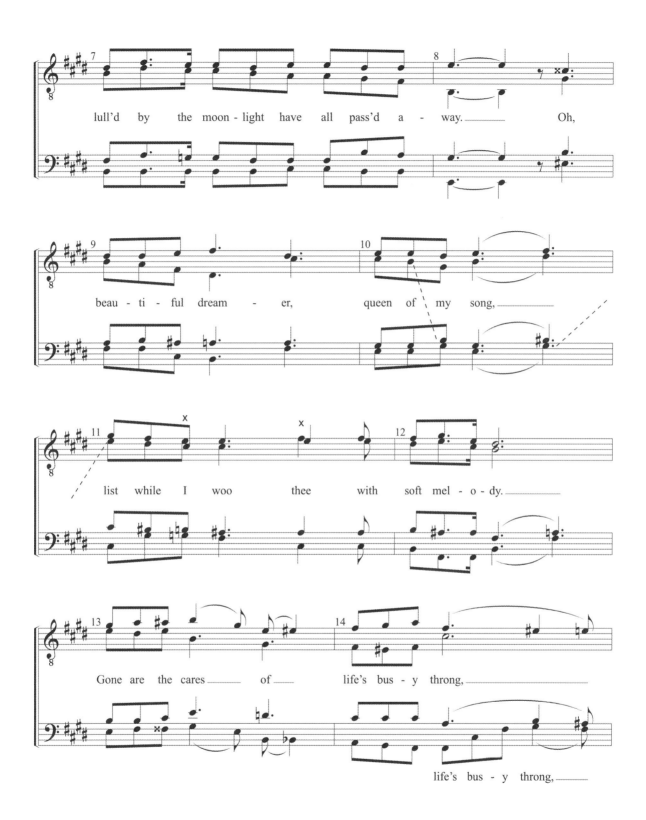

Intro/Verse—Chorus—Tag

Figure 29.2

"Brother, Can You Spare a Dime" as an example of verse—chorus—tag. Arranged by Steve Armstrong.[135]

135 TalkinShop. (2020, May 16). *Toronto Northern Lights - Brother, Can You Spare a Dime?* [Video]. YouTube. https://youtu.be/txJKmwtT3rA

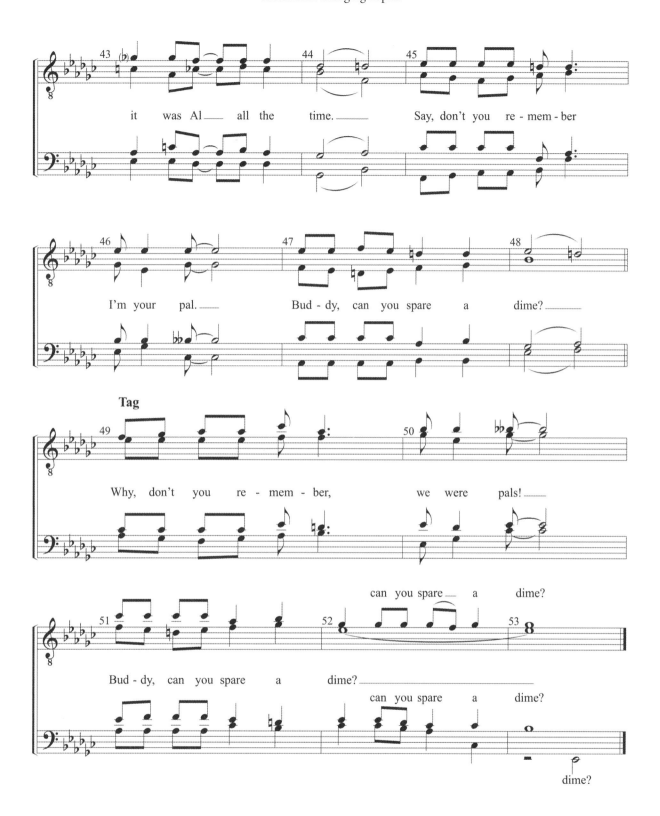

Intro/Verse—Chorus—Half Chorus—Tag

This construction often works if the chorus has AABA form, repeating BA.[136]

Figure 29.3

"Always," as example of a verse–chorus–half chorus–tag form. Words and music by Irving Berlin. Arranged by Mark Hale and Don Gray.

136 Barbershop Harmony Society. (2019, Apr 30). *Vocal Connection - Always* [Video]. YouTube. https://youtu.be/5xEQ_Chh8c8

Other typical examples of form, with YouTube and audio links to the performances available in the Hal Leonard MyLibrary site associated with *Arranging Barbershop Vol 2*, are as follows.

- Intro/Verse—Chorus 1—Chorus 2—Tag
  - "Love Me or Leave Me," arranged by Patrick McAlexander
- Intro—Verse 1—Chorus 1—Verse 2—Chorus 2—Tag
  - "Come What May," arranged by Kevin Keller
- Intro/Verse—Chorus—Interlude—Half chorus—Tag
  - "Ring-a-Ding Ding," arranged by Anthony Bartholomew
- Intro/Verse—Chorus—Interlude—Half chorus—Tag
  - "I Can't Give You Anything But Love," arranged by David Harrington
- Intro/Verse—Chorus 1—Interlude—Chorus 2—Tag
  - "Put Your Arms Around Me," arranged by Aaron Dale
- Intro/Verse—Chorus 1—Chorus 2—Chorus 3—Tag. This kind of construction will likely require variation, key changes, melody transfers.
  - "Cuddle Up A Little Closer," arranged by Clay Hine
- Intro—Verse—Chorus—Tag. This is somewhat rare. Notable examples include:
  - "All the Things You Are," arranged Steve Delehanty
  - "The Sunshine Of Your Smile," arranged Tom Gentry
- Intro—Verse—Chorus 1—Chorus 2—Tag
  - "Redhead," arranged Jim Clancy, Dennis Driscoll, and Ed Waesche

It should be noted that some songs do not have well-defined or easily identifiable segments of equal length, being somewhat through-composed while still having redeeming symmetries. In this case, creating a roadmap like one of the above may not be possible, and usually the arranger will simply adhere to the composer's sequence of events, with possible enhancements, extensions, repetitions, or other adornments. Quite a few songs from contemporary musicals fit into this category. Here is an example in Figure 29.4.[137]

Figure 29.4

"No One Is Alone / Not While I'm Around" Medley. Words and music by Stephen Sondheim. Arranged by Steve Tramack.

137 Barbershop Harmony Society. (2019, Oct 15). *After Hours - Not While I'm Around [from Sweeney Todd]* [Video]. YouTube. https://youtu.be/lEIT8s5LSWg

NOT WHILE I'M AROUND

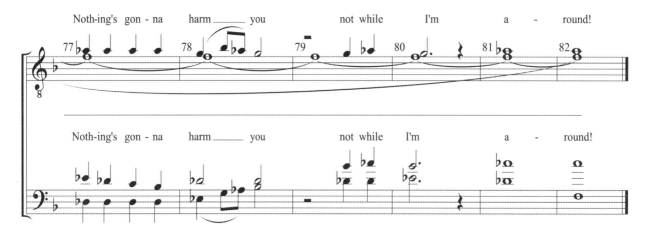

Sometimes arrangers create the arrangement starting at the beginning and going to the tag. It is not necessary, however, to arrange the song chronologically, that is, in the order of the events in the construction plan. Often arrangers start with that portion of the arrangement for which they have the clearest vision. That might be the first entire chorus, the musical climax, or even the tag. Then the missing parts are filled in with the existing pieces in mind, always with the option of modifying what has been written. This approach can lead to new ideas and is often useful when the arranger is still searching for ideas to make the arrangement dynamic.

Medleys

Medleys can sometimes make a musical impression that is stronger than what could be done with the individual songs. This can result if the two or more songs go naturally together because of a common theme or possibly because they contrast with each other.

A classic example is "Liar Medley," which merges two songs, "How Could You Believe Me" and "It's a Sin to Tell a Lie," having diametrically opposite intents to construct the comedic narrative of a rogue who pretends to be pious.[138]

138 Barbershop Harmony Society. (2017, Nov 2). *Keepsake - How Could You Believe Me/It's a Sin to Tell a Lie Medley* [Video]. YouTube. https://youtu.be/vJrkY6tQSIM

Figure 29.5

"How Could You Believe Me," Words and music by Burton Lane and Alan Jay Lerner. "It's a Sin to Tell a Lie," Words and music by Billy Mayhew. Arranged by Renee Craig.

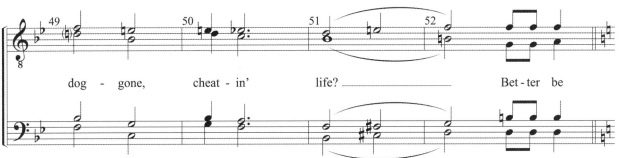

On rare occasions a portion of one song can be used in another to give introductory, transitional, or concluding material. A good example is "No One Is Alone / Not While I'm Around" as found in Figure 29.4. This arrangement largely uses the second song, with the first providing a verse and a tag.

Introductions/Verses:

The most common types of added material are introductions and tags. Hence, we will devote quite a bit of attention to each. We address the former here and the latter in the next section.

Frequently there is a need for the arranger to compose a beginning. This may be because the song only has a chorus that may be too abrupt as an opening, or the composer's verse seems ineffective or out of place for the type of arrangement envisioned.

Sometimes this need is lyrical, sometimes musical, sometimes both. In "Come What May," the introduction is entirely neutral syllable, setting up this poignant song.[139]

---

139 Barbershop Harmony Society. (2017, Aug 18). *After Hours - Come What May [from Moulin Rouge!]* [Video]. YouTube. https://youtu.be/VsAb54zJRcI

Figure 29.6

"Come What May," Words and music by Kevin Gilbert and David Baerwald. Arranged by Kevin Keller.

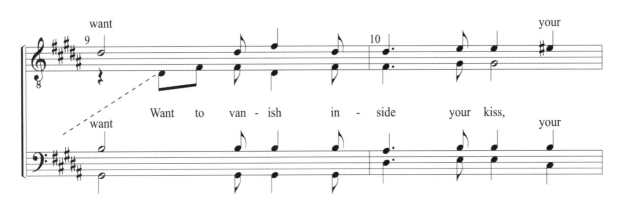

Note how effectively the very simple introduction of "If I Give My Heart to You," beginning with neutral syllables going into lyrics, gets us into the song by asking the pertinent question.

Figure 29.7

"If I Give My Heart to You," Words and music by By Jimmie Crane, Jimmy Brewster, and Al Jacobs. Arranged by Jim Clancy.

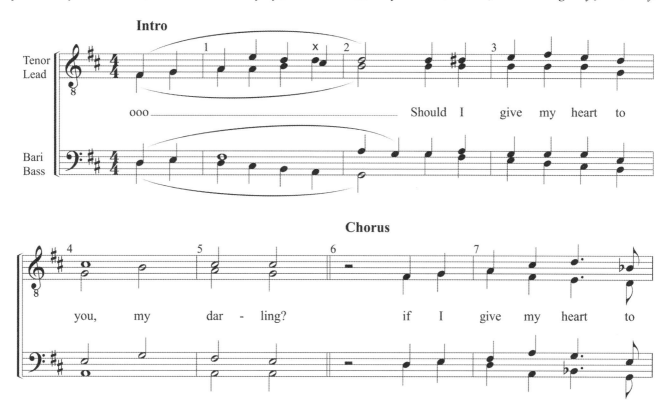

The composed verse in the arrangement of "Bright Was the Night" gives the needed substance and musical interest to transform a simple "polecat" song into a power ballad.[140]

Figure 29.8

"Bright Was the Night" original verse. Words, music and arrangement by David Wright.

140 Barbershop Harmony Society. (2018, Sep 14). *The Gas House Gang - Bright Was the Night* [Video]. YouTube. https://youtu.be/k-q3Opw3DDw

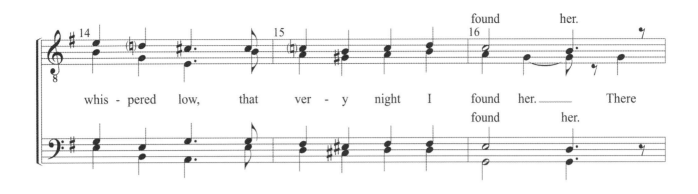

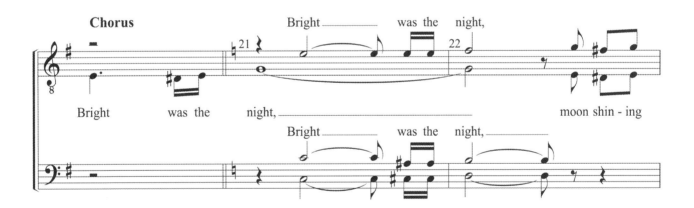

The brief neutral syllable introduction in the arrangement of "She's Got a Way" serves to establish the mood as well as the harmonic motif, comprising swipes and harmonies foreshadowing what comes later in the arrangement's transitional passages.[141]

141 Barbershop Harmony Society. (2019, Mar 27). *Zero8 - She's Got a Way (Billy Joel cover)* [Video]. YouTube. https://youtu.be/gvACHiEFNqg

Figure 29.9

"She's Got a Way." Words and music by Billy Joel. Arranged by David Wright.

Note how effectively the introduction of "All the Way" brings the listener into this classic ballad, both lyrically and musically.[142]

Figure 29.10

"All the Way." Words and music by Sammy Cahn and James Van Hausen. Arranged by Tom Gentry.

142 Barbershop Harmony Society. (2018, Oct 5). *Flipside - All the Way* [Video]. YouTube. https://youtu.be/8TBXMuR7wp4

Similarly, the introduction in "Auld Lang Syne" leads us into the song naturally, giving context and facilitating the transformation of this folk song into a power ballad. This introduction is referenced later in an interlude, giving the arrangement strong binding symmetry.[143]

Figure 29.11

"Auld Lang Syne" introduction. Words, music, and arrangement by Clay Hine.

The arranger of "If Ever I Would Leave You" dealt with a well-known song that has no verse. The arrangement could possibly start with the chorus. However, the well-crafted composed verse removes any vestige of abruptness and leads us naturally into the song, both lyrically and musically.[144]

Figure 29.12

"If Ever I Would Leave You" original verse. Words and music by Richard Rodgers and Oscar Hammerstein II. Original verse and arrangement by Clay Hine.

144 Barbershop Harmony Society. (2019, Oct 7). *Heralds of Harmony - If Ever I Would Leave You [from Camelot]* [Video]. YouTube. https://youtu.be/y-7ltWdvK9g

2   *If Ever I Would Leave You*

The same can be said for the arranger-composed verse of "Jeanie With the Light Brown Hair," now a classic, which paints a mournful context for the song.[145]

Figure 29.13

"Jeanie with the Light Brown Hair" original verse. Words, music, and arrangement by Ed Waesche.

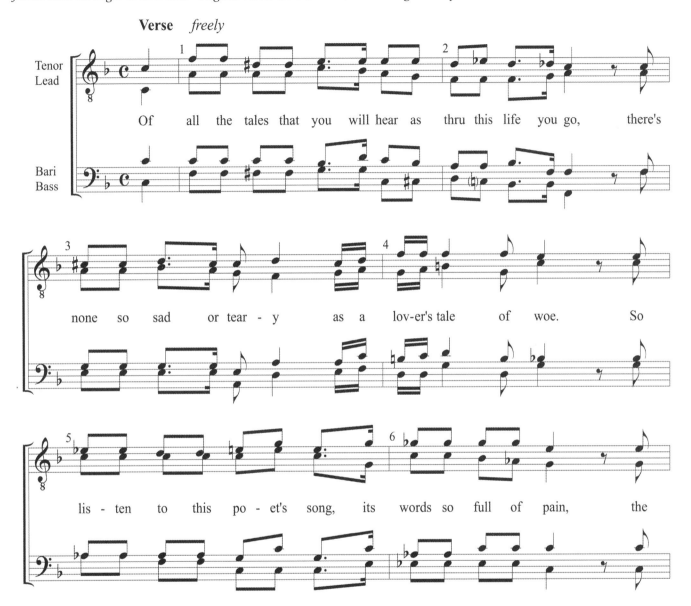

145 Barbershop Harmony Society. (2018, Sep 13). *Second Edition - Jeanie with the Light Brown Hair* [Video]. YouTube. https://youtu.be/p9PGxnY9rE0

emp - ti - ness of love gone wrong, the love I loved in vain.

Chorus

I dream of Jean - ie with the light brown __ hair, born like a va - por

And another classic exemplifying the same characteristic is "If I Had My Way," where the beautiful arranger-composed verse gives a dramatic setup to an old song, starting in the relative minor mode, migrating to major, followed by a temporary tonal shift up a major third.[146]

Figure 29.14

"If I Had My Way." Words and music by Lew Klein and James Kendis. Original verse and arrangement by David Harrington.

146 Barbershop Harmony Society. (2015, Nov 4). *Signature - If I Had My Way (International 2015)* [Video]. YouTube. https://youtu.be/NKipzF7iDf4

Yet another example is "What Kind of Fool Am I," where the composed verse avoids abruptness and adds context to the story.

Figure 29.15

"What Kind of Fool Am I" original verse. Words and music by Leslie Bricusse and Anthony Newly. Original verse, words, and music by Joel Lancaster and Kevin Keller. Arranged by Kevin Keller.

In "Cry Me a River," the arranger-composed verse creates the backdrop of drama that sets up a powerful treatment of this iconic song. Note how cleverly the lead post at the end of this verse becomes the first melody note of the chorus.[147]

Figure 29.16

"Cry Me a River" original introduction. Words and music by Arthur Hamilton. Original introduction and arrangement by Brent Graham.

---

147 Barbershop Harmony Society. (2019, Oct 11). *Pratt Street Power - Cry Me a River (Julie London cover)* [Video]. YouTube. https://youtu.be/y7zgj_4i8yc

Chorus

Sometimes an arranger feels compelled to write an introduction to precede a composer's verse, as in "California, Here I Come," where the opening chord sequence serves as an onomatopoeia for winter wind.[148]

148 Mike McGee. (2009, Mar 13). *Masters of Harmony 1999 International Performance* [Video]. YouTube. https://youtu.be/7Wjp-rSMBSc?t=281

Figure 29.17

"California, Here I Come" onomatopoeia introduction. Words and music by Al Jolson, Buddy DeSylvia, and Joseph Meyer.
Arranged by David Wright.

In "Redhead," the arranger has provided both an introduction and an original verse, with the brief introduction providing a climactic moment and launching the tempo and the verse slowing into ad lib before the tempo resumes in the chorus.

Figure 29.18

"Redhead" introduction and verse. Words and music by Thomas Jordan and Merrill Gridley. Original verse by Ed Waesche. Arranged by Jim Clancy and Ed Waesche

Another good example is "The Sunshine of Your Smile," where the brief four-bar intro eases us into the verse's somewhat precipitous opening line.[149]

Figure 29.19

"The Sunshine of Your Smile" original introduction. Words and music by Leonard Cooke. Original introduction and arrangement by Tom Gentry.

149 Barbershop Archive. (2020, Jun 21). *Power Play & Frontier - The Sunshine of Your Smile (2019 PIOQCA Show)* [Video]. YouTube. https://youtu.be/p08WnYBXMN4

In rare instances, the verse of another song can be extracted; note how seamlessly this works in "Not While I'm Around / No One Is Alone," where the arranger borrows the verse from another song by the same composer, Stephen Sondheim.[150] The arranger said, "I can't write like Stephen Sondheim, so when I needed a verse for 'Not While I'm Around,' I started looking elsewhere in Sweeney Todd. Finding nothing, I began looking at other Sondheim musicals for material that matched thematically and melodically. The first A section from "No One is Alone" from "Into the Woods" was a perfect fit."

Figure 29.20

"No One is Alone" A section serving as a verse for "Not While I'm Around." Words and music by Stephen Sondheim. Arranged by Steve Tramack.

NOT WHILE I'M AROUND

Freely

The arrangement then ties "No One is Alone" into the tag with the lyrics, "hard to see the light now, just don't let it go. We can make it right now, we can make it so."

Figure 29.21

"No One is Alone" recapitulation in the tag of "Not While I'm Around." Arranged by Steve Tramack.

Intros or verses sometimes prepare the listener for an uptune by beginning in ad lib then launching the tempo right before the chorus commences, as in "I Found a Million Dollar Baby."[151]

151 Barbershop Archive. (2019, Oct 10). *Marquis - I Found A Million Dollar Baby (1996 BABS Convention)* [Video]. YouTube. https://youtu.be/aGsQCeWoOUg

Figure 29.22

"I Found a Million Dollar Baby," words and music by Harry Warren, Mort Dixon, and Billy Rose. Arranged by Billy Mitchell, Ed Waesche, and Rob Hopkins.

Some introductions are solely neutral syllables, providing an instrumental beginning that mimics the known version of the song. Such is the case with "The Next Ten Minutes;" here, note that the neutral syllable enters again near the tag, giving cohesiveness and a satisfying bookending effect.[152]

152 Barbershop Harmony Society, (2016, Jul 13). *After Hours - The Next Ten Minutes [from The Last Five Years]* [Video]. YouTube. https://youtu.be/WgwuDAvLxNE

Figure 29.23

Neutral syllables introduction and tag in "The Next Ten Minutes." Words and music by Jason Robert Brown. Arranged by Theo Hicks.

Some intros exist mainly to generate excitement. Note how the intro of "Seventy Six Trombones" builds to a huge climax before launching the song at a pianissimo, while providing lyrical content that is reiterated in the tag.[153]

Figure 29.24

"Seventy-Six Trombones" original introduction. Words and music by Meredith Willson. Original introduction and arrangement by David Wright.

---

153 Barbershop Harmony Society. (2009, Jul 22). *Ambassadors of Harmony - Seventy-Six Trombones [from The Music Man]* [Video]. YouTube. https://youtu.be/QmDGntpZC3I

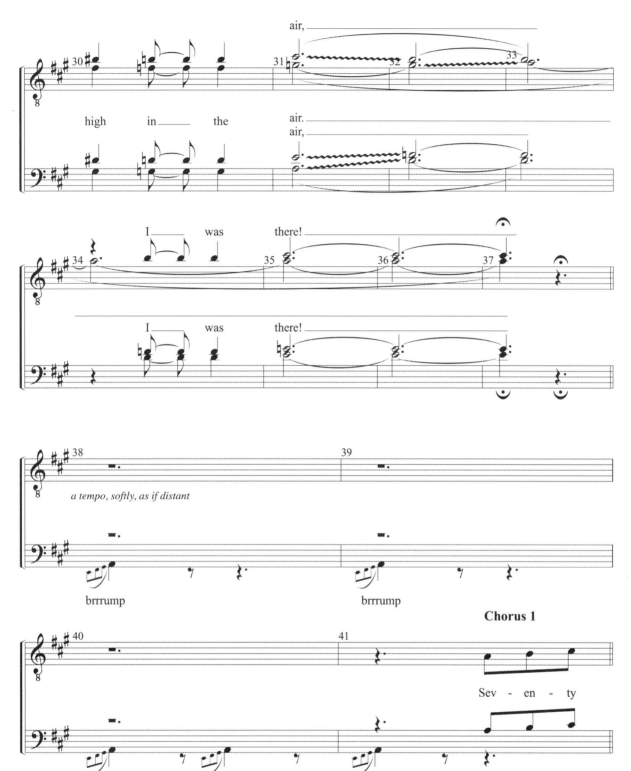

Figure 29.25

"Seventy-Six Trombones" tag. Arranged by David Wright.

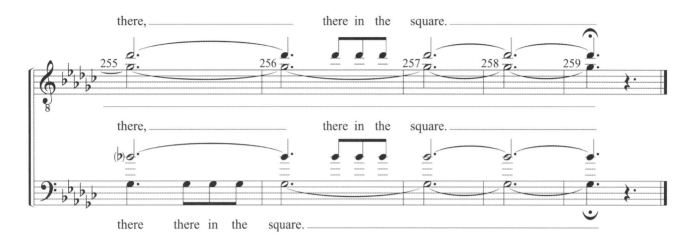

Tags

This second type of added material also deserves special attention. A matter of critical importance in generating a successful arrangement is creating a satisfying ending. The arranger must decide what kind of ending is most appropriate. Does the arrangement call for a high ringing tag, or should the ending set down easy? Which of these is more in line with the musical intent of the arrangement? Is there a driving rhythm with momentum that needs to be diffused in a satisfying way? Should the tag maintain or break the rhythm? Can the tag bookend the introduction? Should the tag be loud or soft, high or low, and should it be the climax of the song? Should it bring in some eleventh-hour surprise? This would be rare but has been known to work, as will be shown by examples below.

Tags can provide an effective wrap-up of a song by repeating lyrics that summarize the song's message or continuing the rhythmic drive. Or they can feature a particular device. Consider the famous lengthy swipe in the tag of "Bright Was the Night," steeped in barbershop tradition, which lifts and propels the song toward its culmination.[154]

---

154 Barbershop Harmony Society. (2018, Sep 14). *The Gas House Gang - Bright Was the Night* [Video]. YouTube. https://youtu.be/k-q3Opw3DDw?t=25

Figure 29.26

"Bright Was the Night" iconic tag. Words and music by Traditional. Arranged by David Wright.

Another example is "Come What May," where the lyrics behind the lead hanger, resting atypically on scale tone five, build up to create a climax at the end.

Figure 29.27

"Come What May" tag. Arranged by Kevin Keller.

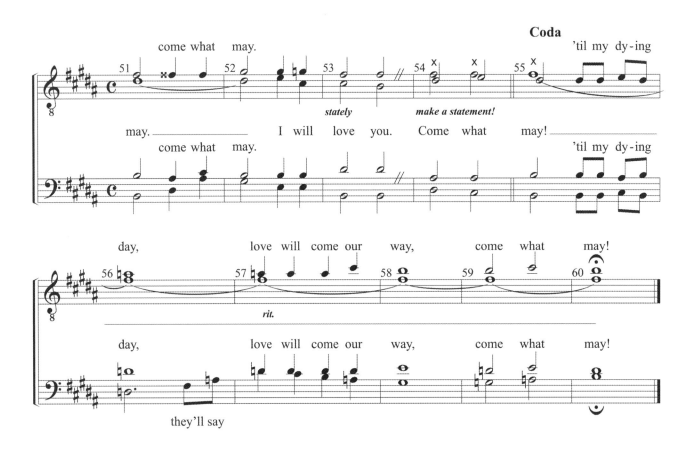

Also consider the classic tag of "Each Time I Fall in Love," which features a traditional scissor followed by a double hanger between tenor and bass with lyrics that cement the song's hopeless resignation.[155]

Figure 29.28

"Each Time I Fall In Love" tag. Words, music, and arrangement by S.K. Grundy.

Then there is the classic use of bell chords in the tag of "Who'll Take My Place When I'm Gone," which finalizes the song's despondent mood.

Figure 29.29

"Who'll Take My Place When I'm Gone" tag. Words and music by Raymond Klages and Billy Fazioli. Arranged by Greg Lyne.

155 Barbershop Harmony Society. (2021, Apr 16). *By Design - Each Time I Fall in Love* [Video]. YouTube. https://youtu.be/1jU50MpkKM4

In "I Can't Give You Anything But Love," the arranger skillfully prolongs the fun of this rollicking song by inserting several brief interpolations in the coda, continuing even as the lead or tenor holds the final post.[156]

Figure 29.30

"I Can't Give You Anything But Love" tag. Words and music by Dorothy Fields and Jimmy McHugh. Arranged by David Harrington.

---

156 Barbershop Harmony Society. (2020, Jul 4). *Ringmasters - I Can't Give You Anything But Love* [Video]. YouTube. https://youtu.be/yj2iY3BSPWs

Often, perform-ability constraints need to be accommodated, such as in tags where the arranger wants to have a long post, or where a part abandons its normal range for some dramatic effect, e.g., the baritone jumping above the tenor as in "Not While I'm Around."

Figure 29.31

"Not While I'm Around" tag. Words and music by Stephen Sondheim. Arranged by Steve Tramack.

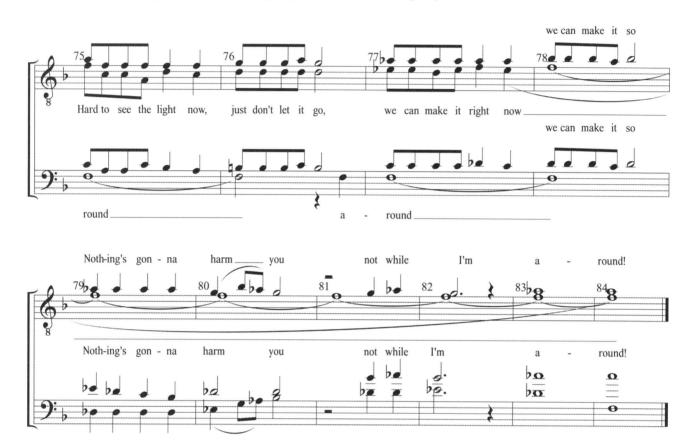

An arranger writing for a particular quartet will usually assign a post to the voice most inclined to take it. Often this is the lead, as in "Butter Outta Cream," but certainly not always.[157]

Figure 29.32

"Butter Outta Cream," Words and music by Mark Shaiman and Scott Wittman. Arranged by Dan Wessler.

Consider "Auld Lang Syne," where it appears in the baritone part.

Figure 29.33

"Auld Lang Syne," Arranged by Clay Hine.

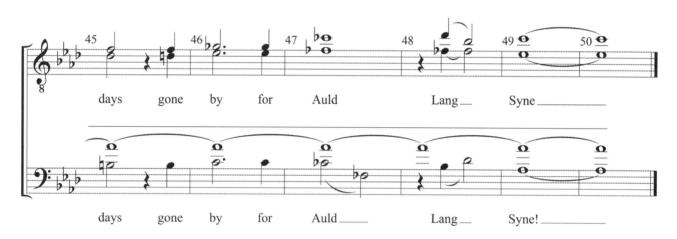

Also consider "Love Me or Leave Me," where the bass takes the post.[158]

Figure 29.34

"Love Me or Leave Me," Words and music by Gus Kahn and Walter Donaldson. Arranged by Patrick McAlexander.

---

158 Barbershop Harmony Society. (2017, Mar 14). *Instant Classic - Love Me or Leave Me (live at the 2016 AIC Show)* [Video]. YouTube. https://youtu.be/v39ERSTk-QY

An extreme example of this is the tag of "Cruella DeVil," where the bottom three parts inexorably continue the story's narrative while the tenor holds an unusually long post.

Figure 29.35

"Cruella DeVil" tag. Words and music by Mel Levin. Arranged by David Wright.

mind is a pile of mal-ice and guile, but kind-ness not e-ven a tad; Cru-

el-la,_____ she's bad! bad!_____ bad, so_____ bad!

It is not unusual for arrangers to transfer a post from one voice to another to allow the effect to be sustained for a longer time, as in the tag of "Not While I'm Around / No One Is Alone."

Figure 29.36

"Not While I'm Around / No One is Alone" tag. Arranged by Steve Tramack.

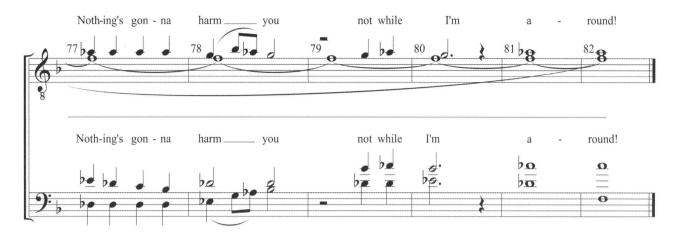

Another example can be found in "I Got Rhythm," where the extended tag maintains and then diffuses the song's momentum.[159]

---

159 Barbershop Harmony Society. (Aug 15, 2016). *Forefront - I Got Rhythm* [Video]. YouTube. https://youtu.be/3frH41TZcaU?si=XWUXZU9W-J2gFm8B

Figure 29.37

"I Got Rhythm." Words and music by George and Ira Gershwin. Arranged by David Wright.

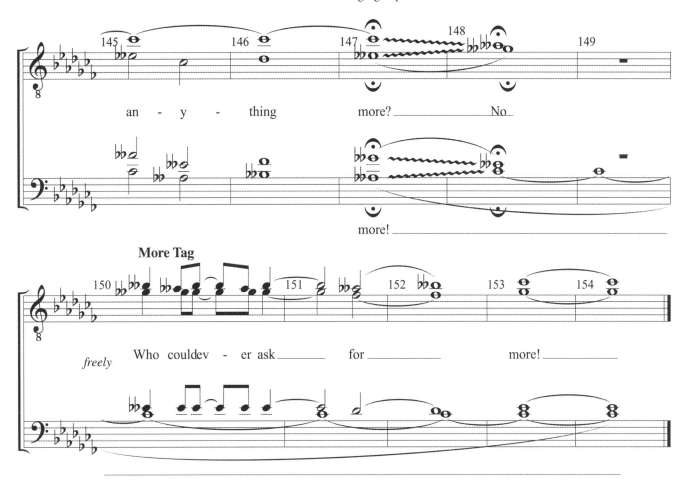

In some cases the tag may actually be called a *coda*. Note the twelve-bar coda in "Stranger in Paradise," which also has some symmetry with the verse.[160]

 A coda is any concluding passage that can be understood as occurring after the structural conclusion of a work and that serves as a formal closing gesture.[161] In barbershop, codas function as tags, but not all tags are codas. Most barbershop tags use material from other structural parts of the song as opposed to being a separate concluding passage with its own new material and unique concepts.

160 Barbershop Harmony Society. (2012, Jan 9). *2011 International Chorus Champion - Masters of Harmony* [Video]. YouTube. https://youtu.be/Hmbm7a94K_w

161 Randall, Don Michael. (1999). *The Harvard Concise Dictionary of Music and Musicians*. Page 146. The Belknap Press of Harvard University Press.

Figure 29.38

"Stranger in Paradise." Words and music by George Forrest and Robert Wright. Arranged by Mark Hale and Rob Campbell.

Also consider the ten-bar coda of "When Day is Done," which extends the song to a beautiful and satisfying ending after a deceptive cadence.[162]

Figure 29.39

"When Day is Done" coda. Words and music by B G De Sylvia and Robert Katscher Arranged by Ed Waesche.

162 Mike McGee. (2009, Mar 13). *Masters of Harmony 1999 International Performance* [Video]. YouTube. https://youtu.be/7Wjp-rSMBSc

Also consider the eight-bar coda in "Cry Me a River," which sets the song down in a soft, low melancholy while referencing the composed verse.[163]

Figure 29.40

"Cry Me a River" coda. Arranged by Brent Graham.

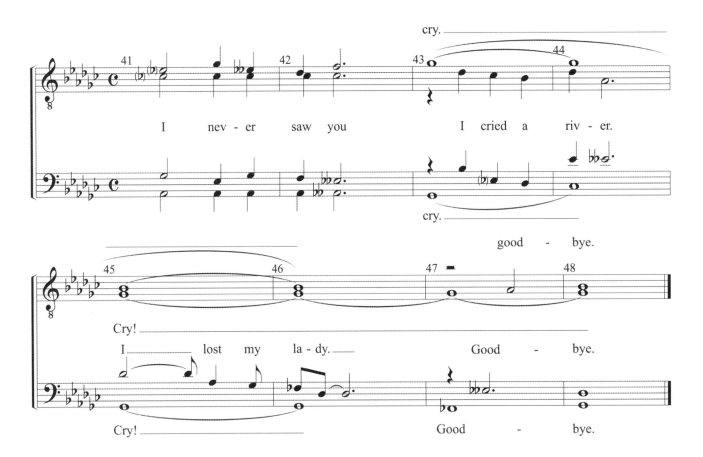

163 Barbershop Harmony Society. (2019, Oct 11). *Pratt Street Power - Cry Me a River (Julie London cover)* [Video]. YouTube. https://youtu.be/y7zgj_4i8yc

Similarly, the tag of "Stormy Weather" wraps up the narrator's melancholy frame of mind.[164]

Figure 29.41

"Stormy Weather." Words and music by Ted Kohler and Harold Arlen. Arranged by Aaron Dale.

164 Barbershop Harmony Society. (Aug 15, 2016). *Da Capo - Stormy Weather* [Video]. YouTube. https://youtu.be/ MIxaOQuw4_4?si=Hai-kpszYiPmkj9Y

Another good example for study is the tag of "If Ever I Would Leave You," which effectively diffuses the climactic moment of the deceptive cadence while recapping the songs lyrical message below the sustained lead tonic.[165]

Figure 29.42

"If Ever I Would Leave You" tag. Arranged by Clay Hine.

165 Barbershop Harmony Society. (Oct 7, 2019). *Heralds of Harmony - If Ever I Would Leave You* [Video]. YouTube. https://youtu.be/y-7ltWdvK9g?si=AHAvyr4jzeuqLJ_Z

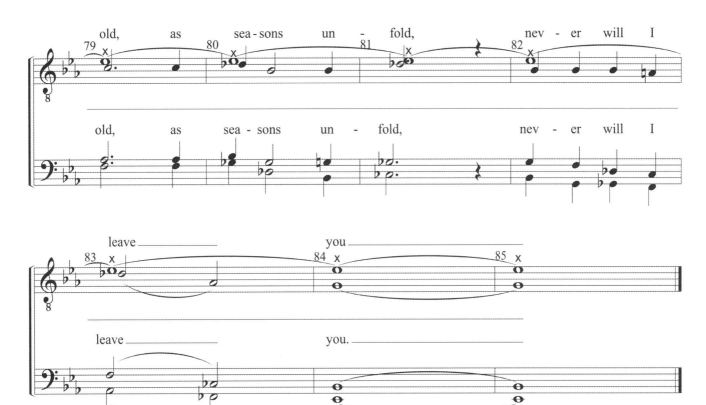

Yet another example is the tag of "Jeannie With the Light Brown Hair," with the transfer of melody to the tenor and the final descending echo over the tenor post. Note the source of the "Waesche 13th" in the second beat of measure 26.[166]

Figure 29.43

"Jeanie with the Light Brown Hair." Arranged by Ed Waesche.

166 Barbershop Harmony Society. (2018, Sep 13). *Second Edition - Jeanie with the Light Brown Hair* [Video]. YouTube. https://youtu.be/p9PGxnY9rE0

An example of the "eleventh hour" surprise is afforded by "Louise," where the development builds the song upward only to have the intensity brought down to a low soft ending.[167]

Figure 29.44

"Louise" tag. Arranged by David Wright.

---

167 Barbershop Harmony Society. (2017, Jun 22). *Michigan Jake - Louise (2000 International)* [Video]. YouTube. https://youtu.be/
GdnIIPzyK2M

In "Brother, Can You Spare a Dime," this effect is accomplished effectively in the last two measures, culminating in the final low bass tonic.[168]

Figure 29.45

"Brother Can You Spare a Dime" tag. Arranged by Steve Armstrong.

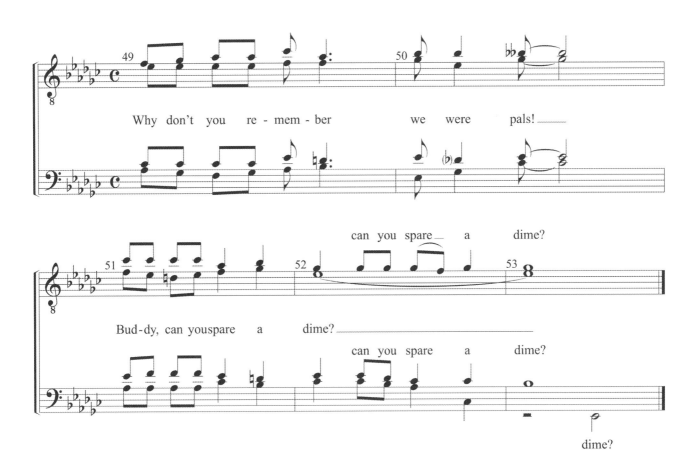

---

168 TalkinShop. (2020, May 16). *Toronto Northern Lights - Brother, Can You Spare a Dime?* [Video]. YouTube. https://youtu.be/ txJKmwtT3rA

In all three of these cases, the final surprise motifs reference textures that were heard earlier in the song. By contrast, sometimes a tag can change the direction of a song that seems to be heading for a soft, low ending, instead bringing it up to a high climactic ending. A good example is "Yesterday I Heard the Rain."[169]

Figure 29.46

"Yesterday I Heard the Rain" tag. Words and music by Gene Lees and Armando Manzanero Canche. Arranged by Brent Graham.

169 The Association of International Champions. (2020, Sep 4). *Realtime I Yesterday I Heard the Rain (Live from the 2015 Westminster Chorus Show)* [Video] YouTube. https://youtu.be/lQZ9C4TgNWM

In rare instances, arrangers have interpolated another song to create a coda. Note how "Do I Love You" does just this, leading to a dramatic climactic ending.[170]

Figure 29.47

"Do I Love You" coda via interpolation, featuring "Do I Love You Because You're Beautiful?." "Do I Love You" words and music by Cole Porter. "Do I Love You Because You're Beautiful" words and music by Richard Rodgers and Oscar Hammerstein II. Arranged by Brent Graham.

170 Barbershop Harmony Society. (2022, Oct 19). *Quorum - Do I Love You? [from Du Barry Was a Lady]* [Video]. YouTube. https://youtu.be/dZGfiPm9wTE

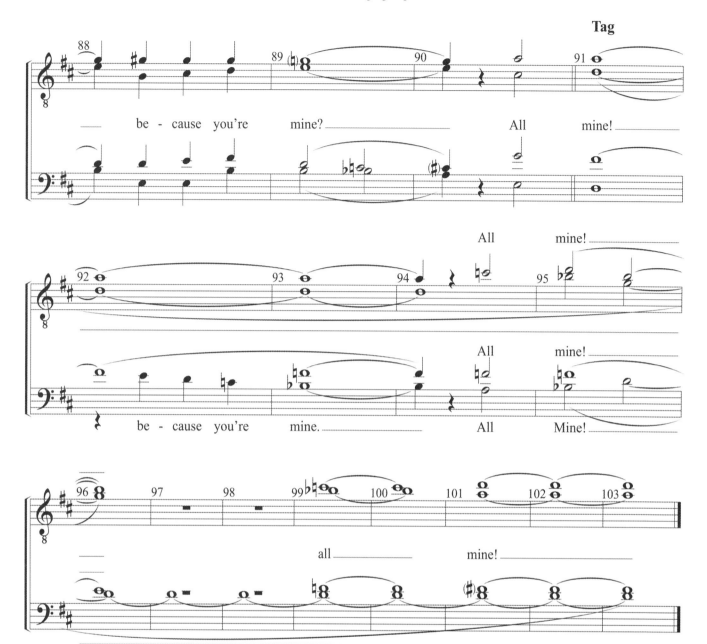

Attention should be given to the final voicing, making sure all parts are in range for the performers and that the voicing is appropriate to the song. Usually the arrangement ends on the tonic triad, but there are examples where other choices work. Note how the open fifth ending of "If You Go Away" closes out the song effectively, in character with the somber mood that has been established.[171]

Figure 29.48

"If You Go Away" open fifth tag. Words and music by Rod Mckuen and Jacques Brel. Arranged by David Wright.

An example in an entirely different song type is the final chord in "Pass Me the Jazz," where the ninth chord fits perfectly with the jazzy flavor.[172]

Figure 29.49

"Pass Me the Jazz" tag. Words and music by Anders Edenroth. Arranged by Jeremy Johnson.

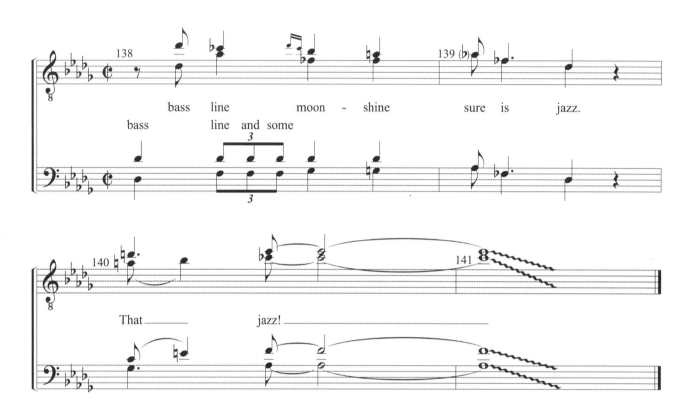

Whatever the intended effect, well-written tags just feel right, perfectly capping off the song.

Interludes/Transitions

There are other kinds of added material commonly used by skilled arrangers other than introductions, verses, and tags. One such type of composed segment is an interlude, which may be used to bridge two choruses, to provide contrast, or just to extend the joy of the song.

172 Barbershop Harmony Society. (2016, Jul 27). *Lemon Squeezy - Pass Me the Jazz* [Video]. YouTube. https://youtu.be/es_TYo7K3yo

A good example of the latter is the instrumental interlude in "Ring-a-Ding Ding!" This simply gives the performer more time to jam in the song where rhythm is paramount, while offering symmetry with the similarly flavored introduction.[173]

Figure 29.50

"Ring-a-Ding-Ding!" interlude. Words and music by Sammy Cahn and James Van Heusen. Arranged by Anthony Bartholomew.

---

173 Barbershop Harmony Society. (2016, Jul 10). *Forefront -Ring-a-Ding-Ding!* [Video], YouTube. https://youtu.be/TbTjlliYU74

In "Auld Lang Syne," the arranger-composed interlude facilitates the emotional lift, ending in a key change that propels the song toward its climactic ending.[174]

Figure 29.51

"Auld Lang Syne" interlude words, music, and arrangement by Clay Hine.

---

174 TalkinShop. (Aug 3, 2011). *Platinum - 1999 International Quartet Final* [Video]. YouTube. https://youtu.be/-kHwxfs7xdk?si=k4-83xLSBMQ3dkUx&t=178

In "I Can't Give You Anything But Love," the interlude's revisit of the lyrical content of the verse includes a clever interpolation of "Happy Birthday."

Figure 29.52

"I Can't Give You Anything But Love" interlude. Arranged by David Harrington.

In "Put Your Arms Around Me, Honey," the arranger's interlude is appended by a partial reprise of the verse, leading into the second chorus and providing excellent contrasting material and musical interest.[175]

Figure 29.53

"Put Your Arms Around Me Honey" original bridge. Words, music, and arrangement by Aaron Dale.

175 Barbershop Harmony Society. (2009, Jan 9). *Max Q - 2007 International Quartet Champions* [Video]. YouTube. https://youtu.be/kwxEHFVHkAM

Sometimes the material inserted by the arranger between sections of the composer's song is more accurately described as a transition, as its main purpose is to connect rather than add to the musical story. An example is in "I Got Rhythm," where the bass run between the verse and first chorus serves to launch the new tempo, as well as add fun. This idea appears again briefly after the second chorus.[176]

Figure 29.54

"I Got Rhythm" interlude. Arranged by David Wright.

176 Barbershop Harmony Society. (Aug 15, 2016). *Forefront - I Got Rhythm* [Video]. YouTube. https://youtu.be/3frH41TZcaU?si=XWUXZU9W-J2gFm8B

Figure 29.55

"I Got Rhythm" recapitulation of the bass riff after the second chorus. Arranged by David Wright.

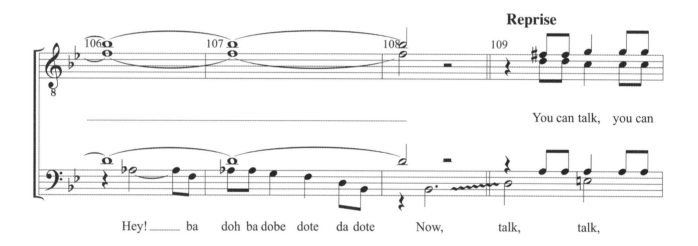

Changing, Appending, Stylizing, and Morphing the Composer's Song

Creative arranging sometimes necessitates changing, adding to, or paring down the composer's song, or presenting it in a way not intended by the composer or expected by the listener. This can be risky if the song is well-known, in which case it behooves the arranger to make a convincing case. Frequently, the composer's melody is stylized in repeated sections of the song to provide interest and contrast. Examples of this have been already seen in the section on harmonic half time, a technique that by definition changes the song.

A simple but effective melody alteration occurs in "Sweet Adeline," at and after the key change, where the high melody notes trigger the drive toward the dramatic ending.[177]

Figure 29.56

"Sweet Adeline" melodic alteration. Arranged by Jay Giallombardo.

---

177 Sweet Adelines International. (2018, Oct 19). *ClassRing, Quartet Finals, 2018* [Video]. YouTube. https://youtu.be/iAwSkvYDPkM?t=259

Another example is in the opening of the second chorus of "Please Don't Talk About Me When I'm Gone," where the jumpy melody is replaced by a smoother line.

Figure 29.57

"Please Don't Talk About Me When I'm Gone" melodic alteration. Words and music by Sam H. Stept and Sidney Clare. Arranged by Buzz Haeger.

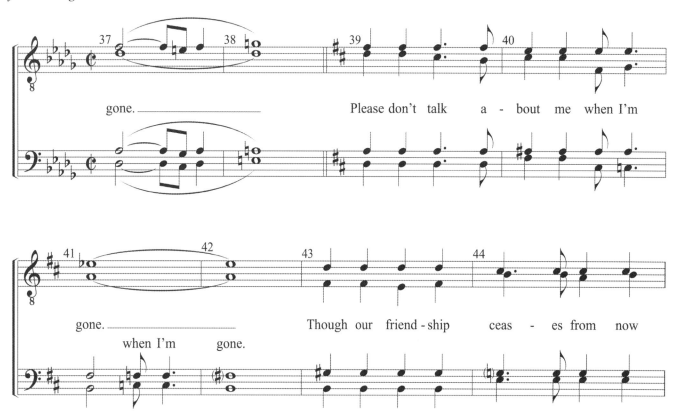

A further example of stylized melody is found in "Louise," when the bridge is repeated with bass melody. Observe how this contrasts with the bridge in the first chorus. Figure 29.58 features the first chorus, where the melody matches the original composer's version.[178]

Figure 29.58

"Louise" first chorus. Arranged by David Wright.

---

178 Barbershop Harmony Society. (2017, Jun 22). *Michigan Jake - Louise (2000 International)* [Video]. YouTube. https://youtu.be/ GdnIIPzyK2M

Figure 29.59 features the second chorus, with a stylized melody as one might hear in a jazz version of the song.

Figure 29.59

"Louise" stylized melody. Arranged by David Wright

Another excellent example is "Love Me."[179] Here, as is noted in the section on rhythmic propellants, the bass propels the first chorus. But in the repeated half chorus, the arranger fills the space with numerous triplets, sung homorhythmically, that stylize the melody.

Figure 29.60

"Love Me" stylized melody. Arranged by Aaron Dale.

179 OCTenor2. (2008, August 24). *OC Times: Love Me* [Video]. YouTube. https://youtu.be/qrvai9qHvEA

Some melodies just beg to be stylized. Note how melodic stylization pervades "Love Me or Leave Me," generating energy and fun as the entire chorus is repeated. In the same example, note how the composer's verse has been modified in the last four measures in the verse to launch the song with a tremendous burst of energy.[180]

Figure 29.61

"Love Me or Leave Me" stylized melody. Arranged by Patrick McAlexander.

180 Barbershop Harmony Society. (2017, Mar 14). *Instant Classic - Love Me or Leave Me (live at the 2016 AIC Show)* [Video]. YouTube. https://youtu.be/v39ERSTk-QY

The stylized melody in the final chorus of "Georgia on My Mind," after the bridge, allows for a dramatic, high-energy outburst, before the song finally winds down.[181]

Figure 29.62

"Georgia on My Mind" stylized melody. Words and music by Stuart Gorrell and Hoagy Carmichael. Arranged by David Harrington.

181 Barbershop Harmony Society. (2019, Oct 15). *Forefront - Georgia on My Mind* [Video]. YouTube. https://youtu.be/xRLUVzcRsGc

Stylized melodies are often static, with the lead singing measures of mostly one note while preserving the harmonic rhythm, a technique often used in jazz and pop. Note the effectiveness of the static melody in "Ring-a-Ding Ding!" in the second chorus right after the final key change, with the lead riding notes around F and G.[182]

Figure 29.63

"Ring-a-Ding-Ding!" stylized melody. Arranged by Anthony Bartholomew.

---

182 Barbershop Harmony Society. (2016, Jul 10). *Forefront - Ring-a-Ding-Ding!* [Video]. YouTube. https://youtu.be/TbTjlliYU74

In "Cuddle Up a Little Closer," study the unfolding stylizations that are necessary to make this three-chorus arrangement work.[183]

Figure 29.64

"Cuddle Up a Little Closer," chorus 1. Arranged by Clay Hine.

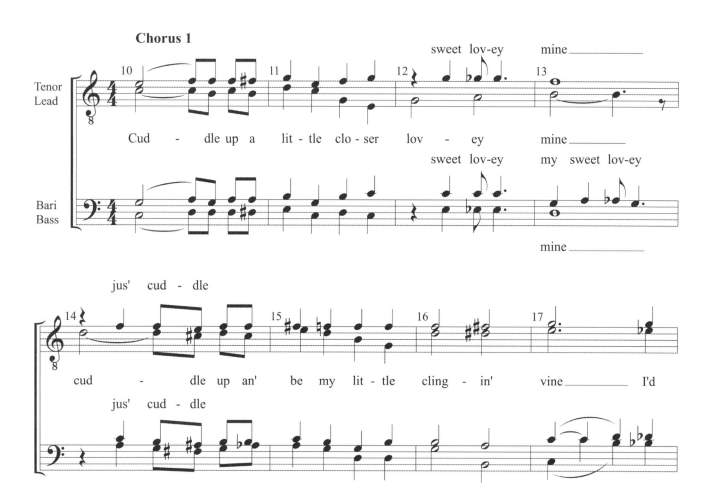

183 Barbershop Harmony Society. (2023, Mar 3). *The Ladies - Cuddle up a Little Closer, Lovey Mine [from Three Twins]* [Video]. YouTube. https://youtu.be/6MvRIHhxKFs

Figure 29.65

"Cuddle Up a Little Closer," chorus 2. Arranged by Clay Hine.

Figure 29.66

"Cuddle Up a Little Closer," chorus 3. Arranged by Clay Hine.

In "Cruella De Vil" the arranger provides alternate lyrics in the second chorus that not only help the story develop, but also furnish syllables for the triplets that create rhythmic interest. Without this the song would have an awkward gap.[184]

Figure 29.67

"Cruella de Vil" with added lyrics. Words and music by Mel Levin. Arranged by David Wright.

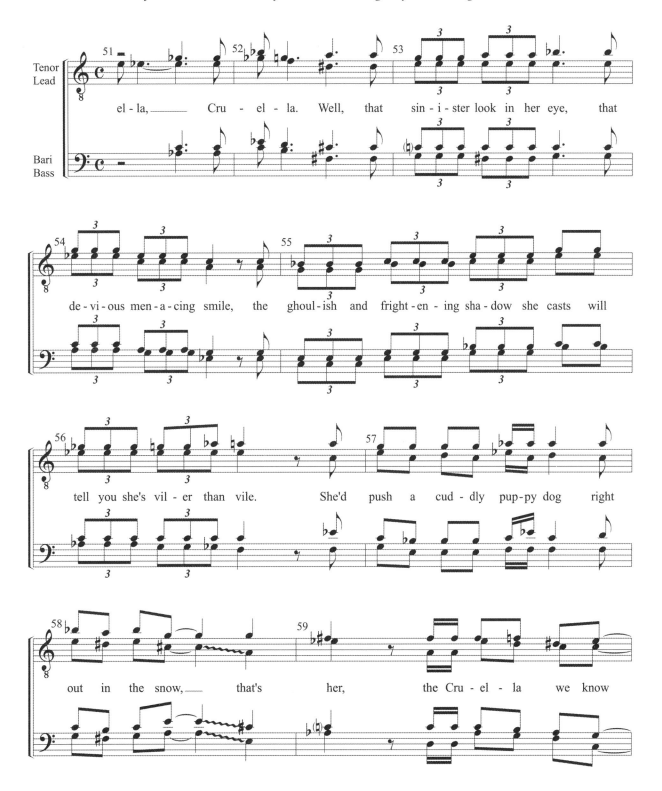

184 Barbershop Archive. (2019, Feb 4). *Vocal Spectrum - Cruella De Vil (2005 BABS Sunday Afternoon Show)* [Video]. YouTube. https://youtu.be/YU9rUXf11zQ?si=EGvM3iynhEfLpuBQ

Changing the composer's intended harmonization is done routinely in barbershop arrangements and in all styles of music; however, in "Cry Me a River," the arranger alters an iconic chord in a well-known melody from the minor ninth rooted on VI to the minor III triad, the first note in each A section in an AABA form, to avoid the dissonance of the minor ninth chord, which is a non-vocabulary chord. This is manifestly dangerous, as it may jolt the listener, but in this case it seems the harmonic flavor is preserved well enough that, along with the skillful disguise of the alteration and the tremendous overall strengths of the chart, the arrangement not only survived but became a classic.

Figure 29.68

"Cry Me a River." Arranged by Brent Graham.

 Caution is advised, though, in arbitrarily changing conspicuous notes in known melodies. The changed melody notes can seem obvious, and fans of the song may feel betrayed hearing changes to the melody they hear in their heads.

Sometimes an arranger will write new lyrics to a repeated portion, either to avoid an unwanted repetition or to help develop the story. In one that has become a classic, "That's An Irish Lullaby" has alternate lyrics and melody alteration in the second chorus. It is followed by a half chorus, giving a powerful culmination to a tender ballad.[185] If the lyrics are well-written this is a more organic choice than simply adding a closing line ending in an *open vowel* that doesn't complete a rhyme, which can sound arbitrary and artificial.

> An *open vowel* is a vowel sound in which the tongue is positioned as far as possible from the roof of the mouth. Open and near-open examples from the International Phoenetic Alphabet include a, œ, ä, and æ.

Figure 29.69

"That's An Irish Lullaby." Words and music by James Royce Shannon. Arranged by Ed Waesche.

185 TalkinShop. (2011, Jul 23). *Acoustix - 1990 International Quartet Semifinal Song #2* [Video]. YouTube. https://youtu.be/ WK9Y4iwfTNE

"If I Only Had a Brain" is a good example of an arrangement that alters the composer's intent by changing the interpretation of the song.[186] The listener expects the song to rollick in six-eight time but this arrangement invites the performer to begin the chorus ad lib, morphing to a slow swing.

Figure 29.70

"If I Only Had a Brain." Arranged by Clay Hine.

186 Central States District. (2021, Jun 7). *Four Voices | If I Only Had a Brain, No No Nora* [Video]. YouTube. https://youtu.be/Ha1ATMRakpQ

Key Changes

Many, perhaps most, arrangements will involve at least one key change. But before launching this discussion we should note that there are classic examples of arrangements that do not have a key change because it is simply not needed and might actually detract. Notable examples, worthy of study by virtue of their lasting success, include "Jeanie with the Light Brown Hair," arranged by Ed Waesche, "Beautiful Dreamer," arranged by David Wright, and "Yesterday I Heard the Rain," arranged by Brent Graham.

However, because key changes of various types are so frequently needed, we will devote quite a bit of attention to this topic. By now the reader is aware of key changes that lift the key by a half step or a step by going to the dominant seventh chord of the new key. Advanced arrangers use not only these, but also other non-standard key changes. Evoking the dominant of the new key is certainly effective in getting to any desired new key. Dramatic key changes up a minor third can arise this way, as in "If I Give My Heart to You."

Figure 29.71

"If I Give My Heart to You" minor third key change. Words and music by Jimmie Crane, Jimmy Brewster, and Al Jacobs. Arranged by Jim Clancy.

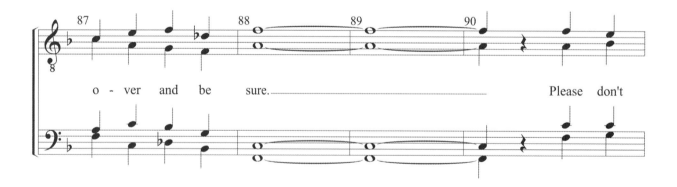

Note how naturally this technique works in "I Want You, I Need You, I Love You" to raise the key by a tritone. Here the change of key almost sounds like a half-step key lift.

Figure 29.72

"I Want You, I Need You, I Love You." Words and music by Maurice Mysels and Ira Kosloff. Arranged by Aaron Dale.

One common key change raises the key by a fourth. This can be perfect for transferring the melody to the bass, moving the melody into the bass's range. A classic example of this is in "Always," where the bass takes the melody briefly in the repeated section of the chorus. Here the duration of the new key is so short it is not notated in the music.

Figure 29.73

"Always" key change with melody transfer to bass. Arranged by Mark Hale and Don Gray.

In "Supercalifragilisticexpialidocious," a key change lowers the key a minor third to allow for a bass melody.[187]

Figure 29.74

"Supercalifragilisticexpialidocious" words and music by Richard and Robert Sherman. Arranged by Anthony Bartholomew.

187 Barbershop Harmony Society. (2017, Aug 18). *The Newfangled Four - Supercalifragilisticexpialidocious [from Mary Poppins]* [Video]. YouTube. https://youtu.be/7BH2CqE5mNQ

Arrangers sometimes make a key change going into a line of the song that is not on the tonic chord, and in that case one might anticipate that chord by hitting its dominant. Note in "Something's Gotta Give," the key change is set up by ♭VI7, so that it sounds like a half-step lift. However, it goes to vi of the new key, thus raising the key a major third.[188]

Figure 29.75

"Something's Gotta Give." Words and music by Johnny Mercer. Arranged by Patrick McAlexander.

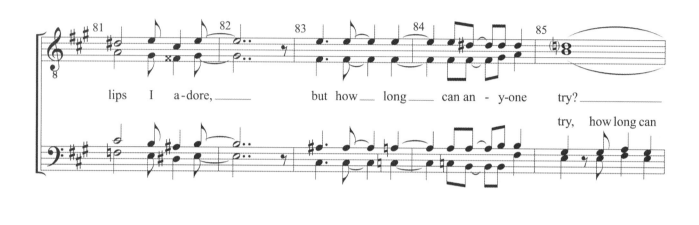

An unusual example is given by "Love Me and the World Is Mine," where, after the lengthy verse, the song makes an unmodulated key change downward a fourth into the first chorus, then returns to the original key for a partial second verse and a concluding half chorus.[189]

---

188 Barbershop Harmony Society. (2022, Oct 11). *The Ladies - Something's Gotta Give* [Video]. YouTube. https://youtu.be/saq-D-uoAdg

189 Barbershop Harmony Society. (2020, Jun 4). *Ringmasters - Love Me and the World is Mine [Video]*. YouTube. https://youtu.be/Q08GyGncjn0

Figure 29.76

"Love Me and the World is Mine" key change. Words and music by Ernest Ball and Dave Reed Jr. Arranged by David Wright.

Key changes are sometimes employed to delineate changes of mood or of character. Note in "Liar Medley" the skillful use of keys to delineate the contradictory identities assumed by the narrator, descending when the person is devious.

Figure 29.77

"Liar Medley" descending key change. Arranged by Renee Craig.

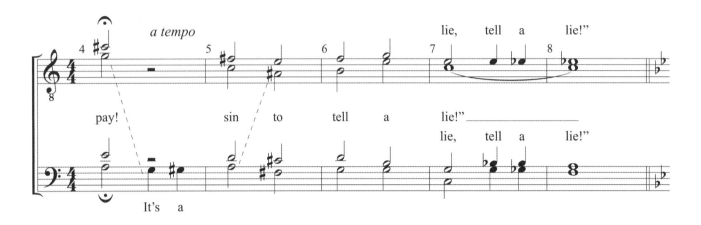

The key change is ascending when virtuous, as shown in figure 29.78.[190]

Figure 29.78

"Liar Medley" ascending key change. Arranged by Renee Craig.

---

190 Barbershop Harmony Society. (Nov 2, 2017). *Keepsake - How Could You Believe Me/It's a Sin to Tell a Lie Medley* [Video]. YouTube. https://youtu.be/vJrkY6tQSIM?si=2_rD66CIAwG1dG2d

When the desired effect is a major lift or a surprise, the experienced arranger often changes the key by a tertian interval, meaning the interval of a major or minor third, upward or downward.

Figure 29.79

"Liar Medley" tertian key change. Arranged by Renee Craig.

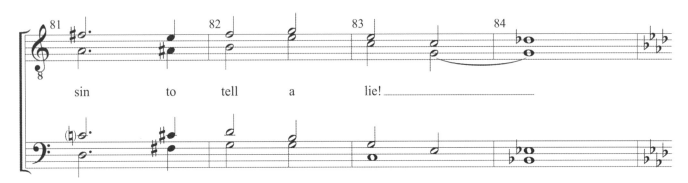

As we said before, key changes often use the dominant chord of the new key as the modulation chord leading to the key change. For example, swiping from the tonic chord I to I7 modulates to raising the key by a fourth. However, sometimes the arranger avoids the expected modulation, either by proceeding directly to the new key or by striking a chord other than the dominant of the new key. This can provide a sudden shift of mood, a dramatic transformation, or a powerful lift. A striking example occurs in "Parade Medley," where in the final chorus the ♭VI7 chord leads directly to a key change up a major third. Note in this example how the arrangement creates the impression that the song is about to end using half time and echo effects, then bursts suddenly into the new key, which justifies the extension of the song.

Figure 29.80

"I Love a Parade" key change. Words and music by Ted Koehler and Harold Arlen. Arranged by Jay Giallombardo.

The classic "Bye Bye Blues" changes the key up a fourth after the intro using III7, not I7, as the modulating chord.[191]

Figure 29.81

"Bye Bye Blues" key change. Words and music by Fred Hamm, Dave Bennett, Bert Lown, and Chauncey Gray. Arranged by Lem Childers.

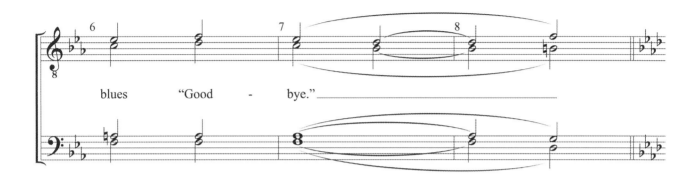

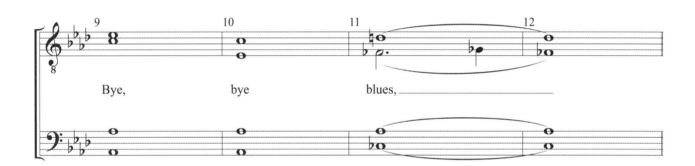

191 Barbershop Harmony Society. (Feb 23, 2018). *The Suntones - Bye Bye Blues (live on the 1988 AIC Show)* [Video]. YouTube, https://youtu.be/42NAaurx4lU?si=cKBJ8ajkcRLaqE5s

Another example is in "She's Got a Way" where, in the second chorus, the key lifts a half step preempted by a high hanging seventh on V.[192]

Figure 29.82

"She's Got a Way." Words and music by Billy Joel. Arranged by David Wright.

192 Barbershop Harmony Society. (2019, Mar 27). *Zero8 - She's Got a Way (Billy Joel cover)* [Video]. YouTube. https://youtu.be/gvACHiEFNqg

And another example occurs in "I Get Along Without You Very Well," where V7 goes directly and beautifully to the first inversion of the tonic chord of the new key, which is up a major third.[193] This is rare but can be effective if skillfully written.

Figure 29.83

"I Get Along Without You Very Well," Words and music by Hoagy Carmichael. Arranged by David Zimmerman.

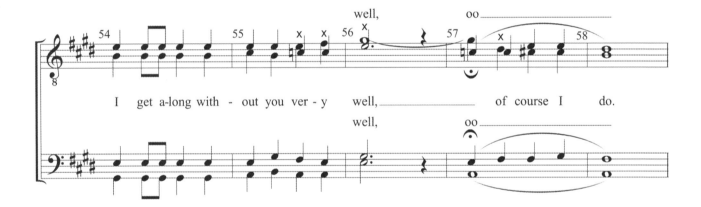

193 Barbershop Harmony Society. (Dec 7, 2018). *Instant Classic - I Get Along Without You Very Well (2018 AIC Show)* [Video]. YouTube. https://youtu.be/1KrZQh-weDo?si=5Tpbt2kryXGxQeXo

Short-term key changes can also make the transition into a desired key more pleasing, less arbitrary sounding. Note in "Not While I'm Around / No One Is Alone" how the arranger lowers the key a minor third by raising the key a major third for a transition, then raising again by a fourth to get to the final key, setting up the tag with a feeling of lift not descent.[194]

Figure 29.84

"Not While I'm Around / No One Is Alone" key changes. Arranged by Steve Tramack.

---

194 Barbershop Harmony Society. (2019, Oct 15). *After Hours - Not While I'm Around [from Sweeney Todd]* [Video]. YouTube. https://youtu.be/lEIT8s5LSWg

Sometimes a subtle key change is created by repeating a section of the song in which a temporary modulation was in progress, but without the modulation. A good example of this is "All the Things You Are," where the song modulates down a half step for a portion of the chorus.[195]

Figure 29.85

"All the Things You Are." Words and music by Oscar Hammerstein II and Jerome Kern. Arranged by Steve Delehanty.

195 Barbershop Harmony Society. (Aug 30, 2019). *Alexandria Harmonizers - All the Things You Are* [Video]. YouTube. https://youtu.be/6xwAX7nUEqg?si=OEzqYIJAAVpV8aEE

After completing the chorus, the arrangement goes to that point but in the original key, thereby eventually lifting the key by a half step. This is far more sophisticated than the standard half-step key lift.

Figure 29.86

"All the Things You Are." Arranged by Steve Delehanty.

A skillful arranger occasionally writes a fairly quick sequence of key changes to generate excitement. This has to be done with care so that it delights rather than confuses the listener. One example of this is "Put Your Arms Around Me," as shown in Figure 29.87. The arrangement features two quick key changes in the verse in measures 4–5 and measures 8–9, then descends a step into the chorus in measures 16–17 after a flurry of echoes and swipes.[196]

Figure 29.87

"Put Your Arms Around Me" key changes. Arranged by Aaron Dale.

196 Barbershop Harmony Society. (2009, Jan 9). *Max Q - 2007 International Quartet Champions* [Video]. YouTube. https://youtu.be/kwxEHFVHkAM

"Stormy Weather" also features three different keys in the verse to help set up a mood of despair.[197]

Figure 29.88

"Stormy Weather" key changes. Arranged by Aaron Dale.

197 Barbershop Harmony Society. (Aug 15, 2016). *Da Capo - Stormy Weather* [Video]. YouTube. https://youtu.be/ MIxaOQuw4_4?si=Hai-kpszYiPmkj9Y

Occasionally the tonal center changes at the very end of the song by eventually settling on a final chord other than the tonic chord. This can be to arrive at a more preferred tessitura for the final voicing or just for a pleasant surprise. Two examples when the key goes up a fifth at the tag are "Put Your Arms Around Me" and "California Here I Come." Note in the latter how the harmony behind the sustained lead hanger serves to cajole the listener into accepting the new tonal center, hopefully without even noticing.

Figure 29.89

"Put Your Arms Around Me." Arranged by Aaron Dale.

Figure 29.90

"California, Here I Come." Words and music by Bud DeSylva, Joseph Meyer, and Al Jolson. Arranged by David Wright.

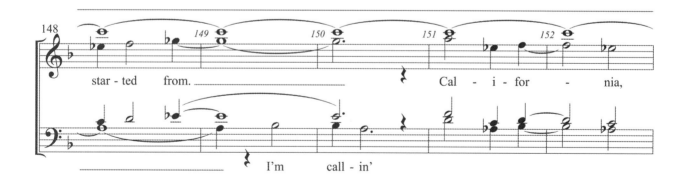

Finally, sometimes a key change can have a practical purpose, as in "Redhead," where the half-step downward key change in the second chorus brings the key back to where it was previously so the high tag isn't too high. It also sounds delightful, effected by a quick sequence of eight circle-of-fifths progressions landing in the new key.

Figure 29.91

"Redhead" key change. Arranged by Jim Clancy. Key change arranged by Dennis Driscoll.

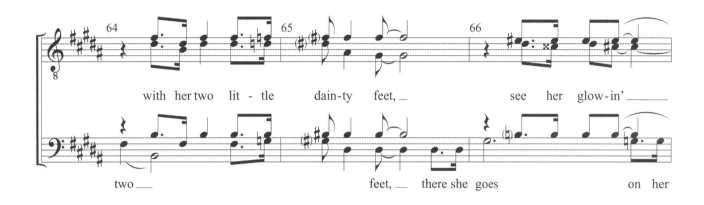

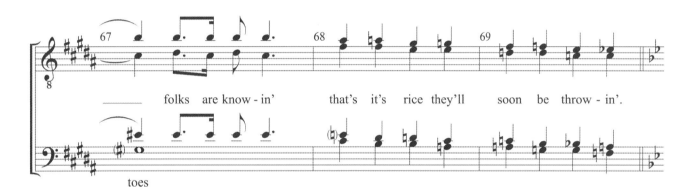

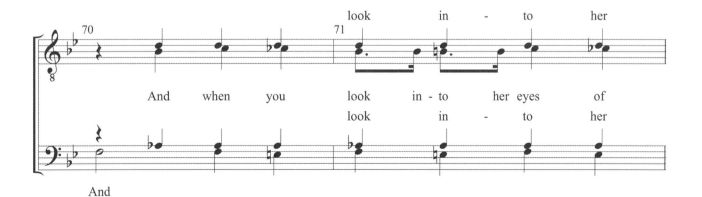

A second example is in the second chorus of "Please Don't Talk About Me When I'm Gone," where a step downward descent makes room for a minor third upward lift to follow.

Figure 29.92

"Please Don't Talk About Me When I'm Gone," Arranged by Buzz Haeger.

Note the sequence of chords, ascending chromatically, leading into the latter.

Figure 29.93

"Please Don't Talk About Me When I'm Gone," arranged by Buzz Haeger.

Rhythmic Propellants

When a song is to be sung in tempo it is usually incumbent on the arranger to supply various devices that serve to define and drive the rhythm, and to fill in beats where the melody is sustained. Examples of such devices include lead-ins, echoes, downbeats, after beats, backtime, added syllables, and alteration of the composer's rhythm. If the song, for example, needs to maintain a slow driving rhythm over a long period of time, these propellants may need to be pervasive to sustain it. In other instances a few well-placed devices may suffice.

A superb example where the arranger provides just the needed propellants, mostly with downbeats and echoes, yet keeps the arrangement uncluttered is "You Make Me Feel So Young."

Figure 29.94

You Make Me Feel So Young." Words and music by Mack Gordon and Josef Myrow. Arranged by Mark Hale.

Another such example is "Pass Me the Jazz," which sustains a jazzy feel throughout, using rhythmic devices when needed and avoiding them when not.[198]

Figure 29.95

"Pass Me the Jazz." Arranged by Jeremey Johnson.

---

198 Barbershop Harmony Society. (Oct 16, 2015). *Lemon Squeezy - Pass Me the Jazz (International 2015)* [Video]. YouTube. https://youtu.be/rytUvA1xJwg?si=_yzFQB0p_UL_KMUY

The slow, bluesy grind of "Georgia on My Mind" is propelled throughout by bass lead-ins and downbeats, as well as walking bass effects.[199]

Figure 29.96

"Georgia On My Mind." Arranged by David Harrington.

Note also the staccato stomp in the non-melodic parts in the second bridge.

199 Barbershop Harmony Society. (2019, Oct 15). *Forefront - Georgia on My Mind* [Video]. YouTube. https://youtu.be/xRLUVzcRsGc

Figure 29.97

"Georgia on My Mind" staccato stomp section. Arranged by David Harrington.

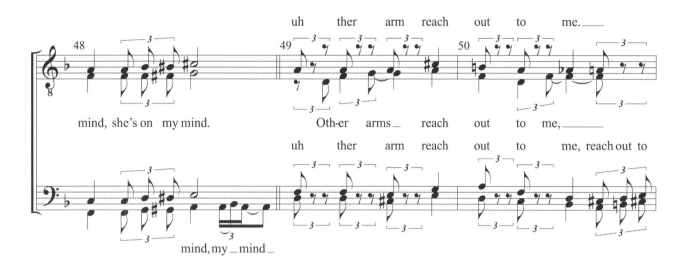

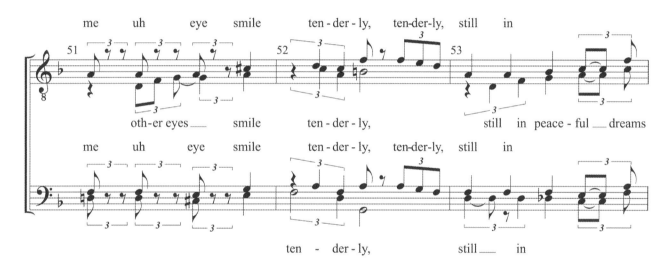

Quite often the main character in rhythmic propellants is the bass, but sometimes other parts are involved, as when the three non melodic parts provide a straight quarter note backtime behind a melody with syncopations and push beats. Note in "I'll Drown In My Own Tears" how the arranger sustains this drive over the course of the entire chorus through a well-chosen combination of swipes, echoes, and backtime.[200]

---

200 Barbershop Harmony Society. (2020, Apr 16). *Signature - Drown in My Own Tears (Lula Reed cover)* [Video]. YouTube. https://youtu.be/rFb3O_2VsHY

Figure 29.98

"I'll Drown in My Own Tears." Words and music by Henry Glover. Arranged by Mark Hale.

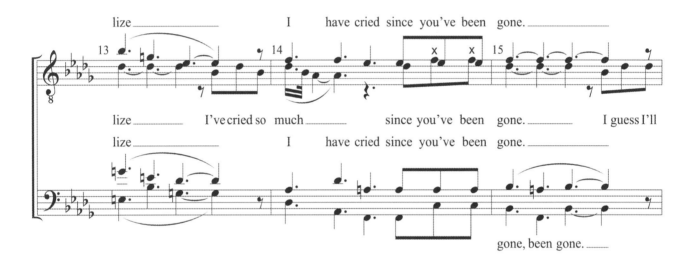

In "I Found A Million Dollar Baby," the appealing slow swing tempo is propelled largely by appropriately placed bass lead-ins.[201]

Figure 29.99

"I Found a Million Dollar Baby." Words and music by Harry Warren, Mort Dixon, and Billy Rose. Arranged by Bill Mitchell, Ed Waesche, and Rob Hopkins.

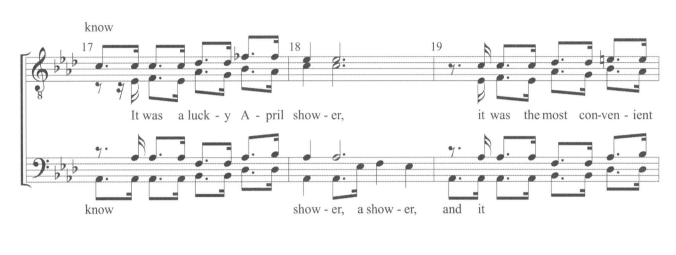

201 Barbershop Archive. (2019, Oct 10). *Marquis - I Found A Million Dollar Baby (1996 BABS Convention)* [Video]. YouTube. https://youtu.be/aGsQCeWoOUg

The same is true for "Love Me," where the bass is the main driver of the slow swing.[202]

Figure 29.100

"Love Me" bass driving the slow swing. Arranged by Aaron Dale.

202 OCTenor2. (2008, August 24). *OC Times: Love Me* [Video]. YouTube. https://youtu.be/qrvai9qHvEA

Note also "Stormy Weather," which utilizes a variety of devices to propel the unhurried tempo. Sometimes a melody that has several phantom downbeats requires frequent lead-ins to reestablish the downbeat.

Figure 29.101

"Stormy Weather." Arranged by Aaron Dale.

Note in the first chorus of "I Got Rhythm" how these are passed around from part to part and to different combinations of parts.[203]

Figure 29.102

"I Got Rhythm." Arranged by David Wright.

Then, in the second chorus with the bass melody, the background lyrics define the rhythm.

203 Barbershop Harmony Society. (Aug 15, 2016). *Forefront - I Got Rhythm* [Video]. YouTube. https://youtu. be/3frH41TZcaU?si=XWUXZU9W-J2gFm8B

Figure 29.103

"I Got Rhythm." Arranged by David Wright.

Chorus 2

Solo

Barbershop is a primarily homorhythmic style, but it departs from it fairly frequently when embellishing features enter the scene, such as rhythmic propellants. The use of solo is another common non-homorhythmic effect, one that is often used to highlight a melody or a particular singer, or just for contrast.

An excellent example where solos are woven throughout the arrangement is "Butter Outta Cream," which deserves careful study. Note how the first chorus features the lead using a combination of neutral syllables and echoes.

Figure 29.104

"Butter Outta Cream" first chorus with lead solo. Words and music by Mark Shaiman and Scott Wittman. Arranged by Dan Wessler.[204]

204 Barbershop Harmony Society. (Aug 18, 2017). *After Hours - Butter Outta Cream [from Catch Me If You Can]* [Video]. YouTube. https://youtu.be/fmE5dsP7z_k?si=JNkvtdewoR4HzwxT

The second chorus changes key and features the bass, but then tosses the melody to the lead, tenor, and baritone. Thereby all four singers become characters in the narrative.

Figure 29.105

"Butter Outta Cream" second chorus with passing solo features. Arranged by Dan Wessler.

The arrangement continually converges back from solo to homorhythm.

Another example is "I'll Drown In My Own Tears," which highlights the lead essentially as a soloist and uses the other parts as propellants to maintain the rhythm's slow grind.[205]

Figure 29.106

"I'll Drown in My Own Tears" lead solo texture. Arranged by Mark Hale.

205 Barbershop Harmony Society. (Aug 15, 2016). *Signature - Drown in My Own Tears* [Video]. YouTube. https://youtu.be/PQn-wpq-21Y?si=8_-kwN1Q7xzVUbDj

Sometimes a simple, brief solo can be effective to reinforce lyrics or generate mood. An example is the two-word solo in "Jeanie With the Light Brown Hair," which begins the last segment of the chorus with a sigh.

Figure 29.107

"Jeanie With the Light Brown Hair," Arranged by Ed Waesche.

Occasionally a barbershop arrangement will contain quite a bit of solo, usually for purposes of characterization. The arranger has to take care that the piece in its entirety is predominantly homorhythmic. An example that lives on this threshold is "If You Go Away;" here the recurring use of solo, interspersed with strong homorhythmic passages, reinforces the storyteller's hopeless plight.

Figure 29.108

"If You Go Away." Arranged by David Wright.

Unison, Duet, and Trio Effects

The use of devices where less than four parts are featured—or even singing—can be useful for many purposes. Solo with neutral syllable background is, of course, one example, but there are others.

Note in "Brother, Can You Spare a Dime" how well the unison sung in the opening line establishes the gaunt mood that is maintained throughout the song.

Figure 29.109

"Brother Can You Spare a Dime" unison effect. Arranged by Steve Armstrong.

Similarly, the solo opening of "Cry Me A River" grabs the listener's attention and dramatically establishes the tone of anger, resentment, and spite that permeates the performance.

Figure 29.110

"Cry Me a River" solo opening line. Arranged by Brent Graham,

A similar example is "Stormy Weather." There are numerous examples of songs opening with solo followed by duet or trio.

Figure 29.111

"Stormy Weather" opening line solo. Arranged by Aaron Dale.

A classic example is "Sweet Adeline," where the opening solo/duet/trio establish effective support and enhance the pensive lyrics.

Figure 29.112

"Sweet Adeline" layered entrance. Arranged by Jay Giallombardo.

Note the haunting opening line of "If You Go Away," which opens with a duet octave in the bass clef, culminating in a four-part swipe.

Figure 29.113

"If You Go Away" Arranged by David Wright.

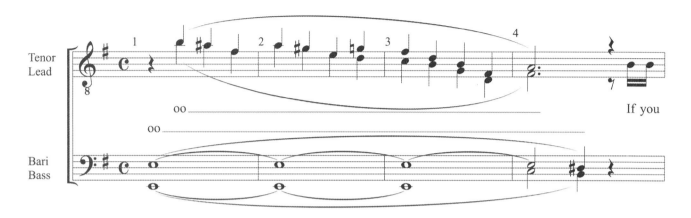

Sometimes a unison note emerging suddenly out of four-part harmony immediately gets the listener's attention. A classic example of this is the striking unison note on "cry," followed by the blossom effect, in the now famous tag of "I'm Sorry I Made You Cry."[206]

Figure 29.114

"I'm Sorry I Made You Cry" tag. Arranged by Brian Beck.

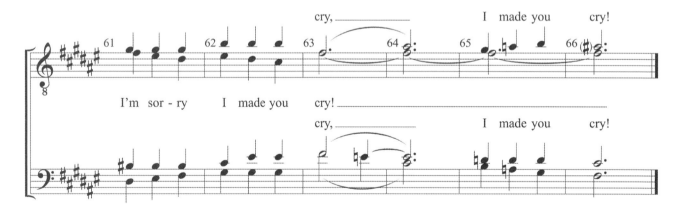

206 Barbershop Harmony Society. (2020, Dec 16). *Side Street Ramblers - I'm Sorry I Made You Cry* [Video]. YouTube. https://youtu.be/zqsKVUV32xc

Duets often impart tenderness and intimacy, exemplified by the lead-baritone and then lead-bass duets in the chorus of "All the Way."

Figure 29.115

"All the Way" lead-baritone duet. Arranged by Tom Gentry.

Figure 29.116

"All the Way" lead-bass duet. Arranged by Tom Gentry.

The arranger of "Bright Was the Night" chooses to use a lead-tenor duet in the second call of the call and echo chorus of this traditional barbershop song. The effect is to help the song evolve towards having a four-part lead-ins in the second half of the chorus, with another duet leading into the tag.

Figure 29.117

"Bright Was the Night" call and response echoes. Arranged by David Wright.

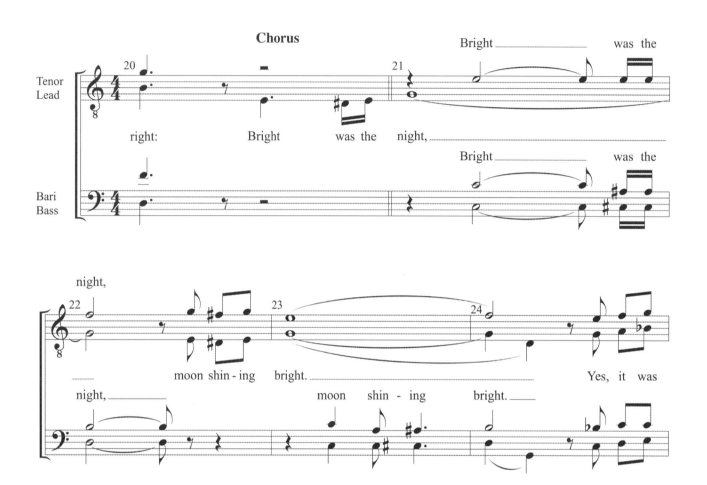

Bass Melody

Brief transfers of melody to the bass can occur to accommodate low lying melody notes and to keep the bass and the other parts in a more comfortable range. Note the cadence at the end of the second A section of "If Ever I Would Leave You," which facilitates a more satisfying echo than what would have been possible otherwise.

Figure 29.118

"If Ever I Would Leave You" bass melody at the end of a cadence. Arranged by Clay Hine.

Also, a bass melody having more duration can also be a good way to provide contrast, as long as the melody is in the lead for most of the arrangement. It works best with melodies that lie predominantly on solid chord tones, namely, roots and fifths. The section in this chapter on key changes mentioned the brief bass melody in "Always," which occurs in the repeated half-chorus, enabled by an un-notated temporary shift of key up a fourth.

Figure 29.119

"Always" bass melody. Arranged by Mark Hale and Don Gray.

Note that "You Make Me Feel So Young" similarly employs bass melody in the second chorus, shifting the key up a fifth, also un-notated.

Figure 29.120

"You Make Me Feel So Young" bass melody. Arranged by Mark Hale.

Another example appears in the "Love Me or Leave Me" second chorus, where the key goes up a fifth into the bass melody, and this also sets up the tessitura for melodic stylizations that ensue.

Figure 29.121

"Love Me or Leave Me" bass melody. Arranged by Patrick McAlexander.

In "She's Got A Way," the eight-bar bass melody after the dramatic key change enables the high neutral syllable chording supplied by the top three parts.

Figure 29.122

"She's Got a Way" bass melody. Arranged by David Wright.

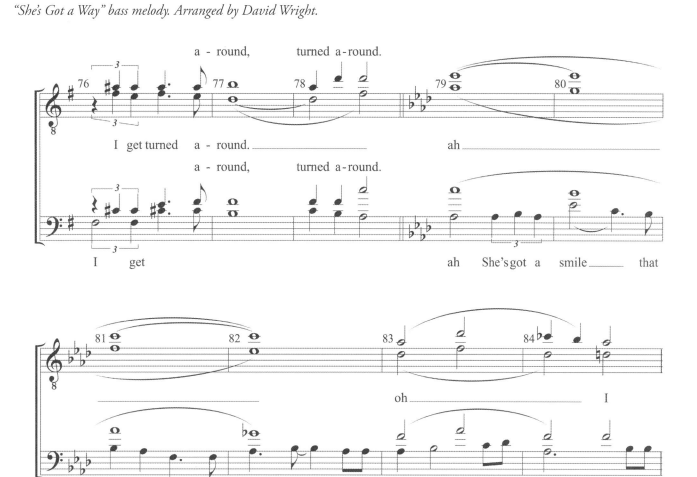

Harmonic Half-Time

A technique that can sometimes be employed to give contrast when a major part of a song is repeated, most commonly a second chorus, is to use half-time. This is called *augmentation* in classical music.

 Augmentation is a compositional device where a melody, theme or motif is extended by lengthening note values—often twice the length of the original note values. This is the opposite of *diminution*, where note values are shortened. This concept is further explored in Chapter 31 of *Arranging Barbershop Vol. 2.*

This simply halves the harmonic rhythm and usually involves adding lyrics rather than just doubling the note values. This can be fairly simple and brief, as when it comes as the song is winding down.

A good example occurs in "All the Way," when the last line of the chorus is repeated before the tag.

Figure 29.123

"All the Way" harmonic half-time. Arranged by Tom Gentry.

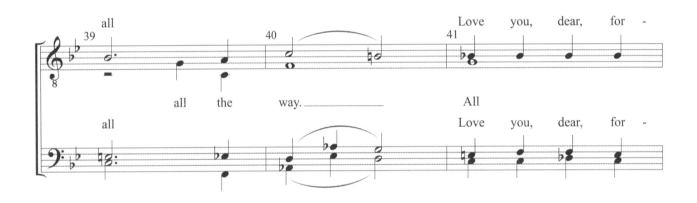

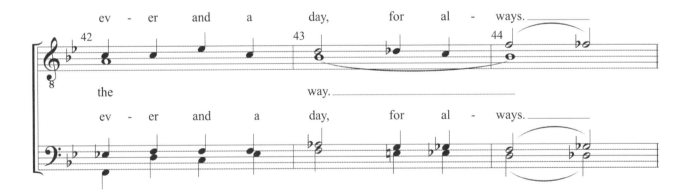

Some traditional barbershop devices necessitate half-time to give them room to operate. One example is the classic "Bye Bye Blues," where the famous bell chord chorus halves the harmonic rhythm to accommodate the bell chords. This is a remarkable use of half-time and embellishment, where the embellishment becomes the focus of the arrangement.

Figure 29.124

"Bye Bye Blues" classic bell chords. Arranged by Lem Childers.

Another device that often calls for half-time is patter. Observe how this works in the well-known patter chorus of "Give Me A Night in June."

Figure 29.125

"Give Me a Night in June" half-time patter. Arranged by Mark Hale.

A more intricate example is heard in "California Here I Come" in the second chorus, following the second verse.

Figure 29.126

"California, Here I Come" harmonic half-time. Arranged by David Wright.

Yet another is "I Got Rhythm," in the third repetition of the chorus where the entire B-section is presented in half-time.

Figure 29.127

"I Got Rhythm" third chorus. Arranged by David Wright.

Note that the latter two examples especially entail a good deal of writing on the part of the arranger to fill the space. In this way the half-time gives opportunity for musical interest and variation.

Adding Harmonic Variety

Barbershop is a style that thrives on harmonic richness and variety. Many songs can be arranged in the style but need harmonic enhancement to give them a satisfying barbershop flavor. Arrangers find various ways to accomplish this, while staying true to the song.

Often static melodic passages will accommodate harmonies that were not a part of the original song. A good example is "Bananaphone," where a children's song built on scale tone six, incorporates circle of fifths movement from VI7 back to tonic.[207]

207 Barbershop Harmony Society. (2017, Jul 28). *The Newfangled Four - Bananaphone* [Video]. YouTube. https://youtu.be/ ESWi63VIAjc

Figure 29.128

"Bananaphone" circle of fifths motion. Words and music by Raffi Cavoukian and Michael Creber. Arranged by Kohl Kitzmiller.

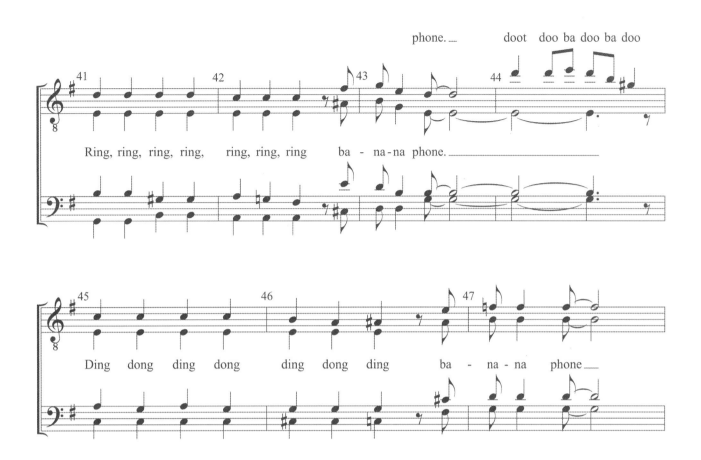

Another excellent example for study is "Auld Lang Syne," where a traditional folk song that implies only three chords is endowed with more than ample harmonic variety by means of using alternate chord choices and the inclusion of added material, i.e. introduction and interlude.

Figure 29.129

"Auld Lang Syne" harmonic variety. Arranged by Clay Hine.

Similarly, the harmonization in "Beautiful Dreamer" adds a great deal of *harmonic interest* that naturally accommodates the melody but is not strictly implied by it.

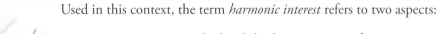

Used in this context, the term *harmonic interest* refers to two aspects:

- Dominant seventh chords built on a variety of roots, i.e., more than just scale tones 1 and 5.
- Alternate harmonizations from what is specified in the original sheet music

Figure 29.130

"Beautiful Dreamer" harmonic interest. Arranged by David Wright.

Review and Final Touches

Before finalizing an arrangement, it is wise to check it over for correctness, inadvertent doubling, and singability. It is advisable to sing through each of the parts making sure the voice leading is conducive to accurate rendering. Ideally, each part flows naturally and even somewhat melodically, making it pleasurable to sing.

It is a good idea to review the overall construction, making sure the arrangement unfolds logically, giving opportunity for development, and maintaining musical interest throughout by virtue of a satisfying sequence of events. One should avoid lengthy sections with no musical highlights where the performer will struggle to sustain musical interest. The best arrangements suggest their own interpretation and musical choices and have clearly defined climaxes and sub-climaxes. That does not mean the performer is totally bound by them, but a plausible plan for shaping, dynamics, tempo choices, and lyrical nuances should be apparent.

One trap to avoid is having repeating passages that are quite similar but slightly different. Of course, variation in repeated sections is often written for good reason to create contrast, but beware the repeated passage where the difference is minuscule, e.g., a difference in the way the baritone dodges the repeated melody for no apparent reason. This can make the arrangement difficult to memorize.

It is a good idea to include breath points for each part, especially if the arrangement is intended for a quartet. This can greatly facilitate the process of learning and refining the performance of the piece. Again, the performer may choose other places to breathe, but if the breath plan is performable and makes sense, they probably will not.

Finally, the arranger should make a final copy of the arrangement that is properly spaced, clear, uncluttered, and easily readable. One should avoid collisions of notes or of note heads with lyrics.

Most arrangers use musical notation software but should not rely on the program's default spacing. Instead, getting a good printout will likely require some manual adjusting. Sometimes, the arranger may decide to include markings that suggest tempo or dynamic changes, especially when a specific musical treatment is intended that is not totally apparent from the context. It is a good idea to label the sections, e.g., verse, chorus 1, chorus 2, interlude, to help the singer understand the construction of the arrangement. These final touches can help educate the singer and better communicate the arranger's intent.

Conclusion

For experienced arrangers, the degree of success of a given arrangement is often dictated by how well the arrangement features the strengths of the ensemble, highlighting and enhancing what makes them unique and special, and minimizes the weaknesses. During the arranging process, the arranger will often be faced with obstacles that will challenge their ability to meet these objectives. This chapter was dedicated to highlighting some of the most frequently-encountered challenges and exploring how expert arrangers overcame the obstacles.

The chapter explored numerous topics: construction and form, fidelity to the composer, added material, use of embellishments, the function of tags, interludes and transitions, advanced key changes, creating harmonic variety, melody passing and improvisation, featuring voices, use of unison/duet/trio, and more. Arrangers will often face these challenges in the development of an arrangement, attempting to create interest and build excitement over the long line of the musical journey. The provided examples represent a small sample of the opportunities for creating interest. Hopefully, these will inspire you in finding the right answer for the ensemble in that musical moment.

Please do take advantage of the reviewing the content from this chapter along with the associated audio and video clips. As a reminder, you can access these clips at www.halleonard.com/mylibrary/ by entering the code from the inside front cover of this book. While there's much to learn from looking at what the arranger did to overcome a given challenge, there's nothing like hearing the result as sung by the ensemble for which the arrangement was intended.

Chapter 30.
Thematic Development Considerations

By Aaron Dale

Introduction

How an arranger develops a song directly influences what emotions a performer can evoke in their listeners. When thinking about your favorite barbershop arrangements, notice how they develop. Look at the techniques and musical elements the arranger used and they contribute to the listening enjoyment.

The source material is an important consideration. How does the form and development of your arrangement compare with the original composer's work? Does it honor the original, but provide opportunities for creativity? Does it feel natural and comfortable?

What you create on paper might be different than how a performer interprets your choices, which might be different than how an audience reacts to the song. Can you imagine hearing this arrangement being performed and feeling a specific way? As you create the arrangement, consider how the techniques you use provide opportunities for a performer.

In this chapter, we'll explore development from several aspects: melodic, harmonic, rhythmic, and textural. We'll also look at some of the differences when arranging for choruses versus quartets, show versus contest, and medleys versus single songs. Chapter 31 will explore rhythmic development in more depth. Let's dive in.

Before You Begin

Before starting to notate, it can help to sketch out a basic outline for the whole arrangement. This concept was discussed in detail in Chapter 12 of *Arranging Barbershop Vol. 1*. Outlining the arrangement could be a good starting point and guide, which you can obviously change as needed.

Points to consider:

- General length
- Key signatures and modulation places
- Meter and time signature options
- Will keys, meter or time signature change at all?
- Large form, e.g., intro, verses, chorus, etc
- Tempo changes
- Climax points

Melodic Development

The melody is one of the most important and identifiable parts of a song. It is likely the melody that we hum long after the song is finished. How an arranger treats the melody is of utmost importance. This section will explore how to develop a melody with melodic alterations and passing the melody to other voices.

Map the Melody

With any new arrangement you should identify the nature of the melody for the entire song. This includes mapping the highest and lowest pitches, repeated motifs, areas of change, *conjunct* versus *disjunct* intervals, and challenging sections. Let's look at each of these a little further.

Melodic Range

Melodic range refers to the distance between the highest and lowest notes in the melody. Melody ranges can be defined as narrow—typically within a fifth—or wide—greater than a fifth. In barbershop, we almost always hear songs with wide-ranging melodies.

Consider "You Make Me Feel So Young." At the beginning of the chorus, the melody seems to exist within a narrow range. It's not until the second phrase and the melodic leap on "time" that we get a sense for the range of the melody and the challenge presented by the surprising melodic leap.

Figure 30.1

"You Make Me Feel So Young" melody structure, demonstrating a narrow range in the first phrases followed by a wide range in the second phrase.

Motifs and Phrases

A *motif*, also called a *motive*, is a musical molecule. It is a recognizable sequence of pitches and rhythms that are often associated with hooks in popular songs. Motifs are often contained within a phrase, that function similar to a musical sentence. When we think of a well-known song, the sequence of pitches you first hear in your head—often associated with the title of the song—is likely a motif or a phrase containing a key motif. Motifs and phrases are repeated, often in a sequence at different pitch level.

Note the melody in the chorus of Irving Berlin's "Always." The first phrase contains the key motif from the composition that starts at the melodic peak of the phrase and descends on the word "Always." Note the repeated, ascending sequence starting with "when the things you've planned," ending with a repeated title motif. Brilliant melodic writing.

Figure 30.2

"Always" sequential phrases and motif. Words and music by Irving Berlin. Arranged by Don Gray and Mark Hale.

Melodic Variation

Variation is a formal technique in music where portions are repeated in an altered form. In the case of melody, a theme in the form of a motif, phrase or entire section of form is established. In subsequent iterations, the material is modified in some fashion. It could be specific melody notes within the melodic contour, the rhythm associated with the melody, or harmonization changes that highlight different aspects of the melody.

Note this example from "Georgia On My Mind." In this case, the arranger, David Harrington, leverages the original melody in the first chorus.

Figure 30.3

"Georgia on My Mind" melodic theme establishment. Arranged by David Harrington.

In the second chorus, reminiscent of a jazz or blues singer stylization, David provides melodic variation following a key change through a melismatic riff, creating a great deal of excitement heading toward the climax of the song.

Figure 30.4

"Georgia on My Mind" second chorus with melodic variation. Arranged by David Harrington.

Intervals and Motion

The concept of intervals, addressing both interval quantity and quality, is addressed in depth in *Arranging Barbershop Vol.1*, Chapter 5: Theory of Barbershop Harmony. The types of intervals that define a section of melody also help define the melodic motion: *conjunct* or *disjunct*.

Conjunct and *disjunct* refer to melodic motion. Conjunct motion moves in smaller steps—chromatic or scale degree—while disjunct motion refers to interval leaps of greater than a major second. A combination of melodic contour and type of motion can imply degree and types of emotion conveyed by the melody.

Consider this passage from the beginning of the chorus from "You Make Me Feel So Young." The first phrase features ascending conjunct motion with growing disjunct qualities, e.g., the full step, then minor third, then major third in measures 15–16. The next four measures feature ascending and descending disjunct leaps, followed by a descending chromatic passage. There is a great sense of symmetry and contrast within the line.

Figure 30.5

"You Make Me Feel So Young" melodic motion examples. Words and music by Mack Gordon and Josef Myrow. Arranged by Mark Hale.

Special Considerations for Challenges

Ask yourself if the entire melody can be sung by an average singer or if it is extreme or diverse in some way that makes it challenging. Generally speaking, most songs have melodic notes that stay with one voice part. Check the original melody to see if all pitches can be sung by the lead(s) of the ensemble. This is especially important when you're tailoring the arrangement to a specific group.

Note the melody at the beginning of the chorus of "On the Sunny Side of the Street." This is certainly a wide-ranging melody, traveling an octave and a third in the first phrase. When arranging this in the key of C, one might consider passing the melody in the first line to the bass in order to keep the overall tessitura manageable.

Figure 30.6

"On the Sunny Side of the Street" rangy melody. Words and music by Jimmy McHugh and Dorothy Fields.

Melodic Alterations

Explore available scores or recorded versions of the song to discover any melodic variations. Sometimes the melody has been altered in a particular recording from what was originally written. The altered versions might fit your arrangement better or could be utilized in developed sections. These options could also fit better in the barbershop style.

 Some copyright holders have rules on whether a melody may be altered from the original. Before doing so, it's best to check, or at least be prepared if the copyright holder requires reverting to the original melody.

Sometimes the melody was written one way but performed slightly differently in an iconic version. Figure 30.7 features a portion of the piano and vocal score for "The Bells of Notre Dame." You'll see this phrase written with pitch G in the melody on the word "use." This allowed an A7 chord to be used in the barbershop version, shown in Figure 30.8.

Figure 30.7

"The Bells of Notre Dame," words and music by Alan Menken and Stephen Schwartz.

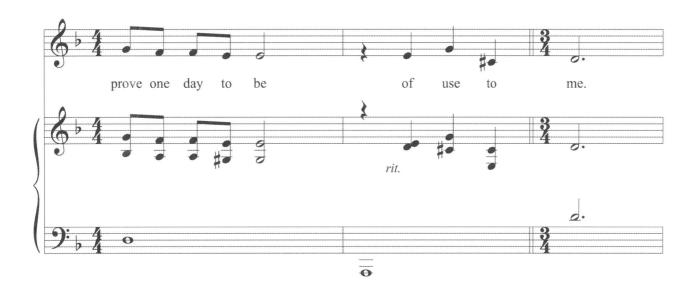

Figure 30.8

"The Bells of Notre Dame," arranged by Aaron Dale.

However, the version of the recording uses F natural there instead, as heard in referenced YouTube clip.[208]

208 disneysoundrack89. (2012, Jun 11). *The Hunchback of Notre Dame OST - 01 - The Bells of Notre Dame* [Audio]. YouTube. https://youtu.be/c4COfl8DMB8?t=323

On occasion, if done tastefully, you might consider altering a few melodic notes to help the harmony. Note the melody in measure 12 in Figure 30.9. The original melody on "a love" is G#–G♮, versus the A–G# in the arrangement.[209] This minor alteration allows for better flow harmonically.[210]

Figure 30.9

"Don't Be a Baby, Baby," words and music by Buddy Kaye and Howard Steiner. Arranged by Aaron Dale.

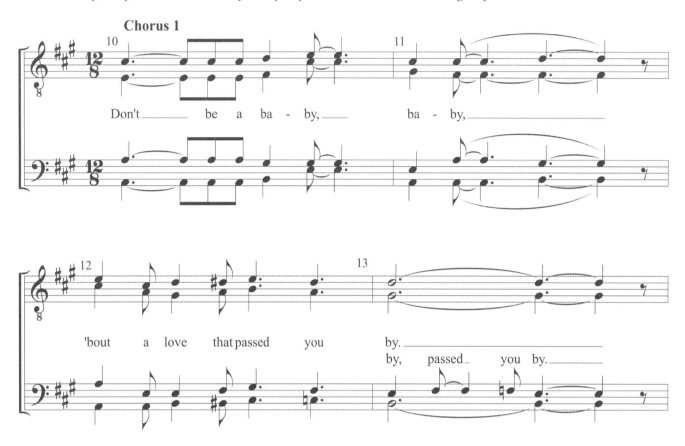

Remember, the melody you use could be what is most famous from a recording; rarely will anyone have seen the original sheet music. Stay true to the established melody the first time through a passage before embellishing

Melody Passing

Be aware of places where the melody might approach the range extremes of the lead singer. Do you want the melody singer to have to switch to their head voice or falsetto if it goes too high or to sing with a breathy or gravelly tone if it goes too low? Passing the melody to another voice can be an excellent solution. If passing the melody to a harmony part, considerations should be made.[211]

209 The 78Prof. (2019, Jun 18). *1946 HITS ARCHIVE: Don't Be A Baby Baby - Mills Brothers* [Audio]YouTube. https://youtu.be/ VBgPz7In7GA

210 Barbershop Harmony Society. (2017, Aug 16). *Parkside Harmony - Don't Be a Baby, Baby* [Video]. YouTube. https://youtu.be/6_ szZ666l00

211 On a related note, finding the right key will affect where you go with the arrangement and can help with range challenges.

When passing the melody to a harmony part, keep in mind three considerations. First, if the melodic range is suitable to allow key modulations, you can start the arrangement in a key appropriately low enough so the melody goes where you desire, intensifying as the song progresses. Second, the baritone voice typically sings pitches in the middle of each chord throughout the song. If the melody is passed to the baritone, it typically will sound just like the lead as long as it stays below the tenor. Last, if you shift the melody to the tenor, those pitches will be heard as the highest note of each chord, so the tenor melody passage should be arranged appropriately for the length of the song for the purpose of contrast and development.

Here is an example of brief passages of bass, baritone, and tenor melody of sufficient length to create the intended contrasting effects within this phrase.

Figure 30.10

An example of melody briefly passing between sections. "Cruella De Vil" melody passing. Arranged by David Wright.

 Extended passages of melody in the highest voice, whether or not it is sung by the tenor, diminish the sense of the barbershop style. The same considerations should be made when passing the melody to the bass: an appropriate length that is suitable for development and contrast.

Melody in an inside voice is one of the immutable laws of barbershop, as discussed in Chapter 2 of *Arranging Barbershop Vol. 1*. If the arrangement is not for use in a barbershop contest, use tenor or bass melody as desired and appropriate for your arrangement.

Here is an example of longer passages of bass and tenor melody of sufficient length to create the intended contrasting effects within this phrase.

Figure 30.11

This excerpt of "Butter Outta Cream," words and music by Mark Shaiman and Scott Wittman and arranged by Dan Wessler, is an example of longer phrases where the melody is passed to other voices.

More details about acceptability of tenor and bass melody can be found in the *Barbershop Harmony Society Contest and Judging Manual*, available at www.barbershop.org. Each barbershop singing organization has a similar set of guidelines for contest suitability. It's always best to confirm the guidelines before arranging with that purpose in mind.

Summary of Melodic Development

Melody is one of the core building blocks of music. So much inherent development is built into what makes melody compelling: range, motion, motifs, sequences, and variation. As an arranger, you can further develop using the melody through form and construction, melodic alterations, and passing to other singers to highlight melodic features.

Harmonic Development

When people hear a song in the barbershop style, there are a few markers that identify it as barbershop rather than some other a cappella style. These include four-part a cappella harmony with the melody sung by an inside voice, leveraging secondary dominants and circle of fifths progressions, delivered through primarily homorhythmic textures. One of the most noticeable characteristics of barbershop is its harmony: both chord vocabulary and chord progressions. When considering developing a song harmonically, an arranger should also consider performance implications of singing the chords, especially as it relates to voice leading and singer range.

Chord Vocabulary

Consonant harmony is a hallmark of the barbershop style. Music can be thought of as simultaneously produced tones, chords, performed in succession over time, phrases, within a hierarchy of perceived relationships, tonality. Chords that produce feelings of pleasantness, rest, or stability are thought to be consonant. Chords that have energy or that produce a feeling of instability can be thought of as dissonant. Phrases of chords can include a variety of qualities from more stable to less stable, or dissonant, but most often result in a stable finish/cadence.

Both dissonance and consonance exist on a spectrum from completely stable to completely unstable. The most stable chords are triads comprising a root and a fifth and some quality of a third—either major or minor. Less stable but still consonant chords comprise a fourth tone beyond the triad. Sixths, sevenths, and ninths are the most common in barbershop.

In barbershop, consonant chords always contain a root, a third of some quality, a fifth of some quality, and many times a flatted seventh. Completely unstable chords are those without a discernible tonality, lacking a third to determine its quality. These are not found in barbershop arrangements.

Of note, the chord that is most characteristic of the barbershop style is one that has the combination of the relatively stable perfect fifth and the tension-filled tritone that comprises the dominant seventh chord—what we call a barbershop seventh. The tritone within a barbershop seventh produces energy that propels the unstable interval tones toward stability, producing a chord change. Our barbershop harmony ears crave that chord progression.

The chord vocabulary found in barbershop arrangements on the contest stage has changed over the years. Still, the style favors consonant harmony, harmonic variety, and strong-voiced chords featuring tritones. The list of chords that are considered to be in the barbershop vocabulary are:

- Major triad
- Major triad with a minor seventh, also known as a barbershop seventh
- Major triad with a major sixth, also known as an add6
- Major triad with a major ninth, also known as an add9
- Minor triad
- Minor triad with a minor seventh
- Half-diminished seventh
- Fully-diminished seventh

Less frequent, but still used:

- Major triad with a major seventh
- Barbershop seventh with flatted fifth
- Dominant ninth with root omitted
- Augmented triad
- Augmented dominant seventh
- Diminished triad

Nonstandard chords such as the dominant 13th, the minor triad with a major seventh, or the minor triad with major ninth are considered non-vocabulary chords and should be avoided except in specific, rare, well-considered instances.

Nonstandard color chords must be used sparingly in an arrangement and only if used appropriately. If used in a contest, judges will evaluate the suitability of the choice. Consider one of the most famous examples in the history of the style: the 13th chord on beat 2 in measure 26 named for the arranger, Ed Waesche.[212]

Figure 30.12

"Jeanie with the Light Brown Hair" with words and music by Stephen Foster and arranged by Ed Waesche. This arrangement features what is now called in the style the Waesche 13th.

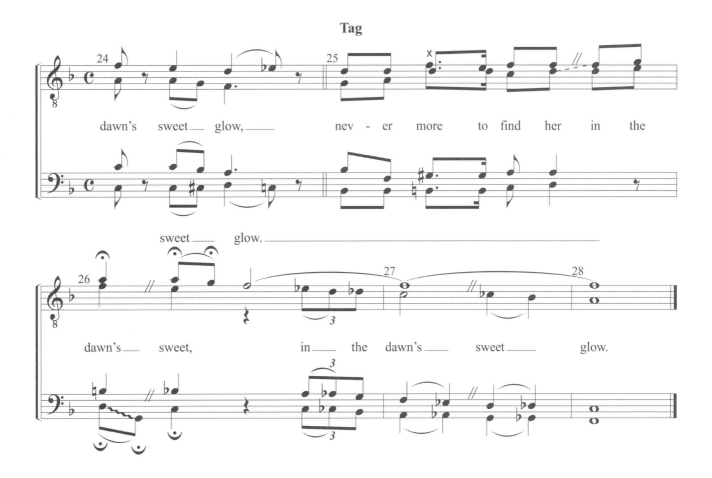

Just because you might hear a non-vocabulary chord in a performance, use caution when deciding to replicate that in your own arrangements. Make sure it is appropriate.

212 Barbershop Harmony Society. (2018, Sep 13). *Second Edition - Jeanie with the Light Brown Hair* [Video]. YouTube. https://youtu.be/p9PGxnY9rE0

Harmonic Rhythm

Harmonic rhythm is, essentially, how quickly the chords change over time. The experienced arranger uses a harmonic rhythm that makes sense and feels right for the song and what you are creating. An audience can feel unsettled if the song is well known and the harmonic rhythm doesn't match what is expected, especially on the first iteration of the material.

Sometimes changes in harmonic rhythm and quick key changes can provide excitement and energy for various portions of a song. In Figure 30.13, the key shifts quickly by half steps within 12 beats.

Figure 30.13

"Put Your Arms Around Me" with words and music by Junie McCree and Albert Von Tilzer. This arrangement by Aaron Dale features several key changes in a relatively short period..

Use of Common Tones

Explore the use of common tones as you progress through a song. A common tone is a tone in one chord that is shared with the next chord. They can offer smooth harmony options. Sometimes the third or fifth of a chord can become a common part of the next chord. When this happens, it can generate a surprise feeling for the listener.

Figure 30.14 shows "Mardi Gras March," as performed by the Scottsdale Chorus, and the common tones used as the key lifts quickly. Measures 1–4 are in A major. The E—the fifth scale degree in A major—becomes the third of the C major chord in measures 5–8. The same E—third in C major—then becomes the root in E major starting in measure 9.

Figure 30.14

"Mardi Gras March," words and music by Paul Francis Webster and Sammy Fain. Arranged by Aaron Dale.

Unless you have a good reason to do otherwise, use the composer's original harmony or what you perceive as widely accepted through recordings and popularity. Sometimes, the composer's originally harmonic progressions will be quite different from what is heard traditionally in a popular recording. This gives you options, but is not a requirement. If the harmony diverts too much from what is expected, or from the original score, the audience might react adversely when hearing your arrangement.

Harmonic Variety

Harmonic variety is the choice of chords an arranger makes as the song is adapted to the barbershop style with regard to the original source material and whether or not those chords change as the song progresses. Harmonic variety is often heard in well-developed arrangements. However, just because various harmonic options are available does not mean they should all be used. Alternate harmonization can be used in a passage to provide contrast and development opportunities and help tricky passages work more suitably in the barbershop style. If possible, alternate harmonizations should be used after the first pass of a section with the original harmony.

Sometimes, alternate harmony might be fitting the first time through a passage. This is usually to set up a stronger feeling of the barbershop style. Reverting to the original harmony for the repeat of that passage can be powerful. Figure 30.15 is an example from the first chorus of "The Man in the Mirror" where more typical circle of fifths progressions are used in the first chorus to lend to the barbershop feel.[213]

Figure 30.15

"The Man in the Mirror," words and music by Siedah Garrett and Glen Ballard. Arranged by Aaron Dale.

213 Barbershop Harmony Society. (2019, Mar 27). *Kentucky Vocal Union - Man in the Mirror (Michael Jackson cover)* [Video]. YouTube. https://youtu.be/FD3M3UMDhh4

Figure 30.16 shows the start of the second chorus, which reverts to the original harmonizations. Note the addition of vocal percussion in the bass line to add more of the rock feeling in the rhythmic subtext.

Figure 30.16

"The Man in the Mirror" second chorus, Arranged by Aaron Dale.

When consistently replacing recognizable chords or passages with alternate harmony, strive to retain the general feeling of the original chords. In "Put Your Head on My Shoulder," shown in Figures 30.17, the original chord on "shoulder" is Cmin.[214]

Figure 30.17

"Put Your Head on My Shoulder" words and music by Paul Anka.

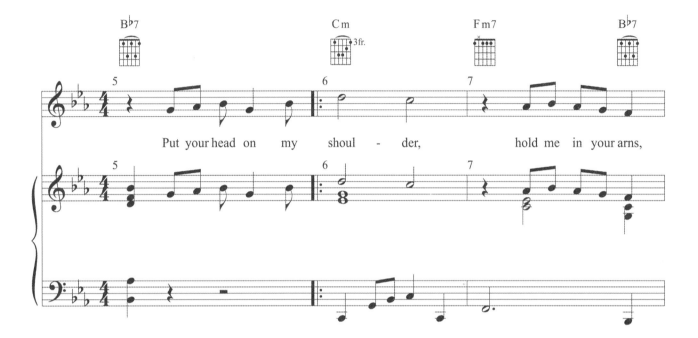

214 PaulAnkaTV. (2014, Dec 31). *Put Your Head on My Shoulder* [Audio]. YouTube. https://youtu.be/kvazBqAlx58

The barbershop arrangement uses a VI dominant ninth chord, which feels more stylistic but doesn't dramatically alter the texture of the song.[215] The alternate major chord of VI7 (no root) with the 9th in the melody, shown in Figure 30.18, is not as dissonant as the original chord, but it could generate a similar feeling for some listeners.

Figure 30.18

"Put Your Head on My Shoulder" with the alternate harmonization in measure 9. Arranged by Aaron Dale.

---

215 bhsstud5565. (2008, Aug 26). *OC Times - Put Your Head on My Shoulder* [Video]. YouTube. https://youtu.be/FV6b4DGyFmg?t=39

Be aware of how you utilize additional secondary dominant resolutions. When dropped into an unexpected place, they can sound pushed or shoehorned. Sometimes you can approach an added secondary dominant by means of a unique rhythm, different inversion, or a melodic line that helps that added passage of circle and feel less jarring.

Figure 30.19

"Rock and Roll is Here to Stay," words and music by David White. Arranged by Aaron Dale.

When harmonizing notes above and below a melody note, be conscious of the tessitura, contour of the line, and the voicings of the chords. Do the chords stay tight and move up together in a similar motion fashion, or stay tight and then spread apart leveraging contrary motion? These options can provide interest and variety within an arrangement.

Note the example from "I Want You to Want Me" in Figure 30.20. The melody line ascends, and the chords stay closely voiced with the harmony parts ascending with similar motion. The bass line descends, creating a walking bass feel during the fill against the sustained melody note.[216]

Figure 30.20

"I Want You to Want Me" ascending motion of the melody line and harmony. Words and music by Rick Nielsen. Arranged by Aaron Dale.

216 Barbershop Harmony Society. (Oct 12, 2022). *Throwback - I Want You to Want Me (Cheap Trick cover)* [Video]. YouTube. https://youtu.be/DJNzKzFZ_xg?si=HOWqEKllxENVq-Af

Here's an example of bass contrary motion, walking down by half steps over two measures while the lead, baritone and tenor move differently. This is an example of using motion in one voice part to convey the subtext of the lyric—in this case, the sense of submission associated with "sleep on your doorstep all night and day."[217]

Figure 30.21

"Ain't Too Proud to Beg" descending bass motion. Arranged by Aaron Dale.

217 Barbershop Harmony Society. (Mar 30, 2019). *Musical Island Boys - Ain't Too Proud to Beg (Temptations cover)* [Video]. YouTube. https://youtu.be/YZ2h7Qeaxww?si=rcl8cqs9gZNWt8DC

Chord Voicing and Voice Leading Considerations

Voicing and tessitura are effective ways to create contrast and subtext within an arrangement. Be aware that low-voiced, close triads of major and minor thirds could sound muddy and be difficult to tune and provide fewer opportunities to produce expansion. Figure 30.22 features several low seventh chords. Tuning could prove challenging for some ensembles.

Figure 30.22

"Sir Duke," words and music by Stevie Wonder. Arranged by Aaron Dale.

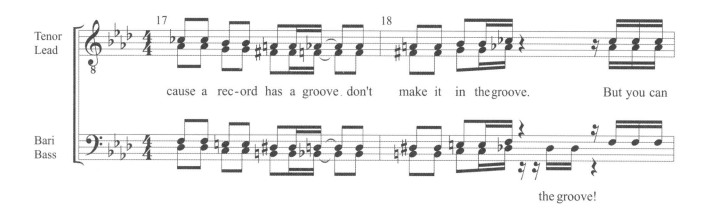

The same can be said of chords with a high tessitura or with notes spread between voices. They might achieve a desired effect from an excitement or climactic perspective, but may create distractions from an execution perspective. High risk, high reward—know your ensemble.

Also consider the choice of vowel—particularly at climactic moments such as the final chord of a tag. The character of the harmony will change based on the vowel. The correlation between frequencies associated with the acoustic properties of the vocal tract in forming the vowel and the range of notes in a chord has an effect on the lock and ring heard. These vowel-specific frequencies are called *formants*.

 *Formants* are resonant frequencies present in many instruments and in the human voice. Formants are often fixed in frequency, with the frequency determined by the physical characteristics of the resonating body. Voices have the additional complication of multiple resonating cavities—the mouth and throat—that constantly change shape to produce different vowel sounds. Each vowel has a characteristic set of formant frequencies, regardless of the sung pitch. Tuning an overtone to match a formant, or the resonant frequency of that resonating cavity, amplifies that overtone and what is known as vowel tuning. Expansion occurs in barbershop when sung pitches, the fundamental frequencies, are in tune and the individual vowels are tuned to their formants.[218]

Voice leading in your harmonic parts should be considered carefully. Awareness of voice leading should be an important part of your arranging process. Monitor all parts so they can be sung successfully. This does not mean avoid all difficult intervals, but consider how difficult the part is overall. Voice leading can make or break the successful learning of a song and eventually a successful performance. Consider:

*   How many parts are making large leaps constantly?
*   Are there incredibly challenging chromatic passages for all parts?
*   Which intervals are sung easier by one voice part and vowel target versus another?

Confident, comfortable performers—especially when under the pressure of a live performance—create compelling music.

218 Indiana University Bloomington Center for Electronic and Computer Music. *Introduction to MIDI and Computer Music.* https://cecm.indiana.edu/361/rsn-neptune.html#:~:text=A%20formant%20is%20a%20resonant,characteristics%20of%20a%20resonating%20body.

Summary of Harmonic Development

Harmonic development can provide constant interest to a listening audience. Paying attention to the chords you use, the speed at which the chords change, and how the voicing of those chords impact the singer can help determine the overall success of the performance.

Rhythmic Development

Compared with other forms of music such as jazz, rhythmic patterns typically associated with songs in the barbershop style are not very complex. Most feature standard meters of 2/4, 4/4 and 3/4 with syncopation occurring within the context of a downbeat feel. Most early examples of the style were derived from folk songs popular in the United States from roughly 1890 through 1930. These songs had simple melodies, harmonies, and rhythm. Take, for example, "Down Our Way." The melody is "sol to sol," the ¾ meter typical for that era, the harmonic rhythm predictable and well-established, and the rhythms straightforward.

Figure 30.23

"Down Our Way," arranged by the Barbershop Harmony Society.

There are many aspects to consider when developing the rhythm of a song:

- Rhythmic impact
- Rhythmic alterations
- Rhythmic drive
- Rhythmic propellants

Finding the right balance between all of these elements will make for an engaging arrangement.

Rhythmic Impact

The arranger should always keep the performer in mind, tailoring the arrangement to the strengths of the intended performer. The audience should also be considered during the arranging process.

Consider the abilities of the performer and what they can successfully execute under pressure. Sometimes the ensemble will be better off with a slight modification of a challenging rhythm. It might divert from the original, but minor modifications may enable better execution and consonance levels for the performer and, if done well, the audience won't mind the change. Consider the example in Figure 30.24, which is an arrangement of "I Want You to Want Me" based on the classic rock anthem by Cheap Trick.[219] The original melody includes several grace notes through this passage, some of which are maintained. However, removing the grace notes in order to provide more homorhythmic texture and complete chords, coupled with retaining the syncopations from the original, provides an overall satisfying experience.

219 Cheap Trick. (2009, Oct 3). *Cheap Trick - I Want You to Want Me (from Budokan!)* [Video]. YouTube. https://youtu.be/-qgpewMCVjs?t=47

Figure 30.24

"I Want You to Want Me" melodic and rhythmic alterations. Arranged by Aaron Dale.

Further, arranging choices made early on set expectations. Rhythm influences energy and forward motion. If the song begins early with many passages of complex rhythmic patterns, you've set certain expectations that may be difficult to continue developing unless the song calls for interest and complexity initially, simplifying in subsequent passages. Consider the overall construction of the song when developing textures from section to section of form.

How do you want to leave the audience? The rhythmic choices at the end of the arrangement will affect how the audience feels. If you want to leave the audience exhilarated, perhaps the arrangement can leverage intricate rhythmic patterns and synchronization all the way to the end. That's a choice that comes with consequences for both performer and audience. Always consider how the arrangement will be perceived once performed.

Rhythmic Alterations

More complex and unique rhythmic combinations that divert from a traditional feel should be used when appropriate for the song. Rhythmic patterns and meters that sound more complex are more difficult to sing and may be more difficult to hear as a listener.

As an arranger, the objective is to keep the basic barbershop sound through hallmarks that can be maintained no matter what rhythmic durations are used. A consonant texture that features primarily homorhythmic unity balanced with contrasting textures for variety is important. Maintaining a primarily homorhythmic texture should guide the degree of rhythmic complexity.

Similar to melody, rhythm patterns in a published piano/vocal version may differ from what is well-known on a popular recording. As an arranger, you have the choice to stay with published rhythms or vary based on your interpretation of the song. The more you stray from the known rhythms—particularly a song with an iconic recording—the more you risk alienating fans of the song. Make sure that if you stray, you do so knowingly and respectfully.

Rhythmic figures can be simplified in a passage if it does not affect the overall feel of the original song. This process was exercised throughout the following arrangement of "Who's Lovin' You."[220]

---

220 Barbershop Harmony Society. (2020, Jul 4). *Musical Island Boys - Who's Lovin' You?* [Video]. YouTube. https://youtu.be/L60br9BILc0

Figure 30.25

"Who's Lovin You" words and music by William 'Smokey' Robinson. Arranged by Aaron Dale.

The first time through a chorus or an A section, consider keeping the rhythmic durations and patterns sounding like the original. This is demonstrated in Figure 30.26, which is the first time the title of the song is introduced.

Figure 30.26

"Who's Lovin' You" first A section. Arranged by Aaron Dale.

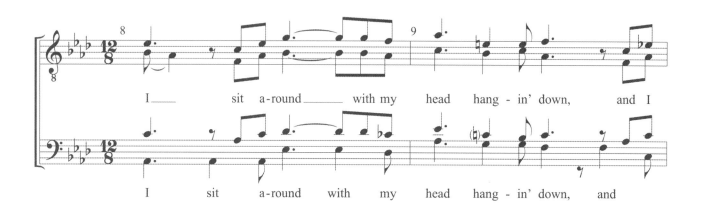

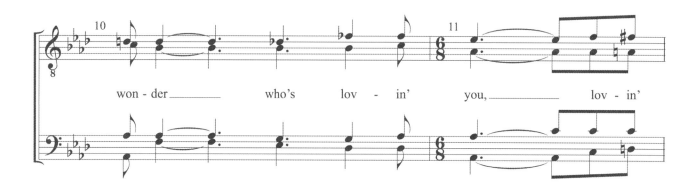

In subsequent instances of the passage, divert from the original feel as you embellish. In songs where rhythm is an important thematic element, consider concepts such as building rhythms or layering in voice parts section by section. Adding additional complexity as a means of development often feels appropriate as the arrangement progresses.

Figure 30.27

"Who's Lovin' You" second A section. Arranged by Aaron Dale.

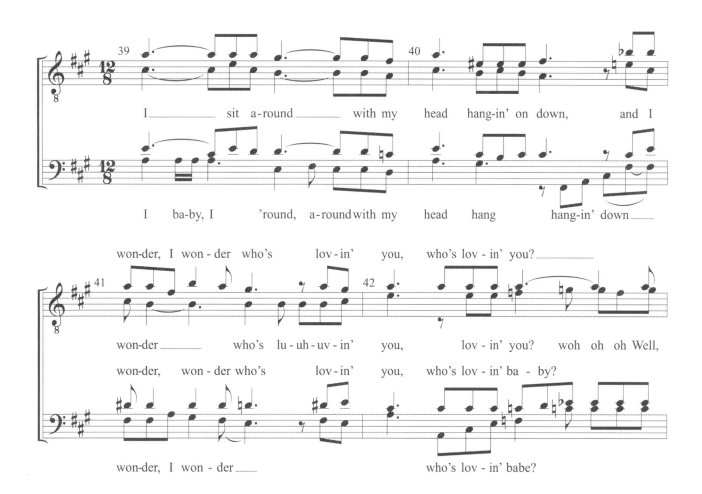

Also consider the abilities of the performer and what they can perform successfully under pressure. Sometimes the ensemble will be more successful with a slight modification of a challenging rhythm. It might divert from the original, but minor modifications may enable better execution and consonance levels for the performer, and the audience won't mind the change.

Always be mindful of the hallmarks of the barbershop sound being created in the arrangement. As you develop the rhythm, consider balancing homorhythm with your newly developed texture. Large portions of a song sung non-homorhythmically can lessen the overall barbershop characteristics.

Rhythmic Drive

If you want a sense of natural, yet driving interest and flow from section to section, one way of accomplishing that is by building in more complex rhythmic patterns. If done in a logical manner, the intensity heightens and not distracts. In Figure 30.28, consider how Mozart first establishes the melody and rhythm of the tune we know as "Twinkle, Twinkle, Little Star," and then builds upon it in successive variations, as shown in Figure 30.29 and Figure 30.30.

Figure 30.28

"12 Variations Über 'Ah, vous dirai-je maman'" K.265/300e (Mozart, Wolfgang Amadeus), original theme.

Figure 30.29

"12 Variations Über 'Ah, vous dirai-je maman'" K.265/300e (Mozart, Wolfgang Amadeus), first variation.

Figure 30.30

"12 Variations Über 'Ah, vous dirai-je maman'" K.265/300e (Mozart, Wolfgang Amadeus), twelfth variation

When approaching a musical and emotional climax in a song where rhythm has been one of the drivers, be careful to not to get too complex and overstimulating with rhythms and texture all the way to the end. Consider rhythmic patterns that feel strong and powerful as you wind back down toward the targeted musical event. This applies whether the event is subtle and soft, cool and mellow, or big and exciting. Figure 30.31 shows an example of lyric, melodic, and rhythmic alterations in "Mardi Gras March" that provide strong harmonic energy heading into a final refrain.

Figure 30.31

"Mardi Gras March" alterations to offset rhythmic drive. Arranged by Aaron Dale.

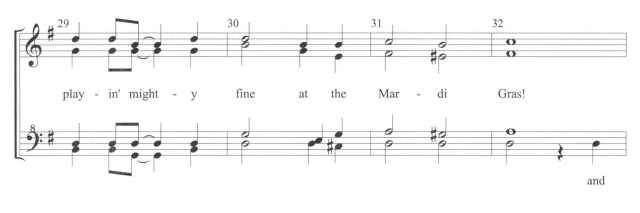

Rhythmic Propellants

Rhythmic propellants are patterns of rhythms that a composer or arranger uses as a device to move the song in a forward direction.

 Rhythmic propellants are defined as a broad category of embellishments that are employed by an arranger to create a sense of motion and reinforce the rhythmic groove in a song. An example of this would be bass nonsense lyrics such as "bum bum bum" which propel a phrase with a sustained melody note into the next phrase. Rhythmic propellants often are used to establish a downbeat

Typically, unless the song demands otherwise, you'll want to start simply and move toward more complex propellants. For example, the first iteration of an A section could feature rhythmic subtext using primarily quarter and half note pulses. The next section could introduce more eighth note pulses and utilizing sixteenth note and other syncopated rhythms.

Figure 30.32 highlights rhythmic development as the echoes and bass propellants change slightly as the chorus progresses.

Figure 30.32

"My Blushin' Rosie," words and music by Edgar Smith and John Stromberg. Arranged by Aaron Dale.

Embellishments

Embellishments are covered in detail in Chapters 23 and 29 of *Arranging Barbershop Vol. 2*. Embellishments are often used for the purpose of propelling the rhythm. For general balance, consider how you introduce embellishments. This could be rhythmic variations, echoed lyrics, swipes, etc. Perhaps start with few or no embellishments in the beginning, then add embellishments as appropriate to develop what you desire. Often the more complex portions will occur about two-thirds of the way through the arrangement. This "golden mean" moment is also discussed in Chapter 23.

In this example, you'll notice bass propellant embellishments introduced slowly. Rhythmic difficulty increases from one pickup note to many notes in the bass embellishments.

Figure 30.33

"Hey, Good Lookin'" words and music by Chuck Berry. Arranged by David Wright.

Borrowing from Instruments

Establishing the groove and mood of the original song is important to the success of translating songs from this style. Rhythmic interest can help emulate a pop song's instrumental rhythm section.

Yet, derivative works of pop songs in a barbershop setting often need more rhythmic contrast than traditional songs from the Tin Pan Alley era. Figure 30.34 shows the introduction of "Every Breath You Take" that immediately establishes the rhythmic texture of the iconic guitar riff and motif from The Police's original version.[221] The introduction of Figure 30.34 is intended to be sung on neutral syllables.

221 Barbershop Harmony Society. (Jul 3, 2020). *Kentucky Vocal Union - Every Breath You Take (The Police cover)* [Video]. YouTube. https://youtu.be/9RL-hNcXdgI?si=f0htms-i8FDvC38C

Figure 30.34

"Every Breath You Take" words and music by Sting. Arranged by Aaron Dale.

Summary of Rhythmic Development

When modifying and adding new ideas to another composer's song, we should approach our choices differently than when composing our own original material. We have gained permission to use another composer's original work. We harmonize, embellish, and often modify it to be sung in the barbershop style with four voices. It is a process best approached with both creativity and respect.

Textural Development

Texture is defined as "how the tempo, melodic, and harmonic materials are combined in a musical composition, determining the overall quality of the sound in a piece. The texture is often described in regard to the density, or thickness, and range, or width, between lowest and highest pitches, in relative terms as well as more specifically distinguished according to the number of voices, or parts, and the relationship between these voices."[222]

With barbershop texture being limited to four voice parts, the thickness of textures capable in an orchestra are not possible. However, that doesn't mean that barbershop textures can't be rich. Barbershop textural development is typically created through melodic and rhythmic variances, performed simultaneously. For instance, a passage with three or four melodic or rhythmic lines woven over each other could still be perceived as simple. It depends on the execution of the performer. A variety of textures in a song can create a more interesting and fulfilling performance.

Here's an example of a layered textural approach, with each voice part acting as independent melodic lines converging to homorhythm.[223] Lyrics and instrumental emulation are also intertwined.

---

222 https://en.wikipedia.org/wiki/Texture_(music). June 30, 2023.
223 Barbershop Harmony Society. (2015, Jul 17). *Westminster Chorus - Seize the Day [from Newsies]* [Video]. YouTube. https://youtu. be/2EZ3k10Hpp4

Figure 30.35

"Seize the Day" words and music by Alan Menken and Jack Feldman. Arranged by Aaron Dale.

A quartet may sing a passage with four separate rhythmic patterns or melodic lines interwoven with ease, but the question is, "How would that be perceived by the audience?" When rhythmic durations and vocalized syllables become less aligned in a quartet setting, a seemingly more complex texture is heard.

Texture is often used to emulate instrumental ensembles, with various parts moving and performing simultaneously. Use of expressive vocal qualities and tone color or timbre changes can emulate instruments and other sounds to help provide texture. Texture differences can help a barbershop song sound like an original pop recording. This approach is often used in other contemporary a cappella styles as well. These texture differences create contrast if balanced appropriately in the context of the whole song. This allows rhythmically diverse sections to exist, though not homorhythmic, and the overall song can still have a feeling of *homophony*.

 Homophony refers to a musical texture based primarily on a single melodic line. The chords supporting the predominating voice part match the rhythmic patterns of the melody. In polyphony, rhythmic differences highlight the different melodic lines.

In general, the arranger should strive to give the audience the perception of four part chords—no matter how complex the rhythm. This live performance feeling of four-part homorhythmic texture can help the audience hear the barbershop style.

Additional Considerations

When developing an arrangement, there are a few more items to consider beyond melodic, rhythmic, and textural changes. These include what to do with repeated sections, treatment of the source material, considerations for ensemble size and composition, and special examination of medleys.

The Pros and Cons of Repeated Sections

When making changes during a repeated section, such as a return of an A section, consider whether the differences are beneficial enough to warrant the change. It can make the arrangement harder to learn when sections vary minimally, e.g., a small rhythm change. Often the audience likely won't notice the subtle differences you chose to use. Therefore, if you choose to alter a repeated section, make sure that the changes are both warranted in the grand scheme of the musical journey and sufficiently different as to not confuse the performer about which pattern is which.

The first, second, and third iterations of the chorus in my arrangement of "Sir Duke" are the same; Figure 30.36 shows the second chorus. This is to provide something familiar to the audience. The chorus then varies in the reprise, shown in Figure 30.37.

Figure 30.36

"Sir Duke" second chorus, arranged by Aaron Dale.

Figure 30.37

"Sir Duke" reprise. Note the different textural approaches for the harmony parts

Source Material and Popular Music

Today we can find music to arrange from various sources, including audio or video recordings of iconic performances, a composer's score or original sheet music, and live performances.

Modern popular songs are typically written for prolific vocalists and are often created just to be dance music. These songs become tough to sing if you notate four parts for four singers on the same words at the same time. This is likely because in the original song, soloists on the melody often jump around quickly in pitch in addition to the rhythmic difficulty level.

When arranging a section that is mostly homorhythmic with all four parts singing the same syllables at the same time, it's helpful to consider how the passage could eventually be received by an audience. Sometimes the four-part homorhythmic texture looks good on paper for pop songs, but doesn't sound as pleasing once vocalized. This is especially true if the original song contained a solo with a lot of rhythmically challenging words or phrases and a band accompaniment.

In the following example, the original song, performed by The Jacksons, features rhythmic accompaniment to Michael Jackson's solo line. His brothers join him on the lyrics following "don't blame it on the" in the chorus. This barbershop arrangement aims to capture both the feel of the original groove and harmonies, as well as a sense of homophony to satisfy the barbershop listener's ear.

Figure 30.38

"Blame it on the Boogie," words and music by Michael Jackson-clark, Thomas Meyer, Elmar Krohn, Hans Kampschroer, and David Jackson-rich. Arranged by Aaron Dale.

Stylistic pop music can have many sections where a soloist utilizes melodic vocal skills that don't naturally transfer well to a four-part homorhythmic texture. Consider whether harmonizing a complex melody with four parts will sound odd compared to the original song. This may be especially true if the original is well known and features rhythmic devices that create the hook for the song. If that is the case, could you modify or alter some of the rhythmic devices or patterns to allow four-part harmony to sound acceptable without altering the feel of the original song for the audience?

 These questions apply in different degrees for each song you arrange. You should consider the iconic aspects and hooks in well-known songs where the audience wants to sing along in their head or tap their foot. If that's what you are setting up for the audience, you don't want to destroy that connection. You risk judgment from the biggest critics—those who love that original artist!

The same applies when creating your own rhythmic devices and embellishments to provide contrast in a well-known song. Be aware that the audience might recognize things that differ from the original and will internally judge whether they fit. This is especially true of iconic pop music arranged in the barbershop style—think songs by The Beatles. In general, it's typically best to honor the original song and performances. If you divert too much, you risk appearing self-indulgent with your arranging choices, caring less about the original song or performer. Proceed with caution!

Sometimes it is appropriate to use exact passages from an original pop recording. Do this carefully and within the context of the overall arrangement plan. Figure 30.39 gives an example of an arrangement device emulating the iconic guitar lick from the Kenny Loggins song "Footloose."[224]

224 Barbershop Harmony Society. (2016, Mar 1). *Kentucky Vocal Union - Footloose (Kenny Loggins cover)* [Video]. YouTube. https://youtu.be/_2oCPyUdCUs?t=32

Figure 30.39

"Footloose" guitar lick. Words and music by Dean Pitchford and Kenny Loggins. Arranged by Aaron Dale.

"Uptown Funk" by Mark Ronson ft. Bruno Mars has an opening line bass guitar lick that makes it immediately identifiable to fans of the song.[225] In this arrangement of the song, the arranger utilized scat lyrics to emulate the bass guitar, cymbals and rhythm guitars.[226] Note the accent marks in the music that provide even more guidance to the performer.

225 DopeLyrics. (2020, Apr 20). *Mark Ronson - Uptown Funk (Lyrics) ft. Bruno Mars* [Video]. YouTube. https://youtu.be/CeYuFSBkkVw
226 Barbershop Harmony Society. (2016, Jun 10). *Vocal FX - Funk Medley* [Video]. YouTube. https://youtu.be/zrdE15auxlQ?t=5

Figure 30.40

"Funk Medley" opening line from "Uptown Funk." Words and music by Charles Wilson, Rudolph Taylor, Philip Lawrence, Jeff Bhasker, Devon Gallaspy, Mark Ronson, Nicholaus Williams, Bruno Mars, Robert Wilson, Ronnie Wilson, and Lonnie Simmons. Arranged by Aaron Dale.

The horn riff from James Brown's "I Got You (I Feel Good)" is as iconic as the lyrics. It's likely that anyone familiar with the song would emulate the horns after singing the title riff. The barbershop arrangement pays homage to the original, providing scat lyrics for the tenor and baritone to emulate the horns section. The bass lyrics and rhythm, shown in Figure 30.41, emulate the bass guitar riff.[227]

Figure 30.41

"I Got You (I Feel Good)" words and music by James Brown. Arranged by Aaron Dale.

---

227 Barbershop Harmony Society. (2016, Jun 10). *Vocal FX - Funk Medley* [Video]. https://youtu.be/zrdE15auxlQ?t=88

Chorus vs. Quartet Arrangements

Four individual voices in a quartet are unique as they have sole responsibility for vocal quality and performance level of their part. That is quite different from a chorus with multiple singers on each part. Singers in each chorus section work together to create a desired unit sound. Vocal abilities vary from singer to singer, which affects how well each section performs. A few considerations when arranging for a chorus versus quartet.

1. **Length of the song.** Chorus music can often exploit longer phrases because singers can stagger their breathing. This is not always utilized by the chorus director, but is an option depending on the vision of the group.
2. **Section abilities.** Discover the strengths and limitations of each section, and consider that when arranging. This includes range, tessitura, and passaggi. Know the power area of the section's voice and what areas to avoid. This understanding can guide your choices and help the chorus succeed in creating a unit sound. This can even aid in successful chorus rehearsals, where schedules and attendance vary, and every singer's level of preparedness affects the rehearsal.
3. **Consider features for smaller groups.** Solo, duet, and quartet opportunities within a chorus arrangement can help provide contrast and interest. Consult the organization's contest rules before considering this for a chorus contest.

Medleys vs. Single Song Arrangements

The development of a medley is not much different from developing a single song arrangement. Single songs are developed with careful attention to the original song, considering the use of musical thematic elements and concepts appropriate for translating the song to the barbershop style. Medleys are handled similarly, with multiple songs being considered. Explore the various sections of each song—chorus, refrain, verse, etc.—and how you will mesh them together. What is the overall theme? Also, consider how the themes of each individual song in the medley will work together. Consider the transitions between disco-style dance songs.[228]

---

228 Barbershop Harmony Society, (2017, Aug 16). *Kentucky Vocal Union - Boogie Down Medley* [Video]. YouTube. https://youtu.be/ZGI8jU7biCs

Figure 30.42

Songs from the "Boogie Down Medley," "You Make Me Feel Like Dancing" words and music by Leo Sayer and Vini Poncia.
"Boogie Wonderland" words and music by Allee Willis and Jonathan Lind. "Blame it on the Boogie" all arranged by Aaron Dale.

Balance is another important factor when developing a medley. Some medleys will use nearly equal portions of each song. The "Girls Medley," arranged by Ed Waesche for the 1978 BHS International Quartet Champions Bluegrass Student Union, is a primary example of this. The song's structure features an original verse that sets up the premise: the singer is in love with three girls. The medley then launches into a song about each girl, featuring a full chorus of "Margie," "No No Nora," and "My Blushin' Rosie." The medley completes with a tag borrowing melodic structure from the original verse. Figure 30.43 highlights the three songs from the medley. Note the sense of a complete journey for each song, melding seamlessly from one to the next.

Figure 30.43

"Girls Medley" arranged by Ed Waesche.

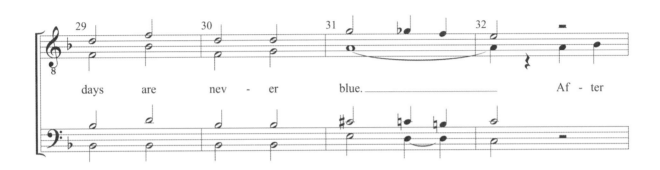

NO NO NORA (1923). Words and music by Ted Fiorito, Gus Kahn and Ernie Erdman

MY BLUSHIN' ROSIE (1923). Words and music by Edgar Smith and John Stromberg

Other medleys will vary in how much each song contributes to the medley. Consider how long you want the overall medley to last. This will affect how much of each song you use. For longer multi-song medleys, sometimes just a few measures of a song can help the medley move forward and provide quick support of the theme.

Summary of Textural Development and Other Considerations

Every arranging journey is different. Beyond the common considerations such as form and construction, melodic and harmonic journey, groove, textural development, key musical events, and overall desired impact, there are unique considerations associated with every performer. Some of these considerations are related to how the source song treats repeated material and how the performer can adapt to these changes. Other considerations are linked to the type of ensemble—chorus versus quartet—and whether the journey involves a single song or several. Treatment and consideration of these factors can help determine the overall success of the eventual performance.

Conclusion

Developing an arrangement which serves dual purposes—honoring the original artist and composer, and exhibiting the core musical elements of the barbershop style—is both a science and an art. Oftentimes, the difference between an arrangement that strikes this balance or not is related to awareness of what best highlights the song and the style. The development considerations in this chapter may help unlock some ideas in helping you find the right balance that delights both fans of the original song and zealots of the barbershop style. When this happens, and the song is performed by an ensemble sensitive to both aspects, a truly magical experience transpires.

Chapter 31.
Advanced Rhythmic Concepts

By Aaron Dale

Introduction

In general, barbershop contest arrangements sound primarily homorhythmic to a listener. That thought should guide your arrangement choices for potential high-level performances. However, songs from other genres—pop, rock, jazz, blues, Motown—leverage multiple rhythmic textures to create their unique character. Balancing fidelity to the original song's layered rhythmic textures with the barbershop style's homorhythmic texture is material to the success of the arrangement. With this in mind, consider the two extremes related to the rhythmic texture when creating a new arrangement:

1. Fully restricted, notating only the composer's original rhythmic durations.
2. No restrictions, notating anything desired.

Typically, you'll find yourself working closer to the fully restricted extreme. This does not mean you're forbidden to change anything, but this is the more typical place to start in order to honor the composer's intent and the feel of the original song. Doing so will help amplify the listener's love of the original onto the performance of this arrangement. Changing iconic rhythmic patterns creates cognitive dissonance in the listener's mind when reconciling the performance of this arrangement with the original artist's performance. Legally, when you obtain the rights to arrange a song, you can make your own derivative work. It allows you to legally change elements of the song within any constraints agreed to in the contract. More often than not, you'll find yourself with greater restrictions. This doesn't mean you can't change anything, but you should always apply constraint and honor the original music. Further, gaining permission to arrange comes with an agreement to limit what you can change, including the original melody, lyrics and even the harmonization and rhythmic schemes..

 Unless the song is in the public domain, or your own composition, you may encounter some publisher- or composer-imposed restrictions. With songs under copyright, the composer already made desired choices for their music, so the rhythmic changes you make should be done respectfully. You are creating a new derivative work from a copyrighted song and not a "new" composition.

Meter and Rhythm

Meter is the underlying pulse/beat that provides structure and motion in a song. Barbershop arrangements are typically heard with standard meters of 2, 3, or 4. The arrangement typically should lead the audience to feel beat one and the downbeats in a song. Diverse or extremely complex rhythmic patterns are not traditionally heard in the barbershop style. When used, they should be crafted purposefully to provide contrast and support a specific idea or theme.

Consider these thoughts about meter:

- Will the downbeat or beat one be recognizable during performance?
- Do the rhythmic patterns always avoid the downbeat and beat one?
- If the rhythmic patterns land consistently on the backbeat, are there places where the performer and audience can feel downbeat for a while? Is that necessary for your song or for selected phrases?

Mood and Rhythm

Mood can be defined various ways based on the context. It could be described as a temporary state of mind or feeling. Music can trigger emotional and sometimes physical feelings in a listener. The combination of musical elements in a song can stir up past life experiences and memories. Unique combinations of rhythmic patterns can help this to happen. Consider these thoughts about mood:

- What do you want the audience to feel from the overall arrangement? From individual passages or sections? Is the purpose to trigger feelings of energy, excitement, sad, happy, etc?
- Does the arrangement do that job consistently?

Groove and Rhythm

A groove could describe something established—like a routine or habit. People can get in a groove when accomplishing something. The beat and subdivision of music can have a feeling of groove—often defined as "sitting in the pocket." Rhythm patterns and pulse might be described as grooving or having a specific style of groove. Musical grooves can make listeners feel a certain way, often evoking movement. Groove is often used to describe the beat and feeling of popular recorded music. The same can apply when discussing rhythm and pulse in barbershop. Consider these guiding questions.

When you hear an existing barbershop arrangement performed:

- How does the rhythm make the song enjoyable or not?
- What feelings do you get when hearing certain rhythmic patterns?
- Is the song full of many complex and complicated rhythmic patterns? Does that fit the song as you perceive it? Does it help the mood or groove feel natural, or does it get in the way?

Now consider these thoughts about groove when creating your own arrangements:

- Do your rhythmic choices make sense and line up on paper to create the specific pattern and pulse you desire?
- Can you imagine an audience hearing these rhythmic patterns and a specific mood being generated? Is it possible to anticipate that happening during a future performance, even while you're now still creating the written arrangement? Also ask yourself whether that is important. If so, is it important throughout the arrangement, or just specific sections, etc? The rhythm might look good on paper, but it may not sound the way you think. Another key question is how do the rhythmic choices for this arrangement compare with the original composer's work? Does the rhythm work in your opinion?
- When creating groove patterns in fast, uptempo songs, there are several considerations. First, choose the feeling and groove you want to create phrase to phrase or section to section. You might do this for the entire arrangement. Notate a skeleton of the grooves desired. Perhaps start with the bass part and some inner harmony parts to bounce back and forth in the pattern. Simplify or embellish it but try not to just settle on something that doesn't quite work. Decide what you want the audience to feel. Is it a similar feeling to a particular original recording of the song?
- Typically we think of groove in reference to fast songs with a lot of rhythmic interest. But you can also think of groove regarding slower songs sung either in tempo or rubato. Ballads and rubato songs should feel in the pocket and not have awkward rhythmic feel or interpretation. If you're arranging a ballad, how does it flow section to section with the rhythms you've chosen—even if rubato?

Utilizing Internal Rhyme for Rhythmic Flow

Often you can find opportunities to create rhythm and pulse through use of lyrics within a phrase. In this example, "Out There" from *Disney's The Hunchback of Notre Dame*, see the composer's use of these lyrics:[229]

If I were in their skin / I'd treasure every instant

The syllables that rhyme are mid phrase: If I WERE in their SKIN, I'd trea-SURE every IN-stant.

Figure 31.1

"Out There" words and music by Alan Menkin and Stephen Schwartz. Arranged by Aaron Dale.

These elements of lyric rhyme and rhythm are often married. A lyric can be repeated for rhythmic emphasis if appropriate. This can help forward motion, excitement, and mood creation. Here you see repetition with "I love, I love, I love ya," providing a giddy sense of overwhelming love right from the start. That ties in later with the lyrics of the main song, "my blushin' Rosie, you are my posie."

---

229 Barbershop Harmony Society. (2017, Feb 1). *Ringmasters - Notre Dame Medley **REMASTERED AUDIO*** [Video]. YouTube. https://youtu.be/Qo_N9_ZFBhs?t=262

Figure 31.2

"My Blushing Rosie," words and music by Edgar Smith and John Stromberg. Arranged by Aaron Dale.

Alternate rhyming words can be utilized when a phrase ends on a long held out vowel or word and you want to keep the rhythm moving. At this point you might choose to fill the long chord with some echo or repeated phrase to maintain forward motion. If you cannot find suitable rhyming words for the echo, you can consider other words that will rhyme on the following echo at the end of the next phrase. Figure 31.3 provides an example of this.

Figure 31.3

"Happy, Happy Birthday, Baby," words and music by Margo Sylvia and Gilbert Lopez. Arranged by Aaron Dale.

Benefits of Exploring Rhythm Notation Options

Changes for Singability

Sometimes subtle rhythm changes can make something easier to sing. Usually small changes won't affect the integrity of the original song and can be used for variety as the arrangement develops.

For example, speak these words: "I'm in a whirl." This could be spoken or sung differently depending on your desired inflection or emphasis. The feel of the phrase can vary greatly based on your notation choices. To illustrate how slight differences can affect the flow of the music and lyrics, analyze the following lyric/rhythm examples. The notation of each varies slightly but can sometimes make a big change. Try them first with a standard straight eighths feel and then with a swing. Small differences in notation could affect the eventual performance.

Figure 31.4

Rhythmic notation differences.

Some lyrics are just easier to sing with one rhythm versus another. Some are easier to sing naturally. So you might use that as a first time through in a passage when establishing the hook or main idea for the audience. But then, in each consecutive repeat of that phrase or lyrics, you might change up the rhythm to create interest. A rhythmic pattern may work well with a given lyric in a given place in a given arrangement but may work better with a different rhythm another time in another arrangement.

Utilizing or Diverting from the Composer's Originally Notated Rhythm

When first looking at a score, the original rhythm and lyrics may appear different from popular recordings. Vocalists often divert from what you see on the paper. Sometimes it could be appropriate to tweak or alter rhythmic notation to make it easier to sing in four parts.

Small alterations to the rhythm could help greatly with singability. But consider two things: audience perception and stability for the performer. If you change the rhythm each time the phrase repeats, what is the benefit? Will it make a difference? Or are the changes so subtle that most people won't hear the difference? Is that little change worth it, or will it go unnoticed in the overall arrangement? Try to anticipate if it could become a trouble spot for the group, creating a challenge for singers to differentiate from one time to the next. It could make the song more difficult to learn and retain.

To avoid creating that situation, consider variations that can generate the most success. Sometimes this means clearly notating rhythm differently with each new pass. Other times, it might mean notating the rhythms identically each time with no variation. The answer is likely somewhere in between.

Lyric alterations can also help generate rhythmic variation. Maybe you keep the idea of the initial lyrical passage, but alter the words slightly when repeated. New word combinations that are still recognized as the song could provide different rhythmic options. Consider these differences:

Rock It for me   *vs.*

Rock it out for me   *vs.*

Rock it all the night for me

They have the same general meaning but have longer and different rhythm patterns from just a few words added. You can keep the message the same with new ways of saying it and new rhythm options.

Cadence Points

Approaching the end of a phrase in a barbershop arrangement provides opportunities to do wonderful things. Much of the magic and artistry in a performance happens in transitions from phrase to phrase or in cadence points. Those are places to consider rhythmic options that help relax the tension of the song or to propel the music forward in some way. Those are A-level opportunities. Ideas for cadence points, transitioning from one phrase to the next, can come from anywhere in your years of listening experience. To get the groove and feel of a song right, you should take time to flood your brain with rhythmic ideas—especially for the transition places.

For example, in a typical driving pop song today, you'll hear phrases of certain length that are completed with a transition rhythm for a measure. This is often played by a drum set and other instruments. It is typically a propelling rhythmic pattern that sets up the next phrase. Different styles have different drum fills. Listen and learn how they start and stop and how they differ from one another, and how they lead in to the next phrase. It's not always the same. These ideas can be good starting points.

- Phil Collins: "In the Air Tonight"[230]
- From the musical Hairspray: "You Can't Stop the Beat"[231]
- Kenny Loggins: "Footloose"[232]

Swipes, Echoes, and Melismas

A *melisma* is a group of notes sung to one syllable of text; typically called a swipe in the barbershop style. They were utilized extensively by baroque and classical composers. In today's world of pop, rock, jazz, blues, and gospel music, melismas are typically improvised as soloists passionately express the message of the song. This can present a challenge to harmonizing four parts in a homorhythmic setting.

In the following example, the opening melisma is key to the style of many original recordings. This is especially true as sung by the original artist, the Jackson 5. The opening passage is solo, then four parts enter.

Measure 2 has four parts initially, with the melisma occurring in the lead line and other parts filling in the triad. This works as it is a major chord; the melisma is all pentatonic. This allows a little more feeling of barbershop at the beginning of the song despite many soloistic passages throughout the piece.[233]

230 Phil Collins. (2010, May 11). *Phil Collins - In The Air Tonight (Official Music Video)* [Video]. YouTube. https://youtu.be/YkADj0TPrJA

231 Hairsprayhome (2011, Jan 9). *You Can't Stop the Beat* [Video]. YouTube. https://youtu.be/AZnt-0fEiT0

232 Kenny Loggins. (2014, Feb 24). *Kenny Loggins - Footloose (Official Video)* [Video]. YouTube. https://youtu.be/ltrMfT4Qz5Y

233 Barbershop Harmony Society. (2020, Jul 4). *Musical Island Boys - Who's Lovin' You?* [Video]. YouTube. https://youtu.be/L60br9BILc0

Figure 31.5

"Who's Lovin' You," words and music by Smokey Robinson. Arranged by Aaron Dale.

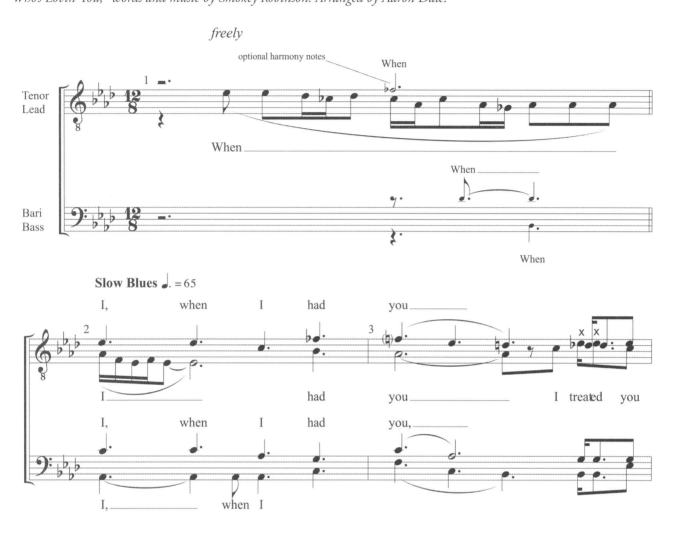

Later we see the lead melisma harmonized with four parts instead of standing as a solo line.

Figure 31.6

"Who's Lovin' You" lead melisma harmonization. Arranged by Aaron Dale.

Beat or Phrase Displacement

One approach to developing an arrangement and creating rhythmic contrast is starting a pattern a beat or more later than usual. This can happen mid phrase or wherever you feel appropriate for rhythmic interest. You can extend the rhythm into the next measure, creating interest. In Figure 31.7, you'll see the phrase "she just got here yesterday, things are hot people say" displaced from the original composer's rhythm.

Figure 31.7

"Sweet Georgia Brown," words and music by Ben Bernie and Maceo Pinkard. Arranged by Aaron Dale.

Entire phrases can be shifted to provide variety and interest. See how the phrase "Seventy Six Trombones caught the (light of the) morning sun" reflect this shift, returning to the normal rhythmic pattern at the second bridge.[234]

Figure 31.8

"Seventy-Six Trombones" melodic displacement. Arranged by David Wright.

234 Barbershop Harmony Society. (2009, Jul 22). *Ambassadors of Harmony - Seventy-Six Trombones [from the Music Man]* [Video]. YouTube. https://youtu.be/QmDGntpZC3I

BRIDGE II

Rhythmic Contrast and Unity

Jazz compositions often use techniques to dynamically change texture every few measures, such as *trading fours* or call and response. This creates natural variety, contrast and unity.

 When *trading fours*, band members exchange improvising solos every four measures. In barbershop, this idea is mirrored in having individual voice take turns being featured every few measures, before returning the returning the melody to the lead.

We can extend this back and forth idea to solo and full group. In this next example, the texture alternates roughly every four measures between trio-against-rhythmic-bass and homorhythmic, creating drive and interest.

Figure 31.9

"Footloose" trading fours section with the bass' rock groove. Arranged by Aaron Dale.

If this balance is carefully monitored, the arranger helps to create more interest for the audience and the performer, while also avoiding very long passages that start to divert from the barbershop style. This ties back to one of the fundamental goals stated at the beginning of this chapter: provide the listener with the perception of homorhythmic texture, even when developing complex rhythmic treatments.

Changing Meter

If you choose to change the meter to create interest, it should be appropriate for the entire form of the arrangement. Sometimes a half-time effect can provide interest in a repeated section. This would involve cutting the initial base rhythmic duration in half for the entire section. The song would continue forward with the same pulse but the melody and harmonic progression is cut in half.

Figure 31.10

"Looking at the World Through Rose-Colored Glasses" half-time effect. Words and music by Jimmy Steiger. Arranged by David Wright.

Augmentation is the lengthening of the rhythmic values, It can signal a feeling of strength, boldness, and climax at the end of a section.

Figure 31.11

Rhythmic augmentation of melody.

In the first chorus of "California, Here I Come," we see the normal rhythmic pattern for the first A section. Each beat of the "Cal-i-for-nia" melody is notated with a half note.[235]

Figure 31.12

"California, Here I Come," words and music by Bud DeSylva, Joseph Meyer, and Al Jolson. Arranged by David Wright.

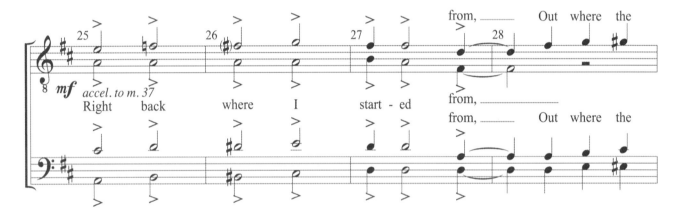

235 Mike McGee. (2009, Mar 13). *Masters of Harmony 1999 International Performance* [Video]. YouTube. https://youtu.be/7Wjp-rSMBSc?t=362

However, at the second chorus at measure 91, the rhythm is augmented in the melody with each melodic half note being doubled. This provides opportunities for excitement and contrast in the original rhythmic pattern from the harmony parts. It then takes a trading fours concept, returning to normal in measure 95. It then transfers the melody to the bass in measure 99 for four more measures of augmentation. This creates a great deal of excitement for the listener.

Figure 31.13

"California, Here I Come" rhythmic augmentation. Arranged by David Wright.

Diminution is the shortening of rhythmic values. This can trigger a feeling of urgency and tension for the listener.

Figure 31.14

Rhythmic diminution of the melody.

Note in Figure 31.15 the normal rhythmic pattern for this section of "California, Here I Come." Once again, the bass melody is notated with half notes for "that's why I can."

Figure 31.15

"California, Here I Come" arranged by David Wright.

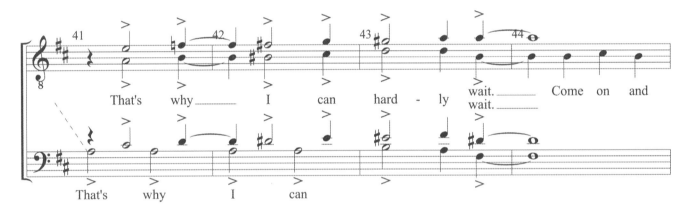

We see a brief passage of rhythmic diminution in the second chorus in measures 127–128. The music at this point in this section is based on half notes and quarter notes, but for a moment, it uses quarter and eighth notes. Even though it's brief, it creates a little extra, syncopated kick in the line. Note that, while in the first chorus with the normal melodic rhythmic pattern the harmony parts feature syncopated rhythms, the texture here in homorhythmic. This is because the rhythmic diminution is already embellished from the listener's expectation, and the ascending harmonic line creates additional excitement. Giving the listener too much contrast at once will only serve to confuse, so this is just the right amount of change.

Figure 31.16

"California, Here I Come" arranged by David Wright.

Percussive Syllables and Perception

"BaCK," "JumP," "SiT," etc. Where do these kinds of phonemes fit rhythmically in the pattern you notate? Do they accentuate the rhythm you desire or do they detract? Hard words sounds can help to give a percussive feel, emulating various drums and cymbals. Figure 31.17 shows an example of this in the bass line and with initial consonant sounds of several words in measures 44–46.[236]

236 Barbershop Harmony Society. (Jul 3, 2020). *Kentucky Vocal Union - Every Breath You Take (The Police cover)* [Video]. YouTube. https://youtu.be/9RL-hNcXdgI?t=96

Figure 31.17

"Every Breath You Take" arranged by Aaron Dale.

Figure 31.18 shows the bass working with other parts to create percussive sounds on echoes and underlying rhythm. Note how the hard consonants in the bass line land on beats 2 and 4 to create a back beat rock snare drum feel.[237]

Figure 31.18

"Footloose" arranged by Aaron Dale.

237 Barbershop Harmony Society. (2016, Mar 1). *Kentucky Vocal Union - Footloose (Kenny Loggins cover)* [Video]. YouTube. https:// youtu.be/_2oCPyUdCUs?t=69

Oftentimes, percussive sounds create rhythm when echoes or repeated words occur. Consider the percussive sound those lyrics will make and the difficulty of the lyrics to sing. Balance percussive consonants between offbeat and downbeat. If the bass part is singing one set of lyrics, how do those rhythmically sound with the other parts above? Within the rhythm you notate, how do the hard and soft syllables blend together? Is the rhythmic pattern too difficult to sing and execute with those words?

For example, the word "scrunch" could be tough to scrunch into a fast rhythmic passage due to the "scr" and "ch" sounds taking up space and time.

Borrowing from Other Styles/Genres

It is possible to incorporate a variety of rhythmic ideas from such other popular styles as rock, jazz, disco, hip-hop, etc.

 When borrowing from other styles as an arranger, the notated rhythms should strive to ensure the eventual performance can still feature the hallmarks of the barbershop style.

Walking Bass: Songs from the rock and jazz genres could have passages where the rhythm and pitch imitate the style of a bass instrument like a string/upright bass, electric bass, tuba, etc. Typically, while the bass notes move separately, the arranger will use the other three parts to fill in the chord and desired harmony. Those parts could be notated with complimentary rhythm patterns using portions of the song lyrics or neutral syllables. Here the bass syllables are neutral and create a jazz bass sound.[238]

Figure 31.19

"Rock This Town" walking bass line. Arranged by Aaron Dale.

238 Barbershop Harmony Society. (2018, Oct 5). *Studio 4 - Rock This Town* [Video]. YouTube. https://youtu.be/sytu4HB-1vU

Rock Bass: In this example, the bass part moves up or down through the notes of a major arpeggio, while the top three parts fill in the chord.

Figure 31.20

"Footloose" arranged by Aaron Dale.

Rock bass line will also often repeat the same note—typically the root of the chord—to provide drive through the phrase when the melody note is sustained or cuts off altogether. Here's an example from Cheap Trick's "I Want You to Want Me."[239]

Figure 31.21

"I Want You to Want Me," words and music by Rick Neilsen. Arranged by Aaron Dale.

239 Barbershop Harmony Society. (2022, Oct 4). *Throwback - I Want You to Want Me (Cheap Trick cover)* [Video]. YouTube. https://youtu.be/DJNzKzFZ_xg

Jazz / Swing Bass: The bass part moves up or down through the notes of a scale—major, minor, blues, etc.—while the top three parts fill in the chord.[240]

Figure 31.22

"'Deed I Do," words and music by Fred Rose. Arranged by Aaron Dale.

240 BarbershopMe. (2013, Jun 28). *BarbershopMe - GQ - Deed I Do* [Video]. YouTube. https://youtu.be/npZu-vUtL6k

Well-Known Rhythmic Patterns

Be careful if you choose to divert from a well-known rhythmic pattern or passage. If you are following a particular version of a song for inspiration, or trying to do a direct "rip" of a song or passage, give more attention to those patterns. Sometimes drum fills or rhythmic patterns are key to the hook, character, or identity for that song.

Figure 31.23 is the introduction from an arrangement of "Just My Imagination," the iconic song by The Temptations. The bass line matches the opening guitar lick from the original version.[241] In this case, changing this iconic lick would serve no artistic purpose; it sets up the song for any fans of the song, and it works well to establish the Motown feel.'

Figure 31.23

"Just My Imagination" words and music by Norman J. Whitfield and Barrett Strong. Arranged by Aaron Dale.

---

241 The Ed Sullivan Show. (2020, Aug 23). *The Temptations "Just My Imagination (Running Away With Me)" on The Ed Sullivan Show* [Video]. YouTube. https://youtu.be/WZ4Ym9Xiw3w

Typically, slight rhythmic alterations from the piano/vocal score won't affect the perception from the audience that it still sounds like what they expect. You can get by with some rhythmic modification for singability purposes. However, if well-known recordings exist that feature a certain rhythmic passage as a key hook, it is recommended that honor that passage. If you do change it, understand the audience is likely to question why. In these next examples you'll see different choices made when arranging a unique passage from the Orleans classic, "Still the One."[242]

Figure 31.24

"Still the One" original melisma on "fun." Words and music by John and Johanna Hall. Arranged by Aaron Dale.

242 Barbershop Harmony Society. (2021, Feb 8). *Quorum - Still the One (Orleans cover)* [Video]. YouTube. https://youtu.be/
TWtOWs-dN7k

Here is what was used for a contestable version where the ensemble wanted to minimize the rhythmic complexity. The melisma is removed, and the word "fun" holds on the II7 longer. When eventually performed, listeners who know the original song might be distracted by the change to this iconic melisma. Those who don't know the song likely won't recognize the change, as it works harmonically and melodically.

Figure 31.25

"Still the One" with the melisma removed. Arranged by Aaron Dale.

In the final version of this particular arrangement, the original melisma passage is used a couple of times to wind up to the tag. This helps to honor and celebrate the moment, recognizing its importance in making the song unique. You'll see and hear it first in the bass melody and then as a unison moment.

Figure 31.26

"Still the One" tag. Arranged by Aaron Dale.

Conclusion

Rhythmic development is an essential part of creating compelling, exciting arrangements in any style of music. There are rhythmic aspects tied to almost every hook from popular music. Sometimes, the rhythm itself is the hook e.g., "In the Air Tonight" by Phil Collins and "We Will Rock You" by Queen. Some key considerations regarding rhythmic development in the barbershop style:

- The barbershop style should sound largely homorhythmic. Allow this to drive your rhythmic development concepts, and consider how passages of rhythmic interest and complexity with non-homorhythmic textures converge to homorhythm.
- Unless you have a good reason for doing so, don't diverge from the original rhythmic highlights and hooks from the original work. This is especially true with iconic popular songs with benchmark recordings.
- Borrow rhythmic fills and transitions from other styles, including jazz, rock, blues and pop.
- Consider meter changes and rhythmic augmentation and diminution, along with concepts like trading fours, to provide interest, balance and structure.

Tag

By Steve Tramack

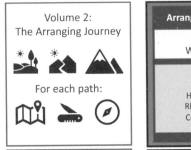

Congratulations on arriving at this point in your arranging journey! If you've consumed all of the content in *Arranging Barbershop Vol. 2*, you've truly skied every trail on the arranging mountain. From the basics of harmonizing a melody to incorporating elements of jazz bass into barbershop arrangements, this book is designed to provide the roadmap with examples from iconic arrangements and insights from expert arrangers. We started all the way back in Chapter 14 discussing approaches for the basic harmonization of a melody and ended in Chapter 31 talking about advanced rhythmic concepts used to develop interest and contrast in expert-level arrangements. Let's review what transpired in between.

Part A: Arranging Fundamentals

Part A provided a foundation for creating successful arrangements. The tools and approaches covered may prove valuable even for more experienced arrangers who have approached arranging from a practical approach as opposed to a theory-based background.

We began with a case study reviewing the process for harmonizing a melody. We looked at an approach for layering voice parts, creating strong voicing and good voice leading. We also looked at identifying non-chord tones and discussed an approach for identifying options to harmonize these NCT melody notes.

We did a deep dive into some fundamental arranging concepts, including harmonic rhythm. Learning how to recognize and implement the implied harmonic rhythm in your arrangements is one of the most important steps in creating a sense of structure and balance.

Distorted harmonic rhythm that moves too fast, too slow, or on weak beats is one of the common mistakes made by beginning arrangers or those who are new to arranging in the barbershop style. Clay Hine reviewed some of these common mistakes by looking at two arrangements with mistakes and compared them to versions without mistakes. This was an exercise used as part of the training of Musicality judges in the Barbershop Harmony Society.

Part B: Developing an Arrangement

Part B represented the very heart of arranging: the development process. Once an arranger becomes proficient in harmonizing a melody and recognizing the basic structure of music, the next step is putting their creative stamp on the arrangement by creating interest and variety. Part B is structured as a reference guide, allowing the reader to focus on different areas and approaches associated with development as their journey grows in experience and expertise.

We explored a case study in development based on "I Have Confidence" from *The Sound of Music*. The case study explored alternate harmonizations, textural development, embellishments, and original material.

We included chapters focused on numerous tools and approaches to developing an arrangement, including key changes, introductions, tags, and embellishments. These chapters feature literally hundreds of examples, intended to provide blueprints and options for developing your next arrangement. Chapters 21 through 26 can serve as a resource for ideas and inspiration for arrangers of all levels.

Part C: Advanced Considerations

Part C provided insights from three of the most prolific arrangers our style has ever known. Imagine yourself spending a month with David Wright, Clay Hine, and Aaron Dale as they share tips, tricks, and lessons they learned for overcoming common challenges when arranging for the very best ensembles in the style.

We took a journey alongside Clay Hine in the development of two gold medal arrangements for the 2017 BHS International Quartet Champions, Main Street. Arranging for the very best ensembles is a different approach than one might take when first harmonizing a melody or developing arrangements, as detailed in Part A and Part B of this book. However, you can't jump to the advanced level unless you've mastered basic skills first. Of particular interest is Clay's explanations of creating original material that sets up the concept of popular songs from the 2000s set in a traditional barbershop context. The result honored both the original song and the barbershop style and has garnered tens of millions of YouTube views.

In Chapter 29, David Wright provided a thorough review of overcoming common challenges facing experienced arrangers in the style. To get the full impact, we recommend going back and reviewing this chapter with all of the audio and video examples uploaded to www.halleonard.com/mylibrary/, using the code on the front inside cover of this book. This chapter is taken from David's 10-hour Advanced Arranging class at Harmony University and allows you to learn from David's years of arranging experiences.

In Chapters 30 and 31, Aaron Dale provided wisdom and guidance on advanced development skills, including a focused session exploring rhythmic development. These chapters are like private arranging lessons with Aaron that will give you insight into how he develops rhythm using songs from the pop and rock genres, resulting in performances that delight all fans.

As with any adventure, one of the ways you grow your skills and hone your craft is by learning from others. *Arranging Barbershop Vol. 3: Visions of Excellence* provides exactly that opportunity. Over thirty arrangers provided thoughtful responses to the same twenty questions. Their responses serve as the chapters. Perhaps one of these responses will unlock new insights, and you'll come back to explore chapters in Volume 2, armed with this fresh insight. Like any adventure, arranging is a lifelong journey and one where the opportunity for growth is both continuous and unexpected. See you in Volume 3!

Permissions

A Nightingale Sang In Berkeley Square
Lyric by Eric Maschwitz
Music by Manning Sherwin
Copyright © 1940 Peter Maurice Music Co., Ltd.
Copyright Renewed
This arrangement Copyright © 2023 Peter Maurice Music Co., Ltd.
All Rights in the United States and Canada Administered by Reservoir Media Management, Inc.
All Rights Reserved   Used by Permission
Reprinted by permission of Hal Leonard LLC

A Handful Of Stars
By Jack Lawrence and Ted Shapiro
© 1939 Leo Feist, Inc.
Copyright Renewed; extended term of Copyright deriving from Jack Lawrence assigned and effective November 28, 1995
to Range Road Music Inc.
This arrangement © 2023 Range Road Music Inc.
All Rights Reserved
Reprinted by permission of Hal Leonard LLC

After the Ball (1891)
Words and music by Charles K Haris
Public Domain

Ain't Too Proud To Beg
Words and Music by Edward Holland Jr. and Norman Whitfield
Copyright © 1966 Stone Agate Music
Copyright Renewed
This arrangement Copyright © 2023 Stone Agate Music
All Rights Administered by Sony Music Publishing (US) LLC, 424 Church Street, Suite 1200, Nashville, TN 37219
International Copyright Secured   All Rights Reserved
Reprinted by permission of Hal Leonard LLC

All About That Bass
Words and Music by Meghan Trainor and Kevin Kadish
Copyright © 2015 Year Of The Dog Music, MTrain Music and Rezven Music
This arrangement Copyright © 2023 Year Of The Dog Music, MTrain Music and Rezven Music
All Rights for Year Of The Dog Music and MTrain Music Administered by Downtown Music Publishing LLC
All Rights for Rezven Music Administered by Amplified Administration
All Rights Reserved   Used by Permission
Reprinted by permission of Hal Leonard LLC

Blame It On The Boogie
Words and Music by Michael George Jackson Clark, David John Jackson Rich, Thomas Meyer, Elmar Krohn and Hans Kampschroer
Copyright © 1978 Edition Delay
This arrangement Copyright © 2023 Edition Delay
All Rights Administered by BMG Rights Management (US) LLC
All Rights Reserved   Used by Permission
Reprinted by permission of Hal Leonard LLC

Boogie Wonderland
Words and Music by Jonathan Lind and Allee Willis
Copyright © 1979 EMI Blackwood Music Inc., Irving Music, Inc. and Big Mystique Music
This arrangement Copyright © 2023 EMI Blackwood Music Inc., Irving Music, Inc. and Big Mystique Music
All Rights on behalf of EMI Blackwood Music Inc. and Irving Music, Inc. Administered by Sony Music Publishing (US) LLC, 424 Church Street, Suite 1200, Nashville, TN 37219
All Rights on behalf of Big Mystique Music Administered by Kobalt Songs Music Publishing
All Rights Reserved   Used by Permission
Reprinted by permission of Hal Leonard LLC

The Bowery (1891)
Words and music by Roy Turk and Fred E. Ahlert
Arranged by the Barbershop Harmony Society
Public Domain
Reprinted by permission of the Barbershop Harmony Society

Bright Was the Night
Words and music by Traditional
Arranged by David Wright
Copyright © 1991 David Wright
Reprinted by permission of David Wright

Brother, Can You Spare A Dime?
Lyric by E.Y. "Yip" Harburg
Music by Jay Gorney
Copyright © 1932 Glocca Morra Music and Gorney Music
Copyright Renewed
This arrangement Copyright © 2023 Glocca Morra Music and Gorney Music
All Rights for Glocca Morra Music Administered by Shapiro, Bernstein & Co., Inc.
All Rights for Gorney Music Administered by Next Decade Entertainment, Inc.
All Rights Reserved   Used by Permission
Reprinted by permission of Hal Leonard LLC

Butter Outta Cream (from Catch Me if You Can)
Words and music by Mark Shaiman and Scott Wittman
Arranged by Dan Wessler
© 2008, 2011 WINDING BROOK WAY MUSIC and WALLI WOO ENTERTAINMENT All Rights Administered by WC MUSIC CORP. All Rights Reserved Used by Permission
Reprinted by permission of Hal Leonard Corporation

Bye Bye Blues (1925)

Words and music by Fred Hamm, Dave Bennett, Bert Lown, and Chauncey Gray
Arranged by Lem Childers
Public Domain
Reprinted by permission of the Barbershop Harmony Society

Bye Bye Bye
Words and Music by Kristian Lundin, Jacob Schulze and Andreas Carlsson
Copyright © 2000 by GV-Maratone and Maratone AB
This arrangement Copyright © 2023 by GV-Maratone and Maratone AB
All Rights Administered by Kobalt Songs Music Publishing
All Rights Reserved   Used by Permission
Reprinted by permission of Hal Leonard LLC

California, Here I Come (1924)
Words and music by Bud DeSylva, Joseph Meyer and Al Jolson
Arranged by David Wright
Public Domain
Reprinted by permission of David Wright

Cheer Up, Charlie
from WILLY WONKA AND THE CHOCOLATE FACTORY
Words and Music by Leslie Bricusse and Anthony Newley
Copyright © 1970, 1971 Downtown DMP Songs and Taradam Music, Inc.
Copyright Renewed
This arrangement Copyright © 2023 Downtown DMP Songs and Taradam Music, Inc.
All Rights for Downtown DMP Songs Administered by Downtown Music Publishing LLC
All Rights Reserved   Used by Permission
Reprinted by permission of Hal Leonard LLC

Come On Get Happy
Theme from THE PARTRIDGE FAMILY
Words and Music by Wes Farrell and Danny Janssen
Copyright © 1972 Screen Gems-EMI Music Inc. and Lovolar Music
Copyright Renewed
This arrangement Copyright © 2023 Screen Gems-EMI Music Inc. and Lovolar Music
All Rights on behalf of Screen Gems-EMI Music Inc. in the United States Administered by Sony Music Publishing (US) LLC, 424 Church Street, Suite 1200, Nashville, TN 37219
All Rights on behalf of Lovolar Music in the United States Administered by Bike Music c/o Concord Music Publishing
All Rights for the World excluding the United States Administered by Sony Music Publishing (US) LLC, 424 Church Street, Suite 1200, Nashville, TN 37219
International Copyright Secured   All Rights Reserved
Reprinted by permission of Hal Leonard LLC

Come What May
from the Motion Picture MOULIN ROUGE
Words and Music by David Baerwald and Kevin Gilbert
Copyright © 2001 ALMO MUSIC CORP., ZEN OF INIQUITY and T C F MUSIC PUBLISHING, INC.
This arrangement Copyright © 2023 ALMO MUSIC CORP., ZEN OF INIQUITY and T C F MUSIC PUBLISHING, INC.
All Rights for ZEN OF INIQUITY Controlled and Administered by ALMO MUSIC CORP.
All Rights Reserved   Used by Permission
Reprinted by permission of Hal Leonard LLC

Cruella De Vil
from 101 DALMATIANS
Words and Music by Mel Leven
© 1961 Walt Disney Music Company
Copyright Renewed.
This arrangement © 2023 Walt Disney Music Company
All Rights Reserved. Used by Permission.
Reprinted by permission of Hal Leonard LLC

Cry Me a River
Words and music by Hamilton Arthur
Arranged by Brent Graham
Copyright © Hamilton Arthur, Chappell & Co
Reprinted by permission of Alfred Music Corporation

Cuddle Up a Little Closer
Words and music by Karl Hoschna and Otto Harbach
Arranged by Clay Hine
Public Domain
Reprinted by permission of Clay Hine

'Deed I Do (1926)
Words and music by Fred Rose and Walter Hirsch
Arranged by Aaron Dale
Public Domain
Reprinted by permission of Aaron Dale

Do I Love You?
Words and music by Cole Porter
Arranged by Brent Graham
© Copyright 1940 Warner/Chappell North America Limited. All Rights Reserved. International Copyright Secured.
Reprinted by permission of Hal Leonard Corporation

Don't Be A Baby, Baby
Words and Music by Buddy Kaye and Howard Steiner
Copyright © 1945 Sony Music Publishing (US) LLC
Copyright Renewed
All Rights Administered by Sony Music Publishing (US) LLC, 424 Church Street, Suite 1200, Nashville, TN 37219
International Copyright Secured   All Rights Reserved
Reprinted by permission of Hal Leonard LLC

From Now On
from THE GREATEST SHOWMAN
Words and Music by Benj Pasek and Justin Paul
Copyright © 2017 Breathelike Music, Pick In A Pinch Music and T C F Music Publishing, Inc.
This arrangement Copyright © 2023 Breathelike Music, Pick In A Pinch Music and T C F Music Publishing, Inc.
All Rights for Breathelike Music and Pick In A Pinch Music Administered Worldwide by Kobalt Songs Music Publishing
All Rights Reserved   Used by Permission
Reprinted by permission of Hal Leonard LLC

Fun, Fun, Fun
Words and Music by Brian Wilson and Mike Love
Copyright © 1964 IRVING MUSIC, INC.
Copyright Renewed
This arrangement Copyright © 2023 IRVING MUSIC, INC.
All Rights Reserved   Used by Permission
Reprinted by permission of Hal Leonard LLC

Gangnam Style
Words and Music by Gun Hyung Yoo and Jai Sang Park
Copyright © 2012 UNIVERSAL TUNES and SONY MUSIC PUBLISHING H.K. KOREA
This arrangement Copyright © 2023 UNIVERSAL TUNES and SONY MUSIC PUBLISHING H.K. KOREA
All Rights for UNIVERSAL TUNES Controlled and Administered by SONGS OF UNIVERSAL, INC.
All Rights for SONY MUSIC PUBLISHING H.K. KOREA in the U.S. and Canada Controlled and Administered by
SONY MUSIC PUBLISHING (US) LLC, 424 Church Street, Suite 1200, Nashville, TN 37219
All Rights Reserved   Used by Permission
Reprinted by permission of Hal Leonard LLC

Georgia May
Words by Andy Razaf
Music by Paul Denniker
© 1934 (Renewed) EDWIN H. MORRIS & COMPANY, A Division of MPL Music Publishing, Inc. and RAZAF
MUSIC
This arrangement © 2023 EDWIN H. MORRIS & COMPANY, A Division of MPL Music Publishing, Inc. and RAZAF
MUSIC
All Rights for RAZAF MUSIC Administered by BMG RIGHTS MANAGEMENT (US) LLC
All Rights Reserved
Reprinted by permission of Hal Leonard LLC

Georgia On My Mind
Words by Stuart Gorrell
Music by Hoagy Carmichael
Copyright © 1930 by Peermusic III, Ltd.
Copyright Renewed
This arrangement Copyright © 2023 by Peermusic III, Ltd.
International Copyright Secured   All Rights Reserved
Reprinted by permission of Hal Leonard LLC

Lida Rose
from Meredith Willson's THE MUSIC MAN
By Meredith Willson
© 1957 (Renewed) FRANK MUSIC CORP. and MEREDITH WILLSON MUSIC
This arrangement © 2023 FRANK MUSIC CORP. and MEREDITH WILLSON MUSIC
All Rights Reserved
Reprinted by permission of Hal Leonard LLC

Livin' La Vida Loca
Words and Music by Desmond Child and Robi Rosa
Copyright © 1999 Desmophobia, A Phantom Vox Publishing and Artemis Muziekuitgenverij B.V.
This arrangement Copyright © 2023 Desmophobia, A Phantom Vox Publishing and Artemis Muziekuitgenverij B.V.
All Rights for Desmophobia Administered by BMG Rights Management (US) LLC
All Rights for A Phantom Vox Publishing and Artemis Muziekuitgenverij B.V. in the United States and Canada
Administered by Warner-Tamerlane Publishing Corp.
All Rights Reserved   Used by Permission
Reprinted by permission of Hal Leonard LLC

Little Patch Of Heaven
from Walt Disney's HOME ON THE RANGE
Music by Alan Menken
Words by Glenn Slater
© 2004 Walt Disney Music Company and Wonderland Music Company, Inc.
All Rights Reserved. Used by Permission.
Reprinted by permission of Hal Leonard LLC

Looking At The World Through Rose Colored Glasses
Words and Music by Tommy Malie and Jimmy Steiger
Copyright © 2023 by HAL LEONARD LLC
International Copyright Secured   All Rights Reserved
Reprinted by permission of Hal Leonard LLC

Louise
from the Paramount Picture INNOCENTS OF PARIS
Words by Leo Robin
Music by Richard A. Whiting
Copyright © 1929 Sony Music Publishing (US) LLC
Copyright Renewed
This arrangement Copyright © 2023 Sony Music Publishing (US) LLC
All Rights Administered by Sony Music Publishing (US) LLC, 424 Church Street, Suite 1200, Nashville, TN 37219
International Copyright Secured   All Rights Reserved
Reprinted by permission of Hal Leonard LLC

Love Me
Words and Music by Jerry Leiber and Mike Stoller
Copyright © 1954 Sony Music Publishing (US) LLC
Copyright Renewed
This arrangement Copyright © 2023 Sony Music Publishing (US) LLC
All Rights Administered by Sony Music Publishing (US) LLC, 424 Church Street, Suite 1200, Nashville, TN 37219
International Copyright Secured   All Rights Reserved
Reprinted by permission of Hal Leonard LLC

Love Me and the World is Mine
Words and music by Ernest Ball and Dave Reed Jr
Arranged by David Wright
Public Domain
Reprinted by permission of David Wright

Love Me Or Leave Me
from LOVE ME OR LEAVE ME
from WHOOPEE!
Lyrics by Gus Kahn
Music by Walter Donaldson
Copyright © 1928 (Renewed) by Donaldson Publishing Company, Gilbert Keyes Music and Larry Spier Music LLC
This arrangement Copyright © 2023 (Renewed) by Donaldson Publishing Company, Gilbert Keyes Music and Larry Spier Music LLC
All Rights for Gilbert Keyes Music Administered by WC Music Corp.
International Copyright Secured   All Rights Reserved
Reprinted by permission of Hal Leonard LLC

Man In The Mirror
Words and Music by Glen Ballard and Siedah Garrett
Copyright © 1987 UNIVERSAL MUSIC CORP., AEROSTATION CORPORATION and YELLOWBRICK ROAD MUSIC
This arrangement Copyright © 2023 UNIVERSAL MUSIC CORP., AEROSTATION CORPORATION and YELLOWBRICK ROAD MUSIC
All Rights for AEROSTATION CORPORATION Controlled and Administered by UNIVERSAL MUSIC CORP.
Worldwide Rights for YELLOWBRICK ROAD MUSIC Administered by BMG RIGHTS MANAGEMENT (US) LLC
All Rights Reserved   Used by Permission
Reprinted by permission of Hal Leonard LLC

Mandy Lee (1899)
Words and music by Thurland Chattaway
Arranged by Clay Hine
Public Domain
Reprinted by permission of Clay Hine

Mardi Gras March
Words and music by Paul Francis Webster and Sammy Fain
Copyright © WB Music
Reprinted by permission of Alfred Music Corporation

Margie (1920)
Words and music by Con Conrad and J. Russel Robinson
Arranged by Ed Waesche
Public Domain
Reprinted by permission of the Barbershop Harmony Society

Marx Brother Opener Intro

Words, music, and arranged by Jay Giallombardo
Reprinted by permission of Jay Giallombardo

Mean To Me
Lyric by Roy Turk
Music by Fred E. Ahlert
TRO - © Copyright 1929 (Renewed) Cromwell Music, Inc., New York, NY, Pencil Mark Music, Inc., Bronxville, NY, Azure Pearl Music, Beeping Good Music and David Ahlert Music
This arrangement TRO - © Copyright 2023 Cromwell Music, Inc., New York, NY, Pencil Mark Music, Inc., Bronxville, NY, Azure Pearl Music, Beeping Good Music and David Ahlert Music
All Rights for Pencil Mark Music, Inc. Administered by Downtown Music Publishing LLC
All Rights for Azure Pearl Music, Beeping Good Music and David Ahlert Music Administered by Bluewater Music Services Corp.
International Copyright Secured
All Rights Reserved Including Public Performance For Profit
Used by Permission
Reprinted by permission of Hal Leonard LLC

Moves Like Jagger
Words and Music by Adam Levine, Benjamin Levin, Ammar Malik and Shellback
Copyright © 2010, 2011 by Universal Music - Careers, Sudgee Music, Matza Ball Music, Where Da Kasz At, Maru Cha Cha and MXM
This arrangement Copyright © 2023 by Universal Music - Careers, Sudgee Music, Matza Ball Music, Where Da Kasz At, Maru Cha Cha and MXM
All Rights for Sudgee Music Administered by Universal Music - Careers
All Rights for Matza Ball Music Administered by Concord Avenue c/o Concord Music Publishing
All Rights for Where Da Kasz At and Maru Cha Cha Administered Worldwide by Songs Of Kobalt Music Publishing
All Rights for MXM Administered Worldwide by Kobalt Songs Music Publishing
International Copyright Secured   All Rights Reserved
Reprinted by permission of Hal Leonard LLC

My Blushin' Rosie (1900)
Words and music by Edgar Smith and John Stromberg
Arranged by Ed Waesche
Public Domain
Reprinted by permission of the Barbershop Harmony Society

My Blushin' Rosie (1900)
Words and music by Edgar Smith and John Stromberg
Arranged by Aaron Dale
Public Domain
Reprinted by permission of Aaron Dale

On The Sunny Side Of The Street
Lyric by Dorothy Fields
Music by Jimmy McHugh
Copyright © 1930 Shapiro, Bernstein & Co., Inc., New York and Cotton Club Publishing
Copyright Renewed
This arrangement Copyright © 2023 Shapiro, Bernstein & Co., Inc., New York and Cotton Club Publishing
All Rights for Cotton Club Publishing Administered by Sony Music Publishing (US) LLC, 424 Church Street, Suite 1200, Nashville, TN 37219
All Rights for Shapiro, Bernstein & Co., Inc. Administered by Reservoir Media Management, Inc.
All Rights Reserved   Used by Permission
Reprinted by permission of Hal Leonard LLC

Oops!...I Did It Again
Words and Music by Martin Sandberg and Rami Yacoub
Copyright © 1999 MXM and Anthem Music Publishing II
This arrangement Copyright © 2023 MXM and Anthem Music Publishing II
All Rights for MXM Administered by Kobalt Songs Music Publishing
All Rights Reserved   Used by Permission
Reprinted by permission of Hal Leonard LLC

Out There
from THE HUNCHBACK OF NOTRE DAME
Music by Alan Menken
Lyrics by Stephen Schwartz
© 1996 Wonderland Music Company, Inc. and Walt Disney Music Company
All Rights Reserved. Used by Permission.
Reprinted by permission of Hal Leonard LLC

Pass Me the Jazz
Words and music by Anders Edenroth
Arranged by Jeremy Johnson
Copyright © Walton Music Corp
Reprinted by permission of Walton Music Corporation

Play that Funky Music
Words and music by Robert Parissi
Arranged by Clay Hine
© 1976 (Renewed) by Bema Music, a division of Sweet City Records, Inc. and RWP Music
Reprinted by permission of Hal Leonard Corporation

Please Don't Talk About Me When I'm Gone
Words and music by Sam H. Stept and Sidney Clare
Arranged by Buzz Haeger
© Copyright Copyright Control (50%)/Francis Day & Hunter Limited
Reprinted by permission of Hal Leonard Corporation

Poker Face
Words and Music by Stefani Germanotta and RedOne
Copyright © 2008 Sony Music Publishing (US) LLC, House Of Gaga Publishing Inc. and RedOne Productions, LLC
This arrangement Copyright © 2023 Sony Music Publishing (US) LLC, House Of Gaga Publishing Inc. and RedOne Productions, LLC
All Rights Administered by Sony Music Publishing (US) LLC, 424 Church Street, Suite 1200, Nashville, TN 37219
International Copyright Secured   All Rights Reserved
Reprinted by permission of Hal Leonard LLC

Put on a Happy Face (from Bye Bye Birdie)
Words and music by Lee Adams and Charles Strouse
Arranged by Kevin Keller
Copyright © Strada Music; WB Music Corp
Reprinted by permission of Alfred Music Corporation

Put Your Arms Around Me (1910)
Words and music by Albert Von Tilzer and Junie McCree
Arranged by Aaron Dale
Public Domain
Reprinted by permission of Aaron Dale

Put Your Head On My Shoulder
Words and Music by Paul Anka
Copyright © 1958 Chrysalis Standards, Inc.
Copyright Renewed
This arrangement Copyright © 2023 Chrysalis Standards, Inc.
All Rights Administered by BMG Rights Management (US) LLC
All Rights Reserved   Used by Permission
Reprinted by permission of Hal Leonard LLC

Redhead
Words and music by Dorothy Fields and Albert Hague
Arranged by Jim Clancy and Ed Waesche
Chappell & Co.
Reprinted by permission of Alfred Music Corporation

Ring-A-Ding Ding
Words by Sammy Cahn
Music by James Van Heusen
Copyright © 1961 Cahn Music Co. and Van Heusen Music Corp.
Copyright Renewed
This arrangement Copyright © 2023 Cahn Music Co. and Van Heusen Music Corp.
All Rights for Cahn Music Co. Administered by Concord Music Publishing
All Rights for Van Heusen Music Corp. Administered by Universal Music Corp.
All Rights Reserved   Used by Permission
Reprinted by permission of Hal Leonard LLC

Someone Like You
from the Broadway Musical JEKYLL & HYDE
Words and Music by Leslie Bricusse and Frank Wildhorn
Copyright © 1997 Painted Desert Music Corp. on behalf of Stage And Screen Music Inc., BMG Ruby Songs, Scaramanga Music, Inc. and Reservoir Media Music
This arrangement Copyright © 2023 Painted Desert Music Corp. on behalf of Stage And Screen Music Inc., BMG Ruby Songs, Scaramanga Music, Inc. and Reservoir Media Music
All Rights for BMG Ruby Songs and Scaramanga Music, Inc. Administered by BMG Rights Management (US) LLC
All Rights for Reservoir Media Music Administered by Reservoir Media Management, Inc.
International Copyright Secured   All Rights Reserved
Used by Permission
Reprinted by permission of Hal Leonard LLC

Something's Gotta Give
Words and music by Johnny Mercer
Arranged by Patrick McAlexander
1954 (Renewed) WB Music
Reprinted by permission of Hal Leonard Corporation

Stormy Weather (Keeps Rainin' All The Time)
from COTTON CLUB PARADE OF 1933
Words and Music by Ted Koehler and Harold Arlen
Copyright © 1933 BMG Gold Songs and S.A. Music Co.
Copyright Renewed
This arrangement Copyright © 2023 BMG Gold Songs and S.A. Music Co.
All Rights for BMG Gold Songs Administered by BMG Rights Management (US) LLC
All Rights Reserved   Used by Permission
Reprinted by permission of Hal Leonard LLC

Stranger in Paradise
Words and music by George and Ira Gershwin
Arranged by Mark Hale and Rob Campbell
Copyright © 1953 Frank Music Corp. Copyright Renewed and Assigned to Scheffel Music Corp., New York, NY All Rights Controlled by Scheffel Music Corp.
Reprinted by permission of Hal Leonard Corporation

Strike Up the Band
Words and music by George and Ira Gershwin
Arranged by Aaron Dale
Copyright © WB Music
Reprinted by permission of Alfred Music Corporation

Supercalifragilisticexpialidocious
from MARY POPPINS
Words and Music by Richard M. Sherman and Robert B. Sherman
© 1964 Wonderland Music Company, Inc.
Copyright Renewed.
All Rights Reserved. Used by Permission.
Reprinted by permission of Hal Leonard LLC

Superstar
Words and Music by Leon Russell and Bonnie Sheridan
Copyright © 1970, 1971 (Renewed) by Embassy Music Corporation (BMI) and Reservoir 416 (BMI)
This arrangement Copyright © 2023 (Renewed) by Embassy Music Corporation (BMI) and Reservoir 416 (BMI)
All Rights for Reservoir 416 Administered by Reservoir Media Management, Inc.
International Copyright Secured   All Rights Reserved
Reprinted by permission of Hal Leonard LLC

Sway (Quien Sera)
English Words by Norman Gimbel
Spanish Words and Music by Pablo Beltran Ruiz and Luis Demetrio Traconis Molina
Copyright © 1954 by Editorial Mexicana De Musica Internacional, S.A. and Words West LLC (P.O. Box 15187, Beverly Hills, CA 90209, USA)
This arrangement Copyright © 2023 by Editorial Mexicana De Musica Internacional, S.A. and Words West LLC (P.O. Box 15187, Beverly Hills, CA 90209, USA)
Copyright Renewed
All Rights for Editorial Mexicana De Musica Internacional, S.A. Administered by Peer International Corporation
International Copyright Secured   All Rights Reserved
Reprinted by permission of Hal Leonard LLC

(You're the Flower of My Heart,) Sweet Adeline (1900)
Words and music by Richard Husch Gerard and Harry Armstrong
Arranged by Jay Giallombardo
Public Domain
Reprinted by permission of Jay Giallombardo

Sweet and Lovely
Words and music by Norman Stars
Arranged by Mac Huff
This Arrangement (c) 1971, 2023 SPEBSQSA, Inc. (ASCAP), 110 7th Avenue North, Nashville, TN 37203 All Rights Reserved   Used by Permission
Reprinted by permission of the Barbershop Harmony Society

Sweet Georgia Brown (1925)
Words and music by Ben Bernie and Maceo Pinkard
Arranged by Aaron Dale
This Arrangement © 2023 by Aaron Dale. All Rights Reserved. Used by Permission
Reprinted by permission of Aaron Dale

Sweet Lorraine
Words and music by Cliff Burwell and Mitchell Parish
Arranged by David Wright
© 1928 (Renewed) EMI MILLS MUSIC INC. All Rights Administered by EMI MILLS MUSIC INC. (Publishing) and ALFRED MUSIC (Print)
Reprinted by permission of Hal Leonard Corporation

Sweetheart of Sigma Chi (1911)
Words and music by Byron Stokes and F. Dudleigh Vernor
Arranged by Steve Tramack
This Arrangement © 2023 by TramackMusic.com. All Rights Reserved. Used by Permission
Reprinted by permission of Steve Tramack

That's an Irish Lullaby (1913)
Words and music by James Royce Shannon
Arranged by Ed Waesche
Public Domain
Reprinted by permission of the Barbershop Harmony Society

The Next Ten Minutes
from THE LAST FIVE YEARS
Music and Lyrics by Jason Robert Brown
Copyright © 2002 by Jason Robert Brown
This arrangement Copyright © 2023 by Jason Robert Brown
All Rights Controlled by Semolina Farfalle Music (ASCAP)
International Copyright Secured   All Rights Reserved
Reprinted by permission of Hal Leonard LLC

The Sunshine of Your Smile (1913)
Words and music by Lilian Ray
Arranged by Tom Gentry
Public Domain
Reprinted by permission of Tom Gentry

These Will Be the Good Old Days (Twenty Years from Now)
Words and music by Jack Fulton and Lois Steele
Arranged by Clay Hine
Copyright © 1951 General Music Publishing Co.
Reprinted by permission of Alfred Music Corporation

Thriller
Words and music by Rod Temperton
Arranged by Aaron Dale
Copyright © Rodsongs (c/o Almo Music Corp.)
Reprinted by permission of Hal Leonard Corporation

Uptown Funk
Words and Music by Mark Ronson, Bruno Mars, Philip Lawrence, Jeff Bhasker, Devon Gallaspy, Nicholaus Williams, Lonnie Simmons, Ronnie Wilson, Charles Wilson, Rudolph Taylor and Robert Wilson
Copyright © 2014 Concord Copyrights and Songs Of Zelig c/o Concord Music Publishing, BMG Onyx Songs, Mars Force Music, New Songs Administration Ltd., Warner Geo Met Ric Music, ZZR Music LLC, Sony Songs LLC, Way Above Music, Sony Ballad, Trinlanta Publishing and KMR Music Royalties II SCSp
This arrangement Copyright © 2023 Concord Copyrights and Songs Of Zelig c/o Concord Music Publishing, BMG Onyx Songs, Mars Force Music, New Songs Administration Ltd., Warner Geo Met Ric Music, ZZR Music LLC, Sony Songs LLC, Way Above Music, Sony Ballad, Trinlanta Publishing and KMR Music Royalties II SCSp
All Rights for BMG Onyx Songs, Mars Force Music and New Songs Administration Ltd. Administered by BMG Rights Management (US) LLC
All Rights for ZZR Music LLC Administered by Warner Geo Met Ric Music
All Rights for Sony Songs LLC, Way Above Music and Sony Ballad Administered by Sony Music Publishing (US) LLC, 424 Church Street, Suite 1200, Nashville, TN 37219
All Rights Reserved   Used by Permission
Reprinted by permission of Hal Leonard LLC

Veni Veni Emanuel
Traditional Latin c. 12th Century. Translated by John Neale
Arranged by Kevin Keller
Public Domain
Reprinted by permission of Kevin Keller

Wait 'Til the Sun Shines, Nellie (1905)
Words and music by Harry Von Tilzer and Andrew B. Sterling
Arranged by Buzz Haeger
Public Domain
Reprinted by permission of the Barbershop Harmony Society

What Kind Of Fool Am I?
from the Musical Production STOP THE WORLD - I WANT TO GET OFF
Words and Music by Leslie Bricusse and Anthony Newley
© Copyright 1961 (Renewed) TRO Essex Music Ltd., London, England, Downtown DMP Songs and Songs Of Steve Peter
This arrangement © Copyright 2023 (Renewed) TRO Essex Music Ltd., London, England, Downtown DMP Songs and Songs Of Steve Peter
TRO - Ludlow Music, Inc., New York, controls all publication rights for TRO Essex Music Ltd. in the U.S.A. and Canada
All Rights for Downtown DMP Songs Administered by Downtown Music Publishing LLC
International Copyright Secured
All Rights Reserved Including Public Performance For Profit
Used by Permission
Reprinted by permission of Hal Leonard LLC

When Day is Done (1925)
Words and music by B G De Sylvia and Robert Katscher
Arranged by Ed Waesche
Public Domain
Reprinted by permission of the Barbershop Harmony Society

When I Lost You (1912)
Words and music by Irving Berlin
Arranged by Steven Armstrong
Public Domain
Reprinted by permission of the Barbershop Harmony Society

When Johnny Comes Marching Home (1863)
Words and music by Patrick Gilmore
Arranged by David Wright
Public Domain
Reprinted by permission of David Wright

When You Wore a Tulip
Words and music by Jack Mahoney and Percy Weinrich
Arranged by Adam Scott
Copyright © 2022 EMI MUSIC PUBLISHING / REDWOOD MUSIC LTD
Reprinted by permission of Hal Leonard Corporation

Where the Southern Roses Grow (1904)
Words and music by Thomas Morse and Richard Buck Henry
Arranged by David Wright
Public Domain
Reprinted by permission of David Wright

Who'll Take My Place (When I'm Gone)
Words and music by Raymond Klages and Billy Fazioli
Arranged by Greg Lyne
Copyright © 1939 Broadway Music Corp. Copyright Renewed All Rights Administered by Sony Music Publishing, 424
Church Street, Suite 1200, Nashville, TN 37219 International Copyright Secured All Rights Reserved
Reprinted by permission of Hal Leonard Corporation

Who's Lovin' You
Words and Music by William "Smokey" Robinson, Jr.
Copyright © 1960 Sony Smash Hits Music Publishing
Copyright Renewed
This arrangement Copyright © 2023 Sony Smash Hits Music Publishing
All Rights Administered by Sony Music Publishing (US) LLC, 424 Church Street, Suite 1200, Nashville, TN 37219
International Copyright Secured   All Rights Reserved
Reprinted by permission of Hal Leonard LLC

Who's Sorry Now? (1923)
Words and music by Ted Snyder, Bert Kalmar and Harry Ruby
Arranged by Tom Gentry
Public Domain
Reprinted by permission of Hal Leonard Corporation

Yes Sir That's My Baby (1925)
Words and music by Walter Donaldson and Gus Kahn
Arranged by Clay Hine
Public Domain
Reprinted by permission of Clay Hine

Yesterday I Heard The Rain
Words and Music by Armando Manzanero Canche
English Words by Gene Lees
Copyright © 1968 by Universal Music Publishing MGB S.A. de C.V.
Copyright Renewed
This arrangement Copyright © 2023 by Universal Music Publishing MGB S.A. de C.V.
All Rights for the U.S. and Canada Administered by Universal Music - MGB Songs
International Copyright Secured   All Rights Reserved
Reprinted by permission of Hal Leonard LLC

Yona from Arizona
Words and music by Traditional
Arranged by Aaron Dale
This Arrangement © 2023 by Aaron Dale. All Rights Reserved. Used by Permission
Reprinted by permission of Aaron Dale

You Can't Stop The Beat
from HAIRSPRAY
Music by Marc Shaiman
Lyrics by Marc Shaiman and Scott Wittman
Copyright © 2001 UNIVERSAL MUSIC CORP., WINDING BROOK WAY MUSIC and WALLI WOO
ENTERTAINMENT
This arrangement Copyright © 2023 UNIVERSAL MUSIC CORP., WINDING BROOK WAY MUSIC and WALLI
WOO ENTERTAINMENT
All Rights Administered by UNIVERSAL MUSIC CORP.
All Rights Reserved   Used by Permission
Reprinted by permission of Hal Leonard LLC

You Make Me Feel Like Dancing
Words and Music by Vini Poncia and Leo Sayer
Copyright © 1975, 1976 EMI Blackwood Music Inc. and Silverbird Songs Ltd.
Copyright Renewed
This arrangement Copyright © 2023 EMI Blackwood Music Inc. and Silverbird Songs Ltd.
All Rights on behalf of EMI Blackwood Music Inc. Administered by Sony Music Publishing (US) LLC, 424 Church
Street, Suite 1200, Nashville, TN 37219
All Rights on behalf of Silverbird Songs Ltd. in the USA and Canada Administered by Almo Music Corp.
International Copyright Secured   All Rights Reserved
Reprinted by permission of Hal Leonard LLC

You Make Me Feel So Young
Words and music by Mack Gordon and Josef Myrow
Arranged by Mark Hale
© 1946 (Renewed) WB MUSIC CORP.
Reprinted by permission of Hal Leonard Corporation

Glossary of Terms

A Cappella – A term applied to vocal music that is performed without accompaniment.

A tempo – A musical direction indicating a return to a previously established tempo.

Absolute pitch – See *perfect pitch.*

Accelerando – A musical direction indicating a gradual speeding up of the tempo.

Accidentals – The signs (sharp (♯), flat (♭), natural (♮), double sharp (𝄪) and double flat (♭♭) used in musical notation to indicate chromatic alterations of pitches or to cancel them.

Ad lib – Ad libitum. Tempo and rhythm may be altered at the discretion of the performer.

Added ninth – The Major ninth (see ninth) added to a triad (see triad). The chord so obtained, such as C–E–G–D.

Added second – See *Added ninth.*

Added sixth – The Major sixth (see Sixth) added to a triad (see Triad). The chord so obtained, such as C–E–G–A.

Amen (plagal) cadence – The cadence (see *Cadence*) with the subdominant preceding the tonic: IV to I. Known as the Amen or plagal cadence because of its traditional use for "amen" at the close of the hymn.

Arrangement – An adaptation in vocal harmony of a composed song using principles of voicing, voice leading, and harmonization that reveal variety and unity.

Augmentation – A form of rhythmic alteration that lengthens the original note values, usually doubling those values.

Augmented interval – An interval that is a chromatic ½-step larger than a Major second, a Major sixth, a perfect fourth, or a perfect fifth. Other intervals may be augmented but are impractical in ordinary musical usage.

Augmented seventh chord – A seventh chord whose characteristic interval is the augmented fifth; a seventh chord consisting of root, the Major third above, the augmented fifth above, and the minor seventh above, as: C–E–G#–Bb, or F–A–C#-Eb.

Augmented triad – A chord consisting of root, the Major third above and the augmented fifth above, as C–E–G# (or Eb–G–B).

Back time – An arranging device that lengthens the duration of syllables or words in the harmony parts as they support the melody.

Balance – The effect achieved through proper voice volume on each note of a chord.

Bar – A vertical line across the staff, dividing it into measures; sometimes called bar line; a measure (see *measure*).

Barbershop ninth chord – A ninth chord consisting of root, the Major third above, the perfect fifth above, the minor seventh above and the Major ninth above, as C–E–G–Bb–D. Because there are only four parts in barbershop music, either the fifth or the root is omitted. See *dominant ninth chord.*

Barbershop seventh chord – A seventh chord consisting of root, the Major third above, the perfect fifth above, and the minor seventh above, as: D–F#–A–C, or F–A–C–Eb.

Baritone – the inside-harmony voice. Similar range to the lead.

Beat – The unit of measurement in music, the pulse in music. Most music beats are organized in groups of two, three, or four per measure; See *pulse.*

Beats – A pulsation in sound intensity produced by the combination of two or more tones of slightly different frequency. The beat frequency is equal to the difference in frequency between any pair of tones. In a different musical context, a beat refers to the time duration of accented and unaccented pulsations that convey the sense of tempo of a song.

Bell chord – An arranging device by which a chord is constructed by a succession of notes sung by each voice in turn.

Blossom effect – An arranging device in which the four voices start in unison and, in contrary motion, expand to a four-part chord.

Blues style – A jazz style characterized using "blue notes," that is, the lowered third, seventh, and sometimes fifth degrees of the Major scale.

Break - an outdated vocal pedagogy term referring to the span of notes in a given singer's range indicating a register transition. Modern, acceptable terms are *passaggio, register event,* and *area of transition*

Bridge – The middle section of the traditional American Tin Pan Alley song. The B (middle) section of the ABA form of such songs; also called release.

Cadence – A melodic harmonic progression that occurs at the end of a composition, section or phrase, conveying the impression of a momentary or permanent conclusion. See *amen cadence.* Also *deceptive cadence.*

Caesura – This sign (//). indicates that a rather long breath should be taken. Under certain conditions, it may indicate a grand pause, a longer breath taken for dramatic effect.

Cascade effect – An arranging device in which the four voices start in unison and, while the top voice sustains their tone, the three lower voices move downward to the notes of a chord. Opposite of *pyramid.*

Chart – Colloquial term for an arrangement.

Chest Voice – A historical vocal pedagogy term for notes primarily used by a singer that correspond to their speaking voice

Chord – A musical sound consisting of three or more notes sounded together.

Chord progression – A succession or series of chords.

Chorus of a song – That part of a song that normally follows the verse; also called refrain. While there may be more than one verse to a song, there is generally only one chorus that is repeated after each verse. The term refers to either melody or lyrics, or to both together.

Chromatic note – A note that has been raised or lowered by an accidental from its normal position in the scale.

Chromatic scale – A twelve-tone scale with ½-steps between all successive notes.

Circle of Fifths – The twelve tones of the chromatic scale arranged in a sequence of ascending or descending perfect fifths. The circular, clockwise arrangement of the twelve keys in an order of ascending fifths (C, G, D, A, etc.); Of greater concern is its importance as a generator of harmonic progressions, because roots of chords most commonly move to roots of other chords that lie a perfect fifth below, as in the counterclockwise progression: C7 to F7 to B♭7, etc.

Clef – A musical sign placed at the beginning of each line of music to give precise pitch meaning to the staff.

Climax – The high point of a song toward which both music and words build.

Clock system – A chord nomenclature system devised in the early 1940s by veteran Barbershopper Maurice "Molly" Reagan. The system is based on the Circle of Fifths which places the twelve chromatic notes found within the octave and their enharmonic equivalents on the face of a clock. The "12 o'clock" position is the tonic, the "1 o'clock" position is the dominant, etc.

Close position voicing – The distribution of notes in a chord so that all four voices fall on consecutive notes of the chord, and the interval from highest to lowest is an octave or less.

Coda – See *tag.*

Combination tones – Tones perceived by a listener when two or more tones of different frequency are sounded simultaneously to produce a beat rate fast enough to be recognized as a tone of a given pitch. Also called coincident partials. Combination tones contribute significantly to the expansion of sound.

Comma – This sign (,) indicates that a short, quick breath should be taken at the point where it appears in the music.

Common time – Same as four-four meter. Four beats to the measure.

Consonance – A smooth sound resulting from the combination of two or more tones whose frequencies are related as the ratios of small whole numbers whereby the roughness related to the beat phenomenon is reduced to a minimum. See *dissonance.*

Consonant – Harmonious. Also, one of a class of speech sounds (as *p, k, m, d, s*) characterized by constriction or closure at one or more points in the breath channel.

Contrapuntal – Having two or more simultaneous melodies.

Contrary motion – Involving melodic movement by two voices, usually the tenor and bass, in opposite directions.

Crossed voices – Pertaining to the situation where the lead is above the tenor or below the bass or where the baritone is above the tenor or below the bass, or where the bass is above any of the other three parts. The lead below the baritone does not constitute crossed voices as this voicing commonly exists in barbershop music.

Cut time – A meter signature indicating two beats per measure.

Deceptive cadence – The delaying of final harmonic repose by a harmonic progression to an unexpected chord at the point of cadence, as V7 to VI.

Decrescendo – A musical direction indicating a gradual decrease in loudness.

Di – The solmization syllable for raised "do," as C# in the scale of C. See *solmization*; *Sol-Fa*.

Diatonic – The seven tones of the natural Major scale.

Diction – The pronunciation and enunciation of words in singing.

Difference tone – A very faint note resulting from the difference of the frequencies of two notes sounded simultaneously.

Diminished interval – An interval that is a chromatic ½-step smaller than a minor third, a minor seventh, a perfect fourth, or a perfect fifth. Other intervals may be diminished but are impractical in ordinary musical usage.

Diminished seventh chord – A seventh chord whose characteristic interval is the diminished seventh; a seventh chord consisting of root, the minor third above, the diminished fifth above and the diminished seventh above, as F#–A–C–E♭, or B–D–F–A♭, etc.

Diminished triad – A chord consisting of root, the minor third above and the diminished fifth above: as C–E♭–G, or G#–B–D, etc.

Diminution – A form of rhythmic alteration that shortens the original note values, usually halving those values.

Diphthong – A combination of two vowel sounds that form a single word syllable, such as "a" in "way" (ayee) or "i" in "mine" (ah-ih), etc.

Dissonance – The absence of consonance characterized by a rough sound resulting from the beat produced by two or more tones whose frequencies are not simply related. See *consonance*.

Dissonant – Inharmonious. Also, a combination of tones (chord) that requires resolution such as a barbershop seventh chord.

Divorced voicing – The distribution of notes in a chord so that either the tenor or the bass is distantly removed from the other three voices.

Do – The solmization syllable for the first degree of the Major scale. See *Solmization, Sol-Fa*.

Dominant – The fifth degree of either a Major or a minor scale. Also, a chord whose root is on that scale degree.

Dominant ninth chord – A ninth chord built on the fifth scale degree consisting of root, the Major third above, the perfect fifth above, the minor seventh above and the Major ninth above as G–B–D–F–A in the key of C. Because there are only four parts in barbershop music, either the fifth or the root is omitted. See *barbershop ninth chord*.

Dominant seventh chord – The barbershop seventh chord built on the fifth scale degree consisting of root, the Major third above, the perfect fifth above and the minor seventh above, as G–B–D–F in the key of C. See *Barbershop seventh chord*

Double – A condition existing when two voices sing the same letter-named pitch in unison, at the octave or at the double octave.

Doubling – Creating a double.

Double time – At double speed; a tempo twice as fast as the preceding tempo.

Downbeat – The first beat of a measure, so called because the director's motion is made in a downward direction.

Duet – A composition or part of a composition or arrangement for two performers only. In barbershop music it refers also to three or four voices singing only two parts.

Duration – The length of a musical tone. In musical notation duration is indicated using varying note values-half notes, quarter notes, etc.

Diminuendo – A musical direction indicating a gradual decrease in loudness. Same as decrescendo.

Dynamics – Degree of loudness or softness in a musical performance, indicated by the musical directions piano (p), pianissimo (pp), mezzoforte (mf), forte (f), and fortissimo (ff).

Echo – An arranging device used as harmonic and durational fill-in that repeats a word or group of words.

Embellishment – Any arranging device such as a swipe, key change, echo, bell chord, etc., designed to add interest and variety to harmonizations of songs.

Enharmonic – Sounding the same but written differently, as: C# and D♭.

Equal temperament – A system of tuning in which the octave is divided into 12 equal semitones (½-steps), as with a piano, to permit such instruments to be played in any key with only small harmonic inaccuracies.

Expanded sound – One of the hallmarks of barbershop singing is the presence of expanded sound, or the auditory perception of additional notes generated by the energetic interaction between overtones (see combination tones), particularly when harmonics coincide with formants.

Expression – The elements of rubato tempo, phrasing, dynamics, accents, fermatas, and tenutos that are used by performers in interpreting music.

Fa – The solmization syllable for the fourth degree of the Major scale, as E♭ in the scale of B♭ Major. See *solmization, Sol-Fa*.

False cadence – Same as *deceptive cadence*.

False relation – See *cross relation*

Falsetto – A historical vocal pedagogy term for notes above chest and head voice in male-presenting voices.

Fermata – A hold or pause, indicated by the sign "⌒"

Fi – The solmization syllable for raised "fa," as F# in the scale of C Major.

Fifth – The note of a chord lying an interval of a fifth above the root, as G in the chord C–E–G. See *perfect fifth; interval*.

Fifth, interval of a – An interval covering five scale degrees. See *perfect fifth*.

First inversion – The distribution of the notes of a chord so that the third of the chord is the lowest sounding note.

Fine (fee-nay) – The end.

Flat – The musical symbol (♭) that lowers the pitch of a "piano white key" note ½-step. Also, below pitch, as "to sing flat"

Folk song style – A style of harmonization characterized by generally limited harmonic interest, avoidance of chromatic notes, and lack of full four-part chords.

Form – The order of the component parts of an arrangement (introduction, verse, chorus, tag, etc.). Also, the architectural division of the musical material into phrases and sub-phrases.

Formants – A series of broad resonant frequency bands that correspond to the natural resonant frequencies of the vocal tract. The character of distinct vowel and sung consonant sounds is determined by the positioning of the jaw, tongue, lips, etc., during singing whereby unique patterns of resonant formant frequencies are established.

Forte (f) – Dynamic marking meaning loud.

Fortissimo (ff) – Dynamic marking meaning very loud.

Fourth, interval of a – An interval covering four scale degrees. See *perfect fourth*.

Four-three chord – A musical term that indicates a seventh chord in the second inversion. See *second inversion*.

Four-two chord – A musical term that indicates a seventh chord in the third inversion. See *third inversion*.

Free style – See *Ad lib*; free tempo.

Free tempo – Performed without a regularly recurring beat or pulse. Also called free style. See *Ad lib*.

Frequency – The number of periodic vibrations or cycles occurring per second. See *Hertz*.

From the top – Colloquial term for "start at the beginning"; from the first measure. Also "from the edge," "upper left"

Fundamental – The lowest tone, or generator, of a series of harmonies and overtones. It is the first harmonic. See *overtones*. See *harmonics*.

Glee club style – A style of harmonization characterized by melody mostly in the top voice, and consisting primarily of diatonic harmony, often using incomplete chords and unnecessary doublings.

Glissando – See *portamento*.

Grand pause – This sign (//) indicates a long pause, often for dramatic effect. See *caesura*.

Half-diminished seventh chord – A seventh chord whose characteristic interval is the diminished fifth; a seventh chord consisting of root, the minor third above, the diminished fifth above, and the minor seventh above, as B–D–F–A, or D–F–A♭–C . In popular sheet music, m7♭5.

Half-time – At half speed; a tempo half as fast as the preceding tempo. See *stomp time*.

Harmonic anticipation – The premature appearance of a harmony in a chord progression. A chord that appears before the implied harmony requires it.

Harmonic rhythm – The rhythmic pattern with which harmonies change within any given portion of music.

Harmonic series – See *overtones*.

Harmonics – Tones of higher pitch that are present in a regular series in nearly every musical sound, and whose presence and relative intensity determine the timbre of the musical sound. The term also includes the fundamental. See *overtones*.

Harmonization – The basic setting of the melody with three harmonizing parts, faithful to the composer's melody and to the implied harmony.

Harmony – The sounding together of tones. Also, the study of chords and chord progressions.

Head voice – A historical vocal pedagogy term for notes above what is typically called chest voice. When referring to a male-presenting voice, head voice is a lighter chest voice and not falsetto. When referring to female-presenting voice, head voice is analogous to falsetto in male-presenting voices.

Hertz – This term has replaced the older term "vibrations per second." in honor of Heinrich Hertz, German physicist, 1857—1894. Abbreviation Hz.

High baritone voicing – The distribution of the tones of a chord so that the usual tenor note is given to the baritone and the tenor sings the baritone note an octave higher.

Homorhythmic – One of the hallmarks of the barbershop style and differentiating aspects from other a cappella styles, homorhythm is a texture having a similarity of rhythm in all parts, such as all voices parts singing the same words at the same time. Homorhythm is a condition of homophony, which is a blocked chordal texture. Homorhythmic textures deliver lyrics with clarity and emphasis. Textures in which parts have different rhythms are defined as *heterorhythmic*.

Hz. – See *Hertz*.

Implied harmony – A succession of harmonies and chord progressions suggested by the composer's melody.

Inflection – A musical direction indicating a slight accent on a note, chord, or syllable.

In tempo – See *a tempo*.

Interlude – A section, generally newly composed, added to an arrangement to separate or to connect larger sections of the arrangement

Interpolation – The insertion of a small portion of one song into an arrangement of another song.

Interpretation – The personal and creative delivery by a performer of a song's message and emotional content. See *expression*.

Interval – The difference in pitch between two tones.

Intonation – The degree to which the tonal center appropriate to any point in a song remains invariant, and the degree to which consonant interval relationships between the harmony parts and the projected melodic line are maintained.

Introduction – A musical phrase preceding the first main portion (verse or chorus) of a song.

Just diatonic scale – The scale of just intonation. A musical scale containing exact intervals in the harmonic series of a given fundamental tone. It may be constructed by tuning the subdominant, tonic, and dominant triads with true Major thirds and fifths in the ratio 4:5:6.

Just intonation – A system of tuning based on acoustically pure perfect fifths and Major thirds. The "natural" tuning preferred for barbershop singing. See *perfect fifth; Major third*; see *equal temperament*; see *just diatonic scale*.

Just temperament – Same as *just intonation*. See *just diatonic scale*.

Just tuning – Same as *just intonation*. See *just diatonic scale*.

Key – The prevailing tonal center as expressed by a key signature. Also, the scale and all relationships embodied in it.

Key change – A modulation. A change of key during a composition or arrangement

Keynote – The first note of the scale and the central tone of the key. Also called tonic or "do."

Key signature – Sharps or flats placed at the beginning of each line of music to indicate the key.

La – The solmization syllable for the sixth degree of the Major scale, as: A in the scale of C Major; G in the scale of B♭ Major, etc. See *solmization, Sol-Fa*.

Le (lay) – The solmization syllable for lowered "la," as: A♭ in scale of C Major.

Lead – The melody in a barbershop song. Also, the one who sings this part.

Lead-in notes – See *pick-up notes*.

Leading tone – The seventh degree of the scale lying a ½-step below the tonic.

Legato – A manner of performance in which successive notes are joined smoothly without separation.

Li (lee) – The solmization syllable for raised "la," as: A# in the scale of C Major.

Lyric – The words of a song.

Major – A qualifying term denoting specific kinds of intervals, scales, triads, and keys.

Major interval – An interval ½-step larger than a minor interval.

Major key – Having the qualities and relationships of the tones of a Major scale and the chords built on those scale tones.

Major scale – A scale with the whole and ½-step pattern of the white keys from C to C on a piano.

Major seventh chord – A seventh chord whose characteristic interval is the Major seventh. A seventh chord consisting of root, the Major third above, the perfect fifth above and the Major seventh above, as C–E–G–B; or B♭–D–F– A.

Major third, interval of a – An interval covering exactly two whole-steps, as: C to E; F to A; and B♭ to D.

Major triad – A chord consisting of root, the Major third above and the perfect fifth above, as C–E–G, D–F#–A, etc.

Me (pronounced may) – The solmization syllable for lowered "mi," as E♭ in the scale of C Major.

Measure – A metric unit consisting of a specific number of beats delineated by bar lines.

Mediant – The third degree of either a Major or minor scale. Also, a chord whose root is on that scale degree.

Medley – An arrangement containing all or major parts of two or more songs having a unified theme or idea.

Meter – The basic, prevailing pattern of beats and accents in a song, or section of a song; indicated by the meter signature, such as 2/4, 3/4, 6/8, etc.

Meter change – A change of meter during a composition or arrangement

Meter signature – Arabic numerals placed at the beginning of a piece of music to indicate the meter.

Mezze forte (mf) – Dynamic marking meaning moderately loud but not as loud as forte (f).

Mezze piano (mp) – Dynamic marking meaning moderately soft but not as soft as piano (p).

Mi (mee) – The solmization syllable for the third degree of the Major scale, as D in the scale of B♭ Major; or B in the scale of G Major. See *solmization, Sol-Fa.*

Middle C – The C near the middle of the piano keyboard. In the notation of TTBB barbershop music, it is the note on the third space of the treble staff (with the 8 underneath the clef) and the note on the first ledger line above the bass staff. For SSAA barbershop notation, it is the note on the first ledger line below the treble staff and the note on the second space of the bass clef (with the 8 above the clef).

Minor – A qualifying term denoting specific kinds of intervals, scales, triads, and keys.

Minor key – Having the qualities and relationships of the tones of a minor scale and the chords built on those tones.

Minor scale – A scale with the whole and ½-step pattern of the piano white keys from A to A. In actual usage the seventh tone of this scale is almost always raised a ½step to a pitch a ½-step below the tonic. In addition, the sixth scale degree is also sometimes raised.

Minor seventh chord – A seventh chord whose characteristic intervals are the minor third and the minor seventh. A seventh chord consisting of root, the minor third above, the perfect fifth above, and the minor seventh above, as: D–F–A–C, and G–B♭–D–F.

Minor sixth chord – A minor triad with an added Major sixth, such as: C–E♭–G–A, or E–G–B–C#.

Minor triad – A chord consisting of root, the minor third above and the perfect fifth above, such as D–F–A, E–G–B, or G–B♭–D.

Mode – A scale form, such as Major or minor.

Modern style – A style of harmonization characterized by melody usually in the top voice, and harmonies of sixth chords, Major seventh chords, ninth, eleventh, and thirteenth chords, plus other, more dissonant chords. Also considered Jazz style.

Modulation – See *key change.*

Music theory – That part of the study of music consisting of all the elements of harmony and notation.

Natural – The musical symbol (♮) that cancels a sharp, flat, double sharp or double flat.

Neutral vowel – A sound such as "oh" or "ah" that is sung usually by three voices as an accompaniment to a solo, or solo passage, in a barbershop arrangement.

Neutral syllable – A sound such as "bum bum" or "doo wah" that is sung by one or more voices in a barbershop arrangement

Ninth chord – Any chord whose largest interval above the root is a ninth. See dominant ninth chord.

Ninth, interval of a – An interval covering nine scale degrees. It may be a Major ninth, that is, an octave plus a whole step, such as C to D, or E to F#; it may be a minor ninth, that is, an octave plus a ½-step, such as C to D♭, or E to F. See *dominant ninth chord.*

Non-chord tone – A tone that is not part of the prevailing harmony. See *suspension, passing tone and pedal tone.*

Notation – The technique of placing musical symbols on manuscript paper.

Octave, interval of an – An interval covering eight scale degrees, as C to C, F# to F#, etc.

Octet – A group of eight performers. In barbershop music, there are two singers on each voice part.

Open position voicing – The distribution of the notes in a chord so that the interval from the lowest to the highest note is more than one octave.

Over arranged – Colloquial term referring to an arrangement embellished to the extent that the melodic and lyric interest are obscured or lost.

Overtones – Any frequency produced by an acoustical instrument, including the voice, that is higher in frequency than the fundamental. It is customary to refer to the first overtone as the second harmonic, the second overtone as the third harmonic, etc. They are present in a regular series in every musical sound, and the presence, absence, and relative strengths of them determine the quality of musical sound. See *harmonics*.

Parallel harmony – A succession of chords in which all or most of the voices move in parallel melodic lines. Generally undesirable in barbershop music except for special effects or when specifically required by the implied harmony.

Parallel motion – Involving melodic movement by two or more voices in the same direction and maintaining the same basic interval relationship between the voices.

Parody – A satirical imitation, such as may be created in music by replacing the original lyric with a comic one, or by changing the composition itself in a comic manner.

Passing tone – A non-chord tone that occurs in an ascending or descending scale pattern. Not typically characteristic of the barbershop style.

Patter – An arranging device featuring the adaptation or composition of lyrics that are sung in more rapid rhythmic pattern than the melody and lyric that they support. There are several variations of this device.

Pedal tone – A tone that is held by one voice while other voices move freely over, under, or around it. Consonant pedal tones are acceptable in the barbershop style.

Perfect fifth – An interval covering five scale degrees and containing exactly seven half-steps, as C to G, B♭ to F, etc.

Perfect fourth – An interval coveting four scale degrees and containing exactly five half-steps, as G to C, F to B♭, etc.

Perfect octave – An internal covering eight scale degrees, as C to C, F to F, etc.

Perfect pitch – The ability or capacity of an individual to identify a pitch immediately by letter name, without reference to a previously sounded note of different pitch. See *relative pitch*.

Piano (p) – Dynamic marking meaning softly.

Pianissimo (pp) – Dynamic marking meaning very softly.

Pick-up note(s) – A note or series of notes preceding the downbeat of a musical phrase.

Pitch – The sensation of relative highness or lowness of a sound, determined primarily by the frequency of vibration of the sound-producing medium.

Precision – The area of a performance that refers to attacks, releases, and synchronization.

Pop style – A style of harmonization characterized by frequent unison singing and much use of the solo voice with a vocal background consisting of singing neutral vowels or syllables.

Portamento – Sliding smoothly from one tone to another, continuously changing pitch.

Pulse – A rhythmic recurrence of beats; a single beat; a slight emphasis to a syllable or note.

Pyramid – An arranging device that incorporates the gradual expansion of a harmonic texture from a single pitch, sung solo or in unison by two or more voices, to a full chord, by the addition of chord tones above the starting pitch. Opposite of cascade.

Ra (rah) – The solmization syllable for lowered "re," as D♭ in C Major.

Range – The pitches a voice can produce, from lowest to highest Also the span of pitches, from lowest to highest, in a particular song or arrangement

Re (ray) – The solmization syllable for the second degree of a Major scale, as D in the scale of C Major, or C in the scale of B♭ Major. See *solmization, Sol-Fa*.

Refrain of a song – See *chorus of a song*.

Register – A series of tones of similar quality within the range of a voice that are produced by a particular adjustment of the vocal folds.

Relative pitch – The ability to recognize or identify the interval relationship between two different pitches.

Release – The termination or cessation of sound. Also see *bridge*.

Resolution – The process in which a note or chord of lesser consonance (e.g., a barbershop seventh chord) moves to another note or chord of greater consonance.

Resonance – The intensification and enrichment of a musical tone by the acoustical amplification of those harmonic frequencies that lie within the format frequency bands.

Rhythm – The organization of music in respect to time. It is expressed by using notes of various durational values. See *meter, beat, measure, syncopation, meter signature, duration*.

Rhythmic propellant – Any of several arrangement devices (echoes; pick-up notes, backtime, swipes, etc.) whose primary purpose is to help maintain the ongoing rhythmic motion in a song.

Ri (ree) – The solmization syllable for raised "re," as D# in the scale of C Major. See *solmization, Sol-Fa*.

Ritard – Abbreviation for ritardando. Also abbreviated rit. A musical direction indicating a gradual slowing down of the tempo.

Root – The note upon which a chord is built and from which it takes its name.

Root position – The distribution of the tones of a chord so that the root of the chord is the lowest sounding note.

Rubato – A controlled flexibility of tempo within a phrase or measure, characterized by a slight quickening or slight slowing of tempo. Not as free as ad lib.

Scale – A pattern of pitches arranged in ascending or descending order. See *Major scale, minor scale*.

Scat – Derived from vocal jazz, scat is a vocal improvisational style using wordless vocables or nonsense syllables, using the voice as an instrument rather than a lyrical singing mechanism.

Second, interval of a – An interval covering two scale degrees. It may be a Major second, that is, a whole step, such as C to D, or E to F#, or it may be a minor second, that is, a ½-step, such as B to C, or F# to G.

Second inversion – The distribution of the tones of a chord so that the fifth of the chord is the lowest sounding tone.

Secondary dominant ninth chord – A chord with the same interval structure as the dominant ninth chord, but whose root is not the fifth degree of the scale. See *dominant ninth chord*. See *barbershop ninth chord*.

Secondary dominant seventh chord – A chord with the same interval structure as the dominant seventh chord, but whose root is not the fifth degree of the scale. See *dominant seventh chord*. See *barbershop seventh chord*.

Seventh, interval of a – An interval covering seven scale degrees. It may be a Major seventh, such as C to B, or G to F#; a minor seventh, such as C to B♭, or G to F; or a diminished seventh, such as C# to B♮.

Seventh chord – Any chord whose largest interval above the root is a seventh. See *dominant seventh chord, Major seventh chord, augmented seventh chord, minor seventh chord, barbershop seventh chord, diminished seventh chord*.

Sforzando (Sfor-tsahnd' -oh) – A musical direction indicating a strong accent on a note or chord. (**sfz** or **>**)

Sharp – The musical symbol (#) that raises the pitch of a "white key" note ½-step. Also, above pitch, as "to sing sharp."

Six-five chord – A musical term that indicates a seventh chord in first inversion.

Six-four chord – A musical term that indicates a triad in second inversion.

Si (see) – The solmization syllable for raised "sol," such as G# in the scale of C Major.

Sixth, interval of a – An interval covering six scale degrees. It may be a Major sixth, such as: C to A, or E to C#, or a minor sixth, such as C to A♭, or E to C.

Sixth chord – Any chord whose largest interval above the root is a sixth. See added *sixth, interval of a sixth*.

Sol – The solmization syllable for the fifth degree of a Major scale, such as F in scale of B♭ Major. See *solmization, Sol-Fa*.

Sol-Fa – A system of ear training and sight singing in which the notes are sung to syllables and the ear is trained to recognize and reproduce, through the syllables, the notes on the printed page. Also called Solfege.

Solmization – The use of syllables to designate the tones of the scale. See *Sol-Fa*. Also *Do, Re, Mi, Fa, Sol, La, Ti*. Also, *Di, Ri, Fi, Si, Li*, ascending; and *Te, Le, Se, Me, Ra*, descending.

Solo – Alone. A composition or part of a composition or arrangement for one performer with or without accompaniment. In barbershop music, the soloist is often accompanied by the remaining three voices.

Song theme – That component of the song (lyric, melody, harmony, rhythm, or parody) that gives it its entertainment value.

Sound flow – A continuous uninterrupted execution of syllables except where staccato or stress is intentionally used for interpretive purposes.

Spread chord – A chord whose tones are distributed in extreme open position voicing. See *open position voicing.*

Staccato – A manner of performance in which successive notes are detached or separated from one another.

Staff – The set of five lines and four spaces, each representing a different pitch, on which music is written.

Stomp time – A manner of performance characterized by a slow, heavily accented beat, generally performed at half the tempo of the major portion of the performance. Used for contrast or climactic effect

Subdominant – The fourth degree of either a Major or minor scale. Also, a chord whose root is on that scale degree.

Submediant – The sixth degree of either a Major or minor scale. Also, a chord whose root is on that scale degree.

Sub-climax – A point of emphasis in a song, which may be melodic or lyric, that does not take away from the climax (high point); but may enhance it.

Summation tone – A very faint note resulting from the sum of the frequencies of two notes sounded simultaneously.

Supertonic – The second degree of either a major or minor scale. Also, a chord whose root is on that scale degree.

Suspension – The sustaining of one of the notes of a chord while the other notes move so that it demands resolution, usually downward to the next chord tone. Non-chord suspensions are not characteristic of the barbershop style.

Syllables – The component parts of words. In solmization the words Do, Re, Mi, etc. See *solmization, Sol-Fa.*

Synchronization – The degree of coordination achieved in the execution for chord progressions and syllables.

Syncopation – A rhythm having accents that do not agree with the normal metrical accents.

Swipe – A progression of two or more chords sung on a single word or syllable. A characteristic feature of the barbershop style of music.

Tag – The coda or special ending added to a song or to an arrangement

Target vowel – The primary sustained vowel sound of the word being sung.

Te (tay) – The solmization syllable for the lowered below the tonic.

Temperament – See *system of tuning.* See *equal temperament, just intonation.*

Tempered tuning – See *equal temperament.*

Tempo – The speed of a composition determined by the speed of the beat to which it is performed.

Tempo ad lib – A musical direction indicating variable tempo. See *rubato, ad lib.*

Tenor – The top voice in a barbershop quartet or chorus.

Tenuto – Usual definition: to hold a note for its full value. In actual practice it involves a slight lengthening of the note.

Tessitura – From the Italian for "texture," tessitura refers to the general "lie" of a vocal part, whether it is high or low in average pitch. From *A Cappella Arranging,* "a vocal part may cover two octaves: if most of that time is spent in the upper octave, the part has a *high* tessitura. If it's all over the place, it's a *wide* tessitura.[243]

Third, interval of a – An interval covering three scale degrees. It may be a Major third consisting of two whole-steps, such as C to E, or D to F#, or a minor third consisting of a step and a half, such as C to E♭, or D to F.

Third inversion – The distribution of the tones of a seventh chord so that the seventh is the lowest sounding note.

Thirteenth chord – Any chord whose largest interval above the root is a thirteenth. In barbershop usage, four tones of this seven-note chord are omitted (the root usually doubled), leading to some confusion with the sixth chord.

---

243 A Cappella Arranging, Deke Sharon and Dylan Bell, page 332

Ti (tee) – The solmization syllable for the seventh degree of a Major scale. It lies ½-step below the tonic. See *tonic*.

Timbre – A result of the presence and relative strength of overtones that makes one voice resemble, or differ from, another.

Time signature – See *meter signature*.

Tone – A musical sound of definite pitch.

Tonic – The key note. The first note of the scale and the central note of the key.

Transpose – To write or to perform in a different key from the original.

Tremolo – An excessive vibrato that leads to deviation from exact pitch. See *vibrato*.

Triad – A three-note chord composed of alternating scale tones, as C–E–G, F–A–C, etc.

Trio – A composition or part of a composition or arrangement for three performers only. In barbershop music, trio refers to the three parts singing an accompaniment to a solo.

Tritone Substitution – From *A Cappella Arranging*: "A jazz harmonic progression wherein a dominant seventh chord is swapped for a dominant seventh chord a tritone away. That means that a Dm7–G7–C progression would become a Dm7–Db7–C. The reason this works is that the third and the seventh of the G7 chord (B and F) are the seventh and the third of the Db chord, and they will still resolve inward (provided there is good voice leading) to C and E."[244]

True scale – A scale with intervals tuned in just intonation. See *just intonation*.

Tune-up chord – The tonic chord of the key in its characteristic voicing used to tune the quartet or chorus preparatory to singing. Oftentimes, the leads sing the root, basses also the root but an octave lower, baritones sing the fifth of the chord between the leads and basses, and the tenors sing the third of the chord above the lead note.

Tuning – Adjusting pitch to obtain desirable tonal relationships. See *intonation, overtones, just intonation*.

Undertone – See *difference tone*.

Unison – The combined sound of two or more notes at the same pitch.

Upbeat – The final beat of a measure; the beat immediately preceding the downbeat. Sometimes confused with the term pick-up notes. See *downbeat, pick-up notes*.

Verse – The part of a song that normally precedes the chorus or refrain.

Vibrato – A method of giving expressive quality to the sound of a note by means of rapid and minute pitch fluctuations.

Voice – A part, such as tenor, lead, baritone, or bass. Also, the music written for that part.

Voice leading – The principles governing the progression of the various voice parts in an arrangement, especially in terms of the singability of the individual lines.

Voicing – The manner of distribution of the tones of a chord among the four voice parts. See *close position voicing, open position voicing, spread chord*.

Volume – The degree of loudness or softness.

Volume relationship – See balance.

Vowel – One of a class of speech sounds (a, e, i, o, u) in the articulation of which the oral part of the breath channel is not blocked or constricted.

Walking bass – From *A Cappella Arranging*: "A bass line that moves in a scaler and/or chromatic fashion from chord to chord. Frequently found in jazz."[245] This technique is used in barbershop arranging in a 3-against-1 texture with the bass frequently providing the beats in the measure while the trio is syncopating.

Waltz time – Three/four meter. Having a meter signature indicating three beats per measure.

Woodshedding – Impromptu four-part singing without benefit of printed arrangements. A form of creativity in harmonizing.

---

244 A Cappella Arranging, Deke Sharon and Dylan Bell, page 332
245 A Cappella Arranging, Deke Sharon and Dylan Bell, page 332

Contributors

Steven Armstrong has been involved in barbershop singing for nearly 50 years, joining the Oshawa Horseless Carriagemen when he was just 13 years of age. Steve began his early directing career at the age of 19, and by the age of 32 Steve had directed both the Scarborough Dukes of Harmony and the East York Barbershoppers into international competitions. Following that, Steve was a co-founder of the Toronto Northern Lights and directed them to 14 International medals, including the International Chorus Championship in 2013. He earned his Bachelor's Degree in Music Education from the University of Toronto in 1984.

Steve has been a member of three Ontario District Championship Quartets (1988 "Flipside," 1996 "Jukebox" and 2022 "Detour"), all of which have competed at the Barbershop Harmony Society's international competitions. In addition, Steve has been a society judge for over 36 years, served as Music Category Specialist from 2017–2019 and has been the Chair of the Society's Contest and Judging program since 2020. He has served on the judging panel of several International competitions as well as many overseas contests.

An accomplished barbershop arranger, coach and instructor, Steve's skill and experience have been sought after by many quartets and choruses. He has coached throughout the barbershop world and he has taught at the society's Harmony University as well as schools for other barbershop organizations.

Steve lives in Oshawa with his wife Lori and son Joel where they attend the local Salvation Army church

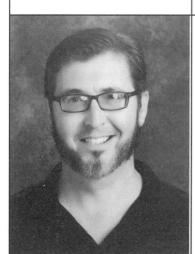

Aaron Dale is the music specialist at G.C. Burkhead Elementary School. Along with elementary music, he has taught percussion ensembles and drumlines all over Kentucky since 1992, and has percussion compositions published with Row-Loff Productions.

Aaron directed the Louisville Times Chorus from 2001 to 2004, and in 2006 co-founded the Kentucky Vocal Union, a male barbershop chorus from Elizabethtown, Kentucky. He was the KVU director and primary vocal arranger their entire existence through 2017, with members joining from all over Kentucky and Indiana. As a successfully entertaining and "cutting edge" ensemble, the KVU finished 3rd place in the world in the 2012 International Chorus Contest of the Barbershop Harmony Society.

Aaron has been active with barbershop music as a judge, performer, coach, and arranger, and in October 2020 the Barbershop Harmony Society recognized him (along with many of his heroes) with an award for LIFETIME ACHIEVEMENT FOR ARRANGERS. "Awarded to an arranger, living or in memorium, in recognition of the profound effect of their contributions on the musical culture of barbershop harmony as an art form through their collective body of work. The 2020 Inaugural Class includes: Renee Craig, Aaron Dale, Tom Gentry, Jay Giallombardo, Don Gray, S.K. Grundy, David Harrington, Val Hicks, Clay Hine, Walter Latzko, Earl Moon, Lou Perry, Sigmund Spaeth, Dave Stevens, Burt Szabo, Greg Volk, Ed Waesche, David Wright, Larry Wright"

Tom Gentry's barbershop career began with The Music Man quartet in high school, and he loved the harmony instantly. Since then, he has arranged roughly 800 songs, worked at the Barbershop Harmony Society in a staff position (1985–1992), sang with two international medalist choruses (Houston Tidelanders and San Diego Sun Harbor Chorus) and many quartets, directed the Akron (Ohio) Derbytown Chorus, and has traveled around the barbershop world.

A charter member (1977) of the woodshedding organization AHSOW and former Arrangement judge (1979–1992), he has served as a Music judge (1993–2023), having once served as the category specialist. He is a 35-year faculty member of Harmony University. In 2006, Tom was inducted into the Johnny Appleseed District Hall of Fame and in 2022 attended my 51st consecutive international convention. Tom is an Honorary Member of BinG! (Barbershop in Germany) and an Honorary Life Member of Harmony, Incorporated.

Rafi Hasib is a software engineer and musician based in New York City. Born in Dhaka, Bangladesh, he immigrated to the US at a young age, where music and art helped him connect with his peers when words alone could not.

As long as he can remember, Rafi enjoyed exploring how different instruments work and blend together, often improvising vocal harmonies with the radio. While studying engineering at the University of Pennsylvania, Rafi was hired as a teaching assistant who embraced the value of making complex concepts understandable in the simplest terms. Inspired by the late composer Dr. Bruce Montgomery, he spent his free time arranging for his university glee club, a cappella group, and barbershop quartet, culminating with scoring an original musical, "The Glee of Clubs," complete with a pit orchestra.

Today, Rafi is a lifelong member of the Barbershop Harmony Society, who has sung in multiple award-winning choruses and served in various administrative roles, focused on the human connection behind technical ideas. He sees this book as the quintessential opportunity to enrich our community through a deeper understanding of the music that draws us together.

Clay Hine, in his own words: "Growing up around folks who were great barbershoppers and even more importantly, great people, was the best kind of brouhaha. That really kicked into full fun fracas mode for me when, at 14 years old, I was finally able to join the chorus my dad directed in Detroit, Michigan. Over the years since then, I've sung with a few quartets—with my dad in Atlanta Forum (1987 Dixie District Quartet Champs), FRED (1999 SPEBSQSA International Quartet Champs), A Mighty Wind (earning a few medals along the way), and most recently, Category 4 (7th place international finalists—for three years in a row; there should be a consistency award). I've also directed the Big Chicken Chorus (described as "poultry in motion" by some—well, just me—on our way to earning three medals in international competition) and am currently the director of the award-winning Atlanta Vocal Project. I've also written over 400 vocal arrangements for many male, female, and mixed ensembles and some of those have created a whole new style of brouhaha. My amazingly patient wife Becki is also very involved in Sweet Adelines International as a judge, coach, and chorus director—her Song of Atlanta Chorus has ballyhooed their way into finishing as high as 4th in the SAI international competition. My daughter, Melody sings with the 2019 Harmony Incorporated quartet champions, Hot Pursuit. Melody—who is a middle school choir teacher—causes quite the entertaining kerfuffle with her arranging brouhaha. When my son, Camden, is not too busy earning college degrees, he also enjoys the brouhaha of singing barbershop."

Kevin Keller has been a society member since 1978. Kevin has won several chorus medals, including multiple gold medals with the Vocal Majority and the Ambassadors of Harmony. Kevin has sung in many quartets as well, winning the Central States District in 1997 with "The EIB Quartet" and placing 6th at the 2003 International Competition with "Cheers!" (doing several of his arrangements).

Kevin is a highly sought-after coach throughout the BHS, SAI, and other international barbershop organizations. He has served on the faculty at numerous district schools and workshops, and has been a fixture on the Harmony University faculty for many years. As a certified MUS judge since 1998, he has served as Category Specialist as well as Chair. He has also produced a video series on the history of BHS judging. For his many contributions in judging as well as other lifetime service, Kevin was inducted into the BHS Hall of Fame in 2020.

Kevin has been arranging for over 30 years and has nearly 300 arrangements to his credit. Although most are barbershop, there are several traditional voicings in both choral and vocal jazz stylings. Numerous barbershop arrangements have been sung at the International level, including champion and medalist choruses and quartets in BHS, SAI, and HI. He has taught arranging classes online and mentors numerous beginning arrangers. He also served on the BHS Music Publications Committee for several years.

Adam Scott works as a music editor for The Church of Jesus Christ of Latter-Day Saints. He holds a M.M. in choral conducting and a B.A. in music composition. Before this he worked as music educator and editor of music publications for the Barbershop Harmony Society. He has collaborated with composers and arrangers including Dr. Kirby Shaw and Deke Sharon. He has been a certified Music judge since 2016. Adam has written/arranged over a thousand pieces of music, composing everything from piano pieces to major works. He specializes in writing custom works to suit individual ensembles. His classical music is sung by various middle / high schools and colleges. He is published by MusicSpoke, Music House Publications, Sheet Music Plus, Hal Leonard, and his own private studio.

Adam lives in Nashville, TN with his wife, Bethany, and four (loud) boys.

Steve Scott is the Director of Harmony University and Education Services for the Barbershop Harmony Society. A barbershopper for over thirty years, Steve taught voice and choir at the college level before joining the BHS staff. His research interests include the biophysiology of the barbershop singing voice, barbershop acoustics, and barbershop history. He is a certified Singing judge, a frequent faculty member for harmony colleges around the world where he teaches voice techniques and vocal pedagogy, a voice teacher, and coach. Steve also serves as the assistant director and principal vocal coach of the 2022 international champion chorus, the Music City Chorus, both in Nashville TN. He enjoys living in the Nashville area with his wife and two children.

Steve Tramack joined the Barbershop Harmony Society in 1983 and proves the adage that barbershopping runs in the blood. Great-grandfather Frank Barker started a chapter in 1946; his father, Dave, was a 40+ year member, and his son Joshua, wife Renee, and daughters Christina and Samantha are all BHS members. Renee, a member of Harmony Inc. since 1982, co-directs New England Voices in Harmony (2014 and 2018 International champions) with Samantha. Renee, Christina and Samantha sing in Taken 4 Granite (2016 Harmony Inc Queens), and Samantha, Christina and Joshua sing in Sweet & Sour (2022 BHS District quartet champions and 2023 international quartet semifinalist)

Steve is actively involved in several facets of barbershopping, including (as of 2023): 10-time international chorus director; 5-time international quartet competitor; Certified Music judge (2010), and BHS Music Category Specialist (2020–2024); Over 300 commissioned arrangements, ranging from international champions (BHS, Harmony Inc, SAI) to chapter quartets and choruses; Active coach of male, female and mixed ensembles worldwide; 19-year Harmony University faculty member and chair of the Arranging Track.

David Wright, from St. Louis, Missouri, is a mathematician, professor, arranger, composer, director, coach, judge (since 1981), Harmony University faculty member, historian, baritone, and member of the Barbershop Harmony Hall of Fame. He helped design the Music Category and served as its first Category Specialist. He is Associate Director of the St. Charles Ambassadors of Harmony, five-time international chorus champions. He is a prolific arranger, having arranged for many top quartets and choruses. More than 100 of his arrangements have been sung in gold medal performances. David's wife Sandi has twice won the quartet gold medal in Sweet Adelines, International, and is a certified judge in SAI, Harmony, Inc., and the Barbershop Harmony Society.